T0214627

Lecture Notes in Computer Science   11421

Commenced Publication in 1973
Founding and Former Series Editors:
Gerhard Goos, Juris Hartmanis, and Jan van Leeuwen

More information about this series at http://www.springer.com/series/7410

Ilia Polian · Marc Stöttinger (Eds.)

Constructive Side-Channel Analysis and Secure Design

10th International Workshop, COSADE 2019
Darmstadt, Germany, April 3–5, 2019
Proceedings

 Springer

Editors
Ilia Polian (iD)
Universität Stuttgart
Stuttgart, Germany

Marc Stöttinger
Continental AG
Frankfurt, Germany

ISSN 0302-9743   ISSN 1611-3349 (electronic)
Lecture Notes in Computer Science
ISBN 978-3-030-16349-5   ISBN 978-3-030-16350-1   (eBook)
https://doi.org/10.1007/978-3-030-16350-1

Library of Congress Control Number: 2019935139

LNCS Sublibrary: SL4 – Security and Cryptology

This Springer imprint is published by the registered company Springer Nature Switzerland AG
The registered company address is: Gewerbestrasse 11, 6330 Cham, Switzerland

Preface

COSADE 2019, the 10th International Workshop on Constructive Side-Channel Analysis and Secure Design, was held in Darmstadt, Germany, April 3–5, 2019. This workshop is a well-established platform for researchers and practitioners from academia, industry, and government to exchange and discuss the state of the art in implementation attacks, e.g., side-channel attacks or fault-injection attacks, and secure implementation of cryptographic algorithms and security controls. The workshop was conducted in cooperation with the International Association for Cryptographic Research. COSADE 2019 was organized by Technische Universität Darmstadt in collaboration with the Collaborative Research Center (SFB) CROSSING.

This year 34 papers were submitted to the COSADE workshop. Each paper was anonymously reviewed in a double-blind peer-review process by at least four Program Committee members. In total, 130 reviews were written by the Program Committee members with the help of 39 additional reviewers. The international Program Committee consisted of 35 members from 13 countries. The members were carefully selected experts in the area of side-channel analysis, fault injection analysis, and secure design to represent academia and industry. The decision process was very challenging and resulted in the selection of 14 papers. These 14 papers were part of the contribution to COSADE 2019 and are contained in these workshop proceedings. We are deeply grateful to all reviewers for their dedication and hard work in reviewing, assessing, and discussing.

Beside the 14 presentations of the selected papers, two keynotes and one invited talk were given at the COSADE 2019. The first invited talk was about RowHammer like exploits given by Onur Mutlu from Carnegie Mellon University and ETH Zürich. This talk provided a comprehensive overview of the various versions of implementation attacks and appropriate countermeasures. The second invited talk was given by Ramesh Karri from New York University about secure high-level synthesis. His talk focused on secure design process for hardware designs with increased resilience against malicious circuits and backdoors. Sylvain Guilley gave an invited talk on detection and prevention of cache-timing attacks. The talks of Mutlu and Guilley are also summarized in a paper and contained in the proceedings of COSADE 2019. In addition, an anniversary talk was given by Sorin A. Huss to mark the tenth edition of COSADE. He presented the highlights and some historical facts of the last nine COSADE workshops as well as the scientific motivation to proceed with research on novel countermeasure strategies and techniques.

We would like to thank the general chair, Stefan Katzenbeisser, and the local organizers, Daniela Fleckenstein and Ursula Paeckel, all of TU Darmstadt, for the local organization, which made this workshop a memorable event. We would also like to thank the two Web administrators, Helmut Haefner and Lothar Hellmeier of the University of Stuttgart, for maintaining the COSADE website for 2019.

We are very grateful for the financial support received from our generous sponsors ALPha NOV, Continental, eshard, FortiyfIQ, Rambus Cryptography Research, Riscure, and Secure-IC.

April 2019

Ilia Polian
Marc Stöttinger

Organization

The 10th International Workshop on Constructive Side-Channel Analysis and Secure Design

Darmstadt, Germany, April 3–5, 2019

Steering Committee

Jean-Luc Danger   Télécom ParisTech, France
Werner Schindler   Bundesamt für Sicherheit in der Informationstechnik (BSI), Germany

General Chair

Stefan Katzenbeisser   Technische Universität Darmstadt, Germany

Program Committee Chairs

Ilia Polian   Universität Stuttgart, Germany
Marc Stöttinger   Continental AG, Germany

Program Committee

Divya Arora	Intel, USA
Navid Asadizanjani	University of Florida, USA
Reza Azarderakhsh	Florida Atlantic University, USA
Josep Balasch	KU Leuven, Belgium
Goerg T. Becker	EMST, Germany
Sonia Belaïd	CryptoExperts, France
Shivam Bhasin	Nanyang Technological University, Singapore
Anupam Chattopadhyay	Nanyang Technological University, Singapore
Elke De Mulder	Cryptography Research, USA
Fabrizio De Santis	Siemens AG, Germany
Wieland Fischer	Infineon Technologies, Germany
Jorge Guajardo	Robert Bosch LLC, Research and Technology Center, USA
Sylvain Guilley	Secure-IC, France
Annelie Heuser	CNRS, IRISA, France
Naofumi Homma	Tohoku University, Japan
Michael Hutter	Cryptography Research, USA
Jens-Peter Kaps	George Mason University, USA

Michael Kasper	Fraunhofer Singapore, Singapore
Elif Bilge Kavun	The University of Sheffield, UK
Osnat Keren	Bar-Ilan University, Israel
Roel Maes	Intrinsic-ID, The Netherlands
Marcel Medwed	NXP Semiconductors, Austria
Nele Mentens	KU Leuven, Belgium
Amir Moradi	Ruhr-Universität Bochum, Germany
Debdepp Mukhopadhyay	IIT Kharagpur, India
Makoto Nagata	Kobe University, Japan
Collin O'Flynn	NewAE Technology, Canada
Axel Poschmann	DarkMatter, United Arab Emirates
Francesco Regazzoni	ALaRi-USI, Switzerland
Kazuo Sakiyama	The University of Electro-Communications, Japan
Patrick Schaumont	Virgina Tech, USA
Georg Sigl	TU München and Fraunhofer AISEC, Germany
Francois-Xavier Standaert	UCL Crypto Group, Belgium
Marc Witteman	Riscure, The Netherlands

Additional Reviewers

Nikolaos Athanasios
  Anagnostopoulos
Melissa Azouaoui
Alexander Bajic
Arthur Beckers
Sarani Bhattacharya
Begul Bilgin
Manuel Bluhm
Joppe Bos
Martin Butkus
Vincent Grosso
Michael Gruber
Amir Jalali
Dirmanto Jap

Kimmo Järvinen
Bernhard Jungk
Mehran Mozaffari
  Kermani
Rami El Khatib
Philipp Koppermann
Bodhisatwa Mazumdar
Hatame Mosanaei
Guilherme Perin
Romain Poussier
Prasanna Ravi
Bastian Richter
Mélissa Rossi
Steffen Sanwald

Pascal Sasdrich
Thomas Schamberger
Hermann Seuschek
Hadi Soleimany
Lars Tebelmann
Michael Tunstall
Rei Ueno
Gilles Van Assche
Vincent Verneuil
Junwei Wang
Felix Wegener
Florian Wilde
Ville Yli-Mäyry

Contents

Keynotes and Invited Talks

RowHammer and Beyond

Onur Mutlu[1,2(✉)]

[1] ETH Zürich, Zürich, Switzerland
onur.mutlu@inf.ethz.ch
[2] Carnegie Mellon University, Pittsburgh, USA

Abstract. We will discuss the RowHammer problem in DRAM, which is a prime (and likely the first) example of how a circuit-level failure mechanism in Dynamic Random Access Memory (DRAM) can cause a practical and widespread system security vulnerability. RowHammer is the phenomenon that repeatedly accessing a row in a modern DRAM chip predictably causes errors in physically-adjacent rows. It is caused by a hardware failure mechanism called read disturb errors. Building on our initial fundamental work that appeared at ISCA 2014, Google Project Zero demonstrated that this hardware phenomenon can be exploited by user-level programs to gain kernel privileges. Many other recent works demonstrated other attacks exploiting RowHammer, including remote takeover of a server vulnerable to RowHammer. We will analyze the root causes of the problem and examine solution directions. We will also discuss what other problems may be lurking in DRAM and other types of memories, e.g., NAND flash and Phase Change Memory, which can potentially threaten the foundations of reliable and secure systems, as the memory technologies scale to higher densities.

1 Summary

As memory scales down to smaller technology nodes, new failure mechanisms emerge that threaten its correct operation [79,80]. If such failures are not anticipated and corrected, they can not only degrade system reliability and availability but also, even more importantly, open up new security vulnerabilities: a malicious attacker can exploit the exposed failure mechanism to take over an entire system. As such, new failure mechanisms in memory can become practical and significant threats to system security.

In this keynote talk, based on our ISCA 2014 paper [55], we introduce the RowHammer problem in DRAM, which is a prime (and likely the first) example of a real circuit-level failure mechanism that causes a practical and widespread system security vulnerability. RowHammer, as it is now popularly referred to, is the phenomenon that repeatedly accessing a row in a modern DRAM chip causes bit flips in physically-adjacent rows at consistently predictable bit locations. It is caused by a hardware failure mechanism called *DRAM disturbance errors*, which is a manifestation of circuit-level cell-to-cell interference in a scaled memory technology. Specifically, when a DRAM row is opened (i.e., activated)

I. Polian and M. Stöttinger (Eds.): COSADE 2019, LNCS 11421, pp. 3–12, 2019.
https://doi.org/10.1007/978-3-030-16350-1_1

and closed (i.e., precharged) repeatedly (i.e., *hammered*), enough times within a DRAM refresh interval, one or more bits in physically-adjacent DRAM rows can be flipped to the wrong value. Using an FPGA-based DRAM testing infrastructure [42,70], we tested 129 DRAM modules manufactured by three major manufacturers in seven recent years (2008–2014) and found that 110 of them exhibited RowHammer errors, the earliest of which dates back to 2010. Our ISCA 2014 paper [55] provides a detailed and rigorous analysis of various characteristics of RowHammer, including its data pattern dependence, repeatability of errors, relationship with leaky cells, and various circuit-level causes of the phenomenon.

We demonstrate that a very simple user-level program [3,55] can reliably and consistently induce RowHammer errors in commodity AMD and Intel systems using vulnerable DRAM modules. We released the source code of this program [3], which Google Project Zero later enhanced [4]. Using our user-level RowHammer program, we showed that both read and write accesses to memory can induce bit flips, all of which occur in rows other than the one that is being accessed. Since different DRAM rows are mapped to different software pages, our user-level program could reliably corrupt specific bits in pages belonging to other programs. As a result, RowHammer errors can be exploited by a malicious program to breach memory protection and compromise the system. In fact, we hypothesized, in our ISCA 2014 paper, that our user-level program, with some engineering effort, could be developed into a *disturbance attack* that injects errors into other programs, crashes the system, or hijacks control of the system.

RowHammer exposes a *security threat* since it leads to a serious breach of memory isolation: an access to one memory row (e.g., an OS page) predictably modifies the data stored in another row (e.g., another OS page). Malicious software, which we call *disturbance attacks* [55], or *RowHammer attacks*, can be written to take advantage of these disturbance errors to take over an entire system. Inspired by our ISCA 2014 paper's fundamental findings, researchers from Google Project Zero demonstrated in 2015 that RowHammer can be effectively exploited by user-level programs to gain kernel privileges on real systems [94,95]. Tens of other works since then demonstrated other attacks exploiting RowHammer. These include remote takeover of a server vulnerable to RowHammer via JavaScript code execution [40], takeover of a victim virtual machine by another virtual machine running on the same system [92], takeover of a mobile device by a malicious user-level application that requires no permissions [103], takeover of a mobile system by triggering RowHammer using the WebGL interface on a mobile GPU [35], takeover of a remote system by triggering RowHammer through the Remote Direct Memory Access (RDMA) protocol [67,101], and various other attacks (e.g., [8,13,14,39,45,85–87,102,108]). Thus, RowHammer has widespread and profound real implications on system security, as it destroys memory isolation on top of which modern system security principles are built.

We provide a wide variety of solutions, both *immediate* and *longer-term*, to RowHammer, starting from our ISCA 2014 paper [55]. A popular *immediate* solution we describe and analyze, is to increase the refresh rate of memory such that the probability of inducing a RowHammer error before DRAM cells get refreshed is reduced. Several major system manufacturers have adopted this solution and released security patches that increased DRAM refresh rates (e.g., [11,34,43,66]) in memory controllers deployed in the field. While this solution is practical and effective in reducing the vulnerability, assuming the refresh rate is increased enough to avoid the vulnerability, it has the significant drawbacks of increasing energy/power consumption, reducing system performance, and degrading quality of service experienced by user programs. Our paper shows that the refresh rate needs to be increased by 7X if we want to eliminate *every single* RowHammer-induced error we saw in our tests of 129 DRAM modules. Since DRAM refresh is already a significant burden [31,33,46,47,49,69,70,84,89] on energy, performance, and QoS, increasing it by any significant amount would only exacerbate the problem. Yet, increased refresh rate is likely the most practical *immediate* solution to RowHammer that can protect vulnerable chips that are already deployed in the field.

After describing and analyzing six solutions to RowHammer, our ISCA 2014 paper shows that the long-term solution to RowHammer can actually be simple and low cost. We introduce a new idea, called *PARA (Probabilistic Adjacent Row Activation)*: when the memory controller closes a row (after it was activated), with a very low probability, it refreshes the adjacent rows. The probability value is a parameter determined by the system designer or provided programmatically, if needed, to trade off between performance overhead and vulnerability protection guarantees. We show that this solution is very effective: it eliminates the RowHammer vulnerability, providing much higher reliability guarantees than modern hard disks provide today, while requiring no storage cost and having negligible performance and energy overheads [55]. Variants of this solution are currently being adopted in DRAM chips and memory controllers [5,6].

The RowHammer problem leads to a new mindset that has enabled a renewed interest in hardware security research: real memory chips are vulnerable, in a simple and widespread manner, and this causes real security problems. We believe the RowHammer problem will worsen over time since DRAM cells are getting closer to each other with technology scaling. Other similar vulnerabilities may also be lurking in DRAM and other types of memories, e.g., NAND flash memory or Phase Change Memory, that can potentially threaten the foundations of secure systems [80]. Our work advocates a principled system-memory co-design approach to memory reliability and security research that can enable us to better anticipate and prevent such vulnerabilities.

2   Significance, Impact and the Future

RowHammer has spurred significant amount of research and industry attention since its publication in 2014. Our ISCA 2014 paper [55] is the first to demonstrate the RowHammer vulnerability, its characteristics, and its prevalence in real DRAM chips. RowHammer is a prime (and likely the first) example of a hardware failure mechanism that causes a practical and widespread system security vulnerability. Thus, the implications of RowHammer and our ISCA 2014 paper on systems security is tremendous, both in the short term and the long term: it is the first work we know of that shows that a real reliability problem in one of the ubiquitous general-purpose hardware components (DRAM memory) can cause practical and widespread system security vulnerabilities.

Since its publication in 2014, RowHammer has already had significant real-world impact on both industry and academia in at least four directions. These directions will continue to exert long-term impact for RowHammer, as memory cells continue to get closer to each other while the technology scaling of memory continues.

First, our work has inspired many researchers to exploit RowHammer to devise new attacks. As mentioned earlier, tens of papers were written in top security venues that demonstrate various practical attacks exploiting RowHammer (e.g., [8, 13, 14, 35, 39, 40, 45, 85, 87, 92, 103, 108]). These attacks started with Google Project Zero's first work in 2015 [94, 95] and they continue to this date, with the latest ones that we know of being published in Summer 2018 [67, 86, 101, 102]. We believe there is a lot more to come in this direction: as systems security researchers understand more about RowHammer, and as the RowHammer phenomenon continues to fundamentally affect memory chips due to technology scaling problems [80], researchers and practitioners will develop different types of attacks to exploit RowHammer in various contexts and in many more creative ways. Some recent reports suggest that new-generation DDR4 DRAM chips are vulnerable to RowHammer [8, 10, 58, 85], so the fundamental security research on RowHammer is likely to continue into the future.

Second, due to its prevalence in real DRAM chips, as demonstrated in our ISCA 2014 paper, RowHammer has become a popular phenomenon [1, 2, 9, 37, 41, 58, 83, 95, 105], which, in turn, has made hardware security "mainstream" in media and the broader security community. It enabled hardware security vulnerabilities as mainstream conversation and a serious threat that has to be defended against. A well-read article from the Wired magazine, all about RowHammer, is entitled "Forget Software – Now Hackers are Exploiting Physics!" [38], indicating the shift of mindset towards hardware security vulnerabilities in the popular mainstream security community. Many other popular articles in press have been written about RowHammer, many of which pointing to the fundamental discovery of RowHammer in our ISCA 2014 work [55]. Making hardware security vulnerabilities mainstream and pulling them to the popular discussion space, and thus changing the mainstream discourse, creates a very long term impact for the RowHammer problem.

Third, our work inspired many solution and mitigation techniques for RowHammer from both researchers and industry practitioners. *Apple* publicly mentioned, in their critical security release for RowHammer, that they increased the memory refresh rates due to the "original research by Yoongu Kim et al. (2014)" [11]. Memtest86 program was updated, including a RowHammer test, acknowledging our ISCA 2014 paper [83]. Many academic works developed solutions to RowHammer, working from our original research (e.g., [12, 15, 36, 39, 44, 50, 65, 96, 97, 104]). Multiple industrial solutions (e.g., [5, 6]) were inspired by our new solution to RowHammer, Probabilistic Adjacent Row Activation. We believe such solutions will continue to be generated in both academia and industry, extending RowHammer's impact into the very long term.

Fourth, and perhaps most importantly, RowHammer enabled a shift of mindset among mainstream security researchers: general-purpose hardware is fallible (in a very widespread manner) and its problems are actually exploitable. This shift of mindset enabled many systems security researchers to examine hardware in more depth and understand its inner workings and vulnerabilities better. We believe it is no coincidence that two of the groups that concurrently discovered the Meltdown [68] and Spectre [56] vulnerabilities (Google Project Zero and TU Graz InfoSec) have heavily worked on RowHammer attacks before. We believe this shift in mindset, enabled in good part by the existence and prevalence of RowHammer, will continue to be very be important for discovering and solving other potential vulnerabilities that may appear as a result of both technology scaling and hardware design.

3   Other Potential Vulnerabilities

We believe that, as memory technologies scale to higher densities, other problems may start appearing (or may already be going unnoticed) that can potentially threaten the foundations of secure systems. There have been recent large-scale field studies a well as small-scale controlled studies of real memory errors on real devices and systems, showing that both DRAM and NAND flash memory technologies are becoming less reliable [17, 25, 27, 28, 73, 74, 77–80, 82, 84, 93, 98–100]. As detailed experimental analyses of real DRAM and NAND flash chips show, both technologies are becoming much more vulnerable to cell-to-cell interference effects [17, 20–23, 26–28, 55, 72, 79–82], data retention is becoming significantly more difficult in both technologies [17–19, 21, 25, 27, 28, 31, 46–49, 69–71, 73–75, 79, 81, 82, 89], and error variation within and across chips is increasingly prominent [17, 21, 29, 30, 51–53, 63, 64, 70]. Emerging memory technologies [76, 79], such as Phase-Change Memory [59–61, 88, 90, 91, 106, 109–111], STT-MRAM [32, 57], and RRAM/ReRAM/ memristors [107] are likely to exhibit similar and perhaps even more exacerbated reliability issues. We believe, if not carefully accounted for and corrected, these reliability problems may surface as security problems as well, as in the case of RowHammer, especially if the technology is employed as part of the main memory system that is directly exposed to user-level programs. We believe future work examining these vulnerabilities, among others, is promising for both fixing the vulnerabilities and enabling the effective scaling of memory technology.

Acknowledgments. This short paper and the associated keynote talk are heavily based on two previous papers we have written on RowHammer, one that first introduced the phenomenon in ISCA 2014 [55] and the other that provides an analysis and future outlook on RowHammer [80]. They are a result of the research done together with many students and collaborators over the course of the past 7–8 years. In particular, three PhD theses have shaped the understanding that led to this work. These are Yoongu Kim's thesis entitled "Architectural Techniques to Enhance DRAM Scaling" [54], Yu Cai's thesis entitled "NAND Flash Memory: Characterization, Analysis, Modeling and Mechanisms" [24] and his continued follow-on work after his thesis, summarized in [27,28], and Donghyuk Lee's thesis entitled "Reducing DRAM Latency at Low Cost by Exploiting Heterogeneity" [62]. We also acknowledge various funding agencies (NSF, SRC, ISTC, CyLab) and industrial partners (AliBaba, AMD, Google, Facebook, HP Labs, Huawei, IBM, Intel, Microsoft, Nvidia, Oracle, Qualcomm, Rambus, Samsung, Seagate, VMware) who have supported the presented and other related work in my group generously over the years. The first version of this talk was delivered at a CMU CyLab Partners Conference in September 2015. Another version of the talk was delivered as part of an Invited Session at DAC 2016, with a collaborative accompanying paper entitled "Who Is the Major Threat to Tomorrow's Security? You, the Hardware Designer" [16]. The most recent version is the invited talk given at the Top Picks in Hardware and Embedded Security workshop, co-located with ICCAD 2018 [7], where RowHammer was selected as a Top Pick among hardware and embedded security papers published between 2012–2017. I would like to also thank Christina Giannoula for her help in preparing this manuscript.

References

1. RowHammer Discussion Group. https://groups.google.com/forum/#!forum/rowhammer-discuss
2. RowHammer on Twitter. https://twitter.com/search?q=rowhammer
3. Rowhammer: Source Code for Testing the Row Hammer Error Mechanism in DRAM Devices. https://github.com/CMU-SAFARI/rowhammer
4. Test DRAM for Bit Flips Caused by the RowHammer Problem. https://github.com/google/rowhammer-test
5. ThinkPad X210 BIOS Debugging. https://github.com/tadfisher/x210-bios
6. Tweet about RowHammer Mitigation on x210. https://twitter.com/isislovecruft/status/1021939922754723841
7. Top Picks in Hardware and Embedded Security - Workshop Collocated with ICCAD 2018 (2017). https://wp.nyu.edu/toppicksinhardwaresecurity/
8. Aga, M.T., Aweke, Z.B., Austin, T.: When good protections go bad: exploiting anti-DoS measures to accelerate rowhammer attacks. In: HOST (2017)
9. Aichinger, B.: The Known Failure Mechanism in DDR3 Memory referred to as Row Hammer, September 2014. http://ddrdetective.com/files/6414/1036/5710/The_Known_Failure_Mechanism_in_DDR3_memory_referred_to_as_Row_Hammer.pdf
10. Aichinger, B.: DDR memory errors caused by row hammer. In: HPEC (2015)
11. Apple Inc., About the security content of Mac EFI Security Update 2015-001, June 2015. https://support.apple.com/en-us/HT204934
12. Aweke, Z.B., et al.: Anvil: software-based protection against next-generation rowhammer attacks. In: ASPLOS (2016)
13. Bhattacharya, S., Mukhopadhyay, D.: Curious case of RowHammer: flipping secret exponent bits using timing analysis. In: Gierlichs, B., Poschmann, A.Y. (eds.) CHES 2016. LNCS, vol. 9813, pp. 602–624. Springer, Heidelberg (2016). https://doi.org/10.1007/978-3-662-53140-2_29
14. Bosman, E., et al.: Dedup Est Machina: memory deduplication as an advanced exploitation vector. In: S&P (2016)

15. Brasser, F., Davi, L., Gens, D., Liebchen, C., Sadeghi, A.-R.: Can't touch this: practical and generic software-only defenses against RowHammer attacks. In: USENIX Security (2017)
16. Burleson, W., et al.: Who is the major threat to tomorrow's security? You, the hardware designer. In: DAC (2016)
17. Cai, Y., et al.: Error patterns in MLC NAND flash memory: measurement, characterization, and analysis. In: DATE (2012)
18. Cai, Y., et al.: Flash correct-and-refresh: retention-aware error management for increased flash memory lifetime. In: ICCD (2012)
19. Cai, Y., et al.: Error analysis and retention-aware error management for NAND flash memory. ITJ **17**(1), 140–165 (2013)
20. Cai, Y., et al.: Program interference in MLC NAND flash memory: characterization, modeling, and mitigation. In: ICCD (2013)
21. Cai, Y., et al.: Threshold voltage distribution in MLC NAND flash memory: characterization, analysis and modeling. In: DATE (2013)
22. Cai, Y., et al.: Neighbor-cell assisted error correction for MLC NAND flash memories. In: SIGMETRICS (2014)
23. Cai, Y., et al.: Vulnerabilities in MLC NAND flash memory programming: experimental analysis, exploits, and mitigation techniques. In: HPCA (2017)
24. Cai, Y.: NAND flash memory: characterization, analysis, modeling and mechanisms. Ph.D. thesis, Carnegie Mellon University (2012)
25. Cai, Y., et al.: Data retention in MLC NAND flash memory: characterization, optimization and recovery. In: HPCA (2015)
26. Cai, Y., et al.: Read disturb errors in MLC NAND flash memory: characterization, mitigation, and recovery. In: DSN (2015)
27. Cai, Y., Ghose, S., Haratsch, E.F., Luo, Y., Mutlu, O.: Error characterization, mitigation, and recovery in flash-memory-based solid-state drives. Proc. IEEE **105**, 1666–1704 (2017)
28. Cai, Y., Ghose, S., Haratsch, E.F., Luo, Y., Mutlu, O.: Errors in Flash-Memory-Based Solid-State Drives: Analysis, Mitigation, and Recovery (2017). arXiv preprint: arXiv:1711.11427
29. Chandrasekar, K., et al.: Exploiting expendable process-margins in DRAMs for run-time performance optimization. In: DATE (2014)
30. Chang, K., et al.: Understanding latency variation in modern DRAM chips: experimental characterization, analysis, and optimization. In: SIGMETRICS (2016)
31. Chang, K., et al.: Improving DRAM performance by parallelizing refreshes with accesses. In: HPCA (2014)
32. Chen, E., et al.: Advances and future prospects of spin-transfer torque random access memory. IEEE Trans. Magn. **46**, 1873–1878 (2010)
33. Das, A., et al.: VRL-DRAM: improving DRAM performance via variable refresh latency. In: DAC (2018)
34. Fridley, T., Santos, O.: Mitigations Available for the DRAM Row Hammer Vulnerability, March 2015. http://blogs.cisco.com/security/mitigations-available-for-the-dram-row-hammer-vulnerability
35. Frigo, P., et al.: Grand Pwning unit: accelerating microarchitectural attacks with the GPU. In: IEEE S&P (2018)
36. Gomez, H., Amaya, A., Roa, E.: DRAM Row-hammer attack reduction using dummy cells. In: NORCAS (2016)
37. Goodin, D.: Once thought safe, DDR4 memory shown to be vulnerable to Rowhammer (2016). https://arstechnica.com/information-technology/2016/03/once-thought-safe-ddr4-memory-shown-to-be-vulnerable-to-rowhammer/

38. Greenberg, A.: Forget Software – Now Hackers are Exploiting Physics (2016). https://www.wired.com/2016/08/new-form-hacking-breaks-ideas-computers-work/
39. Gruss, D., et al.: Another flip in the wall of rowhammer defenses. In: IEEE S&P (2018)
40. Gruss, D., et al.: Rowhammer.js: a remote software-induced fault attack in Javascript. CoRR, abs/1507.06955 (2015)
41. Harris, R.: Flipping DRAM bits - maliciously, December 2014. http://www.zdnet.com/article/flipping-dram-bits-maliciously/
42. Hassan, H., et al.: SoftMC: a flexible and practical open-source infrastructure for enabling experimental DRAM studies. In: HPCA (2017)
43. Hewlett-Packard Enterprise. HP Moonshot Component Pack Version 2015.05.0 (2015). http://h17007.www1.hp.com/us/en/enterprise/servers/products/moonshot/component-pack/index.aspx
44. Irazoqui, G., Eisenbarth, T., Sunar, B.: MASCAT: stopping microarchitectural attacks before execution. IACR Cryptology ePrint Archive (2016)
45. Jang, Y., Lee, J., Lee, S., Kim, T.: SGX-bomb: locking down the processor via rowhammer attack. In: SysTEX (2017)
46. Kang, U., et al.: Co-architecting controllers and DRAM to enhance DRAM process scaling. In: The Memory Forum (2014)
47. Khan, S., et al.: The efficacy of error mitigation techniques for DRAM retention failures: a comparative experimental study. In: SIGMETRICS (2014)
48. Khan, S., et al.: A case for memory content-based detection and mitigation of data-dependent failures in DRAM. CAL 16(2), 88–93 (2016)
49. Khan, S., et al.: PARBOR: an efficient system-level technique to detect data-dependent failures in DRAM. In: DSN (2016)
50. Kim, D.-H., et al.: Architectural support for mitigating row hammering in DRAM memories. IEEE CAL 14, 9–12 (2015)
51. Kim, J.S., Patel, M., Hassan, H., Mutlu, O.: Solar-DRAM: reducing DRAM access latency by exploiting the variation in local bitlines. In: ICCD (2018)
52. Kim, J.S., Patel, M., Hassan, H., Mutlu, O.: The DRAM latency PUF: quickly evaluating physical unclonable functions by exploiting the latency-reliability tradeoff in modern commodity DRAM devices. In: HPCA (2018)
53. Kim, J.S., Patel, M., Hassan, H., Orosa, L., Mutlu, O.: D-RaNGe: using commodity DRAM devices to generate true random numbers with low latency and high throughput. In: HPCA (2019)
54. Kim, Y.: Architectural techniques to enhance DRAM scaling. Ph.D. thesis, Carnegie Mellon University (2015)
55. Kim, Y., et al.: Flipping bits in memory without accessing them: an experimental study of DRAM disturbance errors. In: ISCA (2014)
56. Kocher, P., et al.: Spectre attacks: exploiting speculative execution In: S&P (2018)
57. Kultursay, E., et al.: Evaluating STT-RAM as an energy-efficient main memory alternative. In: ISPASS (2013)
58. Lanteigne, M.: How Rowhammer could be used to exploit weaknesses in computer hardware, March 2016. http://www.thirdio.com/rowhammer.pdf
59. Lee, B.C., et al.: Architecting phase change memory as a scalable DRAM alternative. In: ISCA (2009)
60. Lee, B.C., et al.: Phase change memory architecture and the quest for scalability. CACM 53, 99–106 (2010)
61. Lee, B.C., et al.: Phase change technology and the future of main memory. IEEE Micro 30, 143 (2010)

62. Lee, D.: Reducing DRAM latency by exploiting heterogeneity. ArXiV (2016)
63. Lee, D., et al.: Adaptive-latency DRAM: optimizing DRAM timing for the common-case. In: HPCA (2015)
64. Lee, D., et al.: Design-induced latency variation in modern DRAM chips: characterization, analysis, and latency reduction mechanisms. In: POMACS (2017)
65. Lee, E., Lee, S., Edward Suh, G., Ahn, J.H.: TWiCe: time window counter based row refresh to prevent Row-hammering. CAL **17**, 96–99 (2018)
66. Lenovo. Row Hammer Privilege Escalation, March 2015. https://support.lenovo.com/us/en/product_security/row_hammer
67. Lipp, M., et al.: Nethammer: inducing rowhammer faults through network requests (2018). arxiv.org
68. Lipp, M., et al.: Meltdown: reading kernel memory from user space. In: USENIX Security (2018)
69. Liu, J., et al.: RAIDR: retention-aware intelligent DRAM refresh. In: ISCA (2012)
70. Liu, J., et al.: An experimental study of data retention behavior in modern DRAM devices: implications for retention time profiling mechanisms. In: ISCA (2013)
71. Luo, Y., et al.: WARM: improving NAND flash memory lifetime with write-hotness aware retention management. In: MSST (2015)
72. Luo, Y., et al.: Enabling accurate and practical online flash channel modeling for modern MLC NAND flash memory. JSAC **34**, 2294–2311 (2016)
73. Luo, Y., Ghose, S., Cai, Y., Haratsch, E.F., Mutlu, O.: HeatWatch: improving 3D NAND flash memory device reliability by exploiting self-recovery and temperature awareness. In: HPCA (2018)
74. Luo, Y., Ghose, S., Cai, Y., Haratsch, E.F., Mutlu, O.: Improving 3D NAND flash memory lifetime by tolerating early retention loss and process variation. In: POMACS (2018)
75. Mandelman, J., et al.: Challenges and future directions for the scaling of dynamic random-access memory (DRAM). IBM J. Res. Dev. **46**, 187–212 (2002)
76. Meza, J., et al.: A case for efficient hardware-software cooperative management of storage and memory. In: WEED (2013)
77. Meza, J., et al.: A large-scale study of flash memory errors in the field. In: SIGMETRICS (2015)
78. Meza, J., et al.: Revisiting memory errors in large-scale production data centers: analysis and modeling of new trends from the field. In: DSN (2015)
79. Mutlu, O.: Memory scaling: a systems architecture perspective. In: IMW (2013)
80. Mutlu, O.: The RowHammer problem and other issues we may face as memory becomes denser. In: DATE (2017)
81. Mutlu, O.: Error analysis and management for MLC NAND flash memory. In: Flash Memory Summit (2014)
82. Mutlu, O., Subramanian, L.: Research problems and opportunities in memory systems. In: SUPERFRI (2014)
83. PassMark Software. MemTest86: The Original Industry Standard Memory Diagnostic Utility (2015). http://www.memtest86.com/troubleshooting.htm
84. Patel, M., Kim, J.S., Mutlu, O.: The Reach Profiler (REAPER): enabling the mitigation of DRAM retention failures via profiling at aggressive conditions. In: ISCA (2017)
85. Pessl, P., Gruss, D., Maurice, C., Schwarz, M., Mangard, S.: DRAMA: exploiting dram addressing for cross-CPU attacks. In: USENIX Security (2016)
86. Poddebniak, D., Somorovsky, J., Schinzel, S., Lochter, M., Rösler, P.: Attacking deterministic signature schemes using fault attacks. In: EuroS&P (2018)

87. Qiao, R., Seaborn, M.: A new approach for rowhammer attacks. In: HOST (2016)
88. Qureshi, M.K., et al.: Scalable high performance main memory system using phase-change memory technology. In: ISCA (2009)
89. Qureshi, M.K., et al.: AVATAR: a Variable-Retention-Time (VRT) aware refresh for DRAM systems. In: DSN (2015)
90. Qureshi, M.K., et al.: Enhancing lifetime and security of phase change memories via start-gap wear leveling. In: MICRO (2009)
91. Raoux, S., et al.: Phase-change random access memory: a scalable technology. IBM J. Res. Dev. **52**, 465–479 (2008)
92. Razavi, K., et al.: Flip Feng Shui: hammering a needle in the software stack. In: USENIX Security (2016)
93. Schroeder, B., et al.: Flash reliability in production: the expected and the unexpected. In: USENIX FAST (2016)
94. Seaborn, M., Dullien, T.: Exploiting the DRAM Rowhammer Bug to Gain Kernel Privileges (2015). http://googleprojectzero.blogspot.com.tr/2015/03/exploiting-dram-rowhammer-bug-to-gain.html
95. Seaborn, M., Dullien, T.: Exploiting the DRAM rowhammer bug to gain kernel privileges. In: BlackHat (2016)
96. Seyedzadeh, S.M., Jones, A.K., Melhem, R.: Counter-based tree structure for row hammering mitigation in DRAM. CAL **16**, 18–21 (2017)
97. Son, M., Park, H., Ahn, J., Yoo, S.: Making DRAM stronger against row hammering. In: DAC (2017)
98. Sridharan, V., et al.: Memory errors in modern systems: the good, the bad, and the ugly. In: ASPLOS (2015)
99. Sridharan, V., Liberty, D.: A study of DRAM failures in the field. In: SC (2012)
100. Sridharan, V., Stearley, J., DeBardeleben, N., Blanchard, S., Gurumurthi, S.: Feng Shui of supercomputer memory: positional effects in DRAM and SRAM faults. In: SC (2013)
101. Tatar, A., et al.: Throwhammer: rowhammer attacks over the network and defenses. In: USENIX ATC (2018)
102. Tatar, A., Giuffrida, C., Bos, H., Razavi, K.: Defeating software mitigations against rowhammer: a surgical precision hammer. In: Bailey, M., Holz, T., Stamatogiannakis, M., Ioannidis, S. (eds.) RAID 2018. LNCS, vol. 11050, pp. 47–66. Springer, Cham (2018). https://doi.org/10.1007/978-3-030-00470-5_3
103. van der Veen, V., et al.: Drammer: deterministic rowhammer attacks on mobile platforms. In: CCS (2016)
104. van der Veen, V., et al.: GuardION: practical mitigation of DMA-based rowhammer attacks on ARM. In: Giuffrida, C., Bardin, S., Blanc, G. (eds.) DIMVA 2018. LNCS, vol. 10885, pp. 92–113. Springer, Cham (2018). https://doi.org/10.1007/978-3-319-93411-2_5
105. Wikipedia. Row hammer. https://en.wikipedia.org/wiki/Row_hammer
106. Wong, H.-S.P., et al.: Phase change memory. Proc. IEEE **98**, 2201–2227 (2010)
107. Wong, H.-S.P., et al.: Metal-oxide RRAM. Proc. IEEE **100**, 1951–1970 (2012)
108. Xiao, Y., et al.: One bit flips, one cloud flops: cross-VM row hammer attacks and privilege escalation. In: USENIX Security (2016)
109. Yoon, H., et al.: Row buffer locality aware caching policies for hybrid memories. In: ICCD (2012)
110. Yoon, H., et al.: Efficient data mapping and buffering techniques for multi-level cell phase-change memories. In: TACO (2014)
111. Zhou, P., et al.: A durable and energy efficient main memory using phase change memory technology. In ISCA (2009)

Cache-Timing Attack Detection and Prevention
Application to Crypto Libs and PQC

Sébastien Carré[1,2], Adrien Facon[1,3], Sylvain Guilley[1,2,3(✉)],
Sofiane Takarabt[1,2], Alexander Schaub[2], and Youssef Souissi[1]

[1] Secure-IC S.A.S., 15 Rue Claude Chappe, Bât. B, 35 510 Cesson-Sévigné, France
`sylvain.guilley@secure-ic.com`
[2] LTCI, Télécom ParisTech, Institut Polytechnique de Paris, 75 013 Paris, France
[3] École Normale Supérieure, département d'informatique, 75 005 Paris, France

Abstract. With the publication of Spectre & Meltdown attacks, cache-timing exploitation techniques have received a wealth of attention recently. On the one hand, it is now well understood which patterns in the source code create observable unbalances in terms of timing. On the other hand, some practical attacks have also been reported. But the exact relation between vulnerabilities and exploitations is not enough studied as of today. In this article, we put forward a methodology to characterize the leakage induced by a "non-constant-time" construct in the source code. This methodology allows us to recover known attacks and to warn about possible new ones, possibly devastating.

Keywords: Cache-timing attacks · Leakage detection ·
Leakage attribution · Discovery of new attacks

1 Introduction

Writing secure cryptographic software is notoriously hard, since mistakes can often be turned as a advantage by attackers to really extract the secrets. For instance, corruption of computations is known to allow for catastrophic failures [15]. Consider for instance:

- the Bellcore [3] attack on RSA with Chinese Remainder Theorem (CRT-RSA),
- the differential fault analysis (DFA [2]) on AES (ISO/IEC 18033-3),
- verification skips in signature schemes (recall the case of the double `goto` inadvertent copy-and-paste [14]).

Any bug in the implementation (e.g., possibility to perform a buffer overflow) which allows for replacing an intermediate value (as for Bellcore and DFA) does lead to a successful cryptanalysis. In the case of the verification skip in signature schemes, the bug is already in the source code and allows the attacker to bypass the cryptography.

© Springer Nature Switzerland AG 2019
I. Polian and M. Stöttinger (Eds.): COSADE 2019, LNCS 11421, pp. 13–21, 2019.
https://doi.org/10.1007/978-3-030-16350-1_2

Therefore, it is essential to write correct (bug-free) cryptographic software. But this is not sufficient, since other attacks can still be applied. Typically, side-channel attacks are also known as particularly threatening. Indeed, they exploit some non-functional albeit observable side-effects caused by computations to profile the cryptographic code, and to come back to the secret non-invasively. The reason for these attacks to be feared is that, in most of the time, they cannot be detected.

One particular side-channel attack which received a great deal of attention are the so-called cache-timing attacks. Indeed, the observation is carried out directly by the machine which executes the victim code. Therefore, the resolution is high and the noise is low. Furthermore, it is not necessary for the attacker to possess the machine. The pre-condition for the attack is simply to be able to use a cryptographic service, just as the victim would.

By monitoring the time shared resources react, the attacker learns whether or not the victim has been soliciting such resources. Shared resources are typically the multiple pipelines allowing for HyperThreaded computations, the use of cache memories for data, code, address translations (as in Memory Management Units or MMUs), the optimized management at the Dynamic Random Access Memory (DRAM) side, etc. Not all those resources are termed "caches", but still the exploitation of the fact they can be contended by the concurrent usage request of a victim and an attacker have them leak observable information. This information is often measured as a timing variation, except for those situations where it is sufficient to directly measure the side-channel, e.g., in a hardware performance counter. Sometimes, the attacks are refined in that some hardware peculiarity (e.g., branch prediction, out-of-order execution, etc.) enable indirectly the observable variability, correlated to some internal variable handled by the attacker. The operational use of cache-timing attacks is illustrated for instance to bypass kernel-level protections [12], to create covert-channels [19], to attack code in enclaves (CacheQuote [5]), etc. A big picture for so-called cache-timing vulnerabilities (at C code level) is depicted in Fig. 1.

In this figure, attacks are related to the contended resources which leak. The survey paper [11] also details the relationship between micro-architecture and exploits. But as of today, it is unclear how seriously a timing bias can be effectively exploited. This is precisely the intent of this paper.

The rest of this article is structured as follows. Known exploitation methods are presented in Sect. 2, and they are attributed to a purported hardware bias. Then comes our contribution in Sect. 3: we show a methodology to assess the severity of a cache-timing leakage. Finally, the conclusion is given in Sect. 4. Some examples of codes are relegated to the Appendix A.

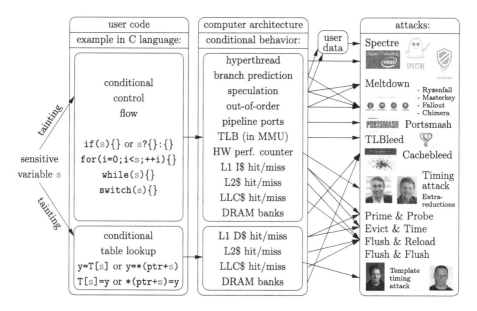

Fig. 1. Illustration how conditional code in one secret can manifest as observable side-channel leakage, and some renown exploitations

2   Cache-Timing Issues

Issues related to cache-timing dependency on sensitive variables can lead to a variety of attacks, namely:

- On RSA:
  - Simple power analysis [17] (horizontal leakage)
  - Extra-reduction analysis [7]
  - BigMac Attack on windowed exponentiation [22]
- On ECDSA:
  - LLL cryptanalysis due to short nonces [4,10]
- On AES:
  - Timing attack [16]
  - Higher-order timing attacks [6]
  - Template attacks [21]

3   Cache-Timing Analysis Methodology

3.1   State-of-the-Art

Cryptographic libraries are thoroughly analyzed for vulnerabilities, and despite a lot of efforts devoted to this topic, libraries need more checking. Indeed, the application of protection can really affect strongly the performances. For instance, the use of sliding-window algorithm for exponentiation is known to leak but is believed hard to exploit. Still, using a perfectly regular exponentiation algorithms would collapse the performances. Hence the question whether or not the countermeasure is practically needed. This has pushed attackers to try harder, and actually a not so abstract on a key extraction has been put forward [1].

The Post-quantum cryptographic (PQC) algorithms have been analyzed for leakages. The affected parts contributing to leakages have already been classified systematically in [9, §5]:

- noise sampling operations, amongst them Gaussian noise is really sensitive,
- insecure Galois Field operations, especially in fields of characteristic two,
- variable time error correction algorithms,
- use of insecure large number libraries, such as GMP (GNU Multi-Precision, https://gmplib.org/).

Let us now explore a systematic leakage discovery methodology.

3.2   Methodology Presentation

The presented methodology combines on the one hand *static* and *dynamic* analyses, and on the other hand *source* and *assembly* analyses.

$\boxed{\text{Step 1}}$: **Static Analysis.** The first step is a static analysis on source code. The code is represented as an abstract syntax tree (AST), and the sensitive variables (secret keys, but also all parameters whose knowledge would allow to recover the secret keys, such as random numbers/noise involved in cryptographic protocols) are propagated in the tree. A vulnerability is the coincidence of a sensitive variable s and of either a conditional control flow operation (recall if(s){}, for(i=0;i<s;++i){}, while(s){}, and switch(s){} constructs illustrated in Fig. 1) or a conditional table lookup (recall y=T[s] and y=*(ptr+s), or vice-versa, constructs illustrated in Fig. 1).

Let us illustrate in Fig. 2 the vulnerabilities found in RSA signature of MbedTLS. The Listing 1.2 in Appendix A shows one practical leakage. As illustrated in Fig. 2, the list of vulnerabilities can be regrouped according to their calling patterns. Indeed, for a versatile routine, there can be many functions actually requesting it. This is of great interest, since the more often a vulnerability is executed, the more likely it will leak exploitable information. Actually, one has to keep in mind that cache-timing attacks face a practical challenge, as:

- when applied against asymmetrical cryptography, which is typically randomized, the attack must succeed in one single trace;
- when applied against symmetrical cryptography (refer for instance to [21]), the key is unchanged for multiple operations, but the algorithms are very fast (around thousand clock periods, where the attackers aims at extracting hundreds of bits).

$\boxed{\text{Step2}}$: **Assembly Code Analysis.** The second step consists in analyzing the generated assembly code after compilation of the C source code. The purpose if to check whether the vulnerability is still present. In some cases, the compiler

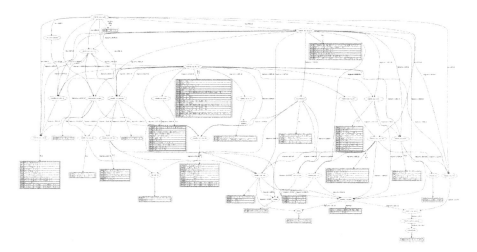

Fig. 2. Vulnerabilities identified in MbedTLS source code for RSA signature (courtesy of [20])

Table 1. Translation of cache-timing vulnerable C operations into assembly

C construct	Pseudo-assembly construct	Vulnerable?
if(s){}	cmov s or setcc s	no
if(s){}, for(i=0;i<s;++i){}, while(s){}, and switch(s){}	test s, jump *address*	yes
y=T[s] or y=*(ptr+s)	load s	yes
T[s]=y or *(ptr+s)=y	store s	yes

manages to remove (unintentionally though) the problem upon assembly code generation. Table 1 illustrates typical translation of C structures into assembly.

It can be seen in Table 1 that some conditional operations can be translated in constant-time assembly instructions, such as cmov (conditional move, atomic) or such as setcc (set conditional, atomic). Indeed, these translations benefit the execution speed: as they do not break the control flow, they can be executed without risking a cache or a speculation fault, thereby accelerating the execution. Furthermore, those translations happen only (paradoxically enough) when the code is compiled with optimization options.

The access to tables are almost certainly not fixed, since the techniques to make unconditional table accesses (bitslicing, extrapolation of table using Lagrange polynomial, lookup of all elements and subsequent addition of values after Boolean mask by the address indicator, etc.) are way too evolved. Additionally, the known tactics to protect table lookups feature extremely high timing

18   S. Carré et al.

overhead, hence shall be added manually. The vulnerability due to pointer deref-
erencing (except for tables with very small, e.g., two, number of entries) thus
remains from C to assembly. For further reference on vulnerabilities at assembly-
level, we redirect the reader to [18].

Step 3 : **Statistical Analysis.** Finally, the code is executed dynamically, and
`breakpoints` are set on the assembly lines previously identified as vulnerable.
The information to be extracted is as follows:

– Count the number of occurrences while running the code—as mentioned, the
  more often the leak is executed, the more chance it is exploitable;
– Check for execution patterns. If they are too fast (e.g., as bursts), it might
  be hard to measure them individually.

The temporal distribution of vulnerabilities identified in static analysis is
represented in Fig. 3 (obtained with Intel PIN), for the 800 first instructions
(out of 3,679,883 making up a complete RSA 2048-bit).

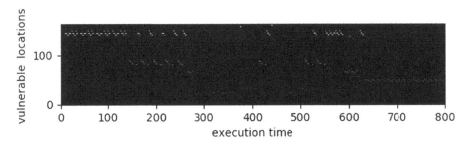

Fig. 3. Activation times (labelled in number of instructions) of vulnerabilities found
by static analysis, for RSA signature.

Step 4 : **Real-World Exploitation.** Ideally, this method is complemented
by a real world measurements (e.g., using FLUSH+FLUSH [13] methodology, as
that from the Catalyzr™ tool [8]), so as to assess in which respect the leakages
are exploitable. Actually, regarding lookup tables, some accesses are indistinguishable, since they occur in the same line of cache. The final check allows to
validate whether the risk is real.

3.3 Methodology Application

The latest version of MbedTLS library (version `2.14.0`) at the time of writing
this paper is studied. It is written with security in mind. Indeed, as an example,
it features some functions allowing for conditional operations to be carried in a
way which cannot be exploited by cache-attacks. An illustration is provided by
function `mbedtls_mpi_safe_cond_assign` (where `mpi` stands for multiprecision
interger), located in `library/bignum.c` and given for reference as Listing 1.1
in Appendix A.

4   Conclusion

This paper has introduced a practical methodology to analyse observable cache-timing biases with respect to their possible exploitation. The methodology consists in several steps, namely: vulnerability identification in source code, vulnerability tracking in assembly code, statistics on the dynamic occurrence of the vulnerability, and eventually, real measurements using FLUSH+FLUSH methodology.

We have shown how known attacks are recovered in a software cryptographic library, and we point towards numerous new (uncovered yet albeit possibly devastating) ones.

Acknowledgments. This work has benefited from a funding via the French PIA (Projet d'Investissment d'Avenir) RISQ (Regroupement de l'Industrie pour la Sécurité post-Quantique). Besides, this work has been partly financed via TEAMPLAY (https://teamplay-h2020.eu/), a project from European Union's Horizon20202 research and innovation programme, under grant agreement N° 779882.

A   Some Excerpts From Secure and Vulnerable Functions From mbedTLS

```
int mbedtls_mpi_safe_cond_assign( mbedtls_mpi *X, const mbedtls_mpi *Y, unsigned char assign )
{
    int ret = 0;
    size_t i;

    assign = (assign | (unsigned char)-assign) >> 7;

    MBEDTLS_MPI_CHK( mbedtls_mpi_grow( X, Y->n ) );

    X->s = X->s * ( 1 - assign ) + Y->s * assign;

    for( i = 0; i < Y->n; i++ )
        X->p[i] = X->p[i] * ( 1 - assign ) + Y->p[i] * assign;

    for( ; i < X->n; i++ )
        X->p[i] *= ( 1 - assign );
cleanup:
    return( ret );
}
```

Listing 1.1. Conditional assignment function, which does not reveal whether the assignment has been completed or not

```
void mbedtls_mpi_init( mbedtls_mpi *X )
{
    if( X == NULL )
        return;

    X->s = 1;
    X->n = 0;
    X->p = NULL;
}
```

Listing 1.2. Example of vulnerable code, as identified statically (the leakage is in the if statement)

References

1. Bernstein, D.J., et al.: Sliding right into disaster: left-to-right sliding windows leak. In: Fischer, W., Homma, N. (eds.) CHES 2017. LNCS, vol. 10529, pp. 555–576. Springer, Cham (2017). https://doi.org/10.1007/978-3-319-66787-4_27
2. Biham, E., Shamir, A.: Differential fault analysis of secret key cryptosystems. In: Kaliski, B.S. (ed.) CRYPTO 1997. LNCS, vol. 1294, pp. 513–525. Springer, Heidelberg (1997). https://doi.org/10.1007/BFb0052259
3. Boneh, D., DeMillo, R.A., Lipton, R.J.: On the importance of checking cryptographic protocols for faults. In: Fumy, W. (ed.) EUROCRYPT 1997. LNCS, vol. 1233, pp. 37–51. Springer, Heidelberg (1997). https://doi.org/10.1007/3-540-69053-0_4
4. Brumley, B.B., Tuveri, N.: Remote timing attacks are still practical. In: Atluri, V., Diaz, C. (eds.) ESORICS 2011. LNCS, vol. 6879, pp. 355–371. Springer, Heidelberg (2011). https://doi.org/10.1007/978-3-642-23822-2_20
5. Dall, F., et al.: CacheQuote: efficiently recovering long-term secrets of SGX EPID via cache attacks. IACR Trans. Cryptogr. Hardw. Embed. Syst. **2018**(2), 171–191 (2018)
6. Danger, J.-L., Debande, N., Guilley, S., Souissi, Y.: High-order timing attacks. In: Proceedings of the First Workshop on Cryptography and Security in Computing Systems, CS2 2014, pp. 7–12. ACM, New York (2014)
7. Dugardin, M., Guilley, S., Danger, J.-L., Najm, Z., Rioul, O.: Correlated extra-reductions defeat blinded regular exponentiation. In: Gierlichs, B., Poschmann, A.Y. (eds.) CHES 2016. LNCS, vol. 9813, pp. 3–22. Springer, Heidelberg (2016). https://doi.org/10.1007/978-3-662-53140-2_1
8. Facon, A., Guilley, S., Lec'hvien, M., Marion, D., Perianin, T.: Binary data analysis for source code leakage assessment. In: Lanet, J.-L., Toma, C. (eds.) SECITC 2018. LNCS, vol. 11359, pp. 391–409. Springer, Cham (2019). https://doi.org/10.1007/978-3-030-12942-2_30
9. Facon, A., Guilley, S., Lec'hvien, M., Schaub, A., Souissi, Y.: Detecting cache-timing vulnerabilities in post-quantum cryptography algorithms. In: 3rd IEEE International Verification and Security Workshop, IVSW 2018, Costa Brava, Spain, 2–4 July 2018, pp. 7–12. IEEE (2018)
10. García, C.P., Brumley, B.B., Yarom, Y.: Make sure DSA signing exponentiations really are constant-time. In: Weippl, E.R., et al. [22], pp. 1639–1650
11. Ge, Q., Yarom, Y., Cock, D., Heiser, G.: A survey of microarchitectural timing attacks and countermeasures on contemporary hardware. J. Cryptographic Eng. **8**(1), 1–27 (2018)
12. Gruss, D., Maurice, C., Fogh, A., Lipp, M., Mangard, S.: Prefetch side-channel attacks: bypassing SMAP and kernel ASLR. In: Weippl, E.R., et al. [22], pp. 368–379
13. Gruss, D., Maurice, C., Wagner, K., Mangard, S.: Flush+Flush: a fast and stealthy cache attack. In: Caballero, J., Zurutuza, U., Rodríguez, R.J. (eds.) DIMVA 2016. LNCS, vol. 9721, pp. 279–299. Springer, Cham (2016). https://doi.org/10.1007/978-3-319-40667-1_14
14. iOS 7.0.6. CVE-ID CVE-2014-1266. Description: Secure Transport failed to validate the authenticity of the connection. This issue was addressed by restoring missing validation steps. Impact: An attacker with a privileged network position may capture or modify data in sessions protected by SSL/TLS, February 2014. https://nvd.nist.gov/vuln/detail/CVE-2014-1266

15. Joye, M., Tunstall, M. (eds.): Fault Analysis in Cryptography. Information Security and Cryptography. Springer, Heidelberg (2012). https://doi.org/10.1007/978-3-642-29656-7. ISBN: 978-3-642-29655-0
16. Kocher, P.C.: Timing attacks on implementations of Diffie-Hellman, RSA, DSS, and other systems. In: Koblitz, N. (ed.) CRYPTO 1996. LNCS, vol. 1109, pp. 104–113. Springer, Heidelberg (1996). https://doi.org/10.1007/3-540-68697-5_9
17. Kocher, P., Jaffe, J., Jun, B.: Differential power analysis. In: Wiener, M. (ed.) CRYPTO 1999. LNCS, vol. 1666, pp. 388–397. Springer, Heidelberg (1999). https://doi.org/10.1007/3-540-48405-1_25
18. Clémentine Maurice and Moritz Lipp. What could possibly go wrong with <insert x86 instruction here>?, December 2016. 33rd Chaos Communication Congress (33c3), Hamburg, Germany. https://lab.dsst.io/slides/33c3/slides/8044.pdf
19. Maurice, C., et al.: Hello from the other side: SSH over robust cache covert channels in the cloud. In: 24th Annual Network and Distributed System Security Symposium, NDSS 2017, San Diego, California, USA, 26 February–1 March 2017. The Internet Society (2017)
20. Takarabt, S., et al.: Cache-timing attacks still threaten IoT devices. In: Codes, Cryptology and Information Security - Third International Conference, C2SI 2019, Rabat, Morocco, 22–14 April 2019, Proceedings. Springer (2019, to appear)
21. Tromer, E., Osvik, D.A., Shamir, A.: Efficient cache attacks on AES, and countermeasures. J. Cryptol. **23**(1), 37–71 (2010)
22. Walter, C.D.: Sliding windows succumbs to big Mac attack. In: Koç, Ç.K., Naccache, D., Paar, C. (eds.) CHES 2001. LNCS, vol. 2162, pp. 286–299. Springer, Heidelberg (2001). https://doi.org/10.1007/3-540-44709-1_24
23. Weippl, E.R., Katzenbeisser, S., Kruegel, C., Myers, A.C., Halevi, S., (eds.): Proceedings of the 2016 ACM SIGSAC Conference on Computer and Communications Security, Vienna, Austria, 24–28 October 2016. ACM (2016)

Side-Channel Attacks

Fast Side-Channel Security Evaluation of ECC Implementations

Shortcut Formulas for Horizontal Side-Channel Attacks Against ECSM with the Montgomery Ladder

Melissa Azouaoui[1,2]([⊠]), Romain Poussier[3], and François-Xavier Standaert[1]

[1] Université Catholique de Louvain, Louvain-la-Neuve, Belgium
melissa.azouaoui@nxp.com
[2] NXP Semiconductors, Hamburg, Germany
[3] Temasek Laboratories, Nanyang Technological University, Singapore, Singapore

Abstract. Horizontal attacks are a suitable tool to evaluate the (nearly) worst-case side-channel security level of ECC implementations, due to the fact that they allow extracting a large amount of information from physical observations. Motivated by the difficulty of mounting such attacks and inspired by evaluation strategies for the security of symmetric cryptography implementations, we derive shortcut formulas to estimate the success rate of horizontal differential power analysis attacks against ECSM implementations, for efficient side-channel security evaluations. We then discuss the additional leakage assumptions that we exploit for this purpose, and provide experimental confirmation that the proposed tools lead to good predictions of the attacks' success.

Keywords: Elliptic Curve Cryptography (ECC) ·
Side-channel attacks · Side-channel security evaluations ·
Horizontal Differential Power Analysis (HDPA)

1 Introduction

Elliptic curve cryptography (ECC) relies on the intractability of the elliptic curve discrete logarithm problem. Due to the efficiency of elliptic curve based cryptosystems in comparison to other public-key cryptosystems such as RSA, they have been widely deployed in modern information systems, and thus are targeted by Side-Channel Attacks (SCAs). One of the most important ingredients of ECC protocols is the Elliptic Curve Scalar Multiplication (ECSM). As a result, various types of SCAs have been introduced against their implementations.

First, Simple Power Analysis (SPA) [16] exploits the fact that the sequence of operations depends on the secret scalar. A regular execution can thwart these attacks [14]. Next, Differential Power Analysis (DPA) [7,15] recovers the secret scalar from multiple side-channel traces, and thus can be prevented by scalar randomization [7]. Template Attacks (TA) [5] have also been used to break ECC

I. Polian and M. Stöttinger (Eds.): COSADE 2019, LNCS 11421, pp. 25–42, 2019.
https://doi.org/10.1007/978-3-030-16350-1_3

implementations [20]. They rely on the knowledge of the input point and can be thwarted by point randomization [7,13]. Attacks against ECSM algorithms additionally include Horizontal Collision Attacks (HCA) [4] which take advantage of the observation that for a certain scalar bit value, identical operands are manipulated at different instants of the execution. These attacks can be hindered by the shuffling countermeasure [17] or randomization techniques [13]. Finally, Horizontal DPA (HDPA) [6] exploits multiple time samples of one side-channel trace, as opposed to the classical vertical DPA described above. Besides, attacks against ECSM algorithms usually follow one out of two standard strategies: *divide-and-conquer* or *extend-and-prune*. In a divide-and-conquer attack, the bits of the scalar are recovered independently, while in an extend-and-prune attack they are recovered recursively.

We are particularly interested in HDPA following an extend-and-prune strategy. Attacks such as in [21] are powerful and suitable for (nearly) worst-case side-channel security assessments, since their horizontal nature allows extracting most of the information from a leakage trace. However, they are intricate to mount, due to the fact that they rely on the knowledge of the implementation, and the exploitation of many time samples from one single noisy side-channel trace. As a result, and inspired by evaluation strategies considered for implementation security in symmetric cryptography (e.g., [10,12,23]), we propose shortcut formulas and derive an efficient approximation of the Success Rate (SR) of an HDPA as function of the number of leaking registers exploited and the noise level of the implementation. For this purpose, we first describe our method and its underlying assumptions, and then confirm its practical relevance based on an experimental case study.

The rest of the paper is organized as follows. Section 2 introduces our notations and background on ECC and the extend-and-prune HDPA by Poussier et al. [21]. Section 3 explains the rationale behind our approach and the goal of our research. Section 4 details the efficient derivation of the success rate. Section 5 reports results from simulated experiments and Sect. 6 shows the relevance of the proposed approach on a real target.

2   Background

2.1   Notations

We use capital letters for random variables and small caps for their realizations. We use sans serif font for functions (e.g., F). We denote the conditional probability of a random variable A given B with $\Pr[A|B]$. We use $\mathcal{U}(\mathbb{F})$ to denote the uniform distribution over a field $\mathbb{F}$ and $\mathcal{N}(\mu, \sigma^2)$ to denote the Gaussian distribution with mean μ and variance σ^2. We use $\sim$ to denote that a random variable follows a given distribution (e.g., $A \sim \mathcal{N}(\mu, \sigma^2)$). We also denote by Φ the Cumulative Distribution Function (CDF) of the normal distribution.

2.2 Elliptic Curve Scalar Multiplication

We denote by $\mathbb{F}_p$ a finite field of characteristic $p > 3$ and $\mathcal{E}(\mathbb{F}_p)$ the set of points $(x, y) \in \mathbb{F}_p^2$ that satisfy the elliptic curve with the Weierstrass equation: $y^2 = x^3 + ax + b$ along with the point at infinity O. For a scalar $k \in \mathbb{F}_p$ we denote by $(k_0, k_1, ..., k_{n-1})$ its binary representation where k_0 is the most significant bit. For $P, Q \in \mathcal{E}(\mathbb{F}_p)$, $P + Q$ denotes the point addition, and kP the k-repeated addition $P + ... + P$, i.e., the ECSM. Elliptic curve cryptosystems (such as ECDH and ECDSA [22]) require to perform a scalar multiplication kP where k is a secret and P a public curve point. A popular method to implement ECSM securely consists in using the Montgomery ladder [14], shown in Algorithm 1. Its regular operation flow makes it naturally resistant against SPA [14].

Algorithm 1. Montgomery ladder

    Input P , $k = (k_0, ..., k_{n-1})$
    Output kP

1:   $R_0 \leftarrow O$
2:   $R_1 \leftarrow P$
3:   **for** $i = 0$ to $n - 1$ **do**
4:      $R_{1-k_i} \leftarrow R_{1-k_i} + R_{k_i}$
5:      $R_{k_i} \leftarrow 2R_{k_i}$
6:   **end for**
7:   **return** R_0

2.3 Horizontal Differential Power Analysis

As shown by Algorithm 1, the Montgomery ladder ECSM processes the bits of k iteratively, updating the internal state (R_0 and R_1) of the algorithm accordingly. At bit position i of k, the internal state depends on bits $\{0, ..., i\}$ of k. As a result, attacks against Montgomery ladder ECSM implementations are naturally performed by using an extend-and-prune strategy, and recovering the key bits in a recursive manner: the recovery of the i-th bit relies on the correct recovery of the previous bits $\{0, ..., i - 1\}$ in order to make a hypothesis on the state [3,6]. Following this strategy, the HDPA attack presented in [21] divides a constant time ECSM execution into a sequence of predictable operations at each abstraction level of the ECSM as shown in Fig. 1. The last layer consists of $n \times N$ register multiplications, where N is the number of register multiplications required to process one scalar bit[1]. We consider the same reference Montgomery ladder ECSM as in [21] on a 32-bit device, using Jacobian coordinates and the point addition and doubling routines given in Appendix A on the NIST P-256 curve [22]. This implementation requires 25 field multiplications per scalar bit and they are performed with a Long Integer Multiplication (LIM) followed by a

---

[1] While we only consider register multiplications, the framework can be applied to any operation.

reduction. Knowing the i previous bits of k and the input point P, the attacker succeeds if he can infer the correct sequence of register values $(r_j)_{0 \leq j < N}$ out of the two possibilities for k_i. For efficiency reasons, the attack assumes the Independence of the Operations' Leakages (IOL) [12]. Besides, a leakage of the form $l_j(r_j) = \delta_j(r_j) + b_j$, where δ_j is the leakage function of r_j. The term b_j represents the noise and is distributed according to $\mathcal{N}(0, \sigma^2)$ is usually assumed for simplicity [19] (yet, any noise distribution could theoretcially be analyzed in a maximum likelihood manner). The correct bit value is then recovered as the one maximizing the product of the probabilities of the register leakages:

$$\prod_j \Pr[l_j \mid (r_j | k_i, P)] = \prod_j \mathcal{N}(l_j \mid (r_j | k_i, P), \sigma^2).$$

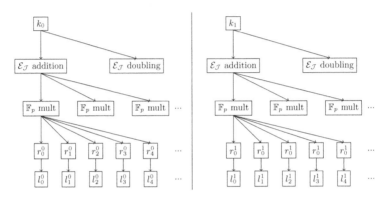

Fig. 1. Leveled view of a regular scalar multiplication. First level (top): scalar bit handling. Second: elliptic curve arithmetic. Third: Field arithmetic. Fourth: register operations. Fifth: leakages on register operations. (Taken from [21]).

3 Problem Statement and Challenges

One recurrent problem of side-channel security evaluations is the large amount of different state-of-the-art attacks [25] which makes it prohibitive to try all of them: ECC implementations are no exception to this issue. In this context, the HDPA described above is an interesting one to investigate, since it belongs to the most powerful type of attacks against ECC implementations. However, it comes at the cost of a complicated instantiation. First, it requires a precise knowledge of the implementation under attack. Second, it requires to profile every single operation of the ECSM. This step is computationally intensive and requires several manual optimizations in order to process the large ECSM traces in a reasonable time. In the following, we describe how this generic framework can be used for systematizing security evaluations and reducing their cost, by providing shortcut formulas to estimate the success rate of HDPA without performing it.

For this purpose, we draw our inspiration from the associated literature on symmetric cryptography. Indeed, shortcut formulas for success rate estimation in the case of block ciphers are already a deeply investigated topic. In the simpler case of unprotected (more precisely, unmasked) implementations, efficient approximations of the success rate can typically rely on easy-to-compute metrics such as the Signal-to-Noise Ratio (SNR) [10,23]. By contrast, for masked implementations, additional assumptions and/or metrics (e.g., the mutual information) are needed [8,9,18]. Since considering unprotected ECC implementations, we will next be in the former case and additionally exploit some of the ideas used in [12] for the analysis of multivariate/horizontal attacks. Precisely, we will adapt the SNR metric to the context of ECSM implementations and exploit it for the estimation of the success rate as a function of the number of targeted register leakages and the noise level.

3.1   SNR Definitions

In general, the SNR of a device depends on the size of the bus (which defines the maximum signal), the adversary's guessing power (which defines the part of the bus that generates exploitable signal and the part that generates algorithmic noise) and the physical noise. It is defined as the variance of the (exploitable) signal divided by the noise variance. In this paper, we consider a 32-bit device and therefore assume that all the bits of the bus can be predicted (so no algorithmic noise). In the context of a standard DPA attack where the full bus is targeted [19], this would lead to an SNR32 defined for a register indexed j as:

$$\mathrm{SNR32}_j = \frac{\underset{r_j \in \mathbb{F}_{2^{32}}}{\mathrm{var}} \; \delta_j(r_j)}{\sigma^2}, \tag{1}$$

where δ_j is the deterministic (noise-free) part of the leakage function for a register r_j, as introduced in Sect. 2.3, and σ^2 is the noise variance. Further assuming an Hamming-weight leakage function for illustration, this leads to $\mathrm{SNR32} = \frac{8}{\sigma^2}$ (with 8=32/4 the variance of a random 32-bit Hamming weight).

When considering a 32-bit implementation of the Montgomery ladder ECSM, the situation slightly differs from this standard DPA context. Indeed, in this case the register content typically depends on a single key bit (rather than 32 ones in the standard DPA case). Therefore, each target register can only take two values instead of every value of $\mathbb{F}_{2^{32}}$. A vertical DPA against an ECSM therefore boils down to distinguishing the leakage of two 32-bit values, whereas a HDPA tries to exploit multiple registers. Concretely, this means that certain registers lead to easier-to-distinguish leakages. Yet, in order to improve the efficiency of the security evaluations, we will also use an average metric to estimate the success rate (and track the distance between this estimate and the success rate of concrete attacks). For this purpose, a first natural idea would be to consider a modified $SNR2_j$ that captures the difference between the (noise-free) leakages of a register r_j for two scalar bit values:

$$SNR2_j = \frac{\underset{P \in \mathcal{E}(\mathbb{F}_p)}{\mathbb{E}} (\delta_j(r_j|k_i = 0, P) - \delta_j(r_j|k_i = 1, P))^2}{\sigma^2}. \tag{2}$$

3.2   Preliminary Observations and Caveats

HDPA aims at exploiting the leakages of a large number of leaking registers for a single key bit. In the symmetric case, this can be viewed as targeting several leakage samples for a single subkey (e.g., both the input and the output of a S-box). As a result, in this case we have that $\delta_i = \delta_j$ trivially implies $SNR32_i = SNR32_j$. This basically means that under the assumption $\delta_i = \delta_j$, the estimation of the SNR32 is only required for a single register. Grosso and Standaert use this same assumption (of similar leakage functions for all their target intermediate computations) to speed up the computation of a multivariate mutual information to an univariate one [12].

Following this approach, a tempting strategy for ECSM evaluation would thus be to also assume that the leakage functions are similar for all the registers, leading to a constant SNR2. To evaluate the soundness of this approach, Fig. 2 illustrates the $SNR2_j$ for each register r_j corresponding to the high 32-bit words of multiplication results. Our reference implementation introduced in Sect. 2 requires $N = 1600$ register multiplications to process one key bit. The SNR2 is evaluated for a Hamming weight leakage model, so exactly fulfilling the assumption of identical leakage functions, and averaged over 10,000 randomly sampled elliptic curve points. We observe that $SNR2_j$ is not constant even when the leakage function is the same for all registers. These differences can be explained by the algebraic relations between the values computed when the scalar bit equals 0 and the values when this bit equals 1. For example, the regions of high SNR2 on Fig. 2 observed in the register index intervals [512,576] and [704,768] respectively correspond to the 9th and 12th field multiplication in the point addition algorithm described in Appendix A. For a bit value, it performs the operations E^2 and H^2 or the operations $(-E)^2$ and $(-H)^2$ when the bit is flipped. This leads to bigger differences in the side-channel leakage, as the bits of the opposite of a field element modulus the NIST P-256 prime [22] are almost all flipped. The peaks of zero SNR2 in register index interval [896,960] correspond to the 15th field multiplication in the point addition algorithm. It performs the operation $Z_1 Z_2$ or $Z_2 Z_1$ when the bit is flipped. Since the same elements are multiplied in both cases, 8 equal cross products appear during the computation of the Long Integer Multiplication, thus leading to no information (SNR2 = 0).

These observations imply that, as opposed to the symmetric case, a single register cannot be used to evaluate the security of ECSM implementations with respect to vertical DPA, even if the leakage function is the same for all the registers. This variation of the SNR2 highlights the fact that when performing these attacks, some leakage points are more interesting than others. So strictly speaking, such a simple evaluation is not possible for HDPA either.

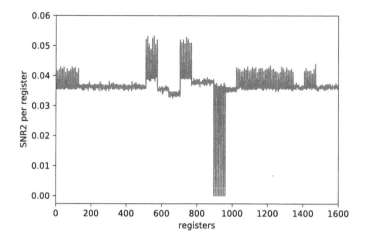

Fig. 2. Average SNR2 for the 1600 targeted registers of field multiplications in the Montgomery ladder.

3.3   The Single Trace Attack Scenario

Besides the previous caveat, another difficulty arises from the contradiction between HDPA that are essentially designed to succeed in a single-trace attack context (e.g., against a randomized key or an unknown scalar nonce) and the SNR2 metric which corresponds to an average amount of information collected over multiple points (and is therefore more in line with a vertical DPA).

In order to deal with this issue, we therefore start by defining the register-specific amount of information that corresponds to the distance between a register value when the scalar bit equals 0 and its value when the scalar bit equals 1, for a fixed EC point. For register r_j and a point P, we denote this distance by $d_j(P)$, whose definition is given by Eq. 3:

$$d_j(P) = (\delta_j(r_j|k_i = 0, P) - \delta_j(r_j|k_i = 1, P))^2. \tag{3}$$

Perfectly characterizing the security of an ECSM against HDPA naturally requires characterizing all the distances $d_j(P)$. Yet, and interestingly, we will next show that the two challenges described in this section (i.e., the fact that the SNR2 metric is register-dependent and that HDPA is primarily designed for single-trace attacks) can be mitigated concurrently. For this purpose, the main observation is that in view of the number of registers in ECSM implementations, it seems reasonable that the success of an attack targeting all the registers at once actually gets close to the average one. We next formalize this idea and describe the additional assumptions it requires.

4 Efficient Success Rate Approximation

In this section, we show how to derive an approximation of the success rate with respect to the HDPA framework for one scalar bit recovery. Since we consider two equally likely Gaussian hypotheses, the SR when targeting a single register r_j for a given point P is computed as in [5] and given by Eq. 4:

$$\text{SR} = \Phi\left(\frac{\sqrt{(\delta_j(r_j|k_i = 0, P) - \delta_j(r_j|k_i = 1, P))^2}}{2\sigma}\right). \tag{4}$$

We recall that the HDPA described in the previous section assumes IOL for computational efficiency. It was also noted by Poussier et al. [21] that fully characterizing the traces' covariance does not improve the attack results in case of profiling with bounded number of measurements. So we next leverage this assumption and recall that it is a conservative one (deviations can only reduce the attack effectiveness). It allows us to easily extend the previous formula to the case where an attacker would exploit N registers at once. Interestingly, it also re-enforces the analogy between vertical and horizontal DPA. Indeed, the IOL assumption divides the side-channel trace into N univariate samples, which roughly corresponds to a vertical DPA using N traces. As a result, similarly to the vertical DPA case [8], the SR of the horizontal DPA exploiting N samples, denoted by SR^N, is given by Eq. 6.

$$\text{SR}^N = \Phi\left(\frac{\sqrt{N \cdot \underset{j}{\mathbb{E}} \ (\delta_j(r_j|k_i = 0, P) - \delta_j(r_j|k_i = 1, P))^2}}{2\sigma}\right), \tag{5}$$

$$= \Phi\left(\frac{\sqrt{N \cdot \underset{j}{\mathbb{E}} \ d_j(P)}}{2\sigma}\right). \tag{6}$$

As shown by Fig. 2, the vertical signal SNR2 is not constant across all registers as opposed to the symmetric case. This is also true for the horizontal signal $d_j(P)$, which will inevitably vary depending on the point and the targeted register. As a result, a strict approximation of the SR^N using Eq. 6 would require to compute $d_j(P)$ for every single register. This requires a first step of leakage characterization [5,24]. This step is quite intensive and the most time and data consuming in HDPA. Using Eq. 6, the SR approximation is just as complex and tedious as performing HDPA. This observation shows the need of additional assumptions in order to simplify the security evaluation.

4.1 Additional Assumptions

Identical Leakage Functions Assumption (ILF): We first assume that the leakage function is identical across all registers: $\delta_i = \delta_j = \delta$, for $i, j \in [0, N - 1]$. Note that this is a common assumption that is also used in the security evaluation of masked implementations of block ciphers [12].

Asymptotic Uniformity Assumption (AU): We define the notion of *ideal distance* d_{id} as the square difference between the noise-free leakages of two uniformly distributed values $V_1, V_2 \sim \mathcal{U}(\mathbb{F}_{2^{|r|}})$. More formally, given a leakage function δ, the ideal distance is given by Eq. 7:

$$d_{id} = \mathop{\mathbb{E}}_{v_1, v_2} \left(\delta(v_1) - \delta(v_2) \right)^2. \tag{7}$$

Naturally, d_{id} can be seen as the *vertical* information provided by a register whose values are uniformly distributed when the input point varies. Our main assumption, the AU, states that the mean of the distances $d_j(P)$ over a large number of registers tends towards d_{id}, as given by Eq. 8. Informally, it means that the average horizontal information $d_j(P)$ for a fixed point P of a big enough number of registers is equal to the vertical information of a single uniformly distributed register:

$$\mathop{\mathbb{E}}_{j=0}^{N-1} d_j(P) \xrightarrow[N \to +\infty]{} d_{id}. \tag{8}$$

4.2   Efficient Success Rate Approximation

Using the two assumptions introduced in the previous subsection, we can efficiently estimate the SR of HDPA against an ECSM implementation. For the AU assumption, we further assume that the number N of exploited registers is big enough so that $\mathop{\mathbb{E}}_j d_j(P)$ is close to d_{id}. As a result, the SR^N approximation is boiled down to the computation of d_{id} and the estimation of the noise level σ. The success rate formula of Eq. 6 is then trivially adapted to d_{id} as:

$$SR^N = \Phi \left(\frac{\sqrt{N \cdot d_{id}}}{2\sigma} \right). \tag{9}$$

Hamming Weight Leakage Example: We illustrate this formula with an example based on a Hamming weight leakage function HW. The HW of a uniform random variable on $\mathbb{F}_{2^{|r|}}$ is approximately distributed as $\mathcal{N}(\frac{|r|}{2}, \frac{|r|}{4})$. For $U_1, U_2 \sim \mathcal{U}(\mathbb{F}_{2^{|r|}})$, we have $HW(U_1) - HW(U_2) \sim \mathcal{N}(0, \frac{|r|}{2})$ and $(HW(U_1) - HW(U_2))^2 \sim \Gamma(\frac{1}{2}, |r|)$, where Γ denotes the Gamma distribution, here with shape parameter $\frac{1}{2}$ and scale parameter $|r|$. If the AU assumption holds, then the ideal distance d_{id} is equal to $\frac{|r|}{2}$. The corresponding success rate is given by Eq. 10:

$$SR^N = \Phi \left(\frac{\sqrt{N \cdot |r|}}{2\sqrt{2}\sigma} \right). \tag{10}$$

4.3   Potential Invalidation of the Assumptions

The previous equations express the SR of a HDPA as a function of its main parameters, which allows gaining intuition about how the complexity of such attacks scales. Yet, the concrete correctness of this proposal depends on the ILF and AU assumptions. In this subsection, we discuss how realistic these assumptions are, and identify issues that may contradict them in practice.

Algorithmic Issue. Even if the leakage model is the same for all targeted registers, the SNR2 is not identical for all registers, as seen on Fig. 2. The SNR2 and the distances $d_j(P)$ depend on the distribution of the intermediate values, the ECSM algorithm, the curve representation and the finite field arithmetic.

Physical Issue. While commonly used in SCAs, the ILF assumption is never fully verified in practice [11]. We might observe $\delta_i \neq \delta_j$ when $i \neq j$. This can introduce additional discrepancies among the registers' distances. It can impact the convergence of the mean distance to the ideal distance and thus the accuracy of the SR approximation using the AU assumption.

In the next sections, we show the validity of our approximations with respect to both issues. First, in section 5, simulations are used to show that the AU assumption provides a valid approximation of the behavior of ECSM intermediate values. Next, in section 6, we use real measurements to show that the physical errors are not too problematic for the accuracy of the SR approximation.

5   Simulated Experiment: The Algorithmic Issue

In this section, we tackle the algorithmic issue due to the distribution of the intermediate values of the ECSM and to what extent it deviates from a uniform distribution. For that purpose we use a perfect setting with a HW leakage function using simulated traces, to fulfill the ILF assumption so that conclusions are not affected by any physical aspect of a real device's leakages. We consider our reference implementation of the Montgomery ladder described in Sect. 2. We consider an attacker targeting all the $N = 1600$ multiplication results. For each execution with a random point P and a random scalar bit k_i, we are provided with the register values $(r_j^i)_{0 \leq j < 1600}$ along with their simulated leakages $l_j^i = \mathsf{HW}(r_j^i) + b_j$ where $b_j \sim \mathcal{N}(0, \sigma^2)$. The noise level is chosen to replicate the target device in Sect. 6: $\sigma^2 = 440$.

Convergence Towards the Ideal Distance: On Fig. 3 we plot the evolution of the average distances of 1000 elliptic curve points. The y axis corresponds to the mean distance computed over the registers indexed by the x axis. Each colored curve corresponds to one randomly chosen elliptic curve point. The horizontal black line represents the ideal distance $d_{\mathrm{id}} = 16$. We can observe that even though we only consider 1600 registers over the large number of leaking registers of an ECSM execution, for different points P of the elliptic curve $\mathcal{E}(\mathbb{F}_p)$,

the average distances $\frac{1}{N} \underset{j=1}{\overset{N-1}{\mathbb{E}}} d_j(P) = \frac{1}{N} \underset{j=1}{\overset{N-1}{\mathbb{E}}} \left(\delta(r_j | k_i = 0, P) - \delta(r_j | k_i = 1, P) \right)^2$

tends towards the ideal distance d_{id} when N gets larger[2]. This result shows that

---

[2] Note that attacking several scalar bits at the same time would also result in increasing the number of registers, thus positively impacting the convergence.

the AU assumption can roughly describe the behavior of the ECSM intermediate values' leakages, and the approximation is more and more accurate as the number of registers required for the success of the attack increases.

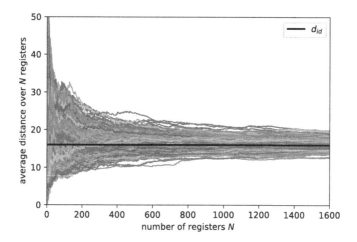

Fig. 3. Convergence of the average HW distances towards the ideal distance.

Success Rate Approximation: The perfect simulated setting allows us to investigate the impact of the AU assumption on the SR approximation. Namely the real success rate is only biased by the distances of register values. The results of the simulated experiments are illustrated in Fig. 4. Each of the 20 colored curves corresponds to the SR of HDPA evaluated for one elliptic curve point (repeated 100 times), and the orange curve is the SR approximation using d_{id}. Knowing the noise variance σ^2, the later is computed using Eq. 10. The figure suggests that the approximation predicts well enough the real SR, showing that the algorithmic issue is not problematic for this particular implementation.

Impact of the Noise: We performed the attack multiple times for different SNR32 values. First, the SNR32 of the target device in Sect. 6 (SNR32 = 0.0182), and additionally for SNR32 $\in \{0.1, 0.5, 1\}$. The results are depicted in Fig. 5. The solid curves represent the SR of HDPA as function of the number of registers, and the dashed curves the corresponding approximations using the AU assumption. We draw attention to the gap between the real SR (solid line) and the SR approximation (dashed line) computed using Eq. 10, which gets tighter as the SNR32 decreases. The bias introduced by the intermediate values of the ECSM makes the average distance over the small number of registers required for the success of HDPA for high SNR32 slightly deviate from the ideal distance. As the SNR32 decreases, this bias becomes smaller compared to the variance of the noise. Moreover, HDPA requires more registers to succeed, and thus requires to sum the distances over multiple registers which would tend towards the ideal distance as shown by Fig. 3. This is an interesting result as we are mainly

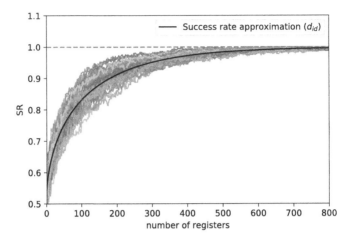

Fig. 4. Comparison of the SR and its approximation on simulated HW leakages. (Color figure online)

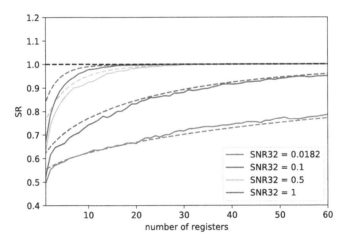

Fig. 5. Impact of the noise on the SR approximation.

interested in the low SNR32 case, as it corresponds to high security devices that require worst-case analysis.

6   Real Experiment: The Physical Issue

In this section, we investigate the impact of the ILF assumption on the accuracy of the SR approximation using the AU assumption. We use real measurements, where a different leakage function δ_j is expected for each leaking register r_j. Our experiments target our reference implementation similarly to the simulated case. The target device is a 32-bit ARM Cortex-M4 micro-controller from the

Atmel SAM4C-EK evaluation kit [1,2] running at 100 MHz. We monitored the voltage variation using a 4.7 Ω resistor inserted in the power supply circuit of the chip. We performed the trace acquisition using a Lecroy WaveRunner HRO 66 ZI oscilloscope running at 200 megasamples per second. We recorded the execution of 10,000 scalar multiplications. For each of them, we triggered the measurement at the beginning of the execution and recorded the processing of one scalar bit. We performed HDPA such as described in Sect. 2 but assuming two different leakage models. First, a linear regression taking as a basis the Hamming Weight of the leaking registers, similarly to the simulated experiment in the previous section. This yields for every register r_j, a leakage function of the form $\delta_j(r_j) = a_j + b_j \cdot \mathsf{HW}(r_j)$. Additionally, we performed HDPA for a linear regression based leakage model using a 32-bit basis, such as described by the original attack by Poussier et al [21].

Hamming Weight Linear Regression: We study the influence of the physical issue on the convergence of the average distance across multiple registers towards the ideal distance. We start by evaluating the distance $d_j(P)$ for each register: $d_j(P) = b_j^2(\mathsf{HW}(r_j|k_i = 0, P) - \mathsf{HW}(r_j|k_i = 1, P))^2$. We aim to compare the ideal distance to the mean distance for multiple different elliptic curve points. We evaluated the leakage model for the ideal distance using 20 random register leakages. Figure 6 depicts the convergence of the average distance over the leaking registers for 1000 random elliptic curve points towards the ideal distance d_{id}. We observe that the distances indeed converge towards the ideal distance similarly to the simulated case in Fig. 3 despite different leakage models for each individual register. Additionally, Fig. 7 shows the comparison between the real SR in blue of HDPA on real traces acquired from the target device previously described and its approximation in orange given by Eq. 9. We averaged the SR over multiple points,

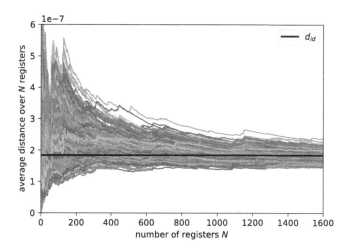

Fig. 6. Convergence towards the ideal distance of the average distances with different HW based real leakage models for each register.

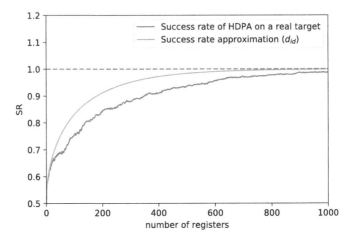

Fig. 7. Comparison of the SR of HDPA and its approximation assuming a HW based linear leakage model.

so that conclusions are not affected by the algorithmic issue. We note that the approximation is still satisfactory but less accurate than in the simulated case. This is expected as the attack is performed on real side-channel measurements and the HW is not the most accurate leakage modeling strategy for this device, while the SR approximation assumes that the leakage model has been perfectly characterized.

32-bit Linear Regession: We plot the convergence towards the ideal distance on Fig. 8 for 1000 random elliptic curve points. We evaluated again the leakage model for the ideal distance using 20 random register leakages. We notice that

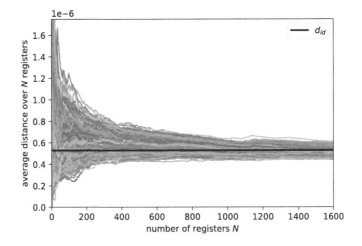

Fig. 8. Convergence towards the ideal distance of the average distances evaluated with a different linear regression function for each register.

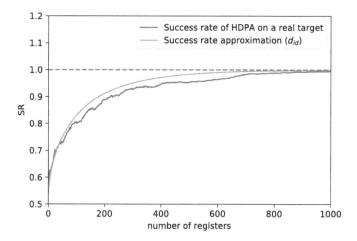

Fig. 9. Comparison of the SR of HDPA and its approximation assuming a linear regression leakage model.

despite having different leakage coefficients for each individual bit of the 1600 registers, the average distances still tend towards the ideal distance. This additional result further highlights the soundness of the AU assumption. Figure 9 shows the comparison between the SR of the HDPA in blue and its approximation in orange evaluated using Eq. 9. First, we notice that the SR approximation for a full basis linear regression attack is more accurate compared to the HW model case. This is due to the fact that the leakage of the considered device is best estimated by the second model.

7   Conclusion

Assessing the SCA security of an implementation is a tedious task. This is particularly true for complex cryptosystems for which numerous attack paths are possible. In this paper, we described a first methodology for analyzing the security of ECSM implementations against (close to) worst-case HDPA It allows us to express the success rate of such attacks based on an easy-to-estimate (ideal distance) metric, in function the number of leakage samples exploited by the adversary (which depends on the register size, the field size and the number of field operations) and the noise level. This shortcut formula trades a bit of accuracy in the success rate estimation for considerable efficiency gains. It could be easily extended to windowed algorithms and to the SR approximation of a full scalar recovery. Future works might investigate the application of this methodology to other implementations of public-key cryptosystems.

Acknowledgement. François-Xavier Standaert is a senior research associate of the Belgian Fund for Scientific Research. This work has been funded in part by the European Commission through the H2020 project 731591 (acronym REASSURE) and by the ERC Consolidator Grant 724725 (acronym SWORD). The authors would like to thank Vincent Verneuil for the valuable comments and the fruitful discussions.

A   Addition and Doubling Formulas

Algorithm 2. Point addition using Jacobian coordinates

Input $P = (X_1, Y_1, Z_1)$, $Q = (X_2, Y_2, Z_2)$

Output $P + Q = (X_3, Y_3, Z_3)$

   $A \leftarrow Z_1^2$, $B \leftarrow Z_2^2$, $C \leftarrow X_1 B$, $D \leftarrow X_2 A$, $E \leftarrow C - D$, $F \leftarrow Y_1 B Z_2$, $G \leftarrow Y_2 A Z_1$,
   $H \leftarrow F - G$, $I \leftarrow E^2$, $J \leftarrow IE$, $K \leftarrow CI$
   $X_3 \leftarrow H^2 + J - 2K$
   $Y_3 = H(K - X_3) - FJ$
   $Z_3 = Z_1 Z_2 E$
   return (X_3, Y_3, Z_3)

Algorithm 3. Point doubling using Jacobian coordinates

Input $P = (X_1, Y_1, Z_1)$

Output $P + P = (X_2, Y_2, Z_2)$

   $A \leftarrow X_1^2$, $B \leftarrow Y_1^2$, $C \leftarrow Z_1^2$, $D \leftarrow 3A + aC^2$, $E \leftarrow B^2$, $F \leftarrow 4X_1 B$
   $X_2 \leftarrow D^2 - 2F$
   $Y_2 \leftarrow D(F - X_2) - 8E$
   $Z_2 = 2Y_1 Z_1$
   return (X_2, Y_2, Z_2)

In the point doubling algorithm described above, the multiplication by $a = -3$ is done using field subtraction, leading to one less field multiplication.

References

1. Atsam4c-ek user guide. http://ww1.microchip.com/downloads/en/DeviceDoc/ Atmel_11251_SmartEnergy_ATSAM4C-EK-User_Guide_SAM4C8-SAM4C16_ User-Guide.pdf
2. Cortex-m4 technical reference manual. http://infocenter.arm.com/help/topic/ com.arm.doc.ddi0439b/DDI0439B_cortex_m4_r0p0_trm.pdf
3. Bauer, A., Jaulmes, E., Prouff, E., Wild, J.: Horizontal and vertical side-channel attacks against secure RSA implementations. In: Dawson, E. (ed.) CT-RSA 2013. LNCS, vol. 7779, pp. 1–17. Springer, Heidelberg (2013). https://doi.org/10.1007/ 978-3-642-36095-4_1

4. Bauer, A., Jaulmes, E., Prouff, E., Wild, J.: Horizontal collision correlation attack on elliptic curves. In: Lange, T., Lauter, K., Lisoněk, P. (eds.) SAC 2013. LNCS, vol. 8282, pp. 553–570. Springer, Heidelberg (2014). https://doi.org/10.1007/978-3-662-43414-7_28

5. Chari, S., Rao, J.R., Rohatgi, P.: Template attacks. In: Kaliski, B.S., Koç, K., Paar, C. (eds.) CHES 2002. LNCS, vol. 2523, pp. 13–28. Springer, Heidelberg (2003). https://doi.org/10.1007/3-540-36400-5_3

6. Clavier, C., Feix, B., Gagnerot, G., Roussellet, M., Verneuil, V.: Horizontal correlation analysis on exponentiation. In: Soriano, M., Qing, S., López, J. (eds.) ICICS 2010. LNCS, vol. 6476, pp. 46–61. Springer, Heidelberg (2010). https://doi.org/10.1007/978-3-642-17650-0_5

7. Coron, J.-S.: Resistance against differential power analysis for elliptic curve cryptosystems. In: Koç, Ç.K., Paar, C. (eds.) CHES 1999. LNCS, vol. 1717, pp. 292–302. Springer, Heidelberg (1999). https://doi.org/10.1007/3-540-48059-5_25

8. Ding, A.A., Zhang, L., Fei, Y., Luo, P.: A statistical model for higher order DPA on masked devices. In: Batina, L., Robshaw, M. (eds.) CHES 2014. LNCS, vol. 8731, pp. 147–169. Springer, Heidelberg (2014). https://doi.org/10.1007/978-3-662-44709-3_9

9. Duc, A., Faust, S., Standaert, F.-X.: Making masking security proofs concrete - or how to evaluate the security of any leaking device. In: Oswald, E., Fischlin, M. (eds.) EUROCRYPT 2015. LNCS, vol. 9056, pp. 401–429. Springer, Heidelberg (2015). https://doi.org/10.1007/978-3-662-46800-5_16

10. Fei, Y., Luo, Q., Ding, A.A.: A statistical model for DPA with novel algorithmic confusion analysis. In: Prouff, E., Schaumont, P. (eds.) CHES 2012. LNCS, vol. 7428, pp. 233–250. Springer, Heidelberg (2012). https://doi.org/10.1007/978-3-642-33027-8_14

11. Gérard, B., Standaert, F.-X.: Unified and optimized linear collision attacks and their application in a non-profiled setting: extended version. J. Cryptogr. Eng. **3**(1), 45–58 (2013)

12. Grosso, V., Standaert, F.-X.: Masking proofs are tight and how to exploit it in security evaluations. In: Nielsen, J.B., Rijmen, V. (eds.) EUROCRYPT 2018. LNCS, vol. 10821, pp. 385–412. Springer, Cham (2018). https://doi.org/10.1007/978-3-319-78375-8_13

13. Joye, M., Tymen, C.: Protections against differential analysis for elliptic curve cryptography — an algebraic approach —. In: Koç, Ç.K., Naccache, D., Paar, C. (eds.) CHES 2001. LNCS, vol. 2162, pp. 377–390. Springer, Heidelberg (2001). https://doi.org/10.1007/3-540-44709-1_31

14. Joye, M., Yen, S.-M.: The montgomery powering ladder. In: Kaliski, B.S., Koç, K., Paar, C. (eds.) CHES 2002. LNCS, vol. 2523, pp. 291–302. Springer, Heidelberg (2003). https://doi.org/10.1007/3-540-36400-5_22

15. Kocher, P., Jaffe, J., Jun, B.: Differential power analysis. In: Wiener, M. (ed.) CRYPTO 1999. LNCS, vol. 1666, pp. 388–397. Springer, Heidelberg (1999). https://doi.org/10.1007/3-540-48405-1_25

16. Kocher, P.C.: Timing attacks on implementations of diffie-hellman, RSA, DSS, and other systems. In: Koblitz, N. (ed.) CRYPTO 1996. LNCS, vol. 1109, pp. 104–113. Springer, Heidelberg (1996). https://doi.org/10.1007/3-540-68697-5_9

17. Le, D.-P., Tan, C.H., Tunstall, M.: Randomizing the montgomery powering ladder. In: Akram, R.N., Jajodia, S. (eds.) WISTP 2015. LNCS, vol. 9311, pp. 169–184. Springer, Cham (2015). https://doi.org/10.1007/978-3-319-24018-3_11

18. Lomné, V., Prouff, E., Rivain, M., Roche, T., Thillard, A.: How to estimate the success rate of higher-order side-channel attacks. In: Batina, L., Robshaw, M. (eds.) CHES 2014. LNCS, vol. 8731, pp. 35–54. Springer, Heidelberg (2014). https://doi.org/10.1007/978-3-662-44709-3_3

19. Mangard, S., Oswald, E., Standaert, F.-X.: One for all - all for one: unifying standard differential power analysis attacks. IET Inf. Secur. 5(2), 100–110 (2011)

20. Medwed, M., Oswald, E.: Template attacks on ECDSA. In: Chung, K.-I., Sohn, K., Yung, M. (eds.) WISA 2008. LNCS, vol. 5379, pp. 14–27. Springer, Heidelberg (2009). https://doi.org/10.1007/978-3-642-00306-6_2

21. Poussier, R., Zhou, Y., Standaert, F.-X.: A systematic approach to the side-channel analysis of ECC implementations with worst-case horizontal attacks. In: Fischer, W., Homma, N. (eds.) CHES 2017. LNCS, vol. 10529, pp. 534–554. Springer, Cham (2017). https://doi.org/10.1007/978-3-319-66787-4_26

22. NIST FIPS PUB. 186–2: Digital signature standard (DSS). National Institute for Standards and Technology (2000)

23. Rivain, M.: On the exact success rate of side channel analysis in the gaussian model. In: Avanzi, R.M., Keliher, L., Sica, F. (eds.) SAC 2008. LNCS, vol. 5381, pp. 165–183. Springer, Heidelberg (2009). https://doi.org/10.1007/978-3-642-04159-4_11

24. Schindler, W., Lemke, K., Paar, C.: A stochastic model for differential side channel cryptanalysis. In: Rao, J.R., Sunar, B. (eds.) CHES 2005. LNCS, vol. 3659, pp. 30–46. Springer, Heidelberg (2005). https://doi.org/10.1007/11545262_3

25. Wagner, M.: 700+ attacks published on smart cards: the need for a systematic counter strategy. In: Schindler, W., Huss, S.A. (eds.) COSADE 2012. LNCS, vol. 7275, pp. 33–38. Springer, Heidelberg (2012). https://doi.org/10.1007/978-3-642-29912-4_3

Side-Channel Analysis of the TERO PUF

Lars Tebelmann[1]([✉]), Michael Pehl[1], and Vincent Immler[2]

[1] Technical University of Munich, Munich, Germany
{lars.tebelmann,m.pehl}@tum.de
[2] Fraunhofer Institute AISEC, Garching bei München, Germany
vincent.immler@aisec.fraunhofer.de

Abstract. Physical Unclonable Functions (PUFs) have the potential
to provide a higher level of security for key storage than traditional
Non-Volatile Memory (NVM). However, the susceptibility of the PUF
primitives to non-invasive Side-Channel Analysis (SCA) is largely unex-
plored. While resistance to SCA was indicated for the Transient Effect
Ring Oscillator (TERO) PUF, it was not backed by an actual assessment. To investigate the physical security of the TERO PUF, we first
discuss and study the conceptual behavior of the PUF primitive to identify possible weaknesses. We support our claims by conducting an EM-
analysis of a TERO design on an FPGA. When measuring TERO cells
with an oscilloscope in the time domain, a Short Time Fourier Transform
(STFT) based approach allows to extract the relevant information in the
frequency domain. By applying this method we significantly reduce the
entropy of the PUF. Our analysis shows the vulnerability of not only the
originally suggested TERO PUF implementation but also the impact on
TERO designs in general. We discuss enhancements of the design that
potentially prevent the TERO PUF from exposing the secret and point
out that regarding security the TERO PUF is similar to the more area-
efficient Ring Oscillator PUF.

Keywords: TERO PUF · Side-Channel Analysis · Non-invasive ·
EM side-channel · Physical Unclonable Function

1 Introduction

Physical side-channel attacks based on power or electromagnetic (EM) analysis, such as Differential Power Analysis (DPA) [10,17], have been subject to
extensive research, especially w.r.t. cryptographic algorithms. Such attacks typically require only moderate resources, e.g., a decent oscilloscope. Therefore, they
create an imminent threat since an attacker is almost guaranteed to have the
necessary equipment at hand to perform the attack. Correspondingly, it is of
utmost importance to protect against physical side-channel attacks.

Equally important is the protection of stored secrets, such as cryptographic
key material. Storing secret data permanently puts it at risk of extraction
by optical analysis upon delayering the Integrated Circuit (IC) or related

© Springer Nature Switzerland AG 2019
I. Polian and M. Stöttinger (Eds.): COSADE 2019, LNCS 11421, pp. 43–60, 2019.
https://doi.org/10.1007/978-3-030-16350-1_4

attacks [19]. To overcome these limitations of non-volatile storage, PUFs have been proposed [5] and are assumed to provide a higher level of security when compared to NVMs. When requested, a PUF leverages the device-inherent manufacturing variation and provides fingerprint-like data for subsequent use, e.g., for key derivation. Extracting the minuscule manufacturing dependent parameters is considered infeasible while the system is powered-off and the PUF can be protected against invasive attacks when the system is powered-on.

For key storage, the PUF utilizes the variations to provide the secret PUF response which is processed to a key during *enrollment*. In this process, public helper data are derived to support later *reconstruction* of the same key from noisy PUF responses. Clearly, securing the processing of secret PUF responses during reconstruction is essential to protect the key. To date, research primarily focused on risks associated with storing helper data [4], algorithmic processing of the PUF responses [20], and (semi-)invasive attacks on the PUF [7,11]. Very few attempts have been made to attack the PUF primitives by means of an even more powerful non-invasive side-channel attack.

In this work, we address the challenge of attacking the Transient Effect Ring Oscillator (TERO) PUF, an FPGA PUF primitive that has been favored independently by several authors [2,14,24] over other PUFs. With regard to Side-Channel Analysis (SCA), its original authors consider the TERO PUF an improvement compared to the Ring Oscillator (RO) PUF that was already known to be vulnerable to SCA at the time. Breaking the TERO PUF by means of SCA entails specific difficulties, e.g., extracting a multi-bit response per TERO cell and measuring the otherwise hard to observe TERO oscillations.

Related Work. Similar to RO PUFs, TERO PUFs are based on observing oscillations of an inverter ring. For RO PUFs, frequencies of two oscillators are compared while for TERO PUFs the difference in settling times of bistable rings is used to derive a secret. In contrast to TERO PUFs, RO PUFs have been subject to substantial analyses regarding side-channels [15,16]. The main observations are: (*i*) The emanated frequencies of the ROs allow for recovering the secret if the same RO is used for multiple comparisons. (*ii*) Single ROs can be distinguished by their EM emanations using on-chip surface measurements, i.e., localized EM analysis of a depackaged chip. (*iii*) Multiplexers and counters show the most significant EM leakage when the instances are spatially separated. Interleaved placement of these components was proposed as a countermeasure.

The possibility to identify and locate ROs by their EM emanations has also been studied in the context of its application in TRNGs [1] and for EM cartography in general [18]. While RO and TERO PUFs share similarities, they also show substantial differences. To the best of the author's knowledge, no work was published regarding the side-channel specifics of the TERO PUF or how its primitive can be attacked by means of a non-invasive side-channel analysis.

Contribution. We are the first to successfully perform an EM-based side-channel attack on the TERO PUF primitive *without* depackaging the chip. As part of this work, we present a new Short-Time Fourier Transform based method to evaluate the oscillations of the TERO primitive. We propose a semi-automatic attack which is able to significantly reduce the entropy of the TERO PUF: While it can recover up to 25% of the response bits without any error, the overall error probability of all estimated bits is less than 18%. The estimate of the failure probability for each bit facilitates an optimal smart guessing strategy. Furthermore, assuming a PUF scenario, where up to 20% errors are corrected, the error probability is sufficiently small to consider the examined TERO PUF design with overlapping comparisons broken by the attack. We also demonstrate that the number of oscillations in TEROs, forming the secret, can be predicted accurately such that the derivation of multiple bits from a single comparison is prone to side-channel analysis. Our method is independent from the specifics of the implementation and is presumably applicable to other implementations of the TERO PUF such as [24], too.

Outline. The remainder of this paper is organized as follows: In Sect. 2, the TERO PUF is introduced. Sect. 3 outlines weaknesses of TERO PUFs by performing a conceptual analysis and by practically discovering the TERO oscillations to tailor the attack. A description of the experimental setup in Sect. 4 is followed by our proposed attack in Sect. 5. We conclude our work in Sect. 6.

2 Transient Effect Ring Oscillator (TERO) Preliminaries

In Sect. 2.1, we reiterate over the TERO PUF architecture. Afterwards, in Sect. 2.2, we describe this work's setting and provide some remarks on the TERO PUF architecture.

2.1 TERO PUF Architecture

The TERO was introduced in 2010 as an entropy source for TRNGs [23]. Each TERO cell comprises two identical branches, consisting of an AND gate and an odd number of inverter gates, that form a metastable ring as depicted in Fig. 1a. When setting the *enable* signal from low to high, two events start to propagate. While in theory the TERO oscillates until the *enable* signal is reset, manufacturing variations of the underlying CMOS structures result in different delays of the two branches and a break down of the oscillation in finite time.

The manufacturing variation-dependent number of oscillations until the TERO reaches its stable state is utilized in [2] to construct the TERO PUF. The proposed architecture of the PUF in [3,13,14] is shown in Fig. 1b. It consists of two blocks of TERO cells and two corresponding counters. One TERO cell is selected from each block by a challenge. The two cells are activated and connected to the counters by multiplexers. Thus, only the two TERO cells that are compared oscillate at a time. The selection of pairs of cells is not restricted in [3,13,14]: Each of the M cells from one block is compared to all M cells from the other block resulting in M^2 challenge-response pairs.

After a fixed acquisition time T_{acq}, the activated TERO cells are stopped. T_{acq} allows for a trade-off between reliability, uniqueness, and run time. It is chosen such that most of the TERO cells are expected to be settled. Therefore,

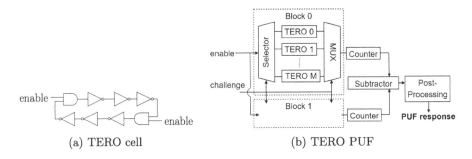

(a) TERO cell   (b) TERO PUF

Fig. 1. TERO cell example and TERO PUF architecture as used in [3,13,14]

T_{acq} is in the range of several hundred nanoseconds depending on the number of inverters in a branch of the TERO cells, e.g., 600 ns for seven inverters [13,14].

To derive the PUF response, the counter values after T_{acq} are subtracted. The Least Significant Bits (LSBs) are unstable due to noise and are ignored. The Most Significant Bits (MSBs), in particular the sign, are variation-dependent and relatively stable over time. Hence, the sign bit and specific unique and steady bits (e.g., Bit 4, Bit 5 or Bit 6 [13,14]) serve as PUF response bits. Gray coding can be applied to the difference to ease further processing and to potentially increase robustness w.r.t. noise [3]. However, the large-scale analysis in [24] suggests that using any counter bits other than the sign drastically decreases reliability.

2.2 Remarks on the TERO PUF Architecture

In the original proposals [2,13] of the TERO PUF, the separation of the two cell blocks is deemed necessary in order to avoid dependencies of the responses. This may lead to bias in the responses though, as spatial gradients in silicon can cause cells of one part of the die to settle faster (or slower) than on other parts. Comparing adjacent cells would largely counteract such spatial effects. In addition, spatially separating the TERO blocks makes them prone to attacks by localized EM measurements. While resolving adjacent cells may not be feasible by localized EM measurements, identifying spatially separated cells is certainly within scope based on attacks on similar structures [8,22]. Due to its architectural limits, we consider the TERO PUF only suited for PUF-based key generation and *not* challenge-response authentication.

Another important design decision is whether to compare TERO outputs among all TERO cells or not. We point out that by comparing a certain cell to multiple other cells enables a similar attack as proposed for RO-PUFs [16]. Also, inherent correlations between PUF bits occur and lower the entropy of the remaining PUF response bits, i.e., the response does not have full entropy as from the comparison of M cells at most $\log_2(M!)$ bits of entropy can be extracted [12]. But restricting the number of derived bits to at the utmost $\log_2(M!)$ changes the evaluation of the efficiency of the TERO PUF significantly so that we take the originally proposed designs as the base for our research.

3   Exploration of the TERO PUF

As a next step, we explore the TERO PUF by identifying suitable attack vectors, discovering the TERO oscillations, estimating their oscillation duration, and briefly introducing the STFT. This corresponds to Sects. 3.1, 3.2, 3.3 and 3.4.

3.1   Attack Vectors

In [6], the temporary oscillations in the TERO structure were modeled. While aimed at providing a stochastic model for the TERO TRNG, the results from the physical model are also useful in the context of the TERO PUF. One key observation of [6] is that equally built TEROs on a device oscillate with constant and similar frequency. Therefore, TERO cells and their location are identifiable by an attacker based on their characteristic frequency. Another result from [6] is that the variation of the duty cycle changes monotonously over time until it reaches 0 % or 100 % and the oscillation collapses. Consequently, in the spectrum an attacker can observe a TERO cell at a constant and approximately known frequency as long as it is oscillating. The number of oscillations per TERO cell that are used to derive the secret can be estimated from the frequency as soon as an attacker observes the beginning and the end of the oscillation. Depending on the TERO implementation the observations lead to two attack vectors:

Multiple Usage of TERO Cells. A comparison of each cell from one TERO block to all cells of the other TERO block and taking the sign of the counter differences was suggested to increase the number of secret bits. However, an attacker that observes the approximate duration of each of the simultaneously oscillating TERO cells from the two blocks knows which cell is reused. Consequently, the assignment of the observed duration to blocks and, given the public challenge, even to cells is possible. Then, similarly to [16], the attacker knows the sign bit derived from the subtractor (i.e., the secret) from the observed oscillation times and the knowledge which time belongs to which cell.

Derivation of Multiple Bits per TERO Cell Pair. Given that an attacker can estimate the oscillation duration per cell, it is evident that approximation of the counter difference is possible. Thus, when deriving multiple bits from a TERO cell as outlined in Sect. 2.1, they are revealed as soon as the attacker observes the oscillations with sufficient precision. An attacker does not have to resolve the counter differences exactly, since only relatively stable bits of the difference can be used. For the difference $\Delta_{cnt,i}$ of counter values cnt_1 and cnt_2, bit i is 1 iff

$$\Delta_{cnt,i} = (cnt_1 - cnt_2) \mod 2^{i+1} \geq 2^i. \tag{1}$$

I.e. the value of distance bit i is revealed when counter values are distinguished with a precision of 2^i. When using Bit 4 and Bit 5 (cf. [13]), an accuracy of 16 is required to learn both bits. This corresponds to a resolution of approx. 85 ns in the time domain for a TERO frequency of 187.5 MHz as found in Sect. 3.2.

Measuring a TERO cell together with exactly one other cell, thereby avoiding the reuse in multiple pairs, improves the situation. It prevents an attacker from resolving the oscillation time to a single cell. Nevertheless, it is still possible to observe the oscillation duration's absolute value. Hence, only the sign bit of the difference remains unknown.

3.2   Discovering TERO Oscillations

An accurate estimate of the number of oscillations is required to enable the discussed attacks. The major obstacle is the very short oscillation time until a TERO cell settles. Figure 2 depicts a practical evaluation of the settling time. The acquisition time in the experiment was varied from 1 to 99 clock cycles and the respective counter values of each TERO cell were stored. Counter values are averaged from 101 repetitions to compensate for noise at room temperature. The break point of a certain curve indicates the end of the oscillation of the corresponding TERO cell.

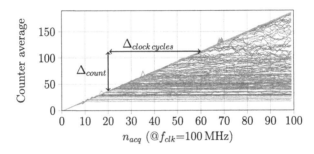

Fig. 2. Evaluation of settling time and counters for $2 \cdot 96 = 192$ TERO cells to estimate the oscillation frequency f_{TERO}, averaged over $N = 101$ measurements. Spikes exceeding the slope are due to measurement artifacts.

The results show that most of the TERO cells settle within less than 600 ns (60 clock cycles at a clock frequency of $f_{\text{clk}} = 100$ MHz). This emphasizes the need for a good time resolution in order to observe the duration of the oscillation. It also motivates the acquisition time of 600 ns which we selected according to [14]. Note that a longer acquisition and oscillation time is beneficial for the attack but is deemed unrealistic for real-world implementations.

In addition to the settling time of the TERO cells, the slope in Fig. 2 confirms that TERO cells indeed oscillate with similar and constant frequency until the oscillation breaks down [6]. The expected frequency

$$f_{\text{TERO}} = \frac{\Delta_{\text{count}}}{\Delta_{\text{acq}}} = \frac{\Delta_{\text{count}}}{\Delta_{\text{clock cycles}}} \cdot f_{\text{clk}} \approx 187.5 \text{ MHz} \qquad (2)$$

for our design is derived from the slope of the counter values, where Δ_{count} is the difference of the counter for a given difference Δ_{acq} of the acquisition time respectively a given difference of clock cycles $\Delta_{\text{clock cycles}}$.

Note that the experiment is only carried out to validate the assumption of a constant oscillation frequency. For an attack, it is not necessary to obtain frequency counter values, as the frequency can be estimated by observing the frequency domain.

3.3   Estimating TERO Oscillation Durations

The experiment in Sect. 3.2 shows a stable oscillation of the TERO cells until the oscillation breaks down. The actual frequency of a certain TERO cell is approximated by f_{TERO} and typically lies in a small interval $f_{\text{TERO}} \pm \Delta_f$. Note that f_{TERO} is device specific and obtained by measuring the frequency domain and Δ_f is the relative deviation on the same device. Given f_{TERO}, the time T_{osc} until a TERO cell settles provides a good estimate of the number of oscillations and thus the TERO counter value n_{TERO}:

$$n_{\text{TERO}} \approx f_{\text{TERO}} \cdot T_{\text{osc}}. \tag{3}$$

All TERO cells are activated for n_{acq} clock cycles of the system clock with frequency $f_{\text{clk}} = \frac{1}{T_{\text{clk}}}$. Therefore, n_{TERO} is upper bounded by

$$n_{\text{TERO}} \leq (f_{\text{TERO}} + \Delta_f) \cdot T_{\text{clk}} \cdot n_{\text{acq}} = \frac{f_{\text{TERO}} + \Delta_f}{f_{\text{clk}}} \cdot n_{\text{acq}}, \tag{4}$$

where equality is reached iff the TERO oscillates until the acquisition time ends.

Note that for many practical cases Δ_f is negligible in Eq. (4). For a deviation Δ_f from the known nominal oscillation frequency f_{TERO}, the difference between actual and estimated counter value for $T_{\text{osc}} \leq T_{\text{acq}} = T_{\text{clk}} \cdot n_{\text{acq}}$ is at most

$$|n'_{\text{TERO}} - n_{\text{TERO}}| \approx |(f_{\text{TERO}} \pm \Delta_f) \cdot T_{\text{osc}} - f_{\text{TERO}} \cdot T_{\text{osc}}| \leq |\Delta_f| \cdot T_{\text{acq}}. \tag{5}$$

E.g., for an accurately known $T_{\text{osc}} = T_{\text{acq}} = 600\,\text{ns}$ and $|\Delta_f| \leq 1.67\,\text{MHz}$ the difference between actual and estimated counter value is 1 when Δ_f is neglected. This is below the expected variations in the measurement due to noise.

Summing up, as long as the counter frequencies lie within a narrow range around the nominal frequency f_{TERO}, the approximation in Eq. (3) holds and the counter values are indeed estimated by the oscillation time T_{osc}.

3.4   Short-Time Fourier Transform (STFT)

To estimate T_{osc}, the visibility of the TERO frequency f_{TERO} in the spectrum is analyzed. The challenge regarding the measurement is the short acquisition time of $T_{acq} = 600\,\text{ns}$ and oscillation times as short as $T_{osc} = 100\,\text{ns}$. In order to resolve time and frequency simultaneously, a Short-Time Fourier Transform (STFT) based approach is taken.

Each time domain signal $x^{\text{TERO}}(t)$ during the activation of a TERO cell is processed via the STFT into the frequency domain. Instead of transforming the entire signal, segments $x^{\text{TERO}}_{(l)}(t)$ of length L are taken from $x^{\text{TERO}}(t)$, where (l)

denotes the index of a segment. Each segment is multiplied by a Hanning window (raised cosine) function $w(t)$ to reduce FFT spectral leakage effects. Windowed segments are transformed individually into the frequency domain:

$$X_{(l)}^{\mathrm{TERO}}(f) = \mathrm{FFT}\left(x_{(l)}^{\mathrm{TERO}}(t) \cdot w(t)\right) = \mathrm{FFT}\left(\hat{x}_{(l)}^{\mathrm{TERO}}(t)\right). \qquad (6)$$

The segments overlap for a number of samples L_{overlap}. In other words, the segments are shifted by $\Delta L = L - L_{\mathrm{overlap}}$ samples along the time axis. The stable frequencies of TERO cells allow averaging in the frequency domain for each segment over N measurements per cell to enhance the Signal-to-Noise Ratio (SNR). This is a valid approach and justified by our preliminary evaluation of the TEROs in Sect. 3.2.

In order to eliminate unwanted signals such as the system clock and other disturbances, a noise floor can be estimated to facilitate the evaluation. For the noise floor estimate, measurements $n(t)$ are taken while the TERO cells are deactivated and the same processing as in Eq. (6) is applied. Averaging over N_{noise} measurements yields the noise frequency spectrum $\bar{N}_{(l)}(f)$ for each segment (l). From the averaged signal $\bar{X}_{(l)}^{\mathrm{TERO}}(f)$ and averaged noise floor $\bar{N}_{(l)}(f)$

$$\bar{X}_{(l)}^{\mathrm{TERO}}(f) = \frac{1}{N}\sum_{i=1}^{N}\mathrm{FFT}\left(\hat{x}_{i,(l)}^{\mathrm{TERO}}(t)\right), \quad \bar{N}_{(l)}(f) = \frac{1}{N_{\mathrm{noise}}}\sum_{i=1}^{N_{\mathrm{noise}}}\mathrm{FFT}\left(\hat{n}_{i,(l)}(t)\right)$$

the frequency- and segment-dependent SNR of segment l is defined as

$$\overline{\mathrm{SNR}}_{(l)}(f) = 10\log\left(\frac{\bar{X}_{(l)}(f)}{\bar{N}_{(l)}(f)}\right) = 10\log\left(\bar{X}_{(l)}(f)\right) - 10\log\left(\bar{N}_{(l)}(f)\right). \quad (7)$$

Our attack evaluates the SNR around the expected TERO frequency f_{TERO}. During the period of activation, $\overline{\mathrm{SNR}}_{(l)}(f_{\mathrm{TERO}})$ is expected to take higher values. Estimating the time of the activation period then translates into measuring the duration of the high SNR.

Note that estimating the noise floor is not a premise for the attack, i.e., instead of evaluating the relative changes defined by the SNR in Eq. (7), absolute values of Eq. (6) could be used to carry out the attack.

Frequency Resolution. For a real valued signal $x(t)$, the spectrum is symmetric and can be reduced to $N_{\mathrm{FFT}}/2 + 1$ bins ranging from DC to f_{max}. Given the sampling frequency f_s, the resolution in the frequency domain is

$$\Delta_{\mathrm{FFT}} = \frac{f_{\mathrm{max}}}{N_{\mathrm{FFT}}/2} = \frac{f_s}{N_{\mathrm{FFT}}} \qquad (8)$$

with f_{max} being the maximum frequency that can be reconstructed according to the Shannon-Nyquist theorem. In general, a narrow frequency resolution Δ_{FFT} is desired. However, the TERO frequency f_{TERO} does not have to be resolved in detail. Instead, an attacker is mostly interested in the duration of the signal. Therefore, a trade-off towards the temporal resolution is acceptable. For the experiments in Sect. 5, $N_{\mathrm{FFT}} = 4096$ resulting in a resolution of $\Delta_{\mathrm{FFT}} \approx 4.88\,\mathrm{MHz}$ for $f_s = 20\,\mathrm{GHz}$ is chosen.

Temporal resolution. The temporal resolution also depends on N_{FFT} and f_s and behaves contrary to the frequency resolution:

$$\Delta_T = \frac{N_{\text{FFT}}}{f_s} = \frac{1}{\Delta_{\text{FFT}}}, \qquad (9)$$

i.e., to get a good temporal resolution, high sampling rates are required. Given $N_{\text{FFT}} = 4096$ and $f_s = 20\,\text{GHz}$, a segment contains $\Delta_T = 204.8\,\text{ns}$. Without overlapping segments, the resolution would be too coarse to analyze the TERO oscillations. As the segments overlap, a certain redundancy between segments exists, i.e., since the same samples are transformed, the resulting amplitudes are similar. Yet, as the oscillations stop after some time, all segments that contain samples during the oscillation provide information, and smaller differences than Δ_T can be resolved as shown in Sect. 5. The offset between segments is chosen as $\Delta L = 200$ as a trade-off between computational cost and temporal resolution.

4   Experimental Setup

In the following, the experimental setup is described in terms of the measurement setup, the design under attack, and a pre-evaluation by means of EM cartography.

Measurement Setup. Measurements are recorded with an oscilloscope of 2.5 GHz analog bandwidth and a sample rate of 20 GS/s. The near-field probes RF-B 0.3-3 and RF-B 3-2 from Langer EMV are used, having <1 mm and ≈ 1 mm resolution respectively. Both probes capture emanations in vertical direction relative to the FPGA package. Two 30 dB amplifiers amplify the signals. Summarizing the results of Sect. 3.4, we set the number of FFT bins N_{FFT} to 4096, corresponding to 204.8 ns segment length and a frequency resolution of 4.88 MHz. A segment offset of $\Delta_L = 200$ samples is selected, corresponding to a full clock cycle length of the system clock with 10 ns. In all experiments in Sect. 5 the number of noise measurements to estimate the noise floor is set to $N_{\text{noise}} = 9600$ and the SNR is evaluated by its maximum in the range from 180 MHz to 190 MHz, corresponding to $f_{TERO} \approx 187.5\,\text{MHz}$ from Sect. 3.2.

Design Under Attack. Our evaluation target is a Xilinx Spartan-6 LX16 FPGA in a 324-pin BGA package mounted on a Nexys3 development board. The package of the FPGA remains unaltered. The design under attack contains two blocks of 96 TERO cells each. For the TERO cells a hard macro [21] for the Spartan-6 by Marchand et al. [13] is used with seven inverters per branch. The number of cells per block is slightly reduced compared to the original TERO PUF proposal in order to include serial communication and an FSM on the same chip.

Figure 3a depicts the floorplan, where the TERO blocks are denoted as PUF_AREA_1 and PUF_AREA_2 respectively. The logic for selecting specific cells in each block and assigning their output to the counters is contained in MAIN, located in the lower right corner in Fig. 3a. The counters are placed separately adjacent to the second block of TERO cells. The separation allows to verify

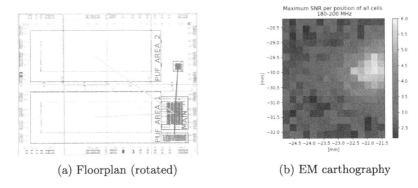

(a) Floorplan (rotated)   (b) EM carthography

Fig. 3. (a) Floorplan of TERO PUF and corresponding SNR heatmap for frequency range 180–200 MHz. (b) Maximum SNR of cells during first 60 ns after the trigger.

whether EM emanations stem from the TERO cells or the counters. The counters are placed side by side to prevent spatial separation of their EM emanations. This thwarts attacks targeting each counter separately.

Pre-evaluation with EM Cartography. Figure 3b depicts a heatmap generated by using the RF-B 0.3-3 probe and an xyz-table. The SNR in the frequency range from 180 MHz to 200 MHz is shown. Measurements were taken on a grid of 0.25 mm × 0.25 mm over the part of the package where the die is located. Each point was only measured $N = 10$ times while a cell from each block was activated, same as for measuring the noise floor, i.e. $N_{noise} = 10$. The SNR according to Eq. (7) is evaluated during the first 60 ns after a trigger signal. In this period, all cells oscillate and no settling effects take place. The maximum SNR in Fig. 3b coincides with the location of the counters in the design. The area spans almost 1 mm², i.e., a fine-grained search over the package is not needed and we position the RF-R 3-2 probe manually for all following experiments. Note, this is in line with previous work on EM analysis of ROs [15] showing that observed EM emanations are most likely caused by multiplexers, counters and wires in between. This is no limitation of our attack, since – similar to the attack on ROs in [16] – we mainly exploit that TERO cells are used for multiple comparisons.

5   Exploitation of the TERO Side-Channel

This section demonstrates that TERO PUFs are vulnerable to a non-invasive side-channel attack. Section 5.1 shows the feasibility of detecting TERO oscillations by activating cells separately. Subsequently, Sect. 5.2 practically exploits the reuse of a certain cell in the derivation of multiple response bits, i.e., two cells under comparison are activated at once. The results illustrate that the oscillation duration is well estimated by our approach. A simple countermeasure is not to reuse a certain TERO cell in multiple comparisons. The analysis in Sect. 5.3

nevertheless shows that if multiple bits are extracted from a single comparison still some counter values are leaked which renders the extraction of more than one bit per TERO cell pair insecure.

5.1 Analysis of Separately Activated Cells

In this experiment only one cell is activated at once. Figure 4 depicts the practical application of our approach outlined in Sect. 3.4. The maximum of the STFT in the frequency range from 180 MHz to 190 MHz is plotted while shifting the segment under transformation in the time domain. The range is chosen according to f_{TERO} from Sect. 3.2. The point where the first sample of the segment in the time domain is aligned with the starting point of the oscillation corresponds to 0 ns. Note that also segments starting before 0 ns can include samples from where the TERO cell oscillates. Thus the increase in SNR starts before this point in time is reached. In addition cells with an oscillation time shorter than the FFT window can cause a maximum before 0 ns.

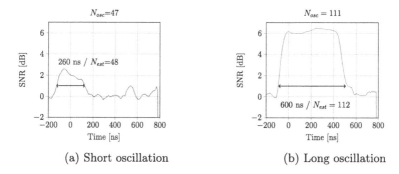

(a) Short oscillation   (b) Long oscillation

Fig. 4. Examples of the SNR according to Eq. (7) for separately activated cells. The estimated oscillation duration is depicted by double arrows.

The activation of the cells causes an increase of SNR in Figs. 4a and b. At approximately -100 ns, i.e., when the oscillation starts in the middle of the segment under transformation, the SNR reaches 0.75 dB. This value is chosen as a threshold to estimate the oscillation duration T_{osc}, i.e., T_{osc} is approximated by the time from exceeding the threshold to falling back below this value. Assuming an oscillation frequency $f_{TERO} = 187.5$ MHz, the counter values are computed according to Eq. (3) as $N_{est} = 48$ and $N_{est} = 112$, respectively. This result fits well to the actual number of oscillations that are $N_{osc} = 47$ and $N_{osc} = 111$. From the experiments we conclude that both short and long oscillations of the TERO are well estimated by our approach.

A comparison of estimated and actual counter values for all TERO cells is depicted in Fig. 5a. The actual counter values, which slightly vary due to noise, are derived from averaging among $N = 100$ measurements. Since the acquisition window is set to $T_{acq} = 600$ ns, the maximum number of oscillations is $N_{\mathrm{osc}}^{\mathrm{max}} = f_{\mathrm{TERO}} \cdot T_{\mathrm{acq}} \approx 112$. Thus, estimated values $N_{\mathrm{est}} > N_{\mathrm{osc}}^{\mathrm{max}}$ can be assumed to be $N_{\mathrm{osc}}^{\mathrm{max}}$. Indeed, in Fig. 5a, almost all estimated values $N_{\mathrm{est}} > N_{\mathrm{osc}}^{\mathrm{max}}$ correspond to the maximum possible value, i.e., the minor overestimation of oscillations does not affect the result. Since it is known that all TERO cells have a minimum oscillation duration, certain values below N_{min} are known to be false.

Entropy Reduction of the TERO PUF. Comparing each cell from one block to all cells of the respective other block and taking the sign bit as a secret results in $96 \cdot 96 = 9216$ response bits. From the $2 \cdot 96 = 192$ estimations of the oscillation durations, four results are deemed unreliable as $N_{\mathrm{est}} < N_{\mathrm{min}} = 10$, i.e., for the corresponding $4 \cdot 96 = 384$ Bits no estimation can be given. For the remaining 8808 bits, the probability of guessing the PUF bit erroneously depends on the difference of the counter estimates $\Delta_{\mathrm{est}} := \left| N_{est}^{Block\,0} - N_{est}^{Block\,1} \right|$ as depicted in Fig. 5b. The graph shows the probability of an error $\bar{p}_e$ if only difference estimates Δ_{est} greater than the value on the x-axis are considered. Clearly, the error probability decreases with an increase of the differences. This is in line with Fig. 5a: The deviation in the average counter value (ordinate) of the scatter plots is an indicator of the estimation accuracy. An inaccurate estimation has more impact if the estimated counter values are close to each other compared to when the estimated counter values are further apart.

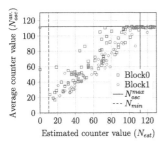   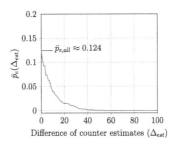

(a) Counter estimation vs. real value   (b) Error of estimated TERO PUF bits.

Fig. 5. (a) Automatically estimated vs. actual counter values for separately activated cells. (b) Probability of guessing a wrong bit using the estimates in (a).

According to Fig. 5b estimated counter differences with $\Delta_{\mathrm{est}} \geq 55$ have an error probability of $\bar{p}_e = 0$, i.e., the 2368 bits corresponding to these estimates are revealed without any errors. Estimated counter differences with $\Delta_{est} \geq 19$ still have an error probability of only $\bar{p}_e \approx 1.5\%$, which applies to 5471 bits. The whole set of 8808 bits has an error probability of $\bar{p}_{e,all} \approx 12.4\%$.

Summing up, automatic estimation of single TERO cell oscillations and using only known error free bits, the entropy of the TERO PUF is reduced by a quarter from 9192 to 6848 bits. In addition, an attacker can take advantage from error probabilities for estimations. They define a confidence for each bit that allows to develop a smart guessing strategy, i.e., the remaining guessing effort is far below an exhaustive search. Also, an attacker can try to adjust the counter values for counters which contribute to unreliable differences, e.g., by visual inspection of the SNR, which provides more precise results than our automatic estimation.

5.2   Analysis of Simultaneously Activated Cells

We now analyze the scenario that each TERO cell in *Block 0* is compared to each cell in *Block 1* where the two cells under comparison are activated in parallel. In this setting, each cell i is measured 96 times, always in combination with a different cell $j \in \{1, \ldots 96\}$. We assume that an attacker can figure out which cell is activated at a certain point in time, e.g., by knowledge of the design. The attacker averages over the SNR of all 96 measurements for cell i. Thus, contributions from other cells are considered noise that results in a distinguishable offset:

$$\mathrm{SNR}^i_{(l)}(f) \approx \mathrm{SNR}^i_{(l)}(f) + \frac{1}{96} \sum_{j=1}^{96} \mathrm{SNR}^j_{(l)}(f) \tag{10}$$

Effectively, the scenario of activating two cells at once is transformed back to the case of separately activated cells. Due to the activation of two cells and an additionally observed noise floor of approx. 1 dB, we increase the threshold in the automatic counter value estimation from 0.75 dB to 2.5 dB. Figure 6 depicts the results for cells of both blocks. For every comparison, a single measurement is taken and the noise floor is subtracted. The $N = 96$ measurements of comparisons containing the same cell are averaged, i.e., the number of traces per cell is in the same range as in the previous experiment.

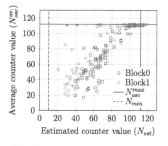

(a) Counter estimation vs. real value

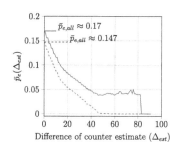

(b) Error of estimated TERO PUF bits.

Fig. 6. (a) Automatically estimated vs. actual counter values for two simultaneously activated cells. (b) Probability of guessing a wrong bit using the estimates in (a); dashed line: result for manually discarding estimates marked in solid red in (a). (Color figure online)

Figure 6a compares automatically estimated counter values against averaged known counter values for this scenario. As expected, the results are slightly degraded compared to Sect. 5.1, since not all effects caused by simultaneously activated cells cancel out. Due to few but substantial deviations of automatically estimated counter values from the actual ones, the resulting error probability for guessing TERO PUF bits in Fig. 6b increases to $\bar{p}_{e,all} \approx 17\%$ compared to $\bar{p}_{e,all} \approx 12.4\%$ in Fig. 5b. While still more than 7600 out of 9216 bits are guessed correctly, this reduces the confidence of the guess for almost all bits.

To significantly improve the result, the underlying SNR is evaluated to eliminate cases showing a distorted SNR over time when compared, e.g., to Fig. 4. The most obviously degraded cases in our results correspond to the two solid red dots in Fig. 6a. Eliminating these yields the dashed line for the error probability in Fig. 6b. Similar to Fig. 5b, bits that are guessed with an estimated counter difference of $\Delta_{est} \geq 62$ are regarded error free. This applies to 831 bits while smart guessing can be used to get remaining bits as suggested above.

In a typical PUF setting, an error correction is applied to the PUF response to compensate variations due to e.g., environmental conditions. Hence, an bit error probability (BER) in the estimated response of up to the correction capability is tolerable for a successful attack. Please note, despite an empirical BER in the range of 5–10% within academic settings [9, 24], it is common practice to consider a substantially larger amount of errors in a commercial setting to ensure a failure free operation throughout the whole lifetime of a product, including industrial temperature ranges from $-40°$ to $+85°$ C, leading to an anticipated BER of 15–20%. Therefore, the examined TERO PUF can be considered broken by our attack even if not all bits are known, e.g., through smart guessing.

5.3   Attack on Multi-bit Responses

The attack in Sect. 5.2 is prevented by using every TERO cell in only one comparison. Then, an attacker cannot assign a counter value to a certain cell as long as the measurements cannot be spatially resolved to cells, which is the case for our setup. Consequently an attacker cannot reveal the secret, i.e., the sign bit of counter differences. But if multiple bits are derived from a comparison of the counters, the difference itself is of interest, since knowing its absolute value reduces the entropy to one bit, as discussed in Sect. 3.1.

While no automatic detection was implemented, visual inspection of the SNRs over time of the measurements reveals the difference of counter values in many cases as depicted in Fig. 7a. Knowing from our previous investigations that the SNR over time develops a plateau while a TERO cell is oscillating, decreases afterwards, and has a knee when no more oscillations are seen in the time segment under observation, the graph can be interpreted: The first peak corresponds to the duration of the first oscillation, while the second oscillation is present until the plateau decays and the SNR vanishes in the noise floor of approx. 1 dB. In Fig. 7a the counter values, and thus the difference, is estimated quite accurately and only the sign bit is still secret when neglecting unreliable LSBs.

In contrast, Fig. 7b shows that revealing the counter differences from the SNR over time is more difficult in other cases. Still, by modelling the behavior of the TERO, the two apparently untypical peaks are explained: (i) The two

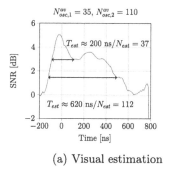

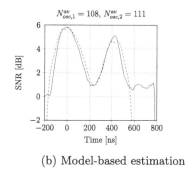

(a) Visual estimation

(b) Model-based estimation

Fig. 7. SNR over time for two simultaneously activated cells ($N = 100$). (a) visually estimated oscillation duration. (b) additional model given as red dashed line. (Color figure online)

TEROs have similar oscillation durations, (ii) we assume in our model that the TERO with the shorter oscillation duration has a 1.5 MHz higher oscillation frequency. Property (i) causes that the end points of the oscillation durations can hardly be distinguished, while (ii) results in a cancellation of the oscillations in the spectrum due to our relatively crude resolution in the frequency domain. The result of our model is marked by the red dashed line in Fig. 7b. Therefore, we suggest one of two approaches to develop automated side-channel analysis of the multi-bit extraction from TERO PUFs: either the frequency resolution is improved, e.g., using a spectrum analyzer, to minimize the probability of cancellation or a model can be fitted to the SNR over time to estimate the counter difference.

5.4   Interpretation and Countermeasures

The results of Sects. 5.2 and 5.3 prove that current methods to derive multiple bits per pair of TERO cells are vulnerable to side-channel attacks. We emphasize that this applies also to the derivation of multi-bit responses from other oscillation-based PUF primitives.

However, TERO PUFs can be protected by similar mechanisms as RO PUFs: (i) Increasing the number of counters decreases the attackers SNR as more TEROs oscillate simultaneously. (ii) Interleaved placement of counters and multiplexers is mandatory to prevent an attacker from spatially resolving them. (iii) The shuffling of compared TERO cells impedes averaging of measurements with the same TERO cell as the attacker does not know to which cell pair a measurement belongs. (iv) Restricting the TERO PUF to non-overlapping pairwise comparisons and using only the sign bit impedes the presented attacks entirely. However, applying (iv) removes the claimed advantages of TERO over RO PUFs: The number of derived bits for TERO PUFs is then equal to the RO PUF, while the latter is more area-efficient due to the lower number of inverters. Alternatively to (iv), if the counter values are stored, comparisons can be made of the stored value. Hence, the oscillation of a single cell can only be observed once revealing no additional side-channel leakage. Yet, this approach can also be applied to RO PUFs, i.e., the comparison above is not altered.

6   Conclusions

In this work, we studied different TERO PUF designs and how they can be attacked. Based on our conceptual analysis and modeling of the TERO PUF, we were able to identify several weaknesses and confirm them by our experiments. Our non-invasive EM measurements and tailored attack methodology exactly recovers up to 25% of the PUF bits without errors while the overall error probability of all estimated bits is below 18%. We point out that our approach is generic and applies to all known TERO designs. Even with our coarse measurement setup, and assuming a typical PUF scenario, where up to 20% errors are corrected, the remaining error probability is sufficiently small to consider the TERO PUF design with overlapping comparisons broken by our attack. With a slightly more advanced measurement setup, e.g., a spectrum analyzer, but applying our proposed technique, we assume that the improvement in terms of measurement enables a complete break of the TERO PUF even without the need of a smart guessing strategy.

Acknowledgement. This work was partly funded by the German Ministry of Education and Research in the project ALESSIO under grant number 16KIS0632.

References

1. Bayon, P., Bossuet, L., Aubert, A., Fischer, V.: Electromagnetic analysis on ring oscillator-based true random number generators. In: 2013 IEEE International Symposium on Circuits and Systems (ISCAS2013), pp. 1954–1957, May 2013
2. Bossuet, L., Ngo, X.T., Cherif, Z., Fischer, V.: A PUF based on a transient effect ring oscillator and insensitive to locking phenomenon. IEEE Trans. Emerg. Top. Comput. **2**(1), 30–36 (2014)
3. Cherkaoui, A., Bossuet, L., Marchand, C.: Design, evaluation, and optimization of physical unclonable functions based on transient effect ring oscillators. IEEE Trans. Inf. Forensics Secur. **11**(6), 1291–1305 (2016)
4. Delvaux, J., Gu, D., Schellekens, D., Verbauwhede, I.: Helper data algorithms for PUF-based key generation: overview and analysis. IEEE Trans. Comput. Aided Des. Integr. Circuits Syst. **34**(6), 889–902 (2015)
5. Gassend, B., Clarke, D., Dijk, M.V., Devadas, S.: Silicon physical random functions. In: ACM CCS (2002)
6. Haddad, P., Fischer, V., Bernard, F., Nicolai, J.: A physical approach for stochastic modeling of TERO-based TRNG. In: Güneysu, T., Handschuh, H. (eds.) CHES 2015. LNCS, vol. 9293, pp. 357–372. Springer, Heidelberg (2015). https://doi.org/10.1007/978-3-662-48324-4_18
7. Helfmeier, C., Boit, C., Nedospasov, D., Seifert, J.: Cloning physically unclonable functions. In: 2013 IEEE International Symposium on Hardware-Oriented Security and Trust (HOST), pp. 1–6, June 2013

8. Immler, V., Specht, R., Unterstein, F.: Your rails cannot hide from localized EM: how dual-rail logic fails on FPGAs. In: Fischer, W., Homma, N. (eds.) CHES 2017. LNCS, vol. 10529, pp. 403–424. Springer, Cham (2017). https://doi.org/10.1007/978-3-319-66787-4_20

9. Katzenbeisser, S., Kocabaş, Ü., Rožić, V., Sadeghi, A.-R., Verbauwhede, I., Wachsmann, C.: PUFs: myth, fact or busted? A security evaluation of physically unclonable functions (PUFs) cast in silicon. In: Prouff, E., Schaumont, P. (eds.) CHES 2012. LNCS, vol. 7428, pp. 283–301. Springer, Heidelberg (2012). https://doi.org/10.1007/978-3-642-33027-8_17

10. Kocher, P., Jaffe, J., Jun, B.: Differential power analysis. In: Wiener, M. (ed.) CRYPTO 1999. LNCS, vol. 1666, pp. 388–397. Springer, Heidelberg (1999). https://doi.org/10.1007/3-540-48405-1_25

11. Lohrke, H., Tajik, S., Boit, C., Seifert, J.-P.: No place to hide: contactless probing of secret data on FPGAs. In: Gierlichs, B., Poschmann, A.Y. (eds.) CHES 2016. LNCS, vol. 9813, pp. 147–167. Springer, Heidelberg (2016). https://doi.org/10.1007/978-3-662-53140-2_8

12. Maes, R., Van Herrewege, A., Verbauwhede, I.: PUFKY: a fully functional PUF-based cryptographic key generator. In: Prouff, E., Schaumont, P. (eds.) CHES 2012. LNCS, vol. 7428, pp. 302–319. Springer, Heidelberg (2012). https://doi.org/10.1007/978-3-642-33027-8_18

13. Marchand, C., Bossuet, L., Cherkaoui, A.: Design and characterization of the TERO-PUF on SRAM FPGAs. In: 2016 IEEE Computer Society Annual Symposium on VLSI (ISVLSI), pp. 134–139, July 2016

14. Marchand, C., Bossuet, L., Mureddu, U., Bochard, N., Cherkaoui, A., Fischer, V.: Implementation and characterization of a physical unclonable function for IoT: a case study with the TERO-PUF. IEEE Trans. Comput. Aided Des. Integr. Circuits Syst. **37**(1), 97–109 (2018)

15. Merli, D., Heyszl, J., Heinz, B., Schuster, D., Stumpf, F., Sigl, G.: Localized electromagnetic analysis of RO PUFs. In: 2013 IEEE International Symposium on Hardware-Oriented Security and Trust (HOST), pp. 19–24, June 2013

16. Merli, D., Schuster, D., Stumpf, F., Sigl, G.: Semi-invasive EM attack on FPGA RO PUFs and countermeasures. In: 6th Workshop on Embedded Systems Security (WESS 2011). ACM, Mar 2011

17. Quisquater, J.-J., Samyde, D.: Electro Magnetic Analysis (EMA): measures and counter-measures for smart cards. In: Attali, I., Jensen, T. (eds.) E-smart 2001. LNCS, vol. 2140, pp. 200–210. Springer, Heidelberg (2001). https://doi.org/10.1007/3-540-45418-7_17

18. Sauvage, L., Guilley, S., Mathieu, Y.: Electromagnetic radiations of FPGAs: high spatial resolution cartography and attack on a cryptographic module. ACM Trans. Reconfigurable Technol. Syst. **2**(1), 4:1–4:24 (2009)

19. Sigl, G., Gross, M., Pehl, M.: Where technology meets security: key storage and data separation for system-on-chips. In: ESSCIRC 2018 - IEEE 44th European Solid State Circuits Conference (ESSCIRC), pp. 12–17, September 2018

20. Tebelmann, L., Pehl, M., Sigl, G.: EM side-channel analysis of BCH-based error correction for PUF-based key generation. In: Proceedings of the 2017 Workshop on Attacks and Solutions in Hardware Security, ASHES@CCS 2017, Dallas, TX, USA, November 3, 2017, pp. 43–52 (2017)

21. The SALWARE Project: Source code of the TERO-PUF implementation on SRAM FPGA (2016). https://perso.univ-st-etienne.fr/bl16388h/salware/tero_puf.htm. Accessed 11 Feb 2019

22. Unterstein, F., Heyszl, J., De Santis, F., Specht, R.: Dissecting leakage resilient PRFs with multivariate localized EM attacks. In: Guilley, S. (ed.) COSADE 2017. LNCS, vol. 10348, pp. 34–49. Springer, Cham (2017). https://doi.org/10.1007/978-3-319-64647-3_3

23. Varchola, M., Drutarovsky, M.: New high entropy element for FPGA based true random number generators. In: Mangard, S., Standaert, F.-X. (eds.) CHES 2010. LNCS, vol. 6225, pp. 351–365. Springer, Heidelberg (2010). https://doi.org/10.1007/978-3-642-15031-9_24

24. Wild, A., Becker, G.T., Güneysu, T.: A fair and comprehensive large-scale analysis of oscillation-based PUFs for FPGAs. In: 2017 27th International Conference on Field Programmable Logic and Applications (FPL), pp. 1–7, September 2017

Fault-Injection Attacks

FIMA: Fault Intensity Map Analysis

Keyvan Ramezanpour$^{(\boxtimes)}$, Paul Ampadu, and William Diehl$^{(\boxtimes)}$

Virginia Tech, Blacksburg, VA 24061, USA
{rkeyvan8,ampadu,wdiehl}@vt.edu

Abstract. We present a new statistical fault analysis technique called fault intensity map analysis (FIMA) that evaluates the responses of cryptographic implementations to biased-fault injections with varying intensities. FIMA exploits information from fault bias, as well as the correlation between fault distribution and intensity, to retrieve the secret key with fewer fault injections than existing techniques. FIMA generalizes several existing statistical fault analysis techniques, such as fault sensitivity analysis (FSA), differential fault intensity analysis (DFIA), ciphertext-only fault analysis (CFA), and statistical ineffective fault analysis (SIFA). FIMA has the flexibility of using different observables, e.g., faulty ciphertexts, correct ciphertexts under ineffective fault inductions, and data-dependent intensity profiles, and is successful against a wide range of countermeasures. In this paper, we use FIMA to retrieve the entire 128-bit secret key of the Ascon authenticated cipher, a CAESAR finalist for lightweight applications. On a software implementation of Ascon, simulations show that FIMA recovers the secret key with fewer than 50% of the fault injections required by previous techniques that rely on fault bias alone; furthermore, in the presence of error-detection and infective countermeasures, FIMA is $6\times$ more efficient than previous bias-based techniques.

Keywords: Authenticated encryption · Fault bias · Fault image · Fault intensity · FIMA · SIFA · Statistical fault analysis

1 Introduction

Increased device connectivity and ubiquitous data transfer in the era of the Internet of Things (IoT) necessitate the improvement of cryptographic security in a wide range of applications from high performance to lightweight computing platforms. Although most standardized cryptographic algorithms are resistant against cryptanalysis, implementation vulnerabilities such as side-channel analysis (SCA) pose serious threats to the security of the system. Passive SCA techniques, such as differential power analysis (DPA), exploit the correlation between a performance measure of the device, such as power consumption and/or electromagnetic radiation, and secret variables processed during execution of the cryptographic algorithms. Fault analysis (FA) is a powerful active SCA technique in which fault injections into the implementation executing the cryptographic

© Springer Nature Switzerland AG 2019
I. Polian and M. Stöttinger (Eds.): COSADE 2019, LNCS 11421, pp. 63–79, 2019.
https://doi.org/10.1007/978-3-030-16350-1_5

algorithm leak information about the secret variables. In this work, we propose a new fault analysis technique that analyzes the response of the system to fault injections more effectively than existing FA techniques.

Differential fault analysis (DFA) techniques analyze the error induced in an intermediate variable of a cipher, as the result of fault injection, using the correct and faulty ciphertexts for the same plaintext. If the type of error induced by the fault injection mechanism is deterministic and known, the attacker can reduce the search space of the secret key to the set of values resulting in the known error. Examples of DFA attacks on different ciphers include AES [1], LED [15], PRINCE [23], Plantlet [17], Trivium [21], Grain [5], and MICKEY 2.0 [2].

While DFA techniques seek to retrieve the secret key with a minimum number of fault injections, they assume strong fault models (i.e., stronger assumptions on the manifestation of the fault) that often make the attack difficult to implement with low-cost fault injection equipment. In contrast, statistical fault analysis techniques seek to reduce the complexity of the fault model, at the cost of requiring more fault injections to recover the secret key. This class of FA techniques is enabled by a property of fault induction called fault bias [10]. The observable used for statistical analysis exhibits a non-uniform, or biased, distribution under fault injection. In order to detect a meaningful bias in the distribution, a larger amount of data is required compared with DFA methods.

In this paper, we present fault intensity map analysis (FIMA) as a new statistical FA method. Compared with existing techniques, FIMA extracts more information about a cryptographic implementation using fault injections, and is thus able to recover the secret key with a fewer number of fault injections – even when a wide range of countermeasures are used to protect implementations against FA. The only requirement is that the attacker be able to inject a biased fault with varying intensities. FIMA can be employed on all ciphers attacked by existing statistical biased-fault techniques in previous works. In this work, we demonstrate a FIMA attack using simulations on a software implementation of the Ascon authenticated cipher, which is a finalist for the lightweight use case in the ongoing Competition for Authenticated Encryption: Security, Applicability, and Robustness (CAESAR) [3].

Our contributions in this paper are as follows: We present (1) a new statistical fault analysis methodology which exploits the bias that faults introduce in the distribution of faulty and/or fault-free values, as well as the correlation between the distribution and fault intensity, in order to reduce the number of fault injections required to recover a secret key, and (2) a methodology by which the attacker can identify the sufficient amount of data to find the correct key with a given probability of success.

This paper is organized as follows: In Sect. 2, we provide a brief background on statistical fault analysis techniques, and the Ascon authenticated cipher. In Sects. 3 and 4, we introduce fault intensity map analysis (FIMA), and describe it in terms of fault model, fault distribution, fault image, and the corresponding test statistics. In Sect. 5 we propose a method for determining the sufficient amount of data to achieve a desired probability of success. We describe a FIMA attack on Ascon in Sect. 6, and summarize results in Sect. 7. We conclude the paper in Sect. 8.

2 Background and Related Work

2.1 Statistical Fault Analysis

Statistical fault analysis techniques exploit the bias a fault injection induces in an observable. Different classes of FA techniques with their corresponding observables used for statistical analysis are shown in Fig. 1. The observables include the intensity of fault induction causing errors, the error induced in an intermediate variable, the faulty values of intermediate variables, as well as the correct values of the intermediate variable under ineffective fault inductions.

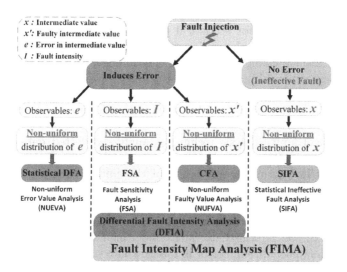

Fig. 1. Taxonomy of statistical fault analysis techniques and their relevant observables.

One class of statistical fault analysis (SFA) techniques uses the biased distribution of intermediate values due to fault injection. Non-uniform error value analysis (NUEVA) and non-uniform faulty value analysis (NUFVA) rely on the data-dependent error and fault value distributions, respectively. A statistical DFA attack on AES is introduced in [13], where it is shown that the distribution of error in one byte of the state, resulting from a clock glitch, is non-uniform. The non-uniform error distribution is exploited in this method to retrieve the key. Although the fault model assumed in this method is simpler than traditional DFA attacks, it still requires differential encryptions to calculate the error. Hence, the attacker requires the correct and faulty ciphertexts for the same plaintext, which is a limitation when attacking nonce-based ciphers [6], or in the presence of countermeasures randomizing the effect of faults.

Ciphertext-only fault attacks (CFA) exploit the non-uniform distribution of faulty values x'. In [8], the error induced by a fault injection is represented by the random-AND model. Here, the effect of fault induction is represented by the AND operation as $x' = x \odot e$. In this model, it is assumed that the error e is uniformly distributed. Due to the nonlinearity of the AND operation, given uniform distribution of the values x, the distribution of faulty values x' is biased. The values of error e with low Hamming weights (HW) will force any x into a low HW value. On the other hand, there is no value of e that will increase the HW of x. Hence, the probability that the faulty variable x' takes values with lower HW is substantially higher in the random-AND model. CFA has been employed in [6] and [14] to attack AES and the LED lightweight block cipher, respectively.

Fault sensitivity analysis (FSA) was the first biased-fault technique that employed fault intensity for statistical analysis. FSA exploits the data-dependent fault intensity at which an error appears in an intermediate variable in AES [16]. Differential fault intensity analysis (DFIA) employs both intensity and faulty values as the observables for statistical analysis. In DFIA, which uses faulty ciphertexts to calculate the change in error values, a slight change in the intensity results in a small change in the error only under a correct key assumption. DFIA has been employed in [11] and [9] to attack AES, LED, and PRESENT. Both FSA and DFIA techniques require encryption on the same set of plaintexts with different intensity values, which is a limitation for attacks on nonce-based ciphers.

Most classical fault analysis techniques analyze collected data from fault injections that induce errors in an intermediate value. Countermeasures that detect an error in intermediate variables of the cipher, such as [12] and [19], or infective countermeasures that randomize the effect of errors, as in [18] and [20], are effective in protecting ciphers against such attacks. Statistical ineffective fault analysis (SIFA), introduced in [7], is based on the observation that the distribution of correct intermediate values under ineffective faults is also biased. Fault inductions that induce no error in intermediate variables are called ineffective faults. Since SIFA uses only fault-free data for statistical analysis, it is able to attack even ciphers protected with a wide range of existing countermeasures.

Since the distributions of faulty values, and correct values of an intermediate variable, are non-uniform, it is implied that the distribution of the variable under fault injection, whether the fault is effective or not, should also be biased. This observation, along with the response of the system to fault intensity variations, are exploited in FIMA. In this work, FIMA is employed to attack the Ascon authenticated cipher.

2.2   Ascon Authenticated Cipher

Authenticated ciphers provide security and authentication in one algorithm suitable for lightweight implementation of authenticated encryption with associated data (AEAD). The Ascon authenticated cipher, selected as a CAESAR finalist for the lightweight use case, is based on a sponge construction shown in Fig. 2. During encryption/decryption, associated data and plaintext/ciphertext

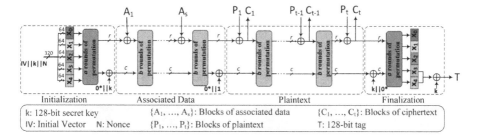

Fig. 2. Authenticated encryption in the sponge-based structure of Ascon.

are divided into blocks of r bits. After initializing the state, the blocks of associated data and plaintext/ciphertext are absorbed into the first r bits of the state in the Associated Data and Plaintext stages, respectively. The remaining c bits of the state are capacity bits determining the security and authentication bounds of the cipher [22]. The blocks of ciphertext/plaintext are squeezed out of the sponge in the Plaintext stage during encryption/decryption. After processing data, the tag for authentication is generated at the Finalization stage.

After updating the state with every block of data, a certain number of rounds of a permutation function are performed on the state. The state of Ascon is organized into 5 words of 64 bits, denoted by $x_i, i = 0, 1, 2, 3, 4$. The permutation function consists of constant addition, a substitution layer (S-box) and a diffusion layer. S-box is a 5-bit nonlinear function with inputs from bits of x_0 to x_4; one bit from each word. After the S-boxes, the state is processed by the diffusion layer. For every word x_i, a particular linear function is defined that mixes the bits within the word. Using the vector representation of the state words x_i, the operation of the diffusion layer can be formulated in matrix form as

$$\Sigma_i(\boldsymbol{x}_i) = (\mathrm{L}_i \boldsymbol{x}_i) \bmod 2, \quad i = 0, 1, \cdots, 4 \qquad (1)$$

In these equations, L_i is a sparse matrix of dimension 64×64 defining the diffusion function corresponding to word x_i. The inverse diffusion functions are simply the inverse matrices L_i^{-1} represented by its rows as

$$\mathrm{L}_i^{-1} = \left[\boldsymbol{l}_0^{(i)T}, \boldsymbol{l}_1^{(i)T}, \cdots, \boldsymbol{l}_{63}^{(i)T} \right]^T, \quad i = 0, 1, \cdots, 4 \qquad (2)$$

We use the matrix representation of inverse diffusion functions in (2) to calculate the output bits at the S-box operation from output tag values for a key candidate.

3   Fault Intensity Map Analysis (FIMA)

3.1   Fault Model

We assume that the attacker is able to inject a biased fault into an intermediate variable of the cipher with varying intensities. The attack is considered successful if any one of the following assumptions holds: (1) The distribution of the intermediate variable under fault injection is biased, or (2) There is a correlation between the fault distribution and fault intensity. Although the first condition, intuitively, implies the second, we specify them as distinct conditions to emphasize that FIMA gains two types of information to detect the secret key; namely, the fault bias, as well as the response of the system to intensity variations.

If both of the above assumptions are true, then FIMA extracts more information about the system than existing statistical techniques. However, even if part of the information is suppressed by any means, FIMA is still successful. For instance, if a particular implementation exhibits the same fault properties under intensity variations, or if the attacker simply opts to use a single intensity value, FIMA can still find the key using the bias information. In this case, FIMA achieves performance equal to or better than techniques based on fault bias, such as CFA and SIFA, as well as techniques such as DFIA.

The above fault model defines the generic assumptions of FIMA. Specific ciphers might require additional assumptions for a successful attack. One specific fault model assumption required to attack the Ascon cipher is that the attacker must be able to inject a biased fault into the operation of any selected pair of S-boxes at the last round of Finalization stage. The fault can be injected with a simple voltage/clock glitch. The distribution of values at the output of the attacked S-box pair is non-uniform.

3.2   Fault Distribution

Non-uniform distribution of data under fault induction, exploited in various statistical techniques, can be explained by the random-AND fault model [7,8]. We use the following modified random-AND model to include the effect of fault intensity variations:

$$
x' = \begin{cases} x, & \text{with probability} \quad 1 - p \\ x \odot e, & \text{with probability} \quad p \end{cases}
\tag{3}
$$

In this equation, e is a random error with uniform distribution. We use the probability p as a measure of the fault intensity. Using this model, it can be shown that the distribution of the intermediate variable, including both faulty and correct values, is non-uniform. This observation is exploited in the proposed FIMA attack to gain information about the secret key. The distribution of an intermediate variable x' under fault injection can be calculated as

$$
p_{X'}(x_0) = (1 - p) \cdot p_X(x_0) + p \cdot \sum_x \sum_e \Pr\{x \odot e = x_0\} p_X(x) p_E(e)
\tag{4}
$$

In this equation, $p_X(\cdot)$ and $p_E(\cdot)$ are probability mass functions of the intermediate variable x and the error e, respectively. The distribution of an intermediate value x for different inputs to a cipher is uniform.

3.3 Fault Image

We define the *fault image* as the map of probability distributions over all possible values of the intermediate variable experiencing the fault, and fault intensity values. The bias of fault distribution, and the correlation of the distribution with fault intensity, are used in FIMA to extract information about the secret key. This information is included in the fault image. Various features of the fault image are analyzed to identify the correct key. The fault image is formed for all candidates of a key subset, and the image with unique features is selected as the one corresponding to the correct key guess.

The fault image for a key candidate is formed by calculating the values of an intermediate variable x using the cipher outputs under fault injection with different intensities, and a key guess. The fault image for a key candidate K, denoted by $p_X(x, I; K)$, is the two-dimensional map of the probabilities that the intermediate variable X takes values x at fault intensity I when the values x are calculated from the cipher output using the key candidate K. The fault images obtained with correct and incorrect key guesses in the Ascon cipher for a 2-bit intermediate variable X are shown in Fig. 3.

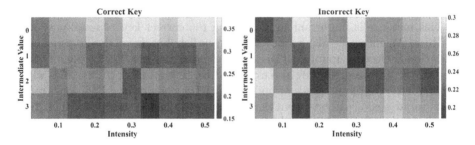

Fig. 3. Fault image showing biased distribution of values with smooth variations under intensity changes for correct key; color code represents the probability of occurrence. (Color figure online)

The distinct features of the fault image corresponding to the correct key that are extracted in FIMA to evaluate the key candidates are as follows; (1) The average probability distribution of the intermediate variable over all intensity values is non-uniform. However, the fault image of an incorrect key exhibits more uniform distribution of data at different fault intensities. (2) The correlation of the probability distribution with the fault intensity is data-dependent. There are values of the intermediate variable with probabilities that either increase, decrease or exhibit no observable variations with increasing intensity. However, this feature is not observed in the fault image of incorrect keys. (3) The probability distribution of the intermediate variable slightly changes with small variations in the fault intensity. Under an incorrect key guess, the distribution varies randomly for different fault intensities.

4   Test Statistics for Fault Image

4.1   Statistics for Fault Bias

Fault bias is defined as a distance measure between the distribution of the inter-mediate variable experiencing the fault and uniform distribution. We choose the proper distance metric based on its capability in distinguishing small variations in fault bias.

The difference between two probability distribution functions $P = \{p_i | i = 1, 2, \cdots, n\}$ and $Q = \{q_i | i = 1, 2, \cdots, n\}$ can be measured with the L_k-norm of the difference between the distribution vectors as $L_k = \sum_i |p_i - q_i|^k$. When Q is the uniform distribution function and $k = 2$, the above distance is called the Square Euclidean Imbalance (SEI) of the distribution P. The distance between distributions P and Q can also be measured with Kullback-Leibler (K-L) divergence [24], or relative entropy, as

$$\mathcal{D}_{KL}(P||Q) = \sum_i p_i \cdot \log(\frac{p_i}{q_i}) \tag{5}$$

We evaluate the sensitivity of the above metrics to fault bias in order to com-pare their effectiveness in detecting the bias in data distribution. The sensitivity of a bias measure is important in identifying the correct key, especially at low fault bias. An incorrect key guess results in a distribution of the intermediate values that is close to uniform. If the fault bias is small, the distribution of data calculated with the correct key also exhibits small bias. To identify the bias with the correct key in the presence of noise, the metric should have high sensitivity to bias variations. It can be shown that norm-based distance metrics with higher orders exhibit higher sensitivity to fault bias. The sensitivity of K-L divergence is similar to SEI (L_2-norm). To achieve high sensitivity at low fault bias, we choose the L_4-norm as the statistic to measure the bias of fault image; i.e.

$$\mathcal{D}_b(p_X; K) = \log\Big(\sum_i (p_i - q_i)^4\Big) \tag{6}$$

In this equation, $p_X = \{p_i\}$ is the average distribution of the intermediate vari-able over all fault intensities, and K is the key candidate by which the interme-diate values are calculated. Also, $Q = \{q_i\}$ is the uniform distribution.

4.2   Statistics for Intensity Correlation

The fault distribution in biased fault techniques has a correlation with fault intensity. Assume that fault injection is started at an infinitesimally low intensity. The distribution of an intermediate variable under such a condition is close to uniform – similar to the case without fault injection. By increasing the fault intensity, stronger bias appears in the distribution. The probability of some intermediate values increases while some other values take lower probability. Hence, the probability distribution is correlated with the fault intensity.

The above discussion implies that the correlation of fault distribution and fault intensity is data-dependent. Values showing positive correlation with the intensity take higher probabilities. This is the generalized concept of the FSA attack. In FSA, the data-dependent fault intensity at which an error occurs, which is called the fault sensitivity, is exploited to gain information about the secret key. This information is captured in the fault bias; at a given intensity, some values are more likely to experience the fault, hence, take lower probability of occurrence. Therefore, the intensity at which all values have the same probability of error is data-dependent. The correlation between fault distribution and intensity also implies smooth variation of the distributions with small changes of intensity under the correct key assumption. This is the generalized concept of DFIA.

In order to measure the variations of fault distribution with intensity changes, we define the *intensity dispersion* as the average of differences between data distribution with incremental intensity variations. For intensity values $\{I_i | i = 1, 2, \cdots, R\}$, the intensity dispersion is defined as

$$D_I(p_X; K) = -\log\left(\frac{1}{R-1} \sum_{i=1}^{R-1} \mathcal{D}_4\left(p_X(x, I_{i+1}; K) \| p_X(x, I_i; K)\right) \right) \quad (7)$$

In this equation $\mathcal{D}_4(P\|Q)$ is the L_4-norm distance between distributions P and Q. Since the dispersion is minimum for the correct key, the negative sign is used in (7) to result in the maximum value for the correct key.

4.3 Score Function

By defining proper metrics to measure the desirable features of the fault image, we can now define a *score function* that takes maximum value only for the fault image of the correct key. We define the score function as a weighted sum of the metrics for fault bias and intensity dispersion. For a fault image $p_X(x, I; K)$ corresponding to the key candidate K, the score function is

$$\mathcal{R}(K, \gamma) = (1 - \gamma) \cdot \mathcal{D}_b(p_X; K) + \gamma \cdot D_I(p_X; K) \quad (8)$$

The parameter $0 < \gamma < 1$ in the score function determines the significance of the fault bias or the intensity correlation in making a decision about the correct key. The attacker can choose the proper γ value based on prior information on which property of the fault injection is more pronounced. When there is no prior knowledge of which of the fault bias or the correlation of fault distribution with intensity contains more information in a given implementation, we treat γ as a learning parameter. In this case, the optimal γ is calculated as

$$\gamma_{opt} = \arg\max_{\gamma} \left| \max_K \mathcal{R}(K, \gamma) - \max_k \left\{ \mathcal{R}(k, \gamma) | k \neq \arg\max_K \mathcal{R}(K, \gamma) \right\} \right| \quad (9)$$

The optimal γ is found as the value that maximizes the difference between the maximum and the second maximum values of the score function over the key space. The correct key guess is then found as

$$K_c = \arg\max_K \mathcal{R}(K, \gamma_{opt}) \tag{10}$$

5   Sufficient Amount of Data

In statistical fault analysis techniques, the correct key can be identified if a sufficient amount of data is collected under fault injection. For biased-fault techniques, it is shown in [7] that the sufficient amount of data is inversely proportional to the fault bias. Since the fault bias is not known a priori, we propose updating the fault images with each newly collected data sample. If successive fault images with the highest score belong to the same key value, then that key is correct with a high probability.

When the fault distribution as well as the distribution of data without fault injection are known, it can be shown that the optimal statistics to detect the correct key among all key candidates is the log-likelihood ratio (LLR), which is closely related to the Kullback-Leibler divergence [7]. The required number of data samples to achieve a given probability of success with the LLR statistics is derived in [4]. Assume N_t data samples are collected up to time instant t and the fault image is constructed with these samples. Using the approximations in [7], the probability of success in detecting the correct key can be calculated as

$$P_t = \Phi_{0,1}\left(\sqrt{N_t \cdot \mathcal{D}_{KL}(P||Q)} - \Phi_{0,1}^{-1}(1 - 2^{-a})\right) \tag{11}$$

In this equation, $\mathcal{D}_{KL}(P||Q)$ is the Kullback-Leibler divergence of the data distribution under fault injection, P, and the distribution without fault, Q. The function $\Phi_{0,1}(\cdot)$ is the cumulative distribution function (CDF) of the normal distribution. Furthermore, the parameter a is the *advantage* of the attack, and is defined as follows: If the search space of key candidates has size 2^n, and the success of the attack is the event that the correct key is among the top ℓ candidates ranked by a given statistic, the advantage of the attack over an exhaustive search is defined as $a = n - \log_2(\ell)$.

We represent the score difference of the correct key and incorrect key guesses with N_t samples by the random variable Δ_t. Detection of the correct key is successful if $\Delta_t > 0$. The random variable Δ_t can be modeled by a traditional Markov process with transition probabilities P_t and $1 - P_t$. The attacker gradually collects samples at successive time instances and keeps track of the correct key guess. At each time instance, the Kullback-Leibler divergence of data distribution with uniform distribution is calculated. The probability of success at every time t with N_t data samples is also calculated using (11). If the correct key guess does not change over L successive time instances, the probability that the key guess is wrong can be calculated as $P\{\text{fail}\} = \prod_{i=t-L+1}^{t}(1 - P_i)$. If $P\{\text{fail}\} < \epsilon$, it means that the obtained key guess is correct with a probability larger than $1 - \epsilon$. The FIMA attack with the proposed approach for detecting the sufficient amount of data is summarized in Algorithm 1.

Algorithm 1. FIMA Attack with Sufficient Data Detection

Inputs: A set of messages $\{M_1, M_2, M_3 \cdots\}$, Intensity values $\{I_1, I_2, I_3 \cdots I_N\}$.

Outputs: Correct key guess

Initialization:

$\quad t = 0, \quad P_{fail} = 1, \quad \gamma_{opt} = 0.5, \quad \beta = 0.1, \quad K_{c,0} = -1,$

while $P_{fail} > \epsilon$ **do**

$\quad$ **for** I in $\{I_1, I_2, I_3 \cdots I_N\}$ **do**

$\quad\quad$ 1. $t := t + 1,$

$\quad\quad$ 2. Encrypt the next message M_t while injecting fault at the intermediate variable X of the cipher with intensity I. The cipher output is C_t.

$\quad\quad$ **for** K in $\{0, 1, \cdots, 2^n - 1\}$ **do**

$\quad\quad\quad$ a. Calculate x (intermediate variable) using C_t and K (key candidate).

$\quad\quad\quad$ b. Update the occurrence probability of x in the fault image $p_X(x, I; K)$.

$\quad\quad$ **end for**

$\quad\quad$ 3. Find the optimum weight from (9) and denote it by γ_o.

$\quad\quad$ 4. Update optimal score weight: $\gamma_{opt} := \beta \cdot \gamma_o + (1 - \beta) \cdot \gamma_{opt}$.

$\quad\quad$ 5. Find the correct key guess from (10) and denote it by $K_{c,t}$.

$\quad\quad$ 6. Find K-L divergence of P (data) and Q (uniform) distributions as in (5).

$\quad\quad$ 7. Find the success probability P_t from (11).

$\quad\quad$ 8. Update failure probability: $P_{fail} := P_{fail} \cdot (1 - P_t)$.

$\quad\quad$ **if** $K_{c,t} \neq K_{c,t-1}$, **then** $P_{fail} = 1$.

$\quad$ **end for**

end while

Return $K_{c,t}$ as the correct key guess.

---

6 FIMA Attack on Ascon

In order to attack Ascon, faults are injected into the operation of selected pairs of S-boxes at the last round of the Finalization stage (refer to Fig. 2). The intermediate variables used for statistical analysis are bits 3 and 4 at the output of the attacked S-boxes. The output tag values are used for calculating the intermediate values with a key candidate.

The operation of Ascon at the last round of the Finalization stage is demonstrated, schematically, in Fig. 4. Using the inverse diffusion functions in (2), bits $i = 3, 4$ at the output of j-th S-box can be calculated from the tag value $T = T_0 \| T_1$ as

$$s_i^{(j)} = \sum_{r=0}^{63} \left[\left(T_{(i-3),r} \oplus k_{64(i-3)+r} \right) \odot l_{j,r}^{(i)} \right] \quad \text{mod } 2 \tag{12}$$

in which, k_r and $T_{s,r}$ are the r-th bit of the key and tag values $T_s, s = 0, 1$, respectively. Also, $l_{j,r}^{(i)}$ is the r-th element in the j-th row of the inverse diffusion matrix L_i^{-1}. We can express the above equations in terms of a combination of key bits as

$$s_i^{(j)} = \left(\sum_{r=0}^{63} T_{(i-3),r} \odot l_{j,r}^{(i)} \right) \oplus K_{i-3}^{(j)} \tag{13}$$

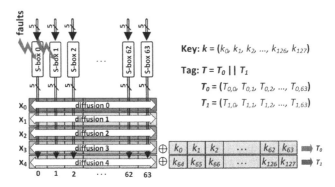

Fig. 4. Last round of the Finalization stage in Ascon with double-fault injection at the targeted pair of S-boxes.

In this equation, $K_0^{(j)}$ and $K_1^{(j)}$ are a linear combination of key bits in the first and second 64-bit halves of the key. The coefficients of the combinations are the j-th row of the inverse diffusion matrices L_3^{-1} and L_4^{-1}, respectively. In other words,

$$K_s^{(j)} = \sum_{r=0}^{63} k_{64s+r} \odot l_{j,r}^{(s+3)} \bmod 2, \quad s = 0, 1 \tag{14}$$

Bits 3 and 4 at the output of S-boxes j and $j + 1$, attacked by a biased fault, are calculated from the tag values using (13) and a 4-bit key candidate $\mathbf{K}^{(j)} = (K_0^{(j)}, K_1^{(j)}, K_0^{(j+1)}, K_1^{(j+1)})$. The two bits calculated at time instant t constitute the first and second bits of the 2-bit intermediate variables $z_t^{(j)}$ and $z_t^{(j+1)}$. The distribution of data $\{z_1^{(j)}, z_2^{(j)}, \cdots, z_t^{(j)}, z_1^{(j+1)}, z_2^{(j+1)}, \cdots, z_t^{(j+1)}\}$ are used for statistical analysis to find the correct key guess.

FIMA finds the correct guess for $\mathbf{K}^{(0)}$ using fault injections at S-box pairs $(0, 1)$. The maximum of the score function is not unique; for every 4 possible values of $(K_0^{(0)}, K_1^{(0)})$, there is a particular value of $(K_0^{(1)}, K_1^{(1)})$ that results in the same bias and intensity correlation. Similarly, by attacking S-box pair $(1, 2)$, FIMA finds 4 guesses of $\mathbf{K}^{(1)}$ in which for every value of $(K_0^{(1)}, K_1^{(1)})$ there is a corresponding value for $(K_0^{(2)}, K_1^{(2)})$. Continuing the attack on S-box pairs $(2, 3)$ up to $(62, 63)$, a unique sequence of $\{K_0^{(0)}, K_0^{(1)}, \cdots, K_0^{(63)}\}$ and $\{K_1^{(0)}, K_1^{(1)}, \cdots, K_1^{(63)}\}$ are obtained for every value of $(K_0^{(0)}, K_1^{(0)})$. These sequences form two sets of 64 linear binary equations for the first and second 64-bit halves of the key, as in (14). By solving these equations, the individual key bits are calculated. Thus, starting from each of the 4 guesses of $(K_0^{(0)}, K_1^{(0)})$, one guess for the entire key is obtained. The correct key can be found by comparing the ciphertext computed for a single plaintext and the 4 key guesses with an expected ciphertext from the actual implementation.

7   Results

We demonstrate the proposed FIMA attack on a C implementation of the Ascon cipher. Biased fault injections at selected pairs of S-boxes with different intensities are modeled by the modified random-AND fault model defined in (3). The effect of countermeasures suppressing faulty outputs as well as infective countermeasures that randomize error values at the output are investigated.

7.1   Signature of Score Function over Key Space

The FIMA score function value, defined in (8), over the search space of key combinations $\mathbf{K}^{(0)}$, for attacked S-boxes 0 and 1, is shown in Fig. 5(a). We note that four values of the key exhibit the same score. For every pair of attacked S-boxes, we obtain four key guesses that result in a total of four guesses for the 128-bit Ascon key. The score values of Fig. 5(a) are obtained for a sufficient number of collected data samples with 20 values of fault intensity where $p \in [0, 0.2]$.

The optimal weight of the score function with every data sample is shown in Fig. 5(b). We observe that when there are not enough data samples, more

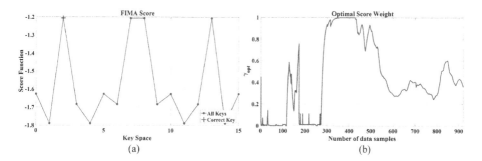

Fig. 5. FIMA score function over key search space; (a) score function with correct key corresponding to one of the four peaks; (b) optimal weight of score function.

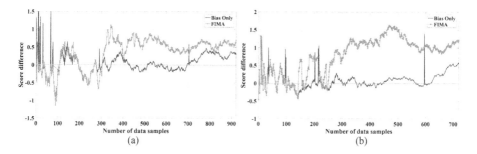

Fig. 6. Differences between correct key score and maximum score of incorrect key guesses, with fault intensities (a) $p \in [0, 0.2]$, (b) $p \in [0, 0.3]$.

weight is assigned to the data bias as the variations over intensity values are noisy and not reliable. By collecting enough data, FIMA uses information from both bias and intensity dispersion to detect the key. The difference between the FIMA score of the correct key, and the maximum score of incorrect key values versus the number of data samples, is shown in Fig. 6(a). In this figure, 20 values of fault intensity ranging in $p \in [0, 0.2]$ are used for FIMA attack.

We note in Fig. 6(a) that using the data bias alone as the score function requires at least 710 data samples to detect the correct key. However, FIMA can detect the key using only 305 samples, which is more efficient by a factor of 2.3×. When the range of fault intensity increases, the required amount of data is decreased. This is shown in Fig. 6(b) when 20 values of fault intensity ranging in $p \in [0, 0.3]$ are used in FIMA. Using only bias information, at least 620 samples are required, while FIMA needs only 250 samples, i.e. ~2.5× fewer samples.

7.2   FIMA with Error-Detection Countermeasures

A widely-used class of countermeasures against DFA attacks consists of error-detection techniques that suppress any output when an error is detected in the cipher operations. Hence, the attacker has no access to faulty values for differential or statistical analysis. However, the biased distribution of fault-free data, used in SIFA, and the correlation of the distribution with intensity, still leak information about the secret. The results of a FIMA attack in the presence of such countermeasures are shown in Fig. 7.

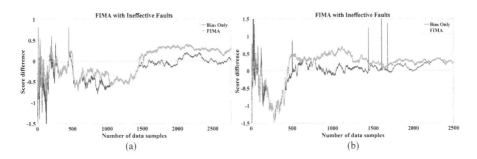

Fig. 7. Score differences between correct key and incorrect key guesses with error-based countermeasures, and fault intensities (a) $p \in [0, 0.2]$, (b) $p \in [0, 0.3]$.

When the faulty values are eliminated, the bias of data distribution decreases. This can be verified by calculating the distribution of fault-free data in the random-AND model of (3). Hence, the required size of data samples increases. This is is observed in Fig. 7. When the fault intensity ranges in $p \in [0, 0.2]$, FIMA requires 1523 samples to successfully recover the key, while by using only the data bias, more than 2710 samples are needed. By increasing the intensity range to $p \in [0, 0.3]$, these values decrease to 460 and 2035, respectively.

7.3   FIMA with Infective Countermeasures

Rather than suppress faulty outputs, infective countermeasures randomize errors so that no information is leaked into observables, which reduces the bias of faulty values. FIMA score differences versus the size of data samples in the presence of infective countermeasures is shown in Fig. 8(a). We simulate infective counter-measures by injecting the fault at an incorrect random round of Ascon. FIMA can detect the key using 453 data samples even with infective countermeasures. The effect of intensity information is observed by noting that the size of data needed to detect the key using only the bias information is about 2880, i.e. larger by a factor of 6. A similar observation is made with noisy fault injection. In this case, the attacker might not have precise control, e.g. on timing or location of the fault injection. The result of FIMA with noisy fault injection at randomly selected pairs of S-boxes with probability 0.7 is shown in Fig. 8(b). Similar to the case of infective countermeasures, the required size of data in FIMA is 690, while at least 2585 samples are needed when using data bias alone. A comparison of FIMA performance with biased-based techniques is given in Table 1.

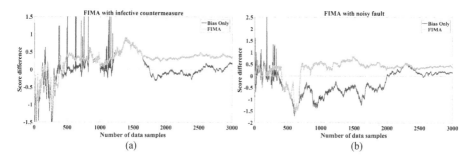

Fig. 8. Score differences between correct key and incorrect key guesses with fault intensities $p \in [0, 0.3]$ and (a) infective countermeasures, (b) noisy fault injection.

Table 1. Comparison of FIMA performance versus biased-based techniques.

Intensity range	$p \in [0, 0.2]$		$p \in [0, 0.3]$		$p \in [0, 0.3]$		$p \in [0, 0.3]$	
Technique	FIMA	Bias	FIMA	Bias	FIMA	Bias (SIFA)	FIMA	Bias
Countermeasure	N/A		N/A		Error-Detection		Infective	
Data size	305	710	250	620	460	2035	453	2880
FIMA improvement	2.3×		2.5×		4.4×		6.3×	

8   Conclusions

In this work, we introduced a new statistical fault analysis technique called fault intensity map analysis (FIMA), which extracts more information from cryptographic implementations than existing techniques, through analysis of fault injections. We analyzed distributions of faulty ciphertexts and correct ciphertexts under ineffective fault inductions, at different fault intensities. We showed that the correlation of distributions with fault intensity represents *extra* information that reduces the size of data samples required for key recovery, especially in the presence of noise and various countermeasures. Additionally, we derived conditions to determine the minimum amount of data required to achieve a given probability of success; this can also be used with other statistical fault analysis techniques. We employed a FIMA attack to retrieve the entire 128-bit secret key of the Ascon authenticated cipher. In simulations on a software implementation of Ascon, we showed that FIMA recovers the secret key with fewer than half of the fault injections required by previous techniques that rely on fault bias alone. Moreover, in the presence of error-detection and infective countermeasures, FIMA is $6\times$ more efficient than previous bias-based techniques.

Acknowledgement. This work was supported by NIST award 70NANB18H219 for Lightweight Cryptography in Hardware and Embedded Systems.

References

1. Ali, S.S., Mukhopadhyay, D., Tunstall, M.: Differential fault analysis of AES: towards reaching its limits. J. Cryptogr. Eng. **3**(2), 73–97 (2013)
2. Banik, S., Maitra, S., Sarkar, S.: Improved differential fault attack on MICKEY 2.0. J. Cryptogr. Eng. **5**(1), 13–29 (2015)
3. Bernstein, D.: Cryptographic competitions (2016). https://competitions.cr.yp.to/caesar.html
4. Blondeau, C., Gérard, B., Nyberg, K.: Multiple differential cryptanalysis using LLR and χ^2 statistics. In: Visconti, I., De Prisco, R. (eds.) SCN 2012. LNCS, vol. 7485, pp. 343–360. Springer, Heidelberg (2012). https://doi.org/10.1007/978-3-642-32928-9_19
5. Chakraborty, A., Mazumdar, B., Mukhopadhyay, D.: A combined power and fault analysis attack on protected grain family of stream ciphers. IEEE Trans. Comput. Aided Des. Integr. Circuits Syst. **36**(12), 1968–1977 (2017)
6. Dobraunig, C., Eichlseder, M., Korak, T., Lomné, V., Mendel, F.: Statistical fault attacks on nonce-based authenticated encryption schemes. In: Cheon, J.H., Takagi, T. (eds.) ASIACRYPT 2016. LNCS, vol. 10031, pp. 369–395. Springer, Heidelberg (2016). https://doi.org/10.1007/978-3-662-53887-6_14
7. Dobraunig, C., Eichlseder, M., Korak, T., Mangard, S., Mendel, F., Primas, R.: SIFA: exploiting ineffective fault inductions on symmetric cryptography. IACR Trans. Cryptogr. Hardw. Embedded Syst. **2018**, 547–572 (2018)
8. Fuhr, T., Jaulmes, E., Lomné, V., Thillard, A.: Fault attacks on AES with faulty ciphertexts only. In: 2013 Workshop on Fault Diagnosis and Tolerance in Cryptography (FDTC), pp. 108–118. IEEE (2013)

9. Ghalaty, N.F., Yuce, B., Schaumont, P.: Differential fault intensity analysis on PRESENT and LED block ciphers. In: Mangard, S., Poschmann, A.Y. (eds.) COSADE 2014. LNCS, vol. 9064, pp. 174–188. Springer, Cham (2015). https://doi.org/10.1007/978-3-319-21476-4_12

10. Ghalaty, N.F., Yuce, B., Schaumont, P.: Analyzing the efficiency of biased-fault based attacks. Embedded Syst. Lett. **8**(2), 33–36 (2016)

11. Ghalaty, N.F., Yuce, B., Taha, M., Schaumont, P.: Differential fault intensity analysis. In: 2014 Workshop on Fault Diagnosis and Tolerance in Cryptography (FDTC), pp. 49–58. IEEE (2014)

12. Kermani, M.M., Jalali, A., Azarderakhsh, R., Xie, J., Choo, K.K.R.: Reliable inversion in GF(2 8) with redundant arithmetic for secure error detection of cryptographic architectures. IEEE Trans. Comput. Aided Des. Integr. Circuits Syst. **37**(3), 696–704 (2018)

13. Lashermes, R., Reymond, G., Dutertre, J.M., Fournier, J., Robisson, B., Tria, A.: A DFA on AES based on the entropy of error distributions. In: 2012 Workshop on Fault Diagnosis and Tolerance in Cryptography, pp. 34–43. IEEE (2012)

14. Li, W., et al.: Ciphertext-only fault analysis on the led lightweight cryptosystem in the internet of things. IEEE Trans. Dependable Secure Comput. (2018)

15. Li, W., et al.: Impossible differential fault analysis on the LED lightweight cryptosystem in the vehicular ad-hoc networks. EEE Trans. Dependable Secure Comput. **13**(1), 84–92 (2016)

16. Li, Y., Sakiyama, K., Gomisawa, S., Fukunaga, T., Takahashi, J., Ohta, K.: Fault sensitivity analysis. In: Mangard, S., Standaert, F.-X. (eds.) CHES 2010. LNCS, vol. 6225, pp. 320–334. Springer, Heidelberg (2010). https://doi.org/10.1007/978-3-642-15031-9_22

17. Maitra, S., Siddhanti, A., Sarkar, S.: A differential fault attack on plantlet. IEEE Trans. Comput. **66**(10), 1804–1808 (2017)

18. Patranabis, S., Chakraborty, A., Mukhopadhyay, D.: Fault tolerant infective countermeasure for AES. J. Hardw. Syst. Secur. **1**(1), 3–17 (2017)

19. Patranabis, S., Chakraborty, A., Mukhopadhyay, D., Chakrabarti, P.P.: Fault space transformation: a generic approach to counter differential fault analysis and differential fault intensity analysis on AES-like block ciphers. IEEE Trans. Inf. Forensics Secur. **12**(5), 1092–1102 (2017)

20. Patranabis, S., et al.: Lightweight design-for-security strategies for combined countermeasures against side channel and fault analysis in IoT applications. J. Hardw. Syst. Secur., 1–29 (2018)

21. Potestad-Ordóñez, F., Jiménez-Fernández, C., Valencia-Barrero, M.: Experimental and timing analysis comparison of FPGA trivium implementations and their vulnerability to clock fault injection. In: 2016 Conference on Design of Circuits and Integrated Systems (DCIS), pp. 1–6. IEEE (2016)

22. Saarinen, M.-J.O.: Beyond modes: building a secure record protocol from a cryptographic sponge permutation. In: Benaloh, J. (ed.) CT-RSA 2014. LNCS, vol. 8366, pp. 270–285. Springer, Cham (2014). https://doi.org/10.1007/978-3-319-04852-9_14

23. Song, L., Hu, L.: Differential fault attack on the PRINCE block cipher. In: Avoine, G., Kara, O. (eds.) LightSec 2013. LNCS, vol. 8162, pp. 43–54. Springer, Heidelberg (2013). https://doi.org/10.1007/978-3-642-40392-7_4

24. Van Erven, T., Harremos, P.: Rényi divergence and kullback-leibler divergence. IEEE Trans. Inf. Theory **60**(7), 3797–3820 (2014)

Differential Fault Attacks on KLEIN

Michael Gruber[1]([⊠]) and Bodo Selmke[2]

[1] Chair of Security in Information Technology,
Technical University of Munich, Munich, Germany
m.gruber@tum.de
[2] Fraunhofer Institute for Applied and Integrated Security, Garching, Germany
bodo.selmke@aisec.fraunhofer.de

Abstract. This paper proposes two *Differential Fault Attacks* on the lightweight block cipher KLEIN. Variant one targets the intermediate state of the cipher. Using at least five faulty ciphertexts, the attacker is able to determine the last round key. The second variant, which works only on KLEIN-64, injects a byte-fault in the key schedule and requires at least four faulty ciphertexts in order to determine the whole key. Furthermore, we demonstrate the efficiency of both attack methods by simulation.

Keywords: Differential fault analysis · Fault attack · Key schedule · Lightweight block cipher · KLEIN

1 Introduction

Exchange of information in computer networks often requires the use of cryptography, to ensure the integrity of messages, the confidentiality of the message or the authenticity of the communication partner. However, the computational effort caused by cryptographic algorithms can be prohibitive for resource constrained devices. A typical example for this class of devices are IoT (Internet of Things) devices. These are often low-power sensor nodes, which are deployed over a large area and submit measurement data to some back-end system. Each node is battery powered and is thus very limited in its energy consumption. For these applications *lightweight block ciphers* were developed in recent years. The idea is to offer a symmetric block cipher (since asymmetric ciphers are always more costly in terms of performance), with a security level that does not have many reserves, but at a much smaller computational overhead. The most prominent example for lightweight block ciphers is PRESENT [2] but many other proposals have been developed, e.g. KLEIN as proposed by Gong et al. [6].

In this paper we investigate *Differential Fault Attacks* on the lightweight block cipher KLEIN. Fault Attacks are a subgroup of *implementation attacks*, which attack the actual implementation of a cryptographic algorithm and not its mathematical properties. Therefore, the attacker disturbs the device while it is executing the cryptographic algorithm. However, the resulting faulty output of the algorithm, can be exploited by an attacker, if the fault was carefully injected

I. Polian and M. Stöttinger (Eds.): COSADE 2019, LNCS 11421, pp. 80–95, 2019.
https://doi.org/10.1007/978-3-030-16350-1_6

at a specific location. Since lightweight block ciphers are often used in devices, where an attacker can easily gain physical access, *implementation attacks* have to be taken into consideration.

Contribution. In this paper we introduce two different fault attacks on the lightweight cipher KLEIN. Both attacks are based on the principle of *differential fault analysis*. The first fault attack requires an attacker to inject faults into the state of the encryption process. This attack method works on all variants of KLEIN. Furthermore, we present a second attack on the key schedule, which works only on the variant of KLEIN using a 64 bit key. This attack enables the attacker to determine the key with 4 fault injections. For both attacks we prove the according efficiency by means of simulations.

Organization. The paper is structured as follows: In Sect. 2 the basic working principle of the KLEIN cipher is described. Subsequently, in Sect. 3, we provide an overview about the existing fault attacks on KLEIN. Section 4 explains the attack based on the fault injection into the encryption, whereas Sect. 5 explains the attack on the key schedule of KLEIN-64. A discussion of the performance of both attack strategies is given in Sect. 6. Section 7 concludes the paper.

2 KLEIN

KLEIN [6] is a SPN-based cipher similar to other state-of-the-art block ciphers (e.g. AES or PRESENT) and features three different security levels with according key sizes of 64, 80 and 96 bit. For all three variants a block size of 64 bit is used, only the number of rounds performed and the key schedule differs. However, in contrast to AES, KLEIN is not operating on bytes, but on 4 bit wide *nibbles*. In the following we will give a very brief description of the general structure and the individual round functions.

2.1 The Round Function

The cipher is composed from $R \in \{12, 16, 20\}$ executions of the round function, depending on the key size of 64, 80 or 96 bit. Each round i utilizes a round key sk^i, which is derived from the previous round key through the *KeySchedule* function. Basic building blocks of each round are the functions *AddRoundKey*, *SubNibbles*, *RotateNibbles* and *MixNibbles*. Algorithm 1 shows the general structure of the KLEIN cipher.

2.2 SubNibbles

The *SubNibbles* function is the nonlinear permutation step of KLEIN. A notable property of the used 4 bit S-Box function S is the fact that it is involutive, i.e. $S(x) = S^{-1}(x) \ \forall \ x \ \in \{0, \ldots, 15\}$. This saves the costs for the implementation of an inverse S-Box. The S-Box is given in Table 1.

Algorithm 1. The structure of the KLEIN cipher.

$sk^1 \leftarrow KEY$
$STATE \leftarrow PLAINTEXT$
for $i = 1$ *to* R **do**
    $AddRoundKey(STATE, sk^i)$
    $SubNibbles(STATE)$
    $RotateNibbles(STATE)$
    $MixNibbles(STATE)$
    $sk^{i+1} \leftarrow KeySchedule(sk^i, i)$
end for
$CIPHERTEXT \leftarrow AddRoundKey(STATE, sk^{R+1})$

Table 1. The 4 bit S-Box of KLEIN.

Input:	0	1	2	3	4	5	6	7	8	9	A	B	C	D	E	F
Output:	7	4	A	9	1	F	B	0	C	3	2	6	8	E	D	5

2.3 RotateNibbles

The *RotateNibbles* function rotates the full 16 Nibbles wide input $[n_0, n_1, \ldots, n_{15}]$ by two bytes (4 Nibbles) to the left:

$$[n_0, n_1, \ldots, n_{15}] \rightarrow [n_4, n_5, \ldots, n_{15}, n_0, n_1, n_2, n_3, n_4]$$

2.4 MixNibbles

The *MixNibbles* function is the linear diffusion step of the KLEIN cipher. It subdivides the input state into two arrays[1] of 4 bytes (8 nibbles $[n_0, \ldots, n_7]$ and $[n_8, \ldots, n_{15}]$) which are interpreted as polynomials in $\mathbb{F}_2^8$. The multiplication with the permutation matrix is calculated modulo the reduction polynomial $x^4 + 1$. MixNibbles uses thereby the exact same 4×4 bytes permutation matrix that is used in the AES:

$$\begin{bmatrix} n_0^{i+1}||n_1^{i+1} & n_8^{i+1}||n_9^{i+1} \\ n_2^{i+1}||n_3^{i+1} & n_{10}^{i+1}||n_{11}^{i+1} \\ n_4^{i+1}||n_5^{i+1} & n_{12}^{i+1}||n_{13}^{i+1} \\ n_6^{i+1}||n_7^{i+1} & n_{14}^{i+1}||n_{15}^{i+1} \end{bmatrix} = \begin{bmatrix} 2 & 3 & 1 & 1 \\ 1 & 2 & 3 & 1 \\ 1 & 1 & 2 & 3 \\ 3 & 1 & 1 & 2 \end{bmatrix} \times \begin{bmatrix} n_0^i||n_1^i & n_8^i||n_9^i \\ n_2^i||n_3^i & n_{10}^i||n_{11}^i \\ n_4^i||n_5^i & n_{12}^i||n_{13}^i \\ n_6^i||n_7^i & n_{14}^i||n_{15}^i \end{bmatrix}$$

2.5 Key Schedule

KLEIN's key schedule reuses the *SubNibbles* functions from the round function. The key schedule is composed from a cyclic left shift by two nibbles (one byte), followed by a Feistel network. Subsequently, four nibbles (two bytes) are substituted by the *SubNibbles* function and the *round constant i* is added to the fifth and sixth nibble (third byte). Figure 2 depicts the structure of the key schedule for 3 iterations. In contrast to the round function the key schedule works in a byte oriented way, as all operations are performed on a multiple of two nibbles.

---

[1] || denotes a concatenation.

2.6   Modified Representation

To simplify the explanation of our attack, it is necessary to slightly change the representation of the last round function, since KLEIN does not omit the *MixNibbles* operation in the last round [6]. The effects of omitting the last *MixColumns* in the AES were extensively studied by Dunkelman et al. in [5]. The final *AddRoundKey* step and the previous *MixNibbles* step are exchanged (cf. Fig. 3) the modified representation of KLEIN is also shown in Algorithm 2. Since *MixNibbles* is a linear function, it holds that $MixNibbles(a + b) = MixNibbles(a) + MixNibbles(b)$, the same reasoning can also be applied to the *AddroundKey* function. Therefore, we can exchange the *AddRoundKey* and the *MixNibbles* step, if we substitute the added round key sk^i with $MixNibbles(sk^i)$. As a result of the exchanged order of *AddRoundKey* and *MixNibbles*, it is also necessary to apply the inverse *MixNibbles* function to the last round key RK^{R+1} prior to the addition to the state RB^R. Furthermore, for the sake of simplicity from now on we will represent KLEIN in a byte-oriented view, in contrast to the originally proposed nibble-oriented view. In fact *SubNibbles* is the only function, which actually operates on nibbles. However, the application of a 4 bit S-Box on two nibbles can be replaced by a compound 8 bit S-Box without loss of generality, if no particular properties of the 4 bit S-Box are considered. Therefore, in the following we represent the KLEIN's state as an array of bytes, which is transformed by the functions *SubBytes*, *MixBytes* and *RotateBytes*.

Algorithm 2. The structure of the modified KLEIN cipher.

$sk^1 \leftarrow KEY$
$STATE \leftarrow PLAINTEXT$
for $i = 1$ **to** $R - 1$ **do**
    $AddRoundKey(STATE, sk^i)$
    $SubNibbles(STATE)$
    $RotateNibbles(STATE)$
    $MixNibbles(STATE)$
    $sk^{i+1} \leftarrow KeySchedule(sk^i, i)$
end for
$AddRoundKey(STATE, sk^R)$
$SubNibbles(STATE)$
$RotateNibbles(STATE)$
$sk^{R+1} \leftarrow KeySchedule(sk^R, R)$
$AddRoundKey(STATE, invMixNibbles(sk^{R+1}))$
$CIPHERTEXT \leftarrow MixNibbles(STATE)$

2.7   Notation

Throughout the remaining sections we will use the following notation. An intermediate state of KLEIN is named according to the abbreviation of the function which was applied to the intermediate state last, i.e. ARK^x is the state after the application of *AddRoundKey* during round x. A subscript refers to a specific byte of the state. The states of the key schedule are abbreviated as RK^x. A multiplication of two bytes is done as defined in the AES [11]. Faulted values are indicated by an overline (e.g. the faulty byte $\overline{ARK}_0^{R-1}$).

3   Related Work

To the best of our knowledge, there are no publications about fault attacks on KLEIN targeting either the state or the key schedule[2]. In contrast, Yoshikawa et al. developed a generic attack based on the manipulation of the control flow [14], where an attacker aims to increase the number of rounds artificially using a fault injection. As shown by Yoshikawa et al. this attack requires one faulty ciphertext and one correct ciphertext to recover the last round key of KLEIN-64. To do so they calculate $K = MixNibbles(RotateNibbles(C)) + \overline{C}$, where K is the additional generated round key and C the correct ciphertext respectively $\overline{C}$ the manipulated ciphertext (the key schedule is invertible).

4   Proposed Attack on the Encryption

The proposed attack strategy is quite similar to those formerly published on AES by Piret et al. [10], Tunstall et al. [12] and Mukhopadhyay [9]. Unlike those, this attack is split up into two separate parts, each revealing 32 bits of the according round key. The attack on the encryption works on all three variants of KLEIN. A random single-byte fault is injected into the state between ARK^{R-3} and MB^{R-1}. We opted for a random single-byte fault model, as KLEIN should be a lightweight cipher [6] which are often implemented on 8-bit platforms. As a result of using a 8-bit platform random, single-byte faults can be achieved easily e.g. due to an instruction skip [7]. This fault will lead to a completely corrupted ciphertext, affecting all 8 bytes. Figure 1 shows the propagation for two different faults, injected either into the left half cf. Fig. 1a or the right half cf. Fig. 1b of the state. The faulted byte is indicated by f. We will now outline the attack for a fault injection which affects the left half of the state MB^{R-1}. After the application of $MixBytes$ in round $R-1$, the former single-byte fault has spread over all four bytes of the left half. Since $MixBytes$ is a linear function (cf. Sect. 2.6), the resulting fault can be described as a bytewise multiple of f: Depending on which byte position before $MixBytes$ was faulted, the individual bytes after $MixBytes$ inherit an additive fault with the values f, $2f$ or $3f$. These multiples of the same value f can be exploited to formulate a set of equations. An attacker cannot obtain f directly by reverse calculating from the ciphertext, as he is only able to observe the transformed version of f i.e. F_i, $i \in \{0, 1, 2, 3\}$ after passing through the four S-Boxes. But the attacker can describe an implicit relationship,

---

[2]   There are two additional publications in chinese: A DFA by Wang et al. [13] and a DFA by Cunyan et al. [4]. However, the latter obviously uses the generic approach of injecting single-bit faults before the last S-Box operation to exploit the differential distribution table (cf. the appendix of the original KLEIN publication [6]) and discard key hypotheses which lead to impossible differentials.

of the S-Box's input and output fault, the following equations demonstrate this for the case depicted in Fig. 1a:

$$SubBytes(ARK_6^{R+1} + RK_6^{R+1}) + SubBytes(\overline{ARK}_6^{R+1} + RK_6^{R+1})$$
$$= 2 \cdot \left(SubBytes(ARK_7^{R+1} + RK_7^{R+1}) + SubBytes(\overline{ARK}_7^{R+1} + RK_7^{R+1}) \right) \quad (1)$$

$$SubBytes(ARK_7^{R+1} + RK_7^{R+1}) + SubBytes(\overline{ARK}_7^{R+1} + RK_7^{R+1})$$
$$= SubBytes(ARK_0^{R+1} + RK_0^{R+1}) + SubBytes(\overline{ARK}_0^{R+1} + RK_0^{R+1}) \quad (2)$$

$$SubBytes(ARK_1^{R+1} + RK_1^{R+1}) + SubBytes(\overline{ARK}_1^{R+1} + RK_1^{R+1})$$
$$= 3 \cdot \left(SubBytes(ARK_7^{R+1} + RK_7^{R+1}) + SubBytes(\overline{ARK}_7^{R+1} + RK_7^{R+1}) \right) \quad (3)$$

Each equation combines two different bytes and therefore uses a hypothesis over two different key-bytes $(RK_i^{R+1}, RK_j^{R+1}) \ \forall \ (i,j) \in \{(6,7),(0,7),(1,7)\}$. Thus, the attacker has a set of three equations depending on four different key-bytes. Since this set is under-determined, there is no unique solution. However, the attacker can use these equations to discard all those 4-byte key-hypotheses, which do not solve the equation. Therefore, all possible keys are stored in a set of hypotheses. Using the result of an additional fault injection with a different fault f, the attacker can discard those keys in the set of hypotheses, which do not fulfill the new equations. The computational complexity of this step can be significantly reduced from 2^{32} by testing only those 4-byte key hypotheses, where the individual four key bytes were tested as valid. Since the attacker usually does not know which of the four possible byte positions were faulted, all four options have to be tested. However, the resulting increase in complexity of a factor of

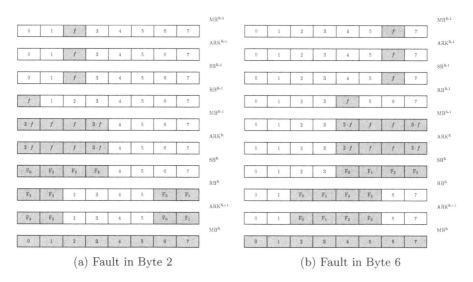

(a) Fault in Byte 2   (b) Fault in Byte 6

Fig. 1. Fault propagation for a single-byte fault injected between MB^{R-2} and MB^{R-1}.

4 does not present a problem. The question of which half of the state was faulted (a single example for both cases is depicted in Fig. 1a and b), can be determined by applying the inverse *MixBytes* function to the observable fault at the output i.e. the addition of the correct and faulty ciphertext. In order to reveal the full 64-bit round key, the attacker can choose to inject another fault at a different position to run the attack on both halves of the key, or to determine the missing 32 bit part with the brute-force approach.

5   Proposed Attack on the Key Schedule

In our proposed attack on the key schedule, the attacker is expected to induce a random byte fault Δ into the key state RK^{R-2}, which corrupts the byte RK_5^{R-2} as shown in Fig. 2. The proposed fault model and location was chosen to be within a path through the key schedule free of nonlinear functions, which results in a partial cancellation of the fault during round R. The fault injection into the key schedule empowers a fault propagation into both halves of the state simultaneously, due to the Feistel-like structure of the key schedule where one half of the key state is added to the other half. One has to keep in mind after a fault injection into the key schedule the fault spreads throughout the key schedule and after an *AddRoundKey* operation also in the state. The approach of the attack can be divided as usual into three parts *fault propagation, fault exploitation* and *state recovery*.

5.1   Fault Propagation

The propagation of the faulty byte is based on two parts, the propagation through the key schedule and the propagation through the state of KLEIN.

Key Schedule: Under the assumption of a random byte fault model, the byte RK_5^{R-2} is perturbed with a fault Δ, as shown in Fig. 2. After the fault injection, both halves are rotated bytewise to the left by 1. During the Feistel step, the faulted byte spreads to both halves of the key state RK^{R-1}. As one can see the path chosen avoids nonlinear functions, therefore the bytes RK_0^{R-1}, RK_4^{R-1} are both under the influence of the same fault Δ. Due to the Feistel structure of the key schedule the fault Δ of byte RK_7^R is canceled out as a result of the addition of both halves ($\Delta + \Delta = 0$). During the last iteration of the key schedule from round R to $R + 1$ the single-byte fault Δ passes through one S-Box, as a result the byte RK_6^{R+1} is the only byte in the key schedule's state with a fault different from Δ. In total there are four distinct locations during the last three iterations of the key schedule where the faults are fed into the state of KLEIN, the four locations are indicated by a lighting symbol under each faulted byte, as shown in Fig. 2.

State: During the round key addition in round $R - 1$ the state ARK^{R-1} is perturbed at first, with the fault Δ at indices 0 and 4 as shown in Fig. 3. After passing through the S-Boxes the fault Δ is transformed into the faults f_1 and f_2.

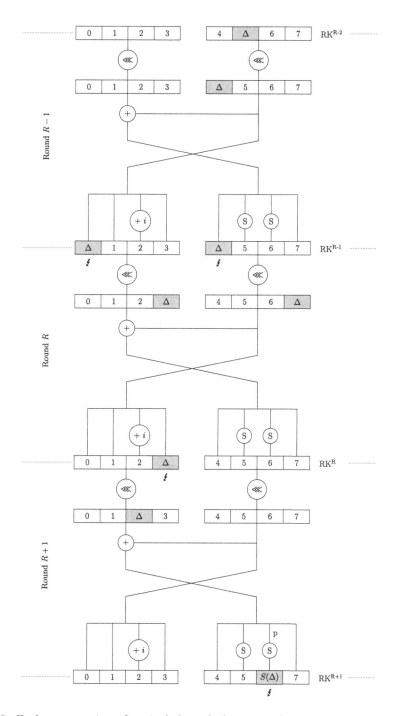

Fig. 2. Fault propagation of a single-byte fault in round 10 of the KLEIN-64 key schedule.

Applying a shift to the state does not change the faults. As a result of passing one faulty byte on each half (i.e. RB^{R-1}) through the *MixBytes* operation, each byte of the state MB^{R-1} is now influenced by multiples of the fault either $\{1, 2, 3\}$ times the original fault f_1, f_2. After the addition with the round key RK^R, the byte ARK_3^R is now faulted with $f_1 + \Delta$. After the application of *SubBytes* the faults are transformed into the faults F_i, $i \in \{0, 1, 2, 3M, 4, 5, 6, 7\}$. As a result of the last *AddRoundKey* operation, the whole right half of the state ARK^{R+1} is perturbed again with a fault coming from the key schedule. After the application of *AddRoundKey* the faults are transformed into the faults which are observable F_i, $i \in \{0M, 1M, 2, 3M, 4, 5, 6M, 7M\}$. The disturbance of the whole right half of the state occurs due to the modified variant of KLEIN where the *AddRoundKey* and *MixBytes* operation are swapped. Swapping both functions requires an application of *MixBytes* to the round key RK^{R+1}, prior to the execution of *AddRoundKey* in round $R + 1$.

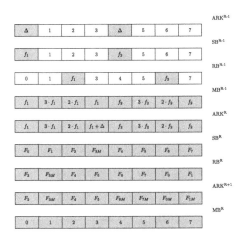

Fig. 3. Fault propagation through the state of KLEIN.

5.2   Fault Exploitation

In order to recover the last round key which is in the case of KLEIN-64 also the master key as the key schedule is invertible, we have to recover the state ARK^R which is KLEIN's state before the *SubBytes* function in round R. After the recovery of ARK^R we can calculate the last round key using the ciphertext C as shown in Eq. (4).

$$RK^{R+1} = RB^R + ARK^{R+1}$$
$$RK^{R+1} = RB^R + inverseMixBytes(C) \qquad (4)$$

Since the S-Boxes are the only nonlinear elements of KLEIN this will provide us a filtering mechanism for wrong state hypotheses. As an example of how to derive the required equations we will demonstrate this for the fault F_0 in detail. The fault F_0 is defined as the result of adding the bytes SB_0^R and $\overline{SB}_0^R$. We can express SB_0^R as an application of $SubBytes$ to ARK_0^R, respectively $ARK_0^R + f_1$ in the faulted case as shown in Eq. (5).

$$
\begin{aligned}
F_0 &= SB_0^R + \overline{SB}_0^R \\
F_0 &= SubBytes(ARK_0^R) + SubBytes(\overline{ARK}_0^R) \\
F_0 &= SubBytes(ARK_0^R) + SubBytes(ARK_0^R + f_1) \\
F_1 &= SubBytes(ARK_1^R) + SubBytes(ARK_1^R + 3 \cdot f_1)
\end{aligned}
\tag{5}
$$

Analogous to F_0 we express F_1 as shown in Eq. (5), both equations depend on the fault f_1, which is not observable. The equations for F_2 and F_3 are constructed similarly, but this time the equation for F_3 depends also on the injected fault Δ as shown in Eq. (6).

$$
\begin{aligned}
F_2 &= SubBytes(ARK_2^R) + SubBytes(ARK_2^R + 2 \cdot f_1) \\
F_3 &= SubBytes(ARK_3^R) + SubBytes(ARK_3^R + f_1 + \Delta)
\end{aligned}
\tag{6}
$$

Equation (7) is a special case, because it is the only equation set where the faults F_4 and F_5 are not overlaid with another fault coming from the key schedule (self cancellation of Δ) therefore this equation set will be the starting point for the state recovery.

$$
\begin{aligned}
F_4 &= SubBytes(ARK_4^R) + SubBytes(ARK_4^R + f_2) \\
F_5 &= SubBytes(ARK_5^R) + SubBytes(ARK_5^R + 3 \cdot f_2)
\end{aligned}
\tag{7}
$$

Equation (8) is constructed similarly to Eq. (7), this time the equations are influenced by the fault f_2 and a multiple of f_2. The faults F_6 and F_7 can not be observed due to the addition of the faulty round key RK^{R+1}, the same holds also for the faults F_0 and F_1.

$$
\begin{aligned}
F_6 &= SubBytes(ARK_6^R) + SubBytes(ARK_6^R + 2 \cdot f_2) \\
F_7 &= SubBytes(ARK_7^R) + SubBytes(ARK_7^R + f_2)
\end{aligned}
\tag{8}
$$

As a result of not being able to observe the output faults F_i where $i \in \{0, 1, 6, 7\}$, we introduce helper variables F_{iM}, which are observable at the output as shown in Eq. (9). These helper variables are composed from the unobservable faults F_i and the addition of the $MixBytes$ transformed fault which passed through the S-Box. Also, we introduce another helper variable p which represents the actual value of RK_6^{R+1} before the application of the S-Box as shown in Fig. 2.

$$
\begin{aligned}
F_{0M} &= F_0 + E \cdot (SubBytes(p) + SubBytes(p + \Delta)) \\
F_{1M} &= F_1 + 9 \cdot (SubBytes(p) + SubBytes(p + \Delta)) \\
F_{6M} &= F_6 + D \cdot (SubBytes(p) + SubBytes(p + \Delta)) \\
F_{7M} &= F_7 + B \cdot (SubBytes(p) + SubBytes(p + \Delta))
\end{aligned}
\tag{9}
$$

Additionally, the relationships between the injected fault and the transformed faults are shown in Eq. (10), which describes the relationships between f_1, f_2, Δ and two state bytes from the round $R - 1$. These equations aim to eliminate wrong hypotheses for the injected fault Δ, the actual values of ARK_0^{R-1} and ARK_4^{R-1} are not of interest.

$$
\begin{aligned}
f_1 &= SubBytes(ARK_4^{R-1}) + SubBytes(ARK_4^{R-1} + \Delta) \\
f_2 &= SubBytes(ARK_0^{R-1}) + SubBytes(ARK_0^{R-1} + \Delta)
\end{aligned}
\tag{10}
$$

Having formulated an equation for every byte of the state ARK^R as shown in Eqs. (5), (6), (7), (8) and (9), and the relationships between the different faults as shown in Eq. (10), we will now provide a description of how to recover the state ARK^{R-1} in several steps.

5.3 State Recovery

To recover the state ARK^R the attacker has to solve several sets of equations. At first, the attacker calculates the fault state F which is composed from the values F_i, $i \in \{0M, 1M, 2, 3M, 4, 5, 6M, 7M\}$. To do so an addition of the correct ciphertext C and the faulty ciphertext $\overline{C}$ is transformed with the inverse *MixBytes* operation as shown in Eq. (11). The position of the faults F_i throughout the state of KLEIN is also shown in Fig. 3.

$$
F = invMB(C) + invMB(\overline{C})
\tag{11}
$$

Throughout the attack's description we use a short hand notation for the addition of a correct S-Box with a faulty one, $filter(x, f) = SubByte(x) + SubByte(x + f)$. The *SubByte* function refers to the substitution of a single-byte using KLEIN's S-Box. As we are unable to recover the whole state at once we apply a divide and conquer strategy. At the beginning we assume every state byte of ARK^R, and the byte p (actual value) as a set of all possible hypotheses i.e. $ARK_i^R = \{0, \ldots, 255\} \ \forall \ i \ \in \{0, \ldots, 7\}$ and $P = \{0, \ldots, 255\}$. While one faulty encryption is processed there will also be sets containing hypotheses for the faults f_1, f_2 and Δ, in contrast to the sets of state bytes these sets are only valid while processing one faulty encryption, as the next encryption is probably under the influence of another fault. The following steps are repeated for all faulty encryptions, in order to decrease the number of hypotheses in the sets. The attacker starts with the recovery of ARK_4^R, ARK_5^R, using Eq. (7). As one can see the equation set depends on five different variables, the known value of the faults F_4, F_5, the unknown values ARK_4^R, ARK_5^R and the unknown fault f_2. The system of equations is then used to reduce the solution space for ARK_4^R, ARK_5^R and f_2 using an exhaustive search with all unknown variables as search space. The first step of the attack is shown in Eq. (12), hypotheses that satisfy both conditions are kept as valid hypotheses.

$$T_{poss} = \{ARK_4^R \times ARK_5^R \times \{1, \ldots, 255\}\}$$
$$T_{valid} = \{(x, y, f) \in T_{poss} \mid F_4 \equiv filter(x, f) \wedge F_5 \equiv filter(y, 3 \cdot f)\}$$
$$ARK_4^R = \{ x \mid (x, y, f) \in T_{valid} \}$$
$$ARK_5^R = \{ y \mid (x, y, f) \in T_{valid} \} \tag{12}$$
$$f_2 = \{ f \mid (x, y, f) \in T_{valid} \}$$

Now that the attacker has gained knowledge of the fault f_2, he can process the second equation of Eq. (10). He iterates through all possible values of $ARK_0^{R-1} \in \{0, \ldots, 255\}$ and stores the valid hypotheses for Δ. The description of the second part of the attack is shown in Eq. (13).

$$T_{poss} = \{f_2 \times ARK_0^{R-1} \times \{1, \ldots, 255\}\}$$
$$T_{valid} = \{(f, x, \delta) \in T_{poss} \mid f \equiv filter(x, \delta)\} \tag{13}$$
$$\Delta = \{ \delta \mid (f, x, \delta) \in T_{valid} \}$$

As a result of having knowledge of Δ the attacker aims now to recover the state bytes ARK_2^R, ARK_3^R to do so the attacker has to solve Eq. (6) in the same manner as in the first step, as a result the attacker gains additional knowledge of the faults f_1. The third part of the attack is shown in Eq. (14).

$$T_{poss} = \{ARK_2^R \times ARK_3^R \times \Delta \times \{1, \ldots, 255\}\}$$
$$T_{valid} = \{(x, y, \delta, f) \in T_{poss} \mid F_2 \equiv filter(x, 2 \cdot f) \wedge F_3 \equiv filter(y, f + \delta)\}$$
$$ARK_2^R = \{ x \mid (x, y, \delta, f) \in T_{valid} \}$$
$$ARK_3^R = \{ y \mid (x, y, \delta, f) \in T_{valid} \} \tag{14}$$
$$f_1 = \{ f \mid (x, y, \delta, f) \in T_{valid} \}$$

Now that the attacker has also knowledge of the fault f_1 he can process the first equation of Eq. (10) using another exhaustive search to shrink the number of possible hypotheses for Δ, under the assumption of $ARK_4^{R-1} \in \{0, \ldots, 255\}$. The algorithmic description of the fourth part of the attack is shown in Eq. (15).

$$T_{poss} = \{f_1 \times ARK_4^{R-1} \times \Delta\}$$
$$T_{valid} = \{(f, x, \delta) \in T_{poss} \mid f \equiv filter(x, \delta)\} \tag{15}$$
$$\Delta = \{ \delta \mid (f, x, \delta) \in T_{valid} \}$$

During the recovery of ARK_0^R, ARK_1^R, ARK_6^R and ARK_7^R the attacker faces the problem that the faults F_i, $i \in \{0, \ldots, 7\} \setminus \{2, 4, 5\}$ do not take into account that the observable faults from the output are composed from several faults coming from the key schedule and the state. Also, the faulted byte p (the *MixBytes* transformed fault) from the key schedule, influences the right half. Therefore, the attacker needs to apply the correction from Eq. (9) and combine the equations with Eqs. (5) and (8). The algorithmic description for the recovery of ARK_0^R, ARK_1^R is shown in Eq. (16).

$$T_{poss} = \{ARK_0^R \times ARK_1^R \times P \times \Delta \times f_1\}$$
$$T_{valid} = \{(x, y, p, \delta, f) \in T_{poss} \mid F_{0M} + E \cdot filter(p, \delta) \equiv filter(x, f)$$
$$\wedge\ F_{1M} + 9 \cdot filter(p, \delta) \equiv filter(y, f)\}$$
$$ARK_2^R = \{\ x \mid (x, y, p, \delta, f) \in T_{valid}\ \}$$
$$ARK_3^R = \{\ y \mid (x, y, p, \delta, f) \in T_{valid}\ \} \tag{16}$$
$$P = \{\ p \mid (x, y, p, \delta, f) \in T_{valid}\ \}$$

The recovery of ARK_6^R and ARK_7^R as shown in Eq. (17) is similar to the bytes ARK_0^R and ARK_1^R.

$$T_{poss} = \{ARK_6^R \times ARK_7^R \times P \times \Delta \times f_2\}$$
$$T_{valid} = \{(x, y, p, \delta, f) \in T_{poss} \mid F_{6M} + D \cdot filter(p, \delta) \equiv filter(x, 2 \cdot f)$$
$$\wedge\ F_{7M} + B \cdot filter(p, \delta) \equiv filter(y, f)\}$$
$$ARK_6^R = \{\ x \mid (x, y, p, \delta, f) \in T_{valid}\ \}$$
$$ARK_7^R = \{\ y \mid (x, y, p, \delta, f) \in T_{valid}\ \} \tag{17}$$
$$P = \{\ p \mid (x, y, p, \delta, f) \in T_{valid}\ \}$$

An attacker has to repeat all the steps mentioned above for each faulted encryption, in order to reduce the number of hypothesis (state bytes) until it becomes feasible to brute force the remaining complexity (key space), which will be discussed in the next section.

6   Simulation and Discussion

In this section we will discuss the performance of the attacks. To do, so we will determine the number of required ciphertexts to reduce the remaining complexity (keyspace) to a certain threshold. We opted to implement the simulation of the faulty ciphers in *Python*, and the attacks as C extension for *Python*. The attacks were performed on an Intel(R) Core(TM) i7-6700 CPU @ 3.40GHz based desktop computer. The amount of RAM required during the attack is negligible, on average the attack takes five minutes on the computer we used depending on the injected fault.

6.1   Simulation

To evaluate the performance of each attack we performed several simulations, using the following approach. For every iteration of the simulation we generated 100 faulty ciphertexts using one random plaintext, 100 was found to be a reliable upper bound for the maximum number of required faulty ciphertexts. Afterwards we launched the attacks and stored the complexity of the key space in bits for every processed faulty ciphertext during the attack. The remaining brute force complexity was defined as power of two of the product of the cardinality of the state byte sets[3]. We then repeated the previous step 500 times to get significant data. Additionally, we have addressed the issue of faults, which do not comply with the required fault model. This results in an empty set of remaining key candidates for both attacks. To overcome this issue an attacker can partition the set of faulty ciphertexts and test the subsets separately until he will find a set containing only ciphertexts according to the fault model. The result of the attack's simulation is shown in Fig. 4, where one can see the number of faulty ciphertexts on the x-axis, and the remaining brute force complexity on the y-axis. The three different plots in each subfigure are either the maximum, mean or minimum complexity. As a result of the simulation it was found out that the attack on the state requires five faulted encryptions on average to reduce the complexity of the last round key from 2^{64} to 2^{32} on average, as shown in Fig. 4a (we opted to attack only on one half of the state therefore the maximum complexity starts at 2^{32}). For the attack on the key schedule it was found out that four faulted encryptions are required on average to reduce the complexity of the last round key from 2^{64} to 2^{32} on average as shown in Fig. 4b.

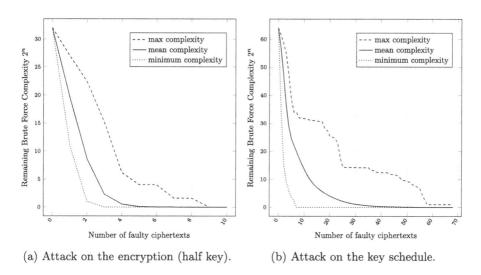

(a) Attack on the encryption (half key).   (b) Attack on the key schedule.

Fig. 4. Remaining brute force complexity (64 bit key length).

6.2   Discussion

As the structure of KLEIN is similar to the AES [11] we will compare the attack on the state with the attacks of [9,10,12], and the attack on the key schedule with the attacks of [1,3,8]. Our attack on the state of KLEIN performs worse in terms of required faulty encryptions than the attack on the state of AES by [9,10,12]. This can be attributed to the structure of KLEIN's round function

---

[3] i.e. for the attack on the key schedule, $complexity = 2^{\prod_{i=0}^{7} |ARK_i^R|}$.

where a fault injected into one half of the state does not spread to the other half, in contrast to the AES. But still only four faulted encryptions (on the same half) are required to deduce the last round key of KLEIN as shown in Fig. 4a. Our attack on the key schedule performs worse in terms of required faulty encryptions if compared to the attacks of [1,3,8]. This can be attributed to the key schedule of KLEIN which is based on a Feistel network where a fault does not create a sufficient avalanche effect which results in an immediate corruption of a whole half of the key schedule. After only one faulty encryption the complexity of the key space was decreased on average to $2^{56.9}$. If we assume a complexity of 2^{32} to be the upper bound for a brute force attack as in [1], this results in four faulty encryptions with a complexity of $2^{29.0}$ on average as shown in Fig. 4b. Additionally, one noteworthy detail of Fig. 4b is the maximum complexity which remains 1 bit, even if we evaluate the simulation up to 100 faulted encryptions, but an increased number of key hypothesis by a factor of two can be neglected. To justify our upper bound of complexity of 2^{32} for both attacks we will focus on the scenario where KLEIN-64 is used to generate a Message Authentication Code (MAC) [6]. The attacker aims to forge a message within a limited amount of time and resources. Therefore, we evaluated how long it takes to perform 2^{32} encryptions, using a C implementation of KLEIN as a result it was found out this takes 4.6 h on average, which seems to be a reasonable tradeoff between complexity and required faulty encryptions.

7   Conclusion

In this paper we proposed a differential fault attack on the round function of KLEIN, and the first key schedule based differential fault attack on KLEIN-64. Furthermore, we validated the performance of our attacks by simulation, and evaluated the remaining brute force complexity, with respect to the number of faulted encryptions. As a result it was found out, an attacker is able to reduce the key space from 64 bit to 32 bit, with only five fault injections into the round function, and with four faults injected into a specific byte in the key schedule. Both attacks can be conducted without knowing the actual plaintext. It is sufficient to know that the same plaintext was processed.

Acknowledgments. We would like to thank the anonymous reviewers for their valuable comments and suggestions on the paper, as these helped us to improve it. This work was partly funded by the German Federal Ministry of Education and Research in the project HQS through grant number 16KIS0616.

References

1. Ali, S.S., Mukhopadhyay, D.: Differential fault analysis of AES-128 key schedule using a single multi-byte fault. In: Prouff, E. (ed.) CARDIS 2011. LNCS, vol. 7079, pp. 50–64. Springer, Heidelberg (2011). https://doi.org/10.1007/978-3-642-27257-8_4
2. Bogdanov, A., et al.: PRESENT: an ultra-lightweight block cipher. In: Paillier, P., Verbauwhede, I. (eds.) CHES 2007. LNCS, vol. 4727, pp. 450–466. Springer, Heidelberg (2007). https://doi.org/10.1007/978-3-540-74735-2_31
3. Chen, C.-N., Yen, S.-M.: Differential fault analysis on AES key schedule and some countermeasures. In: Safavi-Naini, R., Seberry, J. (eds.) ACISP 2003. LNCS, vol. 2727, pp. 118–129. Springer, Heidelberg (2003). https://doi.org/10.1007/3-540-45067-X_11
4. Cunyang, F., Yuechuan, W., Xiaozhong, P.: A differential fault analysis method for KLEIN cipher. Comput. Appl. Softw. **32**, 6 (2015)
5. Dunkelman, O., Keller, N.: The effects of the omission of last round's mixcolumns on AES. Cryptology ePrint Archive, Report 2010/041 (2010). https://eprint.iacr.org/2010/041
6. Gong, Z., Nikova, S., Law, Y.W.: KLEIN: a new family of lightweight block ciphers. In: Juels, A., Paar, C. (eds.) RFIDSec 2011. LNCS, vol. 7055, pp. 1–18. Springer, Heidelberg (2012). https://doi.org/10.1007/978-3-642-25286-0_1
7. Guillen, O.M., Gruber, M., De Santis, F.: Low-cost setup for localized semi-invasive optical fault injection attacks. In: Guilley, S. (ed.) COSADE 2017. LNCS, vol. 10348, pp. 207–222. Springer, Cham (2017). https://doi.org/10.1007/978-3-319-64647-3_13
8. Kim, C.H.: Improved differential fault analysis on AES key schedule. IEEE Trans. Inf. Forensics Secur. **7**(1), 41–50 (2012)
9. Mukhopadhyay, D.: An improved fault based attack of the advanced encryption standard. In: Preneel, B. (ed.) AFRICACRYPT 2009. LNCS, vol. 5580, pp. 421–434. Springer, Heidelberg (2009). https://doi.org/10.1007/978-3-642-02384-2_26
10. Piret, G., Quisquater, J.-J.: A differential fault attack technique against SPN structures, with application to the AES and KHAZAD. In: Walter, C.D., Koç, Ç.K., Paar, C. (eds.) CHES 2003. LNCS, vol. 2779, pp. 77–88. Springer, Heidelberg (2003). https://doi.org/10.1007/978-3-540-45238-6_7
11. NIST FIPS Pub. 197: Advanced encryption standard (AES). Federal Information Processing Standards Publication 197(441):0311 (2001)
12. Tunstall, M., Mukhopadhyay, D., Ali, S.: Differential fault analysis of the advanced encryption standard using a single fault. In: Ardagna, C.A., Zhou, J. (eds.) WISTP 2011. LNCS, vol. 6633, pp. 224–233. Springer, Heidelberg (2011). https://doi.org/10.1007/978-3-642-21040-2_15
13. Wang, Y.-J., Ren, Q.-Y., Zhang, S.-Y.: Differential fault attack on lightweight block cipher KLEIN. Tongxin Xuebao/J. Commun. **37**, 111–115 (2016). 10
14. Yoshikawa, H., Kaminaga, M., Shikoda, A., Suzuki, T.: Round addition DFA on lightweight block ciphers with on-the-fly key scheduling. Int. J. Math. Comput. Sci. **9**(9), 1 (2006)

White-Box Attacks

Another Look on Bucketing Attack to Defeat White-Box Implementations

Mohamed Zeyad[3], Houssem Maghrebi[1(✉)], Davide Alessio[1],
and Boris Batteux[2]

[1] UL Identity Management & Security, La Ciotat, France
{houssem.maghrebi,davide.alessio}@ul.com
[2] Eshard, Marseille, France
boris.batteux@eshard.com
[3] Trusted Labs, Meudon, France
mohamed.zeyad@trusted-labs.com

Abstract. White-box cryptography was first introduced by Chow *et al.*
in 2002 as a software technique for implementing cryptographic algorithms in a secure way that protects secret keys in a compromised environment. Ever since, Chow *et al.*'s design has been subject to mainly
two categories of attacks published by the cryptographic community.
The first category encompasses the so-called differential and algebraic
cryptanalysis. Basically, these attacks counteract the obfuscation process by inverting the applied encoding functions after which the used
secret key can easily be recovered. The second category comprises the
software counterpart of the well-known physical attacks often applied to
thwart hardware cryptographic implementations on embedded devices.
In this paper, we turn a cryptanalysis technique, called statistical bucketing attack, into a computational analysis one allowing an efficient key
recovery from software execution traces. Moreover, we extend this cryptanalysis technique, originally designed to break DES white-box implementations, to target AES white-box implementations. To illustrate the
effectiveness of our proposal, we apply our attack on several publicly
available white-box implementations with different level of protections.
Based on the obtained results, we argue that our attack is not only an
alternative but also a more efficient technique compared to the existing
computational attacks, especially when some side-channel countermeasures are involved as a protection.

Keywords: White-box cryptography · Cryptanalysis ·
Statistical bucketing · Computational analysis · AES · DES · Masking

M. Zeyad and B. Batteux—This work has been done when the authors were working
at UL Identity Management & Security.

© Springer Nature Switzerland AG 2019
I. Polian and M. Stöttinger (Eds.): COSADE 2019, LNCS 11421, pp. 99–117, 2019.
https://doi.org/10.1007/978-3-030-16350-1_7

1   Introduction

White-Box Cryptography. It is a software-based solution for protecting cryptographic keys when the hardware-based secure storage comes at high cost. The main goal of white-box cryptography is to securely implement cryptographic primitives in the presence of a very powerful adversary. The latter has full access to the cryptographic implementation and can modify all resources in the execution environment (*e.g.* intercept system calls, analyze the binary code, collect all the runtime information: addresses, values of accessed memory, . . .). In such a compromised environment, white-box cryptography has been widely adapted in pure software solutions for applications requiring considerable security such as Host-Card Emulation (HCE) for mobile payments and Digital Rights Management (DRM) systems.

White-Box Implementations. In 2003, Chow *et al.* [12,13] introduced the first white-box implementations of AES and DES block ciphers. The main idea behind was to embed the secret key in the implementation using a network of precomputed Look-Up Tables (LUTs) composed with some linear and non-linear random encodings to protect the intermediate states between the LUTs. The knowledge of one or all of these LUTs shall not give any information about the embedded secret key. To implement this design, two types of encodings shall be considered:

- Internal encodings: are non-linear bijections applied to the input and/or the output of each LUT to hide its entries and/or its outputs. This category ecompasses the so-called *mixing bijections* which are linear transformation applied to the input and output of each LUT to add more confusion to the implementation and ensure the cryptographic diffusion property.
- External encodings: are bijective mappings applied to decode the plaintext from the sending process and to encode the resulting ciphertext to the receiving process.

Another similar approach was published by Bringer *et al.* [11]. The idea consists in representing the block cipher as systems of multivariate polynomials over $GF(2^n)$ for some integer value n and adding some perturbations of its algebraic structure. These additional functions are then composed with the random encodings to hide the secret key.

Several white-box designs based on the underlying approaches fell to practical attacks [7,15]. Although some remedial designs have been proposed for improving the security [19,24,30], several of them were broken later on as well [14,22,23,26].

Attacks on White-Box Implementations. Without loss of generality, the published attacks on white-box implementations can be divided into two categories. The first category encompasses the so-called *differential* [17,29] and *algebraic cryptanalysis* [7,23,25]. Specifically, these attacks invert the obfuscation process by recovering the applied encoding functions after which the key can easily be deduced. In 2003, Chow *et al.* [12] proposed the first statistical cryptanalytic attack successfully applied on the seminal DES white-box implementation. This technique is called *Statistical Bucketing Attack* (SBA) and is somehow similar to the Differential Power Analysis (DPA) [20]. Indeed, the adversary has to guess keys and use difference of specific intermediate values to confirm or deny these guesses. The attack's time complexity is about 2^{13} [12]. A detailed description of this attack is provided in Sect. 2.2. This being said, the most common algebraic cryptanalysis approach is the so-called *BGE attack* [7] which enables key extraction from an AES white-box implementation with a 2^{30} time complexity. Later on, Lepoint *et al.* [23] have proposed an improvement of the BGE attack with a time complexity of 2^{22} and also a new collision-based attack with the same work factor. The second category comprises the software counterpart of the well-known *physical attacks* (*i.e.* DPA and fault injection attacks) often applied for attacking hardware cryptographic implementations on embedded devices. These attacks, known as the Differential Computational Analysis (DCA) and the software Differential Fault Analysis (DFA), were first introduced by Bos *et al.* in CHES 2016 [10]. Specifically, the idea of the DCA consists in monitoring the memory addresses (as well as the stack, the CPU instructions, . . .) accessed during the encryption process and to record them in the so-called *computation traces* (*aka* software execution traces). Then, a statistical analysis is performed to extract the secret key. Regarding the DFA, it uses software means in order to inject faults at some specific moments within the execution of the encryption process [5,27]. Later on, the faulty outputted ciphertexts are analyzed to recover the secret key. Almost all the published DES and AES white-box implementations were broken so far using DCA and DFA [10]. As a natural consequence, white-box designers turn towards applying the most common method protecting against side-channel attacks: *masking*. A few masked white-box AES implementations were recently published [21] to resist against DCA. However, these designs are still vulnerable to a new trend of computational attacks: Higher-Order DCA (HO-DCA) [9] and Linear Decoding Analysis (LDA) [18] (*aka* algebraic DCA [8]).

Contribution. In this paper, we first propose a new computational analysis method to recover the secret key from the software execution traces. Our approach is inherently based on the statistical bucketing attack introduced by Chow *et al.* [12]. Indeed, we demonstrate how to turn this cryptanalysis technique into an automated computational attack allowing an efficient key extraction by capturing a few number of computation traces. The execution flow of our attack is quite similar to the DCA. In DCA a chunk of the key is guessed and then the correlation coefficient is computed between the collected traces and the key-dependent sensitive variables to confirm or reject the key guess. Similarly, our proposed attack involves collecting traces and guessing keys, however the key hypotheses are confirmed or rejected based on a new distinguisher: sorting the computation traces based on key-dependent sensitive variables into some clusters (*aka* buckets) and then checking whether this partitioning yield disjoint sets.

As another contribution, we propose a trick to extend this statistical bucketing attack, originally developed to only target DES white-box implementations, to apply it on AES white-box designs. Throughout several practical experiments, we argue that our proposal is an efficient alternative to DCA and LDA attacks. More interestingly, when customized masking is involved to protect white-box implementations, and therefore the HO-DCA and the LDA come at higher-cost in terms of attack complexity, our bucketing computational analysis succeeds to break the white-box design in a reasonable time and by requiring a few number of traces. To ease the reproduction of our results by the white-box community, the source code of our tool is publicly available [3].

Paper Outline. The remainder of this paper is organized as follows. In Sect. 2, we provide an overview of the statistical bucketing attack and we describe how to adapt this cryptanalysis technique to target AES white-box implementations. Then, we introduce our proposed bucketing computational attack in Sect. 3. The experimental results obtained when applying our proposal together with the existing attacks, for comparison purpose, on numerous publicly available white-box implementations are provided in Sect. 4. Finally, Sect. 5 concludes the paper and opens some perspectives.

2   Statistical Bucketing Attack

2.1   Notations and Definitions

In the rest of the paper, the bold block capitals $\mathbf{X}$ denote matrices. The ith column vector of a matrix $\mathbf{X}$ is denoted by $\mathbf{X}[i]$ while its jth row vector is denoted by $\mathbf{X}^j$. The intersection of two sets of values A and B is denoted by $A \cap B$ and is defined as $A \cap B = \{x \mid x \in A \text{ and } x \in B\}$. Two sets are disjoint if they have no elements in common, that is, A and B are disjoint if $A \cap B = \emptyset$. Finally, the ith sub-key defines the portion of the key-round that affects the ith Sbox.

2.2   Overview of the Statistical Bucketing Attack on DES

The Statistical Bucketing Attack (SBA) is a cryptanalysis technique introduced by Chow *et al.* [12] on the *naked version* of their implementation of white-box DES (*i.e.* without external encodings). It is a *chosen-plaintext* attack requiring access to some intermediate states (*i.e.* the input of the second round). The attack recovers the first round key of a DES encryption (or the last round when the decryption is processed[1]). That is, 48 bits of the 56-bit DES key could be revealed and the remaining 8 bits can be determined by exhaustive search.

---

[1] For ease of explanation, we will only consider attacking the first round of the encryption case in this work.

The following steps describe how to apply the SBA to recover the ith sub-key of the first DES round as suggested by Chow *et al.* [12] and detailed in [28]:

1. Select the ith Sbox of the first round S_i^1. Since there are no external encodings, it is straightforward to figure out which Tbox implements the targeted Sbox S_i^1. To do so, one can select plaintext differences that only affect S_i^1 and observe which Tbox is affected.
2. Guess the 6 bits of the first round key that affect S_i^1 and compute 64 plaintexts each corresponding to a different 6-bit input of S_i^1. Please note that this process will set 6 bits of each plaintext and the remaining ones has to be computed such that: (1) the left side of the DES state after the initial permutation must be zero (or any fixed constant) in order to nullify the effect of the *xor* operation in the round function and (2) the remaining 26 bits of the right side of the DES state after the initial permutation should be chosen randomly for each plaintext.
3. Select one bit b of the output of S_i^1 (*aka* the *bucketing bit*) and group the plaintexts into two sets I_0 and I_1 according to the resulting value b, *i.e.* $P \in I_0$ if $b = 0$, while $P \in I_1$ if $b = 1$.
4. Select the zth Tbox T_z^2 from the second round that encodes the jth Sbox S_j^2 which has the bucketing bit b as an input (potentially, the bit b can go to 2 different Sboxes in the second round), and group its inputs into two sets V_0 (resp. V_1) corresponding to the encryption of plaintexts in I_0 (resp. I_1). Figure 1 illustrates this step of the attack.
5. Check if V_0 and V_1 are disjoint sets ($V_0 \cap V_1 = \emptyset$). If the key guess is correct, then V_0 and V_1 must be disjoint sets, because they correspond to the inputs of T_z^2 that are different in at least the bit b.

For a wrong key guess, it might happen that V_0 and V_1 are disjoint sets. However, the probability of this happening is lower than 2^{-6}, when considering 2^6 possible key guesses as stated in [12] which prove the effectiveness of this attack in distinguishing the unique good key value. For the sake of further evidence, we estimated experimentally the probability that for a wrong key guess the sets V_0 and V_1 are disjoints[2]. The obtained results (illustrated in Fig. 3 in Appendix A) demonstrated that this probability is negligible when I_0 (resp. I_1) contains at least 27 plaintexts (*i.e.* 54 chosen plaintexts in total)[3]. Since 64 chosen plaintexts are used (*i.e.* for each key guess I_0 and I_1 contain respectively 32 plaintexts), the good key guess outputted by the distinguisher is unique.

To recover the whole 48 bits of the key, the previous steps should be repeated by targeting the 8 DES Sboxes. Later on, Link and Neumann [24] have proposed a new adaptation of the SBA on DES by considering the whole 4-bit box output instead of a single bit which slightly improve the attack complexity in terms of needed number of traces and execution time to break the implementation. In this work, we mainly focus on the original version of SBA attack as we are

---

[2] The Python script we developed is available on Github [3].
[3] We stress the fact that are our results are inline with those obtained by Chow *et al.* in their seminal work [12, Section 5.4].

P

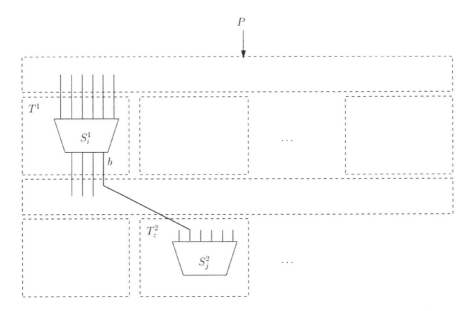

Fig. 1. Statistical bucketing attack on DES white-box implementation [28].

more interested in how to turn this algebraic attack on a computational one. The adaptation of Link and Neumann work [24] is left as a future work.

2.3 Extending the Statistical Bucketing Attack to AES

In this section, we first explain why Chow *et al.*'s proposal cannot be applied straightforwardly on AES algorithm. Then, we propose a trick to adapt the SBA when targeting a naked AES white-box implementation.

Infeasibility of the SBA on AES. We assume that we target the first key byte of an AES implementation. So, the input of the first AES Sbox is the *xor* between the first byte of the plaintext P and the targeted key byte. Then, one can build the set $I = \{P_0, P_1, ..., P_{255}\}$ corresponding to the different 8-bit inputs of the first AES Sbox of the first round. Following the SBA procedure, the plaintexts are grouped into two sets I_0 and I_1 depending on the bucketing bit b (one bit of the first Sbox output). For the sake of simplicity, we shall represent each AES plaintext by its first byte. Then, one can rewrite I_0 and I_1 as:

$$I_0 = \{X_0, X_1, ..., X_{127}\} \quad \text{and} \quad I_1 = \{Y_0, Y_1, ..., Y_{127}\},$$

with X_i and Y_j are respectively the plaintexts yielding to $b = 0$ and $b = 1$ and satisfying $X_i \neq Y_j$ for $0 \leq i, j \leq 127$. Consequently, for each key guess k, the two sets V_0 and V_1 containing the encoded inputs of the zth Tbox T_z^2 rewrite:

$$V_0 = \{E(L(S(X_0 \oplus k))), E(L(S(X_1 \oplus k))), ..., E(L(S(X_{127} \oplus k)))\} \quad \text{and}$$
$$V_1 = \{E(L(S(Y_0 \oplus k))), E(L(S(Y_1 \oplus k))), ..., E(L(S(Y_{127} \oplus k)))\} ,$$

where S is the AES Sbox and E and L denote respectively the encoding function and the AES linear transformations (*i.e.* MixColumns and ShiftRows). Now, since S, E and L are bijective, then we have:

$$X_i \neq Y_j \iff S(X_i \oplus k) \neq S(Y_j \oplus k), \text{ for } 0 \leq i, j \leq 127 \Rightarrow V_0 \cap V_1 = \emptyset .$$

So, due to the bijectivity of S, E and L, the sets V_0 and V_1 are disjoints for all key guesses which demonstrates that the original SBA is not applicable for AES white-box implementations.

Extended SBA for AES. Based on the results from the previous section, we propose to transform the AES Sbox into a non-injective function. The required non-injective transformation S' of the AES Sbox can be any function from $GF(2^8)$ to $\mathcal{F}$ such that (1) $\mathcal{F} \subset GF(2^8)$ and (2) the size of $\mathcal{F}$ should be the size of the applied encodings to protect the implementation. By doing so, we force the sets V_0 and V_1 to have some common values which will enable applying the SBA on AES implementations.

Amongst several possibilities, we choose a high non-injective S' that keeps the least significant 4-bit nibble of an AES Sbox output. The considered S' function in our work is defined as follows:

$$S' : GF(2^8) \rightarrow GF(2^4)$$
$$x \quad \mapsto \text{AES-Sbox}(x)\&0\text{xF} .$$

Our choice of this transformation is motivated by (1) simplicity and (2) the fact that the targeted implementations in our work (see Sect. 4.2) are nibble encoded (which is the most common encoding size used for AES white-box implementations *w.r.t.* to the generated binary code size.). When the targeted implementation is not nibble encoded, then the attacker can perform some reverse engineering on the source code to identify the size of the involved encoding and adapt his choice of the transformation S'. For instance, if the implementation is encoded at the bit level then one has to consider $S'(x) = \text{AES-Sbox}(x)\&1$. We keep the study of the most optimal and suitable non-injective transformations as a future avenue of research.

The following steps describe how to recover the ith key byte of the first round of an AES white-box implementation with our extended SBA:

1. Select the ith AES Sbox of the first round S_i^1.
2. Compute 256 plaintexts P such that the ith byte of each P corresponds to a different byte-input of S_i^1 while the remaining 15 bytes are generated at zero (or a fixed value) for each plaintext.
3. Select two arbitrary distinct values d_0 and d_1 in $\mathcal{F}$ (*i.e.* $GF(2^4)$ in our case)[4].
4. Guess the sub-key K that affects the targeted Sbox S_i^1.

---

[4] We keep the study of the most optimal choice of the pair (d_0, d_1) as a future work. For the sake of simplicity, we considered in this work two fixed values ($d_0 = 0$ and $d_1 = 15$) when targeting the 16 Sboxes of an AES white-box implementation.

5. Group the plaintexts into two sets I_0 and I_1 according to the output value $d = S_i^{'1}(P \oplus K)$ (d is called the *bucketing nibble* in our setting), *i.e.* $P \in I_0$ if $d = d_0$, while $P \in I_1$ if $d = d_1$.

6. Select the zth Tbox T_z^2 from the second round that encodes the jth transformed Sbox $S_j^{'2}$ which has the S_i^1 output bits yielding the value d as input, and group its inputs into two sets V_0 (resp. V_1) corresponding to the encryption of plaintexts in I_0 (resp. I_1). Please note that since we are targeting only two particular values of $S_i^{'1}$ (*i.e.* d_0 and d_1), then for each key guess only 32 plaintexts are used over the 256 selected ones.

7. Check if V_0 and V_1 are disjoints ($V_0 \cap V_1 = \emptyset$). If the key guess is correct, then V_0 and V_1 must be disjoint sets, because they correspond to the inputs of T_z^2 that are different in at least the bits yielding the value d.

To prove the effectiveness of our extension of the SBA for AES, we estimated experimentally the probability that, for a wrong key guess, the sets V_0 and V_1 are disjoints[5]. The obtained results (illustrated in Fig. 4 in Appendix B) demonstrated that this probability is negligible when I_0 (resp. I_1) contains at least 14 plaintexts. Since 256 chosen plaintexts are used (*i.e.* for each key guess I_0 and I_1 contain respectively 16 plaintexts), the good key guess outputted by our proposed distinguisher is unique.

We didn't run this extended SBA cryptanalysis attack in real world scenario since we are more interested on how to turn this technique into a computational one which is described in the following. As a future work, it would be interesting to compare the efficiency of this extended version of SBA to existing algebraic attacks, *e.g.* the BGE attack [7].

3   Bucketing Computational Analysis

In this section, we present our Bucketing Computational Analysis (BCA) for both AES and DES white-box implementations. It is basically inspired from the cryptanalysis techniques described in Sect. 2. As mentioned earlier, the SBA proposed by Chow *et al.* [12] requires a full access to the intermediate state variables. For instance, when considering the SBA on DES, an attacker needs to collect the inputs of a specific Tbox of the second round that has the selected bit b as an input to sort the plaintexts into the buckets V_0 and V_1. However, most of the modern white-box implementations are coupled with several strong software protections (*e.g.* control flow obfuscation, anti-debug protection, *etc.*) making this attack inefficient or difficult in practice. To counter this issue, our approach consists in exploiting the ability of an adversary to recover the intermediate state of the white-box implementation by analyzing the computation traces.

In fact, these collected traces contain, amongst other information, the required inputs of the target Tbox. Indeed, unlike the hardware setting, the software traces contain the *perfect leakage* (*i.e.* noise-free leakage). Thus, an attacker can sort the traces (instead of the inputs of the Tbox as described in

---

[5] The Python script we developed is available on Github [3].

the seminal SBA) into two buckets V_0 and V_1 depending on the bucketing bit b (for DES) or the bucketing nibble d (for AES). At this stage, both sets V_0 and V_1 consists of m computation traces of n samples each and can be represented as two (m, n)-matrices denoted $\mathbf{V_0}$ and $\mathbf{V_1}$ respectively. If the traces in V_0 and V_1 are perfectly synchronized (*i.e.* no random delays is inserted during the acquisition phase), then the adversary can apply recursively the bucketing distinguisher on each column of $\mathbf{V_0}$ and $\mathbf{V_1}$ (*i.e.* checking $\mathbf{V_0}[j] \cap \mathbf{V_1}[j]$ for each j in $[0, n]$). Since the attack will be executed passively on the whole trace samples (due to the fact that the adversary does not have a precise information where the targeted values are processed), some false positive may be obtained[6]. Although from empirical perspectives, the likelihood of observing that some random bucketing will be counted as disjointed for a key guess is quite low, we adapt the bucketing distinguisher to count the whole number of disjoint columns. Then, the good guess of the key is the argument that maximizes the number of disjoint columns. Another practical improvement would consist in considering a small window of the computation trace to minimize this side effect.

We provide in Algorithm 1 the pseudo-code describing the different steps of our proposed attack when applied on AES and DES white-box implementations. Moreover, further details and some practical tricks are presented in the following sections to efficiently apply our attack in real world scenario.

The process of this proposed bucketing computational analysis is somehow similar to DPA. In DPA, a chunk of key is guessed and then we use the difference of power and/or electromagnetic profiles to confirm or deny the key guess. The proposed BCA is a chosen-plaintext attack involving as well guessing keys, but the key assumptions are confirmed or denied by checking whether the columns of the sorted observations into two sets are disjoints or not. Thus, from a conceptual perspective the BCA can be seen as the natural chosen-plaintext software counterpart of DPA (and CPA/DCA more generally). From our point of view, the BCA is more appropriate than the DCA in the context of white-box evaluation since the computation traces are noise-free and the attacker has access to the manipulated values.

The BCA approach can also be considered similar to the Zero Difference Enumeration (ZDE) attack [6]. The ZDE records the computation traces for many well-chosen pairs of plaintexts and performs then a statistical analysis on the effective difference of the traces to extract the secret key. Indeed, the pair of plaintexts are selected such that for the correct key guess many internal state variables in the first rounds of the encryption are the same. Hence, the correct key will corresponds to the key guess for which the number of similar intermediate values in the analyzed traces is maximized. As previously explained, the BCA process is quite similar: the plaintexts are chosen and sorted into two sets such that, for each key guess, the resulting targeted encoded values do not collide. Then, the correct key will corresponds to the key guess for which the

---

[6] For instance, we can consider a time sample in the traces containing the AES input data that takes every value from 0 to 256 which would count as disjointed for every guess whatever the bucketing is.

Algorithm 1. BCA on DES (blue) and AES (red) white-box implementations.

Inputs: a targeted DES/AES Sbox S of the first round and its corresponding S'
Output: good guess of the sub-key
       $* * *$ *Pre-computation phase* $* * *$
1: Compute a set I of $64/256$ plaintexts each corresponding to a different input of S
2: Pick b an output bit of S/Pick two values d_0 and d_1 such that: $0 \leq d_0 < d_1 \leq 15$
3: **for** each key guess $k \in [0, 63/255]$ **do**
4:     Group the plaintexts into two sets I_0 and I_1 according to the resulting value of
       b/the output nibble d of S'
5: **end for**
       $* * *$ *Acquisition phase* $* * *$
6: Acquire a set of $64/256$ traces $\mathbf{T} = (t_{i,j})_{\substack{0 \leq i \leq 63/255 \\ 0 \leq j \leq n}}$ each corresponding to an encryption using a plaintext in I and containing n samples
       $* * *$ *Key-recovery phase* $* * *$
7: Initialize a result vector R with $64/256$ zeros
8: **for** each key guess $K \in [0, 63/255]$ **do**
9:     Group the traces into $\mathbf{V_0}$ and $\mathbf{V_1}$ *w.r.t.* to the sorted plaintexts in I_0 and I_1
10:     **for** each sample j in the trace **do**
11:         **if** $\mathbf{V_0}[j] \cap \mathbf{V_1}[j] = \emptyset$ **then**
12:             $R[K] = R[K] + 1$
13:         **end if**
14:     **end for**
15: **end for**
16: The good sub-key guess corresponds to $K \in [0, 63/255]$ that maximizes $R[K]$

---

number of non-colluded intermediate values in the corresponding analyzed traces is maximized. However, our BCA attack require much less traces than the ZDE when targeting for instance an AES white-box implementation (256 traces *vs* 500×2^{18} traces [6] to recover a byte of the AES key).

Furthermore, the BCA attack (and the SBA in general) can be seen as a variant of the so-called *collision-attack*. Indeed, the principle of BCA is that if two sensitive intermediate variables for two different plaintexts do not collude, then their encodings (using a deterministic bijection) should not collude as well.

3.1   Pre-computation Phase

As described in Algorithm 1, the BCA starts with a pre-calculation phase during which the adversary creates a set of chosen plaintexts I. Then, depending on the bucketing strategy and for each key guess she generates two *template sets* I_0 and I_1. This phase is independent from the targeted white-box implementation and hence the outputted template sets can be hard-coded in the attack source-code (Fig. 2).

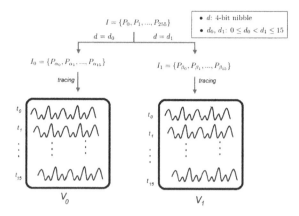

Fig. 2. Sorting the acquired AES traces.

3.2   Acquisition Phase

During this phase, the adversary shall record the most suitable information accessed during the execution of the cryptographic algorithm depending on the specificities of the targeted white-box implementation. Hence, the collected information could be one or a concatenation of the following: the memory read, the memory write, the accessed addresses, the CPU instructions, the stack, *etc.* Indeed, one can use any dynamic binary instrumentation tool (such as PIN, Valgrind, *etc.*) to collect these traces [10].

Tracing an AES Implementation. For AES algorithm, an adversary will need exactly 256 traces for each byte of the key. Since there are 16 bytes, the total number of traces needed to recover the entire key of an AES-128 is 4096 traces. Please note that the number of the required traces to recover the whole AES key can be reduced to 1024 as the AES state bytes are grouped by 4 during the MixColumns operation. Hence, the BCA attack can be performed on 4 key bytes in parallel, *e.g.* by computing 256 plaintexts yielding all possible input values of a group of 4 Sboxes that are not mixed during the MixColumns operation while the other Sboxes inputs are constant. Then, we repeat the same process for the three remaining groups of Sboxes.

Moreover, each recovered value during the acquisition phase (*e.g.* an accessed address) must be decomposed into several nibbles (4-bit values) and then stored in the computation trace. This is required since the considered transformation of AES Sbox (*i.e.* S') in this work has a 4-bit output and the targeted implementations in this work are nibble encoded. As discussed in Sect. 2.3, depending on the size of the involved encoding, one may consider a different transformation of the AES Sbox and adapt the way of representing the acquired values in the computation trace accordingly.

Tracing a DES Implementation. Regarding the DES, we need 64 traces for each sub-key of 6-bit. Hence, the total number of traces needed to recover the 48 bits of the DES key is 512 traces. As discussed previously, the remaining 8 bits can be determined by exhaustive search. Unlike AES, no particular formatting of the traces is needed for the DES. So, compared to other computational attacks (*e.g.* LDA and DCA), the number of traces needed to perform the BCA is fixed independently of the security level of the targeted white-box implementation.

Some Hints on How to Filter the Acquired Traces. When the adversary is not able to accurately localize a small window of interest then she might apply the BCA to the full computational trace. In such case, as highlighted in Algorithm 1 (Lines 10 to 14), for each key guess, the attacker goes through the columns of $\mathbf{V_0}$ and $\mathbf{V_1}$ one by one and count the number of disjoint columns. Hence, if the size of the computation traces is too heavy (*e.g.* the size of targeted traces in [18] is 280 Kbytes), then the BCA complexity might be too huge. To counter this practical issue, the adversary should filter the traces just after the acquisition phase (Line 6) in Algorithm 1. For instance, she has to remove the columns of $\mathbf{T}$ containing constant values (*i.e.* useless for the computational analysis).

3.3   Complexity Improvements

To further improve of the attack complexity when dealing with heavy traces, we propose in Algorithm 2 an optimized key-recovery phase. Therefore, when it applies, an adversary has to replace lines 10 to 14 in Algorithm 1 by the suggested pseudo-code in Algorithm 2. Other hints on how to optimize the computation of matrices intersections are presented in [16] and may be considered to further improve the attack complexity when needed.

Algorithm 2. An optimized key-recovery phase.

Inputs: two (m, n)-matrices $\mathbf{V_0}$ and $\mathbf{V_1}$
Output: the score $R[K]$ for a key guess K
1: $\mathbf{V'_0} = \mathbf{V_0}$
2: $\mathbf{V'_1} = \mathbf{V_1}$
3: **for** each j in $[0, m - 1]$ **do**
4:     $H = \mathbf{V'_0}^j \cap \mathbf{V'_1}^j$
5:     **if** $H \neq \emptyset$ **then**
6:         Remove the columns of $\mathbf{V'_0}$ and $\mathbf{V'_1}$ whose indices correspond to the ones of the intersected values
7:     **end if**
8: **end for**
9: $R[K]$ equals to the number of columns in $\mathbf{V'_0}$

---

4   Practical Experiments

4.1   Experimental Setup

We have developed a tool to perform the BCA on AES and DES implementations following the pseudo-codes provided in Algorithms 1 and 2. To ease the reproduction of our results by the white-box community, the source code of our tool is available [3]. The acquisition of the software execution traces was performed using an internal tool that monitors the memory access during the execution of the target implementations. To evaluate the efficiency of our attack, we targeted several publicly available white-box implementations:

- *ph4r05 white-box*: is an AES white-box implementation based on the design of Chow *et al.* [12] and the approach of dual ciphers introduced by Karroumi [19]. The source-code is available on GitHub [1].
- *The Wyseur* 2007 *Challenge*: is the first public DES white-box implementation [4]. It is based on Chow *et al.*'s design.
- *The CHES* 2016 *Challenge*: is a white-box implementation of AES compiled as an ELF for Linux/x86_64 [2].
- *Lee et al.'s implementation*: is a masked AES white-box implementation [21]. Depending on the security requirement level, three variants of the implementation were presented. In this work, we focus on the first variant (denoted CASE 1 in [21]) which is publicly available on GitHub [2].

For the sake of comparison, we applied the DCA on the same targeted white-box implementations. We decided to not perform the ZDE attack since several traces are required, *e.g.* 500×2^{17} traces are needed to recover 2 key bytes of the CHES 2016 challenge [6]. Both attacks were running on a Linux machine with an Intel Core i7 processor at 3.60 GHz and 16 GB of RAM. The targeted operation was the output of the Sbox during the first round of the encryption. The obtained results are summarized in Table 1. The execution times to recover one key byte are reported in Table 1 and do not include the time required for the acquisition phase.

4.2   Attack Results

From Table 1, one can conclude that when attacking straightforward white-box implementations (*i.e.* Wyseur and ph4r05) both BCA and DCA perform well and the complexity is quite low (*i.e.* few minutes to recover the whole key). In such context, *i.e.* when no particular side-channel countermeasure is applied, the DCA is privileged since it requires less traces.

When targeting more sophisticated white-box implementations the BCA outperforms the DCA. In fact, one has to run two times the DCA attack (by considering two different sensitive operations) in order to extract the full AES key from CHES 2016 challenge [2] while the BCA succeeds to recover it in one run.

The DCA is even unsuccessful on Lee *et al.*'s masked white-box implementation[7]. In this context, our BCA attack is of a great interest since it succeeds to break Lee *et al.*'s implementation in a reasonable time complexity. This result can be explained by the fact that the second round input of Lee *et al.*'s implementation (CASE 1) is not masked[8]. The masking is removed just after the Mixcolumns of the first round. So, to succeed the DCA attack on this implementation, the adversary would have to guess 2^{32} sub-key candidates since each input byte of the second round (*i.e.* output byte of the Mixcolumns of the first round) is the result of a weighted XOR operation between 4 Sbox outputs from the first round[9]. In this case, our BCA attack performs well since the plaintexts are chosen such that one byte is varying and the remaining bytes are generated at zero (or a fixed value). This yields that the targeted input byte of the second round (*i.e.* the targeted output byte of the Mixcolumns of the first round) is the result of a weighted XOR operation between the targeted Sbox output of the first round and a constant value (*i.e.* the weighted XOR result of the three non-targeted Sbox outputs). To fix the vulnerability of CASE 1 implementation, Lee *et al.* have proposed in [21] a new version, denoted CASE 3. Basically, the idea is to use byte encodings on the first round output instead of nibble encodings. Unfortunately, we were not able to evaluate their proposal against our BCA attack since the implementation is not publicly available.

Table 1. Attack results when targeting different white-box implementations.

	DCA			BCA		
	Exec. time (s)	# of traces	Success rate	Exec. time (s)	# of traces	Success rate
Wyseur	30	50	100%	20	512	100%
ph4r05	600	200	100%	280	1024	100%
CHES'16	1080	2000	100%	60	1024	100%
Lee WB	2940	2000	0%	5760	1024	100%

4.3   Discussion and Countermeasures

Regarding the LDA, this attack is efficient when applied against *obscure* white-box implementations [18]. However, depending on the targeted implementation several steps (*e.g.* the so-called single static assignment and data dependency analysis) should be carefully followed in order to successfully apply it. Performing these steps is relatively easy when the source code is available. However when only the compiled binary is available, these steps are more complex and require a

---

[7] Please note that our obtained results are in-line with those published in [2].

[8] Only the first and the last rounds are protected against DCA [21].

[9] This attack is computationally expensive but theoretically feasible. Another approach would consist in performing a DCA in a chosen-plaintext context, *i.e.* varying the plaintext byte corresponding to the targeted Sbox and fix the remaining ones.

lot of preprocessing. Moreover, when the used encoding functions are of higher-degree, a Higher-Degree Decoding Analysis (HDDA) can be applied but the attack complexity exponentially grows with the considered encoding degree [18].

We performed the LDA on Lee *et al.*'s masked white-box implementation when ignoring the pre-analysis steps since only the statically linked binary is available [2] (*i.e.* we only performed the algebraic analysis). The LDA succeeds to extract the last key round when using 200 traces and considering the second degree (a narrow window was selected to run the attack). However, the attack on the first round was unsuccessful even when considering the forth degree and up to 2000 traces. For the sake of comparison, we performed as well a second-order DCA on Lee *et al.*'s proposal using 2000 traces. This attack was unsuccessful on the first round and when targeting the last round, we only recovered 2 bytes of the key. This result could be explained by the fact that the used masks are encoded as explained in [21]. So, compared to the result obtained with the BCA, one can conclude that in the presence of a customized masked implementation, our BCA attack can be a good alternative to consider.

It is obvious that, a properly masked implementation should prevent our BCA attack. However, as demonstrated in the previous section, a customized masking implementation (*e.g.* Lee *et al.*'s proposal) can prevent DCA but may be broken with our BCA attack. To counteract our proposal, another countermeasure would consist in inserting some random delays to misalign the computation traces. This can be done for instance by inserting some dummy operations as suggested in [6]. However, this countermeasure can be defeated during the reverse engineering phase of the targeted implementation binary. Another countermeasure would consist in adding some fake computations with fake keys to increase the score of the corresponding disjoint sets (*i.e.* generating some false positives).

5 Conclusion

In this paper, we presented a new computational analysis method to break white-box implementations. Unlike the DCA, which uses statistic correlations, our approach relies on a cryptanalysis technique based on the statistical bucketing analysis. We have adapted this cryptanalysis technique to AES cipher and we proposed a new key distinguisher for an automated computational analysis which is applicable to both AES and DES white-box implementations. Throughout several practical experiments, we demonstrated that our proposal is an efficient alternative to DCA and LDA attacks. More interestingly, when some side-channel countermeasures (*e.g.* customized masking) are involved to protect white-box implementations, and hence the HO-DCA and the LDA come at higher-cost in terms of attack complexity, our bucketing computational analysis succeeds to break the white-box design in a reasonable time and by requiring very few number of traces.

A future work would consist in extending our bucketing attack to higher-order context and applying it to more complex white-box implementations (*i.e.* that combine higher-order masking, dummy operations, shuffling techniques and rely on higher-order encoding functions). Another avenue of research would be to study the most optimal and suitable non-injective transformations that should be used when targeting an AES white-box implementation.

A   Experimental Estimation of the Probability that for an Incorrect Key Guess the Sets V_0 and V_1 are Disjoints - DES CASE

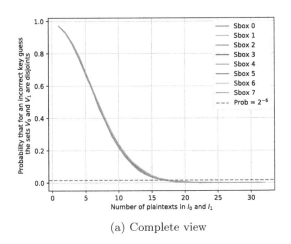

(a) Complete view

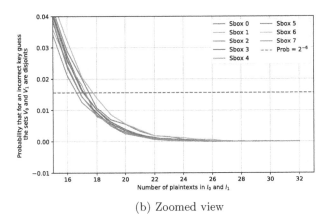

(b) Zoomed view

Fig. 3. Evolution of the probability that for an incorrect key guess the sets V_0 and V_1 are disjoints according to an increasing number of plaintexts in I_0 and I_1 when considering the 8 DES Sboxes.

B   Experimental Estimation of the Probability that for an Incorrect Key Guess the Sets V_0 and V_1 are Disjoints - AES CASE

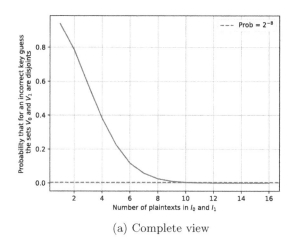

(a) Complete view

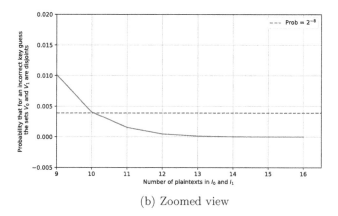

(b) Zoomed view

Fig. 4. Evolution of the probability that for an incorrect key guess the sets V_0 and V_1 are disjoints according to an increasing number of plaintexts in I_0 and I_1.

References

1. Ph4r05 White-Box. https://github.com/ph4r05/Whitebox-crypto-AES
2. SideChannelMarvels Deadpool. https://github.com/SideChannelMarvels/Dead-pool
3. Source code of the Bucketing Computational Analysis for AES and DES. https://github.com/Bucketing/BCA-attack

4. Wyseur Challenge (2007). http://www.whiteboxcrypto.com/challenges.php
5. Allibert, J., Feix, B., Gagnerot, G., Kane, I., Thiebeauld, H., Razafindralambo, T.: Chicken or the egg - computational data attacks or physical attacks. Cryptology ePrint Archive, Report 2015/1086 (2015). https://eprint.iacr.org/2015/1086
6. Banik, S., Bogdanov, A., Isobe, T., Jepsen, M.B.: Analysis of software countermeasures for whitebox encryption. IACR Cryptology ePrint Archive 2017:183 (2017)
7. Billet, O., Gilbert, H., Ech-Chatbi, C.: Cryptanalysis of a white box AES implementation. In: Handschuh, H., Hasan, M.A. (eds.) SAC 2004. LNCS, vol. 3357, pp. 227–240. Springer, Heidelberg (2004). https://doi.org/10.1007/978-3-540-30564-4_16
8. Biryukov, A., Udovenko, A.: Attacks and countermeasures for white-box designs. Cryptology ePrint Archive, Report 2018/049 (2018). https://eprint.iacr.org/2018/049
9. Bogdanov, A., Rivain, M., Vejre, P.S., Wang, J.: Higher-order DCA against standard side-channel countermeasures. Cryptology ePrint Archive, Report 2018/869 (2018). https://eprint.iacr.org/2018/869
10. Bos, J.W., Hubain, C., Michiels, W., Teuwen, P.: Differential computation analysis: hiding your white-box designs is not enough. In: Gierlichs, B., Poschmann, A.Y. (eds.) Cryptographic Hardware and Embedded Systems - CHES 2016, vol. 1717, pp. 215–236. Springer, Heidelberg (2016)
11. Bringer, J., Chabanne, H., Dottax, E.: White box cryptography: another attempt. Cryptology ePrint Archive, Report 2006/468 (2006). https://eprint.iacr.org/2006/468
12. Chow, S., Eisen, P., Johnson, H., van Oorschot, P.C.: A white-box DES implementation for DRM applications. In: Feigenbaum, J. (ed.) DRM 2002. LNCS, vol. 2696, pp. 1–15. Springer, Heidelberg (2003). https://doi.org/10.1007/978-3-540-44993-5_1
13. Chow, S., Eisen, P., Johnson, H., Van Oorschot, P.C.: White-box cryptography and an AES implementation. In: Nyberg, K., Heys, H. (eds.) SAC 2002. LNCS, vol. 2595, pp. 250–270. Springer, Heidelberg (2003). https://doi.org/10.1007/3-540-36492-7_17
14. De Mulder, Y., Roelse, P., Preneel, B.: Cryptanalysis of the Xiao – Lai white-box AES implementation. In: Knudsen, L.R., Wu, H. (eds.) SAC 2012. LNCS, vol. 7707, pp. 34–49. Springer, Heidelberg (2013). https://doi.org/10.1007/978-3-642-35999-6_3
15. De Mulder, Y., Wyseur, B., Preneel, B.: Cryptanalysis of a perturbated white-box AES implementation. In: Gong, G., Gupta, K.C. (eds.) INDOCRYPT 2010. LNCS, vol. 6498, pp. 292–310. Springer, Heidelberg (2010). https://doi.org/10.1007/978-3-642-17401-8_21
16. Ding, B., König, A.C.: Fast set intersection in memory. Proc. VLDB Endow. 4(4), 255–266 (2011)
17. Goubin, L., Masereel, J.-M., Quisquater, M.: Cryptanalysis of white box DES implementations. In: Adams, C., Miri, A., Wiener, M. (eds.) SAC 2007. LNCS, vol. 4876, pp. 278–295. Springer, Heidelberg (2007). https://doi.org/10.1007/978-3-540-77360-3_18
18. Goubin, L., Paillier, P., Rivain, M., Wang, J.: How to reveal the secrets of an obscure white-box implementation. Cryptology ePrint Archive, Report 2018/098 (2018). https://eprint.iacr.org/2018/098
19. Karroumi, M.: Protecting white-box AES with dual ciphers. In: Rhee, K.-H., Nyang, D.H. (eds.) ICISC 2010. LNCS, vol. 6829, pp. 278–291. Springer, Heidelberg (2011). https://doi.org/10.1007/978-3-642-24209-0_19

20. Kocher, P., Jaffe, J., Jun, B.: Differential power analysis. In: Wiener, M. (ed.) CRYPTO 1999. LNCS, vol. 1666, pp. 388–397. Springer, Heidelberg (1999). https://doi.org/10.1007/3-540-48405-1_25

21. Lee, S., Kim, T., Kang, Y.: A masked white-box cryptographic implementation for protecting against differential computation analysis. IEEE Trans. Inf. Forensics Secur. **13**(10), 2602–2615 (2018)

22. Lepoint, T., Rivain, M.: Another nail in the coffin of white-box AES implementations. Cryptology ePrint Archive, Report 2013/455 (2013). https://eprint.iacr.org/2013/455

23. Lepoint, T., Rivain, M., De Mulder, Y., Roelse, P., Preneel, B.: Two attacks on a white-box AES implementation. In: Lange, T., Lauter, K., Lisoněk, P. (eds.) SAC 2013. LNCS, vol. 8282, pp. 265–285. Springer, Heidelberg (2014). https://doi.org/10.1007/978-3-662-43414-7_14

24. Link, H.E., Neumann, W.D.: Clarifying obfuscation: improving the security of white-box DES. In: International Conference on Information Technology: Coding and Computing (ITCC 2005), vol. II, vol. 1, pp. 679–684, April 2005

25. Michiels, W., Gorissen, P., Hollmann, H.D.L.: Cryptanalysis of a generic class of white-box implementations. In: Avanzi, R.M., Keliher, L., Sica, F. (eds.) SAC 2008. LNCS, vol. 5381, pp. 414–428. Springer, Heidelberg (2009). https://doi.org/10.1007/978-3-642-04159-4_27

26. Mulder, Y.D., Roelse, P., Preneel, B.: Revisiting the BGE attack on a white-box AES implementation. Cryptology ePrint Archive, Report 2013/450 (2013). https://eprint.iacr.org/2013/450

27. Sanfelix, E., Mune, C., de Haas, J.: Unboxing the white-box practical attacks against obfuscated ciphers. Black Hat (2015)

28. Wyseur, B.: Software security: white-box cryptography. Ph.D. thesis, K.U.L., March 2009. https://www.esat.kuleuven.be/cosic/publications/thesis-152.pdf

29. Wyseur, B., Michiels, W., Gorissen, P., Preneel, B.: Cryptanalysis of white-box DES implementations with arbitrary external encodings. In: Adams, C., Miri, A., Wiener, M. (eds.) SAC 2007. LNCS, vol. 4876, pp. 264–277. Springer, Heidelberg (2007). https://doi.org/10.1007/978-3-540-77360-3_17

30. Xiao, Y., Lai, X.: A secure implementation of white-box AES. In: 2009 2nd International Conference on Computer Science and its Applications, pp. 1–6, December 2009

Higher-Order DCA against Standard Side-Channel Countermeasures

Andrey Bogdanov[1], Matthieu Rivain[2], Philip S. Vejre[1],
and Junwei Wang[2,3,4(✉)]

[1] Technical University of Denmark, Kongens Lyngby, Denmark
{anbog,psve}@dtu.dk
[2] CryptoExperts, Paris, France
{matthieu.rivain,junwei.wang}@cryptoexperts.com
[3] University of Luxembourg, Esch-sur-Alzette, Luxembourg
[4] University Paris 8, Saint-Denis, France

Abstract. At CHES 2016, Bos *et al.* introduced *differential computational analysis* (DCA) as an attack on white-box software implementations of block ciphers. This attack builds on the same principles as DPA in the classical side-channel context, but uses computational traces consisting of plain values computed by the implementation during execution. It was shown to be able to recover the key of many existing AES white-box implementations.

The *DCA adversary* is *passive*, and so does not exploit the full power of the white-box setting, implying that many white-box schemes are insecure even in a weaker setting than the one they were designed for. It is therefore important to develop implementations which are resistant to this attack. We investigate the approach of applying standard side-channel countermeasures such as *masking* and *shuffling*. Under some necessary conditions on the underlying randomness generation, we show that these countermeasures provide resistance to standard (first-order) DCA. Furthermore, we introduce *higher-order DCA*, along with an enhanced *multivariate* version, and analyze the security of the countermeasures against these attacks. We derive analytic expressions for the complexity of the attacks – backed up through extensive attack experiments – enabling a designer to quantify the security level of a masked and shuffled implementation in the (higher-order) DCA setting.

Keywords: White-box cryptography · Higher-order DCA · Masking · Shuffling

1 Introduction

In the classical cryptanalytic setting, the adversary faces the challenge of breaking the security of *e.g.* an encryption algorithm while only being able to consider the algorithm as a *black box*; she can query the box with inputs and receive the

I. Polian and M. Stöttinger (Eds.): COSADE 2019, LNCS 11421, pp. 118–141, 2019.
https://doi.org/10.1007/978-3-030-16350-1_8

corresponding outputs. While the design of the algorithm is known, the adversary cannot observe the internal state of the algorithm, or affect the execution of the algorithm.

In practice, a cryptographic algorithm has to be implemented somewhere to be useful, *i.e.* in hardware or software. Thus, the adversary has the option of physically interacting with the encryption device. In this case, the adversary has access to implementation specific *side-channel information*. If an implementation is not sufficiently protected, leaking information such as the execution time or the power consumption can be used to extract secret information, *e.g.* encryption keys. The widespread use and success of side-channel attacks show that a cryptographer has to be very careful when operating in this *gray-box* model.

1.1   Shades of Gray

For hardware implementations, the gray-box model is often the limit of what an adversary can achieve. This is not the case for software implementations that are executed in untrusted environments. If an adversary is given full access to the execution environment of the cryptographic software, she can easily observe and manipulate the execution of the primitive, instantiated with some secret key. This setting, introduced by Chow *et al.* in [10], is called the *white-box* model.

In the white-box setting, the adversary can study the logic flow of the implementation, observe any tables the implementation uses, observe intermediate values computed during execution, alter the implementation at run-time, etc. Indeed, *"when the attacker has internal information about a cryptographic implementation, choice of implementation is the sole remaining line of defense"* [10]. Ideally, the aim of a white-box implementation would be to leave the white-box adversary with at most the same advantage as a black-box adversary, but this seems to be very difficult. Instead, the current white-box paradigm aims to provide *practical security*, in the sense that the implementation is difficult enough to attack so that an adversary is forced to attempt other attack vectors.

Several different approaches have been proposed to make white-box secure implementations for standard block ciphers, such as AES [5,6,9,10,17,29]. Sadly, all these designs have been broken by structural attacks [2,19,21–23,27]. Additionally, no provably secure solutions have been reported in the literature. Still, there exists an increasing industrial need for the protection of cryptographic implementations executed in untrusted environments, such as the traditional *digital rights management* use case and the mobile payment applications running on smart devices. This has driven the industry to develop home-made solutions relying on *obscurity* (i.e. secrecy of the underlying obfuscation techniques). In this paradigm, white-box cryptography acts as a moving target based on regular security updates and/or short-term key tokens and is considered a building block of wider security solutions.

1.2 Differential Computational Analysis

The mentioned attacks against *public* white-box implementations exploit flaws in the underlying white-box schemes. However, secret variants of known designs that change a few parameters or combine different techniques would likely thwart these attacks, if exact designs are kept secret. To attack such implementations, the adversary would have to perform reverse engineering, which can take considerable time and effort if various layers of obfuscation have been applied.

A more generic approach was given recently by Bos *et al.* [4] introduced the white-box equivalent of DPA, namely *differential computational analysis* (DCA), and demonstrated how this technique is able to recover the encryption key of several existing white-box implementations of the AES. Notably, the *DCA adversary* is extremely powerful as it is *implementation agnostic* and therefore does not need to exert expensive reverse engineering efforts. Thus, DCA has been devastating for industrial solutions that leverage design secrecy to develop white-box implementations consisting of a mix of various techniques (common white-box techniques, code obfuscation, home-made encodings, etc.).

Moreover, the DCA adversary does not take advantage of the full power of the white-box model. The adversary only needs to be able to observe the addresses and values of memory being accessed during the execution of the implementation. The adversary does not need to reason about the implementation details, or modify the functionality of the code in any way, *e.g.* by disabling RNG functionalities – tasks that could required considerable effort. Thus, the DCA attack is a *passive* and *non-invasive* attack, existing in a setting which is closer to a gray-box than a white-box. Additionally, the attacks presented in [4] have very low complexities.

Following these observations, the current white-box AES implementations are not even secure in a weaker attack context than the one they were designed for, and as a consequence, designing secure white-box implementation seems out of reach. Indeed, DCA seems to be the biggest hindrance to designing practically secure white-box implementations. It is therefore of importance to first explore the design of cryptographic implementations which are secure against DCA.

1.3 Our Contributions

A natural approach when attempting to mitigate the threat of DCA attacks is to apply known countermeasures from the side-channel literature. However, it is not clear how well these countermeasures carry over to the white-box context and what level of security can be achieved by such countermeasures against a DCA adversary. To address these issues, we achieve the following:

– **Side-channel countermeasures in the white-box setting:** In Sect. 3 we discuss how to apply the well known side-channel countermeasures in the white-box setting focusing on the (passive) DCA adversary. Specifically, we focus on *higher-order masking* along with *shuffling of operations* to introduce noise in the DCA traces. We show that if the source of randomness used in the implementation satisfies some specific security properties, then this approach is sufficient to achieve security against standard first-order DCA.

- **Higher-order DCA:** We develop *higher-order DCA* in Sect. 4 to analyze the security of the proposed protection. We show that higher-order DCA is able to break a masked implementation of any order using a couple of traces. However, by introducing noise in the form of shuffling, the security of the implementation can be dramatically increased. As a demonstration, a typical AES implementation with 2nd order masking (and shuffling degree of 16) requires 2^{21} traces to break with 3rd order DCA.

- **Multivariate higher-order DCA:** We extend the above attack by introducing a multivariate version in Sect. 5, which reduces the computational complexity by decreasing the number of required traces for a successful attack. Using this multivariate variant, the number of traces required to successfully attack the AES implementation mentioned above can be reduced to 2^{10}.

- **Formal analysis and experimental verification:** We derive analytic expressions for the success probability and attack complexities of both the higher-order DCA and its multivariate variant. Using these expressions, we are able to give estimates for the security level of a masked and shuffled implementation in the DCA setting. As an example, an AES implementation with 7th order masking would have a security level of about 85 bits in this setting. Then accuracy of our expressions for the success probability of the multivariate higher-order DCA is verified in Sect. 5.2 through extensive experiments for a wide range of implementation and attack parameters. 2 000 attacks of up to order 4 were simulated, using as many as 30 000 traces per attack.

In summary, our result provides formal ground to the study of standard side-channel defenses in the white-box setting. We have analyzed the widely used masking and shuffling countermeasures with respect to the DCA adversary and we have quantified their security against advanced DCA attacks. From our analysis, a designer can choose an appropriate set of implementation parameters to achieve a given security level with respect to DCA, which is a first step towards building security against a stronger white-box adversary.

1.4   Related Works

Two independent and related works have been published since the first version of the present paper which both address masking in the white-box context. First, Biryukov and Udovenko [3] broadly overview how a white-box adversary could attack masked white-box implementations in several aspects, in particular, in an *active* (fault injection) attack setting. Second, Goubin *et al.* [15] proposed a method to attack an *obscure* white-box implementation (in the sense that the adversary has no/limited knowledge on the design), which was successfully applied to break the winning challenge in the recent WhibOx 2017 contest [1]. Particularly, their *linear decoding analysis* can break a noise-free masked implementation with complexity approximately cubic in the size of the computation trace.

Compared to these works, the adversary we consider is *passive*, as such she would not be impacted by fault detection/correction measures. Moreover, [15] demonstrates that masking is a weak countermeasure unless it is composed with some kind of *noise*. Therefore, this work focuses on white-box implementations protected with both masking and shuffling.

2   Differential Computation Analysis

The *DCA adversary* is capable of querying a software implementation of a cryptographic primitive with arbitrary input to obtain a *computational trace* of the execution. The computational trace consists of: any value calculated, written, or read by the implementation, and the address of any memory location read from or written to during execution. Each data point in the computational trace is further annotated with the time it occurred in the execution. When a number of traces have been collected, the adversary calculates correlations between a prediction of a key-dependent intermediate value and computed values.

2.1   DCA Setting

As for hardware side-channel attacks, DCA exploits that the (software) implementation leaks some information about intermediate variables involved in the execution of the cryptographic algorithm. Some of these intermediate variables depend on the plaintext and (part of) the secret key, and knowledge of such variables can therefore reveal the key. We denote such a *secret variable* by $s = \varphi(x, k^*)$, where φ is a deterministic function, x is a public value, *e.g.* (part of) the plaintext, and $k^* \in \mathcal{K}$ is a (secret) subkey over some subkey space $\mathcal{K}$. For instance, k^* could be a byte of the secret key and $\mathcal{K}$ would then be $\{0,1\}^8$.

The DCA attack itself consists of first obtaining a number of computational traces from the execution of the cipher implementation with secret subkey k^* for several (random) plaintexts. We denote a computational trace consisting of t time points by the ordered t-tuple $\boldsymbol{v} = (v_1, v_2, \ldots, v_t)$, with $v_i \in \mathcal{V}$ for some set $\mathcal{V}$. In principle, the traces can be any value exposed to a dynamic binary analysis tool, as explained above. Usually, an attacker will obtain N computational traces, $\boldsymbol{v}_1, \ldots, \boldsymbol{v}_N$, representing N executions of the implementation with different inputs, each corresponding to a value $s_i = \varphi(x_i, k^*)$ of the target secret variable. These traces could *e.g.* arise from the encryption of N different plaintexts. The attacker then performs a classic DPA, in which a *distinguisher* is used to indicate a correct guess of k^*. The distinguisher is a function D which maps the set of computational traces $(\boldsymbol{v}_i)_i$, and corresponding inputs $(x_i)_i$, to a *score vector*:

$$(\gamma_k)_{k \in \mathcal{K}} = \mathsf{D}\big((\boldsymbol{v}_1, \ldots, \boldsymbol{v}_N); (x_1, \ldots, x_N)\big).$$

The adversary then selects the key guess k with the highest score γ_k as candidate for the correct value of k^*. We define the success probability of the attack as

$$p_{\mathrm{succ}} = \Pr(\mathrm{argmax}_{k \in \mathcal{K}} \gamma_k = k^*),$$

where this probability is taken over any randomness supplied to the implementation (including the randomness of the inputs).

2.2   Standard First-Order DCA

The description above does not specify the distinguisher D. Here, we briefly describe the distinguisher used in [4], which we will call the *standard first-order DCA*. Let us denote by $v_{i,j}$ the value at the j'th time point of the i'th trace. The standard first-order DCA attack consists of calculating a correlation coefficient between a vector of predicted values of the secret variable, $(s_1^k, \ldots, s_N^k)$, where $s_i^k = \varphi(x_i, k)$, and the vector $(v_{1,j}, \ldots, v_{N,j})$, for every time index $1 \leq j \leq t$. Then the score γ_k is defined as the maximum correlation obtained over the different time indices, *i.e.*

$$\gamma_k = \max_j C\big((v_{1,j}, \ldots, v_{N,j}), (\psi(s_1^k), \ldots, \psi(s_N^k))\big),$$

for some correlation measure C and some *pre-processing function* ψ. For example, C could be the Pearson correlation coefficient and ψ either the Hamming weight function or the selection of one bit of the predicted variable. If there exists a statistical correlation between the secret variable and the values of the computational trace, we would expect a large absolute value of C for some index j and the correct prediction of the secret variables, *i.e.* the vector $(s_1^{k^*}, \ldots, s_N^{k^*})$. On the other hand, if $k \neq k^*$, we expect a low correlation between all s_i^k and any point in the computational trace. It was shown in [4] that this approach is very effective against a range of different AES and DES white-box implementations.

3   Side-Channel Countermeasures against DCA

The DCA adversary is highly reminiscent of the standard side-channel adversary. It is therefore natural to apply traditional side-channel countermeasures to a white-box implementation, and to evaluate their performance against a DCA adversary. In the following, we specifically study the common software countermeasures of *higher-order masking* and *operation shuffling*. We further discuss the source of randomness necessary to feed these countermeasures and state a few security properties that it should satisfy in this setting. We then show that this approach achieves security against standard first-order DCA. The rest of the paper is dedicated to the study of advanced DCA attacks against these countermeasures.

3.1   DCA is a Passive and Non-invasive Gray-Box Attack

We start by noting that applying the mentioned countermeasures in a strict white-box context might be hazardous – indeed classical countermeasures such as masking and shuffling use fresh randomness throughout the execution of the protected implementation which is usually provided by an external random number generator (RNG). Since a white-box adversary has full control over the execution environment, such an RNG could be detected and disabled, shuffled operations could be re-synchronized (*e.g.* using memory addresses, program counter, etc.), and/or masks could be canceled (if masked variables and corresponding masks are easily identified).

In order to make such disabling difficult, the used randomness should rely on some internal PRNG (see Sect. 3.4) and one should further add some layers of obfuscation countermeasures on top of it. The adversary then has to invest some reverse engineering effort to bypass these countermeasures. Nevertheless, we stress that this is exactly the type of analysis an adversary performing a DCA attack is trying to avoid. While DCA attacks might not be optimal in terms of time and/or data complexity, they are very powerful due to their genericness and the fact that they can be applied in a *black-box* way, *i.e.* without requiring reverse engineering effort. This is an essential property of these attacks in the current white-box cryptography paradigm where designers aim at practical security (as provable security seems out of reach) and use the secrecy of the design as a leverage towards this goal. The main purpose of protecting against DCA is therefore to force an adversary to employ more complicated and dedicated attack techniques, which might take a long time to develop and apply, which is beneficial when combined with a moving target strategy.

3.2 Masking

A widely used countermeasure to standard DPA of hardware implementations is *masking* [7,16]. Since the DCA attack relies on the same ideas as DPA, the prospect of applying masking to secure a software implementation against DCA is promising. To mask a secret variable, it is split into several parts that are then processed independently. Specifically, each secret variable s occurring in the execution of the implementation is split into d *shares* $s_1, \ldots, s_d$ such that $s_1 \oplus \ldots \oplus s_d = s$. The masking must be done such that any subset of less than d shares are statistically independent of s. A simple way to achieve this is by picking $s_1, \ldots, s_{d-1}$ uniformly at random (*the masks*), and setting $s_d = s \oplus s_1 \oplus \ldots \oplus s_{d-1}$ (*the masked variable*). The masking is then said to be of *order* $d - 1$. One important aspect of a masked implementation is therefore that of randomness: the implementation has to use a (P)RNG to generate these $d - 1$ masks.

Knowledge of all d shares is required to recover s, but combining the d shares would reveal the secret variable to the DCA adversary. Thus, the implementation must be able to perform computations on the secret variable s without combining the shares, *i.e.* for a function f, we want to compute shares r_i such that $r_1 \oplus \ldots \oplus r_d = f(s)$, from the original shares $s_1, \ldots, s_d$. The computation is then said to be *secure at the order* τ if no τ-tuple of intermediate variables is statistically dependent on a key-dependent variable. Usually, d'th order masking aims to provide security at the order $\tau = d - 1$. To compute any $\mathbb{F}_2$-linear function on a masked variable s, we simply compute the function on each share separately. Thus, calculation of the linear components of a typical SPN can be easily implemented on the masked state. Computing the non-linear components (*i.e.* typically the S-boxes) is more involved but several masking schemes exist that achieve $(d-1)$'th order security (see for instance [11,13,24]).

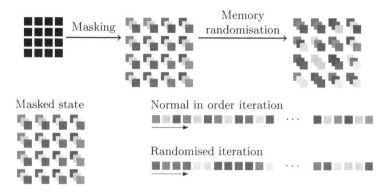

Fig. 1. An illustration of memory (top) and time (bottom) shuffling applied to a second-order masked implementation. The location of each share in memory and the order of iteration is randomised for each execution.

3.3   Shuffling

We will show in Sect. 4 that if masking is the only countermeasure, the DCA adversary can easily recover the key. Indeed, the strength of a masked implementation is directly related to how noisy the adversary's observation of the shares is. Several approaches for introducing and increasing noise in masked implementations have been proposed and analyzed, *e.g.* in [12,25,26,28]. One such approach is shuffling: instead of processing the calculations of the cipher in some fixed order, the order of execution is randomly chosen for each run of the implementation based on the value of the input (*e.g.* the plaintext). The situation is slightly more complicated in the DCA setting. Here, the adversary can make observations in two dimensions, namely *time* and *memory*. Even if the order of execution is shuffled in time, an adversary can choose to order the traces by the memory addresses accessed. Thus, we need to shuffle in both the time and memory dimension (as illustrated in Fig. 1).

Memory Shuffle. In a masked implementation, we will typically have some state in which each element is shared as described in Sect. 3.2. The idea of the memory shuffle is to randomly rearrange the shares of the state in memory. Consider a state consisting of S elements. We assume that the shares $s_{i,j}$, $1 \le i < S$, $1 \le j \le d$, are stored in an array, initially in order. That is, the implementation uses the array $(s_{1,1}, s_{2,1}, \ldots, s_{S-1,d}, s_{S,d})$. Then, we randomly pick a permutation $P : [1, S] \times [1, d] \to [1, S] \times [1, d]$, based on the value of the input. Note that this can be done efficiently using the Fisher-Yates shuffle [14]. Now, instead of using the in-order array, we rearrange the array such that the implementation uses the array $(s_{P(1,1)}, s_{P(2,1)}, \ldots, s_{P(S-1,d)}, s_{P(S,d)})$. Whenever the implementation needs to access share $s_{i,j}$, it simply looks up the element in position $P^{-1}(i,j)$ of the array. A similar randomisation is performed for any key shares.

Time Shuffle. In a typical SPN, there will be several operations that operate on each element of the state in each round. The order of these operations is typically suggested by the cipher designers. As an example, consider the case where we want to apply a linear operation A to each element of the state separately. Since the operation is linear, we can apply it to each share of the masked elements individually. This will normally be done in some "natural" order, e.g. $A(s_{1,1}), A(s_{1,2}), A(s_{1,3}), \ldots, A(s_{S,d})$. However, the exact order of execution does not matter. Thus, we can shuffle in the time dimension by randomly ordering these $S \cdot d$ operations. In general, if a set of λ independent operations exists, we can freely shuffle the order in which we process the $\lambda \cdot d$ shares. Formally, we randomly pick a permutation $Q : [1,\lambda] \times [1,d] \to [1,\lambda] \times [1,d]$. Then, when we normally would have processed share $s_{i,j}$, we instead process share $s_{Q(i,j)}$. Thus, the probability that a specific share is processed in a given step is $1/(\lambda \cdot d)$. We will denote the size of the smallest maximal set of independent operations the *shuffling degree*.

3.4   On the Source of Randomness

A potential issue while applying side-channel countermeasures to the white-box context is randomness generation. Since a white-box adversary can easily get rid of an external RNG, the randomness used by a white-box implementation must be pseudo-randomly generated from the single available source of variation: the input plaintext. In other words, the white-box implementation should embed some kind of pseudo random number generator (PRNG) seeded by the input plaintext. We now (informally) state a few security properties that should be fulfilled by such a PRNG in the white-box setting:

1. *Pseudorandomness:* The output stream of the PRNG should be hard to distinguish from true randomness.
2. *Obscurity:* The design of the PRNG should be kept secret.
3. *Obfuscation:* The PRNG should be mixed with the white-box implementation so that its output stream is hard to distinguish from other intermediate variables.

The pseudorandomness property is required to ensure that the PRNG does not introduce a statistical flaw in the implemented countermeasures. It is well known that a flawed RNG can be a disaster for the security of masking (see for instance [20]). The pseudorandomness property further implies that the generated randomness is *unpredictable* provided that the obscurity property also holds. The unpredictability of the generated randomness is necessary to get DCA resistance, since without it all the intermediate variables can be expressed as (known) deterministic functions of the plaintext and the secret key, which enables the application of standard first-order DCA.[1]

Indeed, if the PRNG design was known to the adversary, then she could predict all the generated randomness from the plaintext. Therefore in order to provide unpredictability, some part of the design must be secret, even if the obscurity concept clearly clashes with the adage of Kerckhoffs's Principle [18]. Nevertheless, it seems almost impossible to provide any security if the full design is known, and we stress that this does not imply that one should forego all good cryptographic engineering practices. One could use a keyed PRNG (or PRNG with secret initial state), but even then if the design was known to the adversary she could mount a DCA attack to recover the PRNG key and we would then face a chicken and egg problem. Alternatively, an implementation could use a known strong PRNG with some sound changes to design parameters, in order to have some confidence in its security. Another approach, which aligns with the moving target strategy, would be to have a set of different PRNG designs that are often changed.

Finally the obfuscation property is required to prevent easy detection of the PRNG output which could facilitate a DCA attack. It is for instance described in [15] how the generated randomness can be easily detected by switching the values of intermediate variables and checking whether this affects the final result. Such a detection is an *active* attack that tampers with the execution (in the same way as *fault attacks*) and is hence out of scope of the DCA adversary. However it should be made difficult (in the same way as fault attacks should be made difficult) to achieve some level of resistance in practice.

In the following, we shall consider that the above security properties are satisfied by the used PRNG so that the DCA adversary cannot easily remove or predict the generated randomness. We will then analyze which level of security is achievable by using masking and shuffling in this context.

3.5   Resistance to First-Order DCA

In Sect. 2 we described the capabilities of the DCA adversary and the standard first-order DCA. For the masked implementation described above with $d > 1$, the d'th order security of the underlying masking scheme implies that any d-tuple of variables from the computation trace $v = (v_1, v_2, \dots, v_t)$ is statistically independent of any key-dependent variable. Assuming that the PRNG embedded in the target implementation outputs strong and unpredictable pseudorandomness (as required in Sect. 3.4) the distribution of any d-tuple of variables from v is indistinguishable from the same distribution with perfect randomness, which makes it (computationally) independent of any key-dependent variable. Therefore, standard first-order DCA as described in Sect. 2.2 is doomed to fail.

---

[1] Following the DCA setting described in Sect. 2.1, the only impact of the countermeasures in presence of a known PRNG is to change the deterministic function φ in the expression of the secret variable s.

4   Introducing Higher-Order DCA

While masking has been proven to be an effective defense against standard DPA, and we have argued for its effectiveness against standard first-order DCA, there are ways to attack such masked implementations. For hardware implementations, it is well known that a $(d-1)$'th-order masked implementation, such as the one described above, can be defeated by d'th-order DPA, if no other protection is employed. We will therefore develop a higher-order version of DCA.

A d'th-order DCA consists of a pre-processing step followed by a first-order DCA. The adversary first pre-processes each computational trace v to obtain a d'th-order computational trace w by applying a so-called (d'th-order) *combination function* ψ. Specifically, the d'th-order computational trace w consists of $q = \binom{t}{d}$ points $(w_1, \ldots, w_q)$ given by

$$w_j = \psi(v_{j_1}, v_{j_2}, \ldots, v_{j_d}), \quad \{j_1, \ldots, j_d\} = \phi(j),$$

where $\phi(j)$ is the j'th subset of $\{1, \ldots, t\}$ of size d (for some ordering). After computing the set of d'th order traces $w_1, \ldots, w_N$, the adversary proceeds as for first-order DCA, using the w_i's as input to the distinguisher D. Specifically, the adversary computes the score vector $(\gamma_k)_{k \in K} = \mathsf{D}\big((w_i)_i; (x_i)_i\big)$ in order to determine a candidate for k^*.

For side-channel analysis of hardware implementations, it has been shown that a good combination function for higher-order DPA is the centered product $\psi : (v_1, \ldots, v_d) \mapsto \prod_j (v_j - \mu_j)$, where μ_j is the average of the leakage point v_j over several encryptions. Nevertheless, since the measurements in this setting are inherently noisy, a larger masking degree will require a larger number of traces to obtain a good success probability. Note that this is not the case in the DCA context, if no noise is introduced in the implementation, *e.g.* by using shuffling as described in Sect. 3.3. In this case, the exact value of each variable that appears in an execution of the implementation appears at the same position of every computational trace v_i. Then there exists a fixed j^*, such that for $\phi(j^*) = (j_1^*, \ldots, j_d^*)$, the elements $v_{j_1^*}, \ldots, v_{j_d^*}$ of the trace are the shares of the target secret variable s. In that case, an optimal choice for the combination function is the XOR sum of the trace values, that is

$$\psi(v_{j_1}, v_{j_2}, \ldots, v_{j_d}) = v_{j_1} \oplus v_{j_2} \oplus \cdots \oplus v_{j_d}.$$

For this combination function, we have that $\psi(v_{j_1^*}, v_{j_2^*}, \ldots, v_{j_d^*}) = s$ for all the d'th-order traces. By counting the number of times this equality holds, we can easily determine the correct key. That is, we set

$$\gamma_k = \max_j \left(C_k(v_{\phi(j)}, (x_i)_i) \right) \text{with} C_k(v_{\phi(j)}, (x_i)_i) = \left| \left\{ i \; ; \; \bigoplus_{l \in \phi(j)} v_{i,l} = \varphi(x_i, k) \right\} \right|.$$

For the correct key k^*, we deterministically have that $\gamma_{k^*} = N$. Thus, if no noise is present, the higher-order DCA is successful when $\gamma_{k^\times} < N$ for all $k^\times \neq k^*$. The probability of this happening is quite close to 1, even for small N. Thus, the introduction of some noise in the traces is required to secure a masked white-box implementation against DCA.

4.1   Higher-Order DCA against Masking and Shuffling

We now consider how well the masked and shuffled implementation resists the higher-order DCA attack described above. Due to the shuffling, the adversary is no longer guaranteed that her prediction for the correct key guess will correspond to a single time point for all traces. Thus, she must compensate by increasing the number of traces. The higher the degree of shuffling, the more traces needs to be collected.

Attack Analysis. In the following, we assume that the adversary knows exactly where in the computational trace to attack. That is, for a masking order $d - 1$ and a shuffling degree λ, she knows the range of the $t = \lambda \cdot d$ time points that contain the shares of the target secret variable. In other words, the length of each computational trace $\boldsymbol{v}$ is t. This, intuitively, represents the optimal situation for the adversary.[2] We seek an expression for the success probability of the attack, *i.e.* the probability that the correct key has a higher score than all other key candidates.

The adversary proceeds as above and computes the d'th-order computational trace. However, there will no longer be a single value j such that $C_{k^*}(\boldsymbol{v}_{\phi(j)}, (x_i)_i) = N$ deterministically for the correct key k^*. Thus, we need to know the distribution of γ_k, both for a wrong and a right guess of the key.

Theorem 1. *Consider a masked white-box implementation of order $d - 1$ with shuffling degree λ. Let $p = \binom{t}{d}^{-1}$ where $t = \lambda \cdot d$, and let $F(x; n, q)$ be the CDF (cumulative distribution function) of the binomial distribution with parameters n and q. Let $|\mathcal{K}|$ be the number of possible key values and define*

$$F^{\times}_{\max}(x) = F(x; N, (1-p)\tfrac{1}{|\mathcal{K}|})^{\binom{t}{d}},$$

$$F^{*}_{\max}(x) = F(x; N, p + (1-p)\tfrac{1}{|\mathcal{K}|})^{\binom{t}{d}}.$$

Then the probability of recovering a key using d'th-order DCA with N traces is

$$p_{succ} = \left(\sum_{i=0}^{N} (F^{*}_{\max}(i) - F^{*}_{\max}(i-1)) \cdot F^{\times}_{\max}(i-1) \right)^{|\mathcal{K}|-1}.$$

We prove Theorem 1 in Appendix A. We can use this formula to calculate the required N to obtain a desired probability of success. The number of traces required to obtain 90% success probability for a range of parameters is shown in Table 1. Here, $|\mathcal{K}| = 256$, and the parameters would be typical choices for *e.g.* a protected AES implementation.

---

[2] In practice, the adversary could exhaustively search the correct location of the $(\lambda \cdot d)$-length subtrace in the full computation trace of length t_{full}, which increases the complexity at most t_{full} times.

Attack Complexity. We consider the time complexity of recovering the secret key k^* using the higher-order DCA attack. For a fixed probability of success p_{succ}, let N_d be the number of computational traces required to obtain this probability for a d'th-order implementation. We again assume that $t = \lambda \cdot d$. The cost of computing the higher-order trace is $N_d \cdot \binom{t}{d}$. Then, for each key guess k and each time point in the higher-order trace, the adversary computes C_k. The complexity of this is $|\mathcal{K}| \cdot N_d \cdot \binom{t}{d}$. Thus, the time complexity is $\mathcal{O}\left(|\mathcal{K}| \cdot N_d \cdot \binom{t}{d}\right)$. Table 1 shows the time complexity of the attack for a range of parameters.

Table 1. The number of traces N and the time needed to successfully attack an implementation with $(d-1)$-order masking and shuffling of degree λ with d'th-order DCA. Here, $|\mathcal{K}| = 256$, and we fix the success probability at 90%. The parameters chosen would be typical for a protected AES implementation.

d	λ	$\log_2 N$	$\log_2$ time	d	λ	$\log_2 N$	$\log_2$ time	d	λ	$\log_2 N$	$\log_2$ time
2	8	8.6	23.5	3	8	15.7	34.7	4	8	23.6	46.7
2	16	11.0	28.0	3	16	21.6	43.7	4	16	31.7	59.0

5   Multivariate Higher-Order DCA

In the higher-order DCA, presented in Sect. 4, the adversary tries to correlate each sample of the higher-order trace with the predicted variable independently, finally taking the maximum over the obtained correlation scores. Such an approach is not optimal, as successive samples may carry joint information on the secret. As in the side-channel context, one can take advantage of this joint information by performing a *multivariate attack*, namely an attack in which the distinguisher exploits the multivariate distribution of different samples in the higher-order trace. Emblematic multivariate attacks in the classical side-channel context are the so-called *template attacks* [8]. In the following section, we describe a similar attack in the setting of the DCA adversary.

5.1   Multivariate Higher-Order DCA against Masking and Shuffling

Our proposed multivariate higher-order DCA attack is based on the principle of maximum likelihood. Similar techniques have been adopted in side-channel template attacks. Let K, $(X_i)_i$, and $(\boldsymbol{V}_i)_i$ be random variables representing the subkey k, the public inputs $(x_i)_i$, and the computational traces $(\boldsymbol{v}_i)_i$. The likelihood distinguisher is then defined as

$$\mathsf{L} : \left((\boldsymbol{v}_i)_i, (x_i)_i\right) \mapsto (\ell_k)_{k \in \mathcal{K}},$$
$$\ell_k \propto \Pr\left(K = k \mid (\boldsymbol{V}_i)_i = (\boldsymbol{v}_i)_i \wedge (X_i)_i = (x_i)_i\right), \qquad (1)$$

where $\propto$ means equal up to some factor constant w.r.t. k. To evaluate this likelihood function, we need a model for the distribution of the traces (also called a *template* in the side-channel context). It is well known that if Eq. 1 is evaluated from the true distributions of $(X_i)_i$ and $(\boldsymbol{V}_i)_i$, then the above distinguisher is optimal. This is sound, as in this case, the score is the exact probability that the target subkey equals a key guess k, for all $k \in \mathcal{K}$.

In the following, we will assume that $\boldsymbol{V}_i$ is composed of t uniformly distributed random variables $V_{i,1}, V_{i,2}, \ldots, V_{i,t}$, with the constraint that for a uniformly chosen j, we have $\bigoplus_{l \in \phi(j)} V_{i,l} = \varphi(X_i, K)$. This assumption matches the setting of a masked and shuffled implementation. The public inputs X_i and the subkey K are also assumed to be uniformly distributed and mutually independent. Under this model, we have the following result (see proof in Appendix B):

Proposition 1. *The likelihood distinguisher, Eq. 1, satisfies:*

$$\ell_k \propto \prod_{i=1}^{N} C_k(\boldsymbol{v}_i, x_i),$$

where $C_k(\boldsymbol{v}, x)$ is the number of d-tuples in a trace $\boldsymbol{v}$ with bitwise sum equals to $\varphi(x, k)$, that is $C_k(\boldsymbol{v}, x) = \left| \{ (v_{j_1}, \ldots, v_{j_d}) \; ; \; v_{j_1} \oplus \cdots \oplus v_{j_d} = \varphi(x, k) \} \right|$.

Remark 1. For practical reasons, it is more convenient to evaluate the log-likelihood, that is $\log \ell_k = \sum_{i=1}^{N} \log C_k(\boldsymbol{v}_i, x_i)$. Note that this does not affect the ranking of the key guesses (as the logarithm is a monotonically increasing function) and therefore has no impact on the success probability of the attack.

5.2   Analysis of the Likelihood Distinguisher

In this section we analyze the success probability of the likelihood distinguisher. For the sake of simplicity, we only consider two key guesses, namely the right key guess k^* and a wrong key guess $k^\times$. We then consider their likelihood scores ℓ_{k^*} and $\ell_{k^\times}$ random variables, since

$$\ell_k = \prod_{i=1}^{N} C_k(\boldsymbol{V}_i, X_i),$$

for $k \in \{k^*, k^\times\}$, where $(\boldsymbol{V}_i)_i$ and $(X_i)_i$ are the random variables defined above for the computational traces and the corresponding public inputs. We then consider the probability $p_{\text{succ}} = \Pr\left(\ell_{k^*} > \ell_{k^\times}\right)$ in Theorem 2.

Theorem 2. *For a multivariate d'th-order DCA attack using the likelihood distinguisher on N traces of length t, the probability that a correct key guess is ranked higher than an incorrect key guess is approximately given by*

$$p_{succ} \approx p_{\mathcal{U}} + (1 - p_{\mathcal{U}}) \left(\frac{1}{2} + \frac{1}{2} \text{erf}\left(\frac{\sqrt{N|\mathcal{V}|}}{2\sqrt{q}} \right) \right)$$

where $q = \binom{t}{d}$ and $p_{\mathcal{U}} = 1 - \left(1 - \left(1 - |\mathcal{V}|^{-1} \right)^q \right)^N$.

The total success probability of the attack $p_{\text{full-succ}}$, *i.e.* the probability that the correct key guess has the largest likelihood, is then heuristically $p_{\text{full-succ}} \approx p_{\text{succ}}^{|\mathcal{K}|-1}$. Moreover, it can be checked that $p_{\mathcal{U}} \approx N \cdot (1 - |\mathcal{V}|^{-1})^q$ becomes negligible as q grows. Theorem 2 then implies

$$p_{\text{succ}} = \Theta \left(\text{erf} \left(\frac{\sqrt{N|\mathcal{V}|}}{2\sqrt{q}} \right) \right),$$

from which we deduce that the data complexity of the attack is $N = \Theta(q)$. Namely, the number of required traces N to achieve certain p_{succ} is linear in the number of combinations $q = \binom{t}{d}$. We also have $N = \Theta(q/|\mathcal{V}|)$ to make appear the impact of the definition set $\mathcal{V}$.

In order to prove Theorem 2, we introduce the concept of the *zero-counter event*. Denoted by $\mathcal{U}_k$, this is the event that $C_k(\boldsymbol{v}_i, x_i) = 0$ for at least one $i \in [1, N]$ for a key guess k. Note that this event can never happen for $k = k^*$, since for all i, there exists a j such that $\bigoplus_{l \in \phi(j)} v_{i,l} = \varphi(x_i, k^*)$. Thus, $\Pr(\ell_{k^*} > \ell_{k^\times} \mid \mathcal{U}_{k^\times}) = 1$, since in this case the likelihood $\ell_{k^\times}$ equals zero (or equivalently, the log-likelihood equals $-\infty$). This is intuitively sound, as the right key guess could not give rise to a zero counter for any of the N computational traces. Then, by the law of total probability, we can write

$$p_{\text{succ}} = \Pr(\mathcal{U}_{k^\times}) + \Pr(\neg \mathcal{U}_{k^\times}) \cdot \Pr(\ell_{k^*} > \ell_{k^\times} \mid \neg \mathcal{U}_{k^\times}). \tag{2}$$

We are therefore interested in the probabilities $\Pr(\mathcal{U}_{k^\times})$ and $\Pr(\ell_{k^*} > \ell_{k^\times} \mid \neg \mathcal{U}_{k^\times})$. These are given in the following lemmas.

Lemma 1. *Given N traces of length t, the probability of the zero-counter event for a wrong key guess $k^\times$ in a d'th-order attack is approximately given by*

$$\Pr(\mathcal{U}_{k^\times}) \approx 1 - \left(1 - \left(1 - |\mathcal{V}|^{-1} \right)^q \right)^N,$$

where $q = \binom{t}{d}$.

Lemma 2. *Given N traces of length t, let $q = \binom{t}{d}$, and assume that the zero-counter event does not occur. The probability that a correct key guess has a higher likelihood score than a wrong key guess in a d'th-order attack is approximately*

$$\Pr(\ell_{k^*} > \ell_{k^\times} \mid \neg \mathcal{U}_{k^\times}) \approx \frac{1}{2} + \frac{1}{2}\text{erf} \left(\frac{\sqrt{N|\mathcal{V}|}}{2\sqrt{q}} \right).$$

We prove Lemma 1 in Appendix C and Lemma 2 in Appendix D. Theorem 2 then follows directly from Eq. 2 and these two results.

6   Experimental Verification and Security Evaluation

The proof of Theorem 2 relies on a number of approximations. We therefore verified the accuracy of the estimate by simulating the multivariate higher-order DCA attack for various choices of the parameters d and t. We chose to simulate traces of a masked and shuffled AES implementation, that is, the target secret variable was taken to be $\varphi(x, k^*) = \mathsf{Sbox}_{\mathrm{AES}}(x \oplus k^*)$. The computational traces

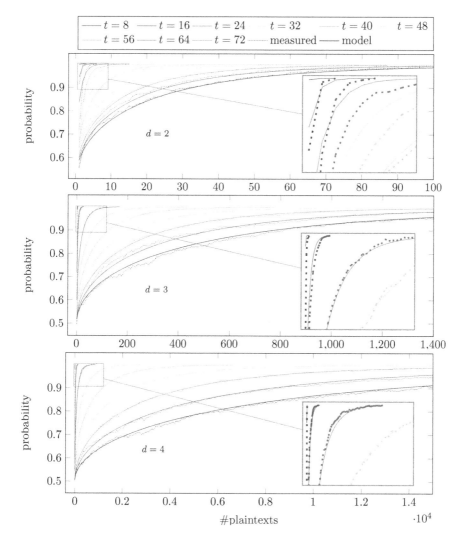

Fig. 2. The measured probability of ranking a correct key higher than an incorrect key in the multivariate higher-order DCA attack, compared to Theorem 2. The measurement is based on 2 000 simulations of the attack. Here, d is the attack order and t is the length of the obtained traces.

were generated according to the model described at the beginning of Sect. 5.1, namely by sampling random values v_j over $\mathcal{V} = \mathbb{F}_{2^8}$ with the constraint that one randomly chosen d-tuple of each trace has XOR-sum $\varphi(x, k^*)$.

We generated traces for $d \in \{2, 3, 4\}$ and $t \in \{8, 16, 24, 32, 40, 48, 56, 64, 72\}$, and calculated the log-likelihood scores for the correct key and a randomly chosen wrong key. This was repeated $2\,000$ times, and the probability $\Pr(\ell_{k^*} > \ell_{k\times})$ was calculated for varying values of N. The results are shown in Fig. 2. The figure shows that the estimate of Theorem 2 is quite accurate in most cases, only deviating from the experimental measurements for very small values of $q = \binom{t}{d}$ ($q < 300$). Note that in practice, this would rarely be a problem. For example, if all shares of the full AES state were shuffled in a first order masked implementation, as described in Sect. 3.3, the smallest trace that would always contain the correct shares would have $q = \binom{2 \cdot 16}{2} = 496$.

The attack complexity of the multivariate higher-order DCA is the same as that of the higher-order DCA, namely $\mathcal{O}\left(|\mathcal{K}| \cdot N_d \cdot \binom{t}{d}\right)$. Using this and Theorem 2 we can provide an estimate of the security level obtained by a masked and shuffled implementation against the DCA adversary. Table 2 shows the complexities of attacking e.g. a protected AES implementation where the operations are shuffled among all 16 state bytes (the shuffling degree is $\lambda = 16$ implying $t = 16 \cdot d$). When fixing $p_{\text{full-succ}}$ at 90%, we see that an implementation which uses 7th order masking will obtain an estimated security level of 85 bits.

Table 2. The number of traces N and the time needed to successfully attack an implementation with $(d-1)$-order masking and shuffling of degree $\lambda = 16$ ($t = 16 \cdot d$) using multivariate d'th-order DCA . Here, $|\mathcal{K}| = 256$, and we fix the success probability at 90%.

d	$\log_2 N$	$\log_2$ time	d	$\log_2 N$	$\log_2$ time	d	$\log_2 N$	$\log_2$ time
3	10.6	32.7	5	21.0	53.5	7	31.6	74.6
4	15.8	43.1	6	26.3	64.1	8	36.9	85.3

Acknowledgment. The fourth author was supported by European Union's Horizon 2020 research and innovation program under the Marie Skłodowska-Curie grant agreement No. 643161.

A Success Probability of Higher-Order DCA (Proof of Theorem 1)

Consider a specific value w_j of the higher-order trace $\mathbf{w}$. Denote by $\mathcal{A}$ the event that w_j corresponds to the combination of the correct shares. The probability of $\mathcal{A}$ occurring, i.e. of choosing the correct d shares out of the t elements of the original computational trace $\mathbf{v}$, is $p = \binom{t}{d}^{-1}$.

Fix some plaintext and the corresponding trace. By the law of total probability, the probability that a value w_j of the d'th order trace is equal to a prediction $s = \varphi(x, k)$ for some key guess k is

$$\Pr(w_j = s) = \Pr(w_j = s|\mathcal{A}) \cdot \Pr(\mathcal{A}) + \Pr(w_j = s|\neg\mathcal{A}) \cdot \Pr(\neg\mathcal{A}).$$

For a wrong key guess, $k^\times \neq k^*$, $\Pr(w_j = s^\times|\mathcal{A}) = 0$, while for a right key guess $\Pr(w_j = s^*|\mathcal{A}) = 1$. In both cases, we have $\Pr(w_j = s|\neg\mathcal{A}) = 1/|\mathcal{K}|$. In total:

$$p^\times = \Pr(w_j = s^\times) = (1 - p)/|\mathcal{K}|,$$
$$p^* = \Pr(w_j = s^*) = p + (1 - p)/|\mathcal{K}|.$$

Thus, for N traces,

$$C_{k^\times}(\boldsymbol{v}_{\phi(j)}, (x_i)_i) \sim \mathrm{Bin}(N, p^\times)$$

for a wrong key guess, and

$$C_{k^*}(\boldsymbol{v}_{\phi(j)}, (x_i)_i) \sim \mathrm{Bin}(N, p^*)$$

for a right key guess. Note that $|\boldsymbol{w}| = \binom{t}{d}$. Let $X_1, \ldots, X_{|\boldsymbol{w}|}$ be distributed as $\mathrm{Bin}(N, p^\times)$. Then $\gamma_{k^\times} \sim \max X_i$, and we denote the CDF by $F^\times_{\max}(x)$. If the X_i were independent, we would have

$$F^\times_{\max}(x) = F(x; N, p^\times)^{\binom{t}{d}}.$$

While the X_i are pairwise independent, they are not mutually independent. However, we find that in practice, the dependence is so weak that $\gamma_{k^\times}$ approximately has CDF $F^\times_{\max}$, even for small values of $|\boldsymbol{w}|$ and N. We define $F^*_{\max}(x)$ similarly.

The attack is successful if $\gamma_{k^*} > \gamma_{k^\times}$ for all $k^\times$. As there are $|\mathcal{K}| - 1$ wrong keys, and all $\gamma_{k^\times}$ are independent and identically distributed, we have $p_{\mathrm{succ}} = \Pr(\gamma_{k^*} > \gamma_{k^\times})^{|\mathcal{K}|-1}$, where

$$\Pr(\gamma_{k^*} > \gamma_{k^\times}) = \sum_{i=0}^{N}(F^*_{\max}(i) - F^*_{\max}(i - 1)) \cdot F^\times_{\max}(i - 1).$$

which concludes the proof.

B   Proof of Proposition 1

Proof. By applying the Bayes' rule, one gets (we skip random variables for the sake of clarity):

$$\Pr\left(k \mid (\boldsymbol{v}_i)_i \wedge (x_i)_i\right) = \frac{\Pr\left((\boldsymbol{v}_i)_i \mid k \wedge (x_i)_i\right) \cdot \Pr\left(k \wedge (x_i)_i\right)}{\Pr\left((\boldsymbol{v}_i)_i \wedge (x_i)_i\right)} \tag{3}$$

By mutual independence of the X_i's and K, we have $\Pr\left(k \wedge (x_i)_i\right) = \frac{1}{|K|}\left(\frac{1}{|X|}\right)^N$ for every $k \in \mathcal{K}$. Moreover, $\Pr\left((v_i)_i \wedge (x_i)_i\right)$ is constant with respect to k. We hence get

$$\Pr\left(k \mid (v_i)_i \wedge (x_i)_i\right) \propto \Pr\left((v_i)_i \mid k \wedge (x_i)_i\right). \tag{4}$$

By mutual independence of the V_i's and the X_i's we further deduce

$$\Pr\left((v_i)_i \mid k \wedge (x_i)_i\right) = \prod_{i=1}^{N} \Pr(v_i \mid k \wedge x_i). \tag{5}$$

For the sake of simplicity we skip the index i in the following. By the law of total probability, we have

$$\Pr(v \mid k \wedge x) = \sum_{\phi(j)} \Pr(\mathcal{S}_{\phi(j)}) \cdot \Pr(v \mid k \wedge x \wedge \mathcal{S}_{\phi(j)}), \tag{6}$$

where $\mathcal{S}_{\phi(j)}$ denotes the event that the set $\phi(j)$ is selected for the sharing of $\varphi(X, K)$. By definition, we have

$$\Pr(\mathcal{S}_{\phi(j)}) = \frac{1}{\binom{t}{d}} \tag{7}$$

and

$$\Pr(v \mid k \wedge x \wedge \mathcal{S}_{\phi(j)}) = \begin{cases} \left(\frac{1}{|V|}\right)^{t-1} & \text{if } \bigoplus_{l \in \phi(j)} v_l = \varphi(x, k) \\ 0 & \text{otherwise} \end{cases} \tag{8}$$

which finally gives

$$\Pr(v \mid k \wedge x) \propto C_k(v, x) . \tag{9}$$

C   Probability of the Zero-Counter Event (Proof of Lemma 1)

We first define $\mathcal{Z}_k$ as the zero-counter event for key k for a *single* computational trace V. Formally,

$$\mathcal{Z}_k = \text{``} \forall j \subseteq \left\{1, \ldots, \binom{t}{d}\right\} : \bigoplus_{i \in \phi(j)} V_i \neq \varphi(X, k) \text{''}.$$

The zero-counter event $\mathcal{Z}_k$ occurs if and only if none of the $q = \binom{t}{d}$ combinations $\bigoplus_{i \in \phi(j)} V_i$ match the predicted value $\varphi(X, k)$. As discussed, $\mathcal{Z}_{k^*}$ never occurs for the correct key guess k^*. For the incorrect key guess $k^\times$, intuitively, the zero-counter probability $\Pr(\mathcal{Z}_{k^\times})$ should quickly become negligible as the number of combinations q grows. While all q combinations are not strictly independent, we can approximate the probability of $\mathcal{Z}_{k^\times}$ by:

$$\Pr(\mathcal{Z}_{k^\times}) \approx \left(1 - \frac{1}{|V|}\right)^q. \tag{10}$$

Table 3. Approximation and estimation of the zero-counter probability.

(t,d)	$(16,2)$	$(16,3)$	$(16,4)$	$(24,2)$	$(24,3)$	$(32,2)$	$(32,3)$
Approximation (10)	0.625	0.112	$8 \cdot 10^{-4}$	0.340	$4 \cdot 10^{-4}$	0.144	$4 \cdot 10^{-9}$
Estimation (prec. $\sim 10^{-3}$)	0.628	0.135	$< 10^{-3}$	0.342	$< 10^{-3}$	0.145	$< 10^{-3}$

We verified this approximation by estimating the zero-counter probability over some sampled computation traces. As illustrated it Table 3, the obtained estimations match the approximation pretty well.

Then, by definition, the zero-counter event for N traces is the union

$$\mathcal{U}_k = \mathcal{Z}_k^{(1)} \vee \mathcal{Z}_k^{(2)} \vee \cdots \vee \mathcal{Z}_k^{(N)},$$

where $\mathcal{Z}_k^{(i)}$ denotes the zero-counter event for k on trace $\boldsymbol{V}_i$. Taking the negation we obtain $\neg \mathcal{U}_{k^\times} = (\neg \mathcal{Z}_k^{(1)}) \wedge (\neg \mathcal{Z}_k^{(2)}) \wedge \cdots \wedge (\neg \mathcal{Z}_k^{(N)})$, and since the zero events $\mathcal{Z}_{k^\times}^{(i)}$ are mutually independent, we get

$$\Pr(\mathcal{U}_{k^\times}) = 1 - \prod_{i=1}^{N} \Pr(\neg \mathcal{Z}_{k^\times}^{(i)}) = 1 - \left(1 - \Pr(\mathcal{Z}_{k^\times})\right)^N.$$

This finishes the proof of Lemma 1.

D   Success Probability with No Zero Counters (Proof of Lemma 2)

If the zero counter event does not occur, we can think of each trace $\boldsymbol{V}_i$ as a random variable uniformly distributed over $\mathcal{V}^t$. Since the public input X_i is also random, the counters $C_k(\boldsymbol{V}, X)$ follow some probability distribution. In order to prove Lemma 2, we first prove the following result regarding these distributions.

Lemma 3. *Let k^* and $k^\times$ be a right and wrong key guess. Let $q = \binom{t}{d}$ and $\kappa = (q-1)\frac{1}{|\mathcal{V}|}$. Then for a trace of length t and a d'th-order attack,*

$$C_{k^*}(\boldsymbol{V}, X) \sim \mathcal{N}(\kappa+1, \kappa) \quad \text{and} \quad C_{k^\times}(\boldsymbol{V}, X) \sim \mathcal{N}(\kappa, \kappa),$$

where $\mathcal{N}(\mu, \sigma^2)$ denotes the normal distribution with mean μ and variance σ^2.

Proof. Let $\delta : \mathcal{V}^2 \to \{0,1\}$ be the function defined as

$$\delta(v_1, v_2) = \begin{cases} 1 & \text{if } v_1 = v_2, \\ 0 & \text{otherwise.} \end{cases}$$

The counter $C_k(\boldsymbol{V}, X)$ can be rewritten as a sum $C_k(\boldsymbol{V}, X) = \sum_{j=1}^{q} \delta(W_j, \varphi(X, k))$, where the variables $(W_j)_j$ are defined as the $q = \binom{t}{d}$ combinations $\bigoplus_{i \in \phi(j)} V_i$. We recall that for one index j we have $W_j = \varphi(X, k^*)$, whereas for the other indices the W_j are randomly distributed independently of X. The counter expectation then satisfies

$$E\big(C_k(\boldsymbol{V}, X)\big) = \sum_{j=1}^{q} E\big(\delta(W_j, \varphi(X, k))\big) = \begin{cases} (q-1)\frac{1}{|\mathcal{V}|} & \text{if } k \neq k^*, \\ (q-1)\frac{1}{|\mathcal{V}|} + 1 & \text{if } k = k^*. \end{cases}$$

On the other hand, the counter variance can be expressed as:

$$Var\big(C_k(\boldsymbol{V}, X)\big) = \sum_{j=1}^{q} Var\big(\delta(W_j, \varphi(X, k))\big)$$
$$+ 2 \sum_{1 \leq j < j' \leq q} Cov\big(\delta(W_j, \varphi(X, k)), \delta(W_{j'}, \varphi(X, k))\big).$$

It can be checked that the covariances will be equal to 0 most of the time. Indeed, the covariances are non-zero only when $W_j \oplus W_{j'} = \varphi(X, k^*)$, which never happens when d is odd and which happens for few pairs (j, j') when d is even. Therefore these covariance terms will only have a small impact on the overall variance. Moreover, it can be checked that this impact is negative, *i.e.* it reduces the variance.[3] Therefore we will ignore the sum of covariances, which yields a correct result when d is odd and a slight overestimation when d is even. We then have

$$Var\big(\delta(W_j, \varphi(X, k))\big) = \begin{cases} \frac{1}{|\mathcal{V}|}\big(1 - \frac{1}{|\mathcal{V}|}\big) & \text{if } j \neq j^*, \\ 0 & \text{if } j = j^*, \end{cases}$$

where j^* denotes the index of the right combination matching $\varphi(X, k^*)$. Combining the two above equations gives:

$$Var\big(C_k(\boldsymbol{V}, X)\big) = (q-1)\frac{1}{|\mathcal{V}|}\left(1 - \frac{1}{|\mathcal{V}|}\right) \approx (q-1)\frac{1}{|\mathcal{V}|}.$$

Since the counter is defined as a sum of *somewhat independent* random variables, we can soundly approximate its distribution by a Gaussian, and setting $\kappa = (q-1)\frac{1}{|\mathcal{V}|}$ concludes the proof.   □

In the above proof, we use that the $\delta(W_j, \varphi(X, k))$ are somewhat independent. By *somewhat independent* we mean that these variables are pairwise independent (for most or all of them, as discussed). Note that variants of the central limit theorem exist that take some form of dependence between the summed variables into account. We have experimentally verified that the Gaussian approximation is sound for various parameters (t, d).

---

[3] Most of the time we have $\varphi(X, k^*) \neq 0$ so that the pairs (j, j') with $W_j \oplus W_{j'} = \varphi(X, k^*)$ are such that $W_j \neq W_{j'}$ with high probability. In that case $\delta(W_j, \varphi(X, k)) = 1$ implies $\delta(W_{j'}, \varphi(X, k)) = 0$ and conversely which yields a negative covariance.

Using Lemma 3, we can now prove Lemma 2. Following Remark 1, we will focus on the log-likelihood, *i.e.* we consider

$$\Pr(\ell_{k^*} > \ell_{k^\times} \mid \neg \mathcal{U}_{k^\times}) = \Pr\left(\log \ell_{k^*} - \log \ell_{k^\times} > 0 \mid \neg \mathcal{U}_{k^\times}\right),$$

$$\log \ell_{k^*} - \log \ell_{k^\times} = \sum_{i=1}^{N} \underbrace{\log C_{k^*}(\boldsymbol{V}_i, X_i) - \log C_{k^\times}(\boldsymbol{V}_i, X_i)}_{Y_i}.$$

As introduced above, we denote by Y_i the difference between the log-counters for the trace $\boldsymbol{V}_i$. Since the Y_i are mutually independent and identically distributed, the central limit theorem implies that, for N sufficiently large,

$$\frac{1}{N}(\log \ell_{k^*} - \log \ell_{k^\times}) \sim \mathcal{N}\left(\mu_Y, \sigma_Y^2 N^{-1}\right) \quad \text{with} \quad \begin{cases} \mu_Y = \mathrm{E}(Y), \\ \sigma_Y^2 = \mathrm{Var}(Y), \end{cases}$$

for $Y = \log C_{k^*}(\boldsymbol{V}, X) - \log C_{k^\times}(\boldsymbol{V}, X)$. Thus

$$\Pr(\ell_{k^*} > \ell_{k^\times} \mid \neg \mathcal{U}_{k^\times}) = 1 - \Phi_{\mu_Y, \sigma_Y^2/N}(0) = \frac{1}{2} + \frac{1}{2}\mathrm{erf}\left(\frac{\sqrt{N}\,\mu_Y}{\sqrt{2}\,\sigma_Y}\right), \qquad (11)$$

where $\Phi_{\mu,\sigma}$ is the CDF of $\mathcal{N}(\mu, \sigma^2)$. By the heuristic assumption that $C_{k^*}(\boldsymbol{V}, X)$ and $C_{k^\times}(\boldsymbol{V}, X)$ are mutually independent, and using the Taylor expansion of the logarithm at $\mathrm{E}(C)$, as well as Lemma 3, we have

$$\mu_Y \approx \log(\kappa + 1) - \frac{\kappa}{2(\kappa+1)^2} - \log \kappa + \frac{\kappa}{2\kappa^2} \approx \frac{1}{\kappa}, \quad \text{and} \quad \sigma_Y^2 \approx 2\frac{\kappa}{\kappa^2} = \frac{2}{\kappa},$$

where the approximation of the mean is sound if κ is large enough (*e.g.* $\kappa > 10$). Inserting these approximations into Eq. 11, remembering that $\kappa = (q-1)\frac{1}{|\mathcal{V}|} \approx \frac{q}{|\mathcal{V}|}$, finishes the proof.

References

1. CHES 2017 Capture the Flag Challenge - The WhibOx Contest, An ECRYPT White-Box Cryptography Competition. https://whibox.cr.yp.to/. Accessed Oct 2017
2. Billet, O., Gilbert, H., Ech-Chatbi, C.: Cryptanalysis of a white box AES implementation. In: Handschuh, H., Hasan, M.A. (eds.) SAC 2004. LNCS, vol. 3357, pp. 227–240. Springer, Heidelberg (2004). https://doi.org/10.1007/978-3-540-30564-4_16
3. Biryukov, A., Udovenko, A.: Attacks and countermeasures for white-box designs. In: Peyrin, T., Galbraith, S. (eds.) ASIACRYPT 2018. LNCS, vol. 11273, pp. 373–402. Springer, Cham (2018). https://doi.org/10.1007/978-3-030-03329-3_13
4. Bos, J.W., Hubain, C., Michiels, W., Teuwen, P.: Differential computation analysis: hiding your white-box designs is not enough. In: Gierlichs, B., Poschmann, A.Y. (eds.) CHES 2016. LNCS, vol. 9813, pp. 215–236. Springer, Heidelberg (2016). https://doi.org/10.1007/978-3-662-53140-2_11

5. Bringer, J., Chabanne, H., Dottax, E.: Perturbing and protecting a traceable block cipher. In: Leitold, H., Markatos, E.P. (eds.) CMS 2006. LNCS, vol. 4237, pp. 109–119. Springer, Heidelberg (2006). https://doi.org/10.1007/11909033_10

6. Bringer, J., Chabanne, H., Dottax, E.: White box cryptography: another attempt. IACR Cryptology ePrint Archive 2006, 468 (2006)

7. Chari, S., Jutla, C.S., Rao, J.R., Rohatgi, P.: Towards sound approaches to counteract power-analysis attacks. In: Wiener, M. (ed.) CRYPTO 1999. LNCS, vol. 1666, pp. 398–412. Springer, Heidelberg (1999). https://doi.org/10.1007/3-540-48405-1_26

8. Chari, S., Rao, J.R., Rohatgi, P.: Template attacks. In: Kaliski, B.S., Koç, K., Paar, C. (eds.) CHES 2002. LNCS, vol. 2523, pp. 13–28. Springer, Heidelberg (2003). https://doi.org/10.1007/3-540-36400-5_3

9. Chow, S., Eisen, P., Johnson, H., van Oorschot, P.C.: A white-box DES implementation for DRM applications. In: Feigenbaum, J. (ed.) DRM 2002. LNCS, vol. 2696, pp. 1–15. Springer, Heidelberg (2003). https://doi.org/10.1007/978-3-540-44993-5_1

10. Chow, S., Eisen, P., Johnson, H., Van Oorschot, P.C.: White-box cryptography and an AES implementation. In: Nyberg, K., Heys, H. (eds.) SAC 2002. LNCS, vol. 2595, pp. 250–270. Springer, Heidelberg (2003). https://doi.org/10.1007/3-540-36492-7_17

11. Coron, J.-S.: Higher order masking of look-up tables. In: Nguyen, P.Q., Oswald, E. (eds.) EUROCRYPT 2014. LNCS, vol. 8441, pp. 441–458. Springer, Heidelberg (2014). https://doi.org/10.1007/978-3-642-55220-5_25

12. Coron, J.-S., Kizhvatov, I.: Analysis and improvement of the random delay countermeasure of CHES 2009. In: Mangard, S., Standaert, F.-X. (eds.) CHES 2010. LNCS, vol. 6225, pp. 95–109. Springer, Heidelberg (2010). https://doi.org/10.1007/978-3-642-15031-9_7

13. Coron, J.-S., Prouff, E., Rivain, M., Roche, T.: Higher-order side channel security and mask refreshing. In: Moriai, S. (ed.) FSE 2013. LNCS, vol. 8424, pp. 410–424. Springer, Heidelberg (2014). https://doi.org/10.1007/978-3-662-43933-3_21

14. Fisher, R.A., Yates, F., et al.: Statistical tables for biological, agricultural and medical research. Statistical tables for biological, agricultural and medical research (1938)

15. Goubin, L., Paillier, P., Rivain, M., Wang, J.: How to reveal the secrets of an obscure white-box implementation. Cryptology ePrint Archive, Report 2018/098 (2018). https://eprint.iacr.org/2018/098

16. Goubin, L., Patarin, J.: DES and differential power analysis the "Duplication" method. In: Koç, Ç.K., Paar, C. (eds.) CHES 1999. LNCS, vol. 1717, pp. 158–172. Springer, Heidelberg (1999). https://doi.org/10.1007/3-540-48059-5_15

17. Karroumi, M.: Protecting white-box AES with dual ciphers. In: Rhee, K.-H., Nyang, D.H. (eds.) ICISC 2010. LNCS, vol. 6829, pp. 278–291. Springer, Heidelberg (2011). https://doi.org/10.1007/978-3-642-24209-0_19

18. Kerckhoffs, A.: La cryptographic militaire. J. Sci. Mil. **IX**, 5–38 (1883). https://www.petitcolas.net/kerckhoffs/crypto_militaire_1.pdf

19. Lepoint, T., Rivain, M., De Mulder, Y., Roelse, P., Preneel, B.: Two attacks on a white-box AES implementation. In: Lange, T., Lauter, K., Lisoněk, P. (eds.) SAC 2013. LNCS, vol. 8282, pp. 265–285. Springer, Heidelberg (2014). https://doi.org/10.1007/978-3-662-43414-7_14

20. Mangard, S., Oswald, E., Popp, T.: Power Analysis Attacks - Revealing Thesecrets of Smart Cards. Springer, Boston (2007). https://doi.org/10.1007/978-0-387-38162-6

21. Michiels, W., Gorissen, P., Hollmann, H.D.L.: Cryptanalysis of a generic class of white-box implementations. In: Avanzi, R.M., Keliher, L., Sica, F. (eds.) SAC 2008. LNCS, vol. 5381, pp. 414–428. Springer, Heidelberg (2009). https://doi.org/10.1007/978-3-642-04159-4_27

22. De Mulder, Y., Roelse, P., Preneel, B.: Cryptanalysis of the Xiao – Lai white-box AES implementation. In: Knudsen, L.R., Wu, H. (eds.) SAC 2012. LNCS, vol. 7707, pp. 34–49. Springer, Heidelberg (2013). https://doi.org/10.1007/978-3-642-35999-6_3

23. De Mulder, Y., Wyseur, B., Preneel, B.: Cryptanalysis of a perturbated white-box AES implementation. In: Gong, G., Gupta, K.C. (eds.) INDOCRYPT 2010. LNCS, vol. 6498, pp. 292–310. Springer, Heidelberg (2010). https://doi.org/10.1007/978-3-642-17401-8_21

24. Rivain, M., Prouff, E.: Provably secure higher-order masking of AES. In: Mangard, S., Standaert, F.-X. (eds.) CHES 2010. LNCS, vol. 6225, pp. 413–427. Springer, Heidelberg (2010). https://doi.org/10.1007/978-3-642-15031-9_28

25. Rivain, M., Prouff, E., Doget, J.: Higher-order masking and shuffling for software implementations of block ciphers. In: Clavier, C., Gaj, K. (eds.) CHES 2009. LNCS, vol. 5747, pp. 171–188. Springer, Heidelberg (2009). https://doi.org/10.1007/978-3-642-04138-9_13

26. Strobel, D., Paar, C.: An efficient method for eliminating random delays in power traces of embedded software. In: Kim, H. (ed.) ICISC 2011. LNCS, vol. 7259, pp. 48–60. Springer, Heidelberg (2012). https://doi.org/10.1007/978-3-642-31912-9_4

27. Tolhuizen, L.: Improved cryptanalysis of an AES implementation. In: Proceedings of the 33rd WIC Symposium on Information Theory, 2012. WIC (Werkgemeenschap voor Inform.-en Communicatietheorie) (2012)

28. Veyrat-Charvillon, N., Medwed, M., Kerckhof, S., Standaert, F.-X.: Shuffling against side-channel attacks: a comprehensive study with cautionary note. In: Wang, X., Sako, K. (eds.) ASIACRYPT 2012. LNCS, vol. 7658, pp. 740–757. Springer, Heidelberg (2012). https://doi.org/10.1007/978-3-642-34961-4_44

29. Xiao, Y., Lai, X.: A secure implementation of white-box AES. In: Computer Science and its Applications, CSA 2009, pp. 1–6. IEEE (2009)

Side-Channel Analysis Methodologies

Gradient Visualization for General Characterization in Profiling Attacks

Loïc Masure[1,2(✉)], Cécile Dumas[1], and Emmanuel Prouff[2,3]

[1] Univ. Grenoble Alpes, CEA, LETI, DSYS, CESTI, 38000 Grenoble, France
{loic.masure,cecile.dumas}@cea.fr
[2] Sorbonne Universités, UPMC Univ Paris 06, POLSYS,
UMR 7606, LIP6, 75005 Paris, France
[3] ANSSI, Paris, France
emmanuel.prouff@ssi.gouv.fr

Abstract. In Side-Channel Analysis (SCA), several papers have shown that neural networks could be trained to efficiently extract sensitive information from implementations running on embedded devices. This paper introduces a new tool called *Gradient Visualization* that aims to proceed a post-mortem information leakage characterization after the successful training of a neural network. It relies on the computation of the gradient of the loss function used during the training. The gradient is no longer computed with respect to the model parameters, but with respect to the input trace components. Thus, it can accurately highlight temporal moments where sensitive information leaks. We theoretically show that this method, based on *Sensitivity Analysis*, may be used to efficiently localize points of interest in the SCA context. The efficiency of the proposed method does not depend on the particular countermeasures that may be applied to the measured traces as long as the profiled neural network can still learn in presence of such difficulties. In addition, the characterization can be made for each trace individually. We verified the soundness of our proposed method on simulated data and on experimental traces from a public side-channel database. Eventually we empirically show that the Sensitivity Analysis is at least as good as state-of-the-art characterization methods, in presence (or not) of countermeasures.

Keywords: Side Channel Analysis · Profiling attacks · Deep Learning · Points of Interest · Characterization

1 Introduction

Side-channel analysis is a class of cryptanalytic attacks that exploits weaknesses of a physical implementation of a cryptographic primitive. During its execution, the primitive processes values, called *sensitive*, that both depend on a piece of public data (*e.g.* a plaintext) and on some chunk of a secret value (*e.g.* a key). As the processing is invertible, knowing the value of this variable (or at least having some information about it) and the plaintext enables an attacker

© Springer Nature Switzerland AG 2019
I. Polian and M. Stöttinger (Eds.): COSADE 2019, LNCS 11421, pp. 145–167, 2019.
https://doi.org/10.1007/978-3-030-16350-1_9

to recover the piece of secret key. Secure cryptographic algorithms such as the *Advanced Encryption Standard* (AES) can then be defeated by recovering each byte of the secret key separately thanks to a *divide-and-conquer* strategy, thereby breaking the high complexity usually required to defeat such an algorithm. This information is usually gathered thanks to physical leakages such as the power consumption or the electromagnetic emanations measured on the target device. Actually, conducting an SCA is equivalent as studying the conditional probability distribution of the sensitive variables given the physical measure. It can be done for example through the computation of statistics such as a difference of means [16] or a correlation coefficient [3].

For the specific type of SCA called *profiling attacks*, an attacker will try to estimate the whole conditional distribution thanks to a profiling phase during which she has access to an open sample for which she knows the value of the target variable. Such an access allows her to estimate the conditional distribution. Historically, *Gaussian Template Attacks* (GTA) have first been proposed in the early 2000's [7]. Their complexity is however strongly impacted by the number of time samples contained in the exploited traces. A first pre-processing step is hence required to extract, from each trace, few points called *Points of Interest* (PoIs). Tools like *Signal-to-Noise Ratio* (SNR) can efficiently extract those PoIs [22] (see Sect. 4.3). Other characterization methods based on statistical tools such as the *T-Test* [24] or the χ^2-*Test* [26] may also be used.[1] However, in presence of countermeasures such as masking or de-synchronization [33], both estimation with GTA and PoIs extraction with SNR are no longer efficient (or at least much less). Likewise, other dimensionality reduction techniques like dedicated variants of Principal Component Analysis (PCA) [4,8,9,11,37] or *Kernel Discriminant Analysis* (KDA) [6] can be used, without guarantee that relevant components will be extracted.

Recently, the SCA community has benefited the resurgence of *Convolutional Neural Networks* (CNNs) in the 2010's [17] to apply them to profiling attacks, as first proposed in [12,20,23]. They are seen as a black-box tool and their results have been afterwards experimentally shown to be robust to the most common countermeasures, namely masking [21] and de-synchronization [5]. Their main advantage is that they do not require pre-processing, and are at least as efficient as the other state-of-the-art profiling attacks. However, from the evaluator's point-of-view, this is not sufficient. On the one hand she wants to make sure that a CNN attack succeeded for good reasons *i.e.* that the learned model can generalize to new data. On the other hand the evaluator also wants to help the developer to localize and understand where the vulnerability comes from in order to remove or at least reduce it. This issue is part of a more general problematic in Deep Learning based systems, namely their *explainability* and *interpretability*. To address it, a theoretical framework has recently been proposed in [25], and several

---

[1] In practice, the latter methods usually emphasize the same PoIs than SNR. This claim has been empirically verified on the data considered in this study. For this reason, we will only focus on the SNR when challenging the effectiveness of our method in the remaining of this paper.

methods have been tested to tackle the issue. In particular, some computer vision research groups have studied the so-called *Sensitivity Analysis* [35,36] which is derived from the computation of the loss function gradient with respect to the input data during the training phase.

In this paper, we propose to apply a particular Sensitivity Analysis method called *Gradient Visualization* (GV) in order to better understand how a CNN can learn to predict the sensitive variable based on the analysis of a single trace. The main claim is that CNN based models succeed in discriminating PoIs from non-informative points, and their localization can be deduced by simply look-ing at the gradient of the loss function with respect to the input traces for a trained model. We theoretically show that this method can be used to localize PoIs in the case of a perfect model. The efficiency of the proposed method does not decrease when countermeasures like masking or misalignment are applied. In addition, the characterization can be made for each trace individually. We verified the efficiency of our proposed method on simulated data and on exper-imental traces from a public Side Channel database. We empirically show that Gradient Visualization is at least as good as state-of-the-art characterization methods, in presence or not of different countermeasures.

The paper is organized as follows. In Sect. 3 we start by considering the optimal model an ideal attacker may get during profiling, and we deduce some properties of its derivatives with respect to the input traces that can be related to the PoIs. In Sect. 4 we use these properties on a model estimated with CNNs and we explain how to practically implement the visualization method. A toy example applied on simulated data is proposed for illustration. Sections 5 and 6 are eventually dedicated to an experimental validation of the effectiveness of our proposal in realistic attacks scenarios.

2 Preliminaries

2.1 Notations

Throughout the paper we use calligraphic letters as $\mathcal{X}$ to denote sets, the corre-sponding upper-case letter X to denote random variables (resp. random vectors $\mathbf{X}$) over $\mathcal{X}$, and the corresponding lower-case letter x (resp. $\mathbf{x}$ for vectors) to denote realizations of X (resp. $\mathbf{X}$). The i-th entry of a vector $\mathbf{x}$ is denoted by $\mathbf{x}[i]$. We denote the probability space of a set $\mathcal{X}$ by $\mathcal{P}(\mathcal{X})$. If $\mathcal{X}$ is discrete, it corresponds to the set of vectors $[0,1]^{|\mathcal{X}|}$ such that the coordinates sum to 1. If a random variable X is drawn from a distribution $\mathcal{D}$, then $\mathcal{D}^N$ denotes the joint distribution over the sequence of N i.i.d. random variables of same proba-bility distribution than X. The symbol $\mathbb{E}$ denotes the expected value, and might be subscripted by a random variable $\mathbb{E}_X$, or by a probability distribution $\underset{X \sim \mathcal{D}}{\mathbb{E}}$ to specify under which probability distribution it is computed. Likewise, Var denotes the variance of a random variable. If $f : x, y \mapsto f(x, y)$ is a multivariate function, $\frac{\partial}{\partial x}$ denotes the partial derivative with respect to the input variable x. Likewise, if f is a function from $\mathbb{R}^n$ to $\mathbb{R}$, then $\nabla f(\mathbf{x})$ denotes the gradient of

f computed in $\mathbf{x} \in \mathbb{R}^n$, which corresponds to the vector of the partial derivatives with respect to each coordinate of $\mathbf{x}$ respectively. If there is an ambiguity, the gradient will be denoted $\nabla_{\mathbf{x}} f(\mathbf{x}, \mathbf{y})$ to emphasize that the gradient is computed with respect to $\mathbf{x}$ only. Eventually if f is a function from $\mathbb{R}^n$ to $\mathbb{R}^m$, then $J_f(\mathbf{x}) \in \mathbb{R}^{m,n}$ denotes the (m, n) matrix whose rows are the transposed gradient of each elementary function $\mathbf{x} \mapsto f(\mathbf{x})[i] \in \mathbb{R}$. The output of a cryptographic primitive $\mathbf{C}$ is considered as the target sensitive variable $Z = \mathbf{C}(P, K)$, where P denotes some public variable, e.g. a plaintext chunk, where K denotes the part of secret key the attacker aims to retrieve, and where Z takes values in $\mathcal{Z} = \{s_1, \ldots, s_{|\mathcal{Z}|}\}$. Among all the possible values K may take, $k^\star$ will denote the right key hypothesis. A side-channel trace will be viewed as a realization of a D-dimensional random column vector $\mathbf{X} \in \mathcal{X} \subset \mathbb{R}^D$.

2.2 Profiling Attacks

We will consider attacking a device through a profiling attack, made of the following steps:

- *Profiling acquisition*: a dataset of N_p *profiling traces* is acquired on the prototype device: $S_p \triangleq \{(\mathbf{x}_1, z_1), \ldots, (\mathbf{x}_{N_p}, z_{N_p})\}$.
- *Model building*: a model that returns a discrete probability distribution (pdf) $F(\mathbf{x})$ is built. If the model is accurate, the returned discrete pdf, viewed as a vector, is assumed to be a good approximation of the conditional pdf $\Pr[Z | \mathbf{X} = \mathbf{x}]$.
- *Attack acquisition*: a dataset of N_a *attack traces* is acquired on the target device: $S_a \triangleq \{(\mathbf{x}_1, z_1), \ldots, (\mathbf{x}_{N_a}, z_{N_a})\}$.
- *Predictions*: a prediction vector is computed on each attack trace, based on the previously built model: $\mathbf{y}_i = F(\mathbf{x}_i), i \in [\![1, N_a]\!]$. It assigns a score to each key hypothesis, for each trace.
- *Guessing*: the scores are combined over all the attack traces to output a *likelihood* for each key hypothesis; the candidate with the highest likelihood is predicted to be the right key.

Let us denote by $g_{S_a}(k^\star)$ the actual rank of the correct key hypothesis returned by the attack. If $g_{S_a}(k^\star) = 1$, then the attack is considered as *successful*. More details about the score vector and the rank definitions can be found in Appendix A. The difficulty of attacking the target device is often defined as the number of traces required to get a successful attack. As many random factors may be involved during the attack, it is preferred to study its expected value, the so-called **G**uessing **E**ntropy (GE) [38]:

$$\mathrm{GE}(N_a) \triangleq \underset{S_a}{\mathbb{E}} \left[g_{S_a}(k^\star) \right]. \tag{1}$$

The goal of an evaluator is therefore to find a model F that minimizes N_a such that $\mathrm{GE}(N_a) < 2$. We will assume that this is equivalent to the problem of accurately estimating the conditional probability distribution $\mathbf{x} \mapsto \Pr[Z | \mathbf{X} = \mathbf{x}]$.

As mentioned in the introduction, we distinguish the security evaluator as a particular attacker who additionally wishes to interpret the attack results. One step of this diagnosis is to temporally localize where the information leakage appeared in **x**. This task is usually called *characterization*. It consists in emphasizing *Points of Interest* (PoIs) where the information leakage may come from. Section 4.3 will present an usual characterization technique while a new method will be introduced through this paper.

3   Study of an Optimal Model

In this section, we address the evaluator interpretation problem in the ideal situation when the conditional distribution is known (*i.e.* when the model is perfect). The latter will be denoted as F^*. We will show how the study of the derivatives of such a model with respect to each coordinate of an input trace can highlight information about our PoIs. To this end, we need two assumptions.

Assumption 1 (Sparsity). *There only exists a small set of coordinates* $\mathcal{I}_Z \triangleq \{t_1, \ldots, t_C | C \ll D\}$ *such that* $\Pr[Z|\boldsymbol{X}] = \Pr[Z|\boldsymbol{X}[t_1], \ldots, \boldsymbol{X}[t_C]]$.

Assumption 2 (Regularity). *The conditional probability distribution* F^* *is differentiable over* $\mathcal{X}$ *and thereby continuous.*

Informally, Assumption 1 tells that the leaking information is non-uniformly distributed over the trace. Both assumptions are realistic in a SCA context (this point is discussed in Appendix B).

Once Assumptions 1 and 2 are stated, we may want to observe their impact on the properties verified by the optimal model derivatives. For such a purpose we start by considering an example on a trace **x**. Figure 1 (left) illustrates such a trace in blue, and the green line depicts a PoI, namely a peak of SNR (in other words the set of PoIs $\mathcal{I}_Z$ is reduced to a single time index). The prediction pdfs $F^*(\mathbf{x})$ are given at the right of the same figure: they are here represented by a histogram over the 256 possible values of a byte. We may fairly suppose that a slight variation on one coordinate that does not belong to $\mathcal{I}_Z$ (dotted in gray in Fig. 1, left) should not radically change the output of the optimal model. The pdf remains the same, as the gray bars and blue bars perfectly match in Fig. 1 (right). However, applying a slight variation on the coordinate from $\mathcal{I}_Z$ (dotted in red in Fig. 1, left) may radically change the output distribution (red bars in Fig. 1, right).

This example illustrates the more general idea that small variations applied to the trace at a coordinate $t \in \mathcal{I}_Z$ should radically change the output prediction whereas small variations at $t \notin \mathcal{I}_Z$ have no impact. As a consequence, if F^* is differentiable with respect to the input trace (according to Assumption 2), there should exist $s \in \mathcal{Z}$ such that:

$$\frac{\partial}{\partial \mathbf{x}[t]} F^*(\mathbf{x})[s] \begin{cases} \neq 0 & \text{iff } t \in \mathcal{I}_Z \\ \approx 0 & \text{iff } t \notin \mathcal{I}_Z \end{cases}. \tag{2}$$

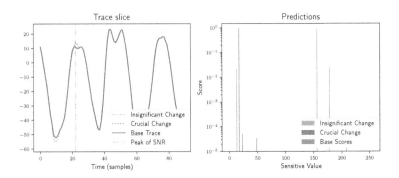

Fig. 1. Illustration of the Sensitivity Analysis principle. Left: a piece of trace. $t \in \mathcal{I}_Z$ is depicted by the green line, and slight variations dotted in red and gray. Right: predictions of the optimal model. (Color figure online)

The latter observation can be stated in terms of the Jacobian matrix of the estimator, denoted as $J_{F^*}(\mathbf{x})$. Its coefficients should be zero almost everywhere, except in columns $t \in \mathcal{I}_Z$:

$$J_{F^*}(\mathbf{x}) = \begin{pmatrix} \mathbf{0} \ldots \mathbf{0} \, \mathbf{Y}_t \, \mathbf{0} \ldots \mathbf{0} \end{pmatrix} \tag{3}$$

where $\mathbf{Y}_t = \left(\frac{\partial}{\partial \mathbf{x}[t]} F^*(\mathbf{x})[s_1], \frac{\partial}{\partial \mathbf{x}[t]} F^*(\mathbf{x})[s_2], \ldots, \frac{\partial}{\partial \mathbf{x}[t]} F^*(\mathbf{x}) \left[s_{|\mathcal{Z}|} \right] \right)^{\mathsf{T}}$ and $\mathbf{0}$ denotes the zero column vector.

The properties verified by the Jacobian matrix in (3) form the cornerstone of this paper, as it implies that we can guess from this matrix whether a coordinate from an input trace belongs to $\mathcal{I}_Z$ or not, *i.e.* whether a coordinate has been recognized as a PoI when designing the optimal model F^*. Such a technique is part of *Sensitivity Analysis*.[2] Moreover, except Assumption 1, no more assumption on the nature of the leakage model is required.

4   Our Characterization Proposal

So far we have shown that the Jacobian of an optimal model may emphasize PoIs. In practice however, the evaluator does not have access to the optimal model, but a trained estimation of it. A natural idea is hence to look at the Jacobian matrix of the model estimation, hoping that its coefficients will be close to the optimal model derivatives. Here we follow this idea in contexts where the approximation is modeled by training *Convolutional Neural Networks*, described in Sect. 4.1 (discussions can be found in Appendix C about this approximation). Section 4.2 illustrates our claim with a toy example. Finally, Sect. 4.3 is dedicated to the comparison of our approach with state-of-the-art methods for leakage characterization.

---

[2] A general definition of *Sensitivity Analysis* is the study of how the uncertainty in the output of a mathematical model or system (numerical or otherwise) can be apportioned to different sources of uncertainty in its inputs [1].

4.1   Gradient Approximation with Neural Networks

Neural Networks (NN) [19] aim at constructing a function $F \colon \mathcal{X} \rightarrow \mathcal{P}(\mathcal{Z})$ composed of several simple operations called *layers*. All the layers are entirely parametrized by (a) a real vector called *trainable weights* and denoted by θ that can be automatically set; (b) other parameters defining the general architecture of the model which are gathered under the term *hyper-parameter*. The latter ones are defined by the attacker/evaluator.

Convolutional Neural Networks (CNN) form a specific type of Neural Network where particular constraints are applied on the trainable weights [18]. The training phase consists in an automatic tuning of the trainable weights and it is done *via* an iterative approach that locally applies the Stochastic Gradient Descent algorithm to minimize a *loss function* that quantifies the classification error of the function F over the training set. For further details, the interested reader may refer to [13].

To accurately and efficiently compute the Jacobian matrix of a CNN, an algorithm called *backward propagation* (or back-propagation) can exactly compute the derivatives with the same time complexity as computing $F(\mathbf{x}, \theta)$ [13]. As a consequence, computing such a matrix can be done with a negligible overhead during an iteration of a Stochastic Gradient Descent. Actually the modern Deep Learning libraries [2,28] are optimized to compute the required derivatives for Stochastic Gradient Descent in the back-propagation, so the Jacobian matrix is never explicitly stored, and it is easier to get the loss function gradient with respect to the input trace $\nabla_{\mathbf{x}}\ell(F(\mathbf{x}, \theta), z^{*})$, where $\ell \colon \mathcal{P}(\mathcal{Z}) \times \mathcal{Z} \rightarrow \mathbb{R}_{+}$ denotes the loss function, and z^{*} denotes the true sensitive value. Hopefully, studying either the latter one or $J_{F}(\mathbf{x})$ is fairly equivalent, as one coordinate of the loss function gradient is a function of elements from the corresponding column in the Jacobian matrix:

$$\nabla_{\mathbf{x}}\ell(F(\mathbf{x}, \theta), z) = J_{F}(\mathbf{x}, \theta)^{T} \nabla_{\mathbf{y}}\ell(F(\mathbf{x}, \theta), z). \tag{4}$$

That is why we propose to visualize the latter gradient to characterize PoIs in the context of a CNN attack, instead of the Jacobian matrix (unless explicit mention). To be more precise, we visualize the absolute value of each coordinate of the gradient in order to get the sensitivity magnitude. In the following, such a method is named *Gradient Visualization* (GV for short).

4.2   Example on Simulated Data

To illustrate and explain the relevance of the GV method, and before going on experimental data, we here propose to apply it on a toy example, aiming at simulating simple D-dimensional leakages from an n-bit sensitive variable Z. The traces are defined such that for every $t \in [\![1, D]\!]$:

$$\mathbf{x}_{i}[t] = \begin{cases} U_{i} + B_{i}, & \text{if } t \notin \{t_{1}, \ldots, t_{m}\} \\ z_{t,i} + B_{i} & \text{otherwise} \end{cases}, \tag{5}$$

where $(U_i)_i, (B_i)_i$ and all $(z_{t,i})_i$ are independent, $U_i \sim \mathcal{B}(n, 0.5)$, $B_i \sim \mathcal{N}(0, \sigma^2)$ and where $(z_{1,i}, \ldots, z_{m,i})$ is a m-sharing of z_i for the bitwise addition law. This example corresponds to a situation where the leakages on the shares are hidden among values that have no relation with the target.

Every possible combination of the m-sharing has been generated and replicated 100 times before adding the noise, in order to have an exhaustive dataset. Therefore, it contains 100×2^{mn} simulated traces. We ran the experiment for $n = 4$ bits, $m \in \{2, 3\}, D = 100$, and a varying noise $\sigma^2 \in [0, 1]$. Once the data were generated, we trained a neural network with one hidden layer made of D neurons. Figure 2 presents some examples obtained for 2 (left) and 3 shares (right). We clearly see some peaks at the coordinates where the meaningful information have been placed. Interestingly, this simulation shows that a second order masking has been defeated, though it required 16 times more simulated data and less noised data ($\sigma^2 \geq 0.1$) than for the same experiment against first order masking. Further works might study how much the noise magnitude σ^2 and the number of shares impact the efficiency of the training. It is however beyond the scope of this paper.

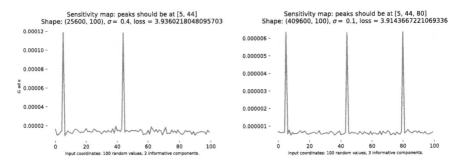

Fig. 2. Gradient of the loss function respectively for two and three shares.

4.3   Comparison with SNR for Characterization

Now we have shown that Gradient Visualization is relevant for characterization on simulated data, one may wonder to what extent this method would be useful compared to other characterization techniques. In this section, we compare our contribution to the SNR used for PoIs selection in SCA. For each time sample t, it is estimated by the following statistics:

$$\text{SNR}[t] \triangleq \frac{\underset{Z}{\text{Var}} \left(\mathbb{E}\left[\mathbf{X}[t] | Z = z\right] \right)}{\underset{Z}{\mathbb{E}} \left[\text{Var} \left(\mathbf{X}[t] | Z = z \right) \right]}, \tag{6}$$

where the numerator denotes the signal magnitude and the denominator denotes the noise magnitude estimate (see [22] for more details on its application in the SCA context). One has to keep in mind that the SNR is a statistical tool, and produces a single characterization from all the profiling traces; whereas our method gives one map for each trace, though we might average them. This observation has two consequences. First, if an SNR characterization is launched in presence of masking, every trace coordinate $\mathbf{X}[t]$ is likely to be independent from Z, which will lead the numerator to converge towards 0. Secondly, if an SNR characterization is launched in presence of de-synchronization (which is likely to introduce a lot of noise in the traces), then the denominator is expected to explode as argued in [33, Section 3.2]. To sum-up, an SNR characterization cannot directly highlight higher order leakages when the random material (used to mask and/or desynchronise the data) is not assumed to be known. Some solutions to deal with this issue have been proposed, *e.g.* by pre-processing the traces with some functions combining tuple of points [31] or by applying realignment techniques [10,27,39].

4.4   Related Works

The idea to use the derivatives of differentiable models to visualize information is not new. Following the emergence of deep convolutional networks, [35] has first proposed the idea of GV to generate a so-called *Sensitivity Map* for image recognition. The approach was motivated by the fact that such a map can be computed for free thanks to the back-propagation algorithm. A derived method, called *Guided Backpropagation* has also been proposed in [36]. The latter one slightly modifies the back-propagation rule in a ReLU layer in order to filter the contributions from the upper layers. Actually [25] states that visualizing the gradient only tracks an explanation to the variation of a final decision ($F(\mathbf{x})$ in our context), and not directly the decision itself. To this end, they propose a visualization method called *Layerwise Relevance Propagation* (LRP). Another method called *Deconvolution* has been proposed in [40] in order to give insight about the regions of an input data that contribute to the activation of a given feature in a model (either in an intermediate layer or in the output layer). In the domain of Image Recognition, these methods have been shown to be more relevant than GV.

However, the SCA and Image Recognition domains differ. In the latter one, the decision is highly diluted among lots of pixels, and the decision surface might be locally flat, though we are in a very determining area. Hopefully in a SCA context, Assumption 1 states that it is reasonable to consider that the information is very localized. That is why we are in a particular case where looking at the output sensitivity may be more interesting than other visualization methods.

5   Experiment Description

So far we have claimed that relevant information can be extracted from the loss gradient of a differentiable model. Following this idea, it has been shown to be efficient to localize PoIs on simulated data and validated that this method might overcome some weaknesses of state-of-the-art techniques. We now plan to experimentally verify these claims. Before introducing the results in Sect. 6, we first describe our investigations. In Sect. 5.1, we present the CNN architecture that will be used for profiling. Finally, Sect. 5.2 gives an exhaustive description of all the considered parameters for our experiments.

5.1   CNN Architecture

For these experiments, we will consider the same architecture as proposed in [5,32], with the same notations since the training will be done on the same dataset (see Sect. 5.2):

$$s \circ [\lambda \circ \sigma]^{n_1} \circ \delta_G \circ [\delta \circ \sigma \circ \mu \circ \gamma]^{n_3}, \tag{7}$$

where γ denotes a convolutional layer, σ denotes an activation function *i.e.* a non-linear function applied elementwise, μ denotes a batch-normalization layer, δ denotes an average pooling layer, λ denotes a dense layer and s denotes the softmax layer. Furthermore, n_1 denotes the number of *dense blocks*, namely the composition $[\lambda \circ \sigma]$. Likewise, n_3 denotes the number of *convolutional blocks*, namely $[\delta \circ \sigma \circ \mu \circ \gamma]$.

As the ultimate goal is not to get the better possible architecture, but rather having a simple and efficient one, a lighter baseline has been chosen compared to the original architecture proposed in the cited papers:

- The number of filters in the first layers has been decreased (10 instead of 64), though it is still doubled between each block; and the filter size has been set to 5.
- The dense layers contain less neurons: 1,000 instead of 4,096.
- A *global pooling layer* δ_G, has been added at the top of the last block. Its pooling size equals the width of the feature maps in the last convolutional layer, so that each feature maps are reduced to one point. While it acts as a regularizer (since it will drastically reduce the number of neurons in the first dense layer), the global pooling layer also forces the convolutional filters to better localize the discriminative features [41].

5.2   Settings

Our experiments have been done with the 50,000 EM traces from the ASCAD database [32]. Each trace is made of 700 time samples.[3] Here-after, the three different configurations investigated in this paper are presented with the notations taken from [32]. For each experiment we precise the label to be learned. This label is known during the training/profiling phase but not during the test/attack phase:

- **Experiment 1 (no countermeasure)**: the traces are synchronized, the label to be learned by the Neural Network is $Z = \text{Sbox}(P \oplus K) \oplus r_{out}$

---

[3] It corresponds to 26 clock cycles.

(in other terms, r_{out} is assumed to be known, like P). The traces correspond to the dataset ASCAD.h5, and the labels are recomputed from the metadata field of the hdf5 structure.

- **Experiment 2 (artificial shift)**: the labels are the same as in Exp. 1 but the traces are artificially shifted to the left of a random number of points drawn from a uniform distribution over $[\![0, 100]\!]$. Concretely, the traces correspond to the dataset ASCAD_desync100.h5.
- **Experiment 3 (synchronized traces, with unknown masking)**: we target $Z = \mathrm{Sbox}(P \oplus K)$, *i.e.* we have no knowledge of the masks r_{out} (neither during profiling or attack phase). Concretely, the traces correspond to the dataset ASCAD.h5 and the labels are directly imported from the field labels in the hdf5 structure.

It is noticeable that in every case, as the key is fixed, and both the plaintext and r_{out} are completely random and independent. Therefore, the labels are always balanced.

The Neural Networks source code is implemented on Python thanks to the Pytorch [28] library and is run on a workstation with a Nvidia Quadro M4000 GP-GPU with 8 GB memory and 1664 cores.

We will use the *Cross-Entropy* (also known as Negative Log Likelihood) as a loss function. It particularly fits our context as it is equivalent as minimizing the Kullback-Leibler divergence, which measures a divergence between two probability distributions, namely $F^*(\mathbf{x})$ and $F(\mathbf{x}, \theta)$ in our case. Therefore, the model $F(., \theta)$ will converge towards F^* during the training.

For each tested neural network architecture, a 5-fold cross-validation strategy has been followed. Namely, the ASCAD database has been split into 5 sets $S_1, \ldots, S_5$ of $10,000$ traces each, and the i-th cross-validation, denoted by CV_i, corresponds to a training dataset $S_p = \cup_{j \neq i} S_j$ and a validation dataset $S_v = S_i$. The given performance metrics and the visualizations are averaged over these 5 folds. The optimization is actually done with a slight modification of Stochastic Gradient Descent called *Adam* [15]. The learning rate is always set to 10^{-4}. Likewise, the batch size has been fixed to 64. For each training, we operate 100 epochs, *i.e.* each couple $(\mathbf{x}_i, z_i)$ is passed 100 times through an SGD iteration, and we keep as the best model the one that has the lowest GE on the validation set.[4]

6 Experimental Results

This section presents experimentations of the GV in different contexts, namely (Exp. 1) when the implementation embeds no countermeasure, (Exp. 2) when traces are de-synchronized and (Exp. 3) when masking is applied. The methods used to train the CNNs, to tune their hyper-parameters and to generate the GV have been presented in Sect. 5.

---

[4] Following the recent work in [29], the classical Machine Learning metrics (accuracy, recall) are ignored, as they are not proved to fit well the context of SCA.

6.1 Application Without Countermeasure

In application context (Exp. 1) (*i.e.* no countermeasure) several CNNs have been trained with the architecture hyper-parameters in (7) specified as listed in Table 1 (left). Since the masked data are here directly targeted (*i.e.* the masks are supposed to be known), no recombination (thereby no dense layer) should be required, according to [32], Sec.4.2.4. The parameter n_1 should therefore be null. However, to validate this intuition we let it vary in $\{0, 1, 2\}$. The validation loss corresponding to these values is given in Table 1 (center), where N^* denotes the minimum number of traces required to have a GE lower than 1. Even if this minimum is roughly the same for the 3 different configurations, we selected the *best* one (i.e. $n_1 = 1$) for our *best* CNN architecture. Figure 3 (left) presents the corresponding GV, and the corresponding SNR (right).[5] It may be observed that the peaks obtained with GV and SNR are identical: the highest point in the SNR is the second highest point in GV, whereas the highest point in GV is ranked 7-th in the SNR peaks. More generally both methods target the same clock cycle (the 19-th). These observations validate the fact that our characterization method is relevant for an unprotected target.

Table 1. Architecture hyper-parameters (left) and performance metrics without countermeasure (center) and with de-synchronization (right).

Parameter	Value	n_1	Validation Loss (bits)	N^*	n_1	Validation Loss (bits)	N^*
n_3	5	0	6.40	3.25	0	6.64	4.0
n_1	$\{0, 1, 2\}$	1	6.15	3	1	6.46	3.6
		2	6.35	3.25	2	6.90	5.4

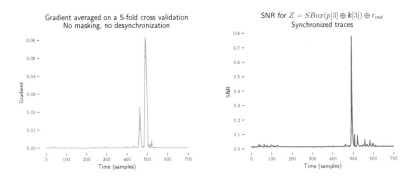

Fig. 3. Case where no countermeasure is considered. Left: GV for the trained model with 1 dense layer. Right: SNR.

---

[5] An alternative representation with the Jacobian matrix is given in Appendix D, Fig. 8.

6.2 Application with an Artificial De-synchronization

We now add a new difficulty by considering the case of de-synchronization as described in Sect. 5.2. The hyper-parameter grid is exactly the same as in Sect. 6.1, and the corresponding loss is given in Table 1 (right). Faced to mis-alignment, the considered architectures have still good performances, and the attacks succeeded in roughly the same number of traces than before. Interestingly, Fig. 4 shows that the GV succeeds to recover the leakage localization while the SNR does not (see Fig. 9 in Appendix D). Actually, the gradient averaged over the profiling traces Fig. 4 (left) shows that, instead of having a small number of peaks, a band is obtained whose width approximately equals the maximum quantity of shift applied in the traces, namely 100 points. Moreover, individual gradients Fig. 4 (right) bring a single characterization for each trace, enabling to guess approximately the shift applied to each trace.

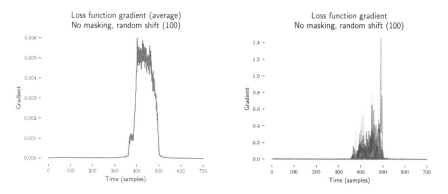

Fig. 4. Case where de-synchronization is considered. GV for each trace separately (right) and averaged (left).

6.3 Application with a First Order Masking

The last experiment concerns the application of GV in presence of masking. Several model configurations have been tested which correspond to the hyper-parameters listed in Table 2 (left). We eventually selected the 8 models that achieved the best GE convergence rate (right).

For the selected architectures, our first attempt to use GV did not give full satisfaction. As an illustration, Fig. 5 (left) presents it for one of the tested architectures (averaged over the 5 folds of the cross-validation). Indeed, it looks difficult to distinguish PoIs (i.e. those identified by our SNR characterization, see the right-hand side of Fig. 6) from *ghost* peaks (*i.e.* peaks a priori independent of the sensitive target). To explain this phenomenon, we decided to study the validation loss of the trained models. Figure 5 (right) presents it for one model and for each of the 5 cross-validation folds CV_i, $i \in [0..4]$.

Table 2. Masking case. Left: architecture hyper-parameters (bold values refer to the best choices). Right: GE for the 8 best architectures.

Parameter	Value
n_3	$\{5, 6, \mathbf{7}, 8\}$
n_1	$\{\mathbf{2}, 3\}$
n_filters_1	10
kernel_size	$\{3, 5, \mathbf{11}\}$

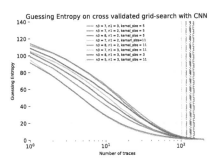

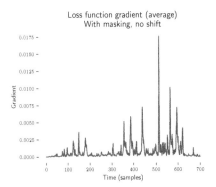

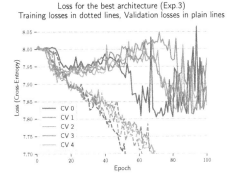

Fig. 5. Left: GV in presence of masking (without early-stopping). Right: validation loss for each fold.

It may be observed in Fig. 5 (right) that the training and validation loss curves proceeded a fast big decrease after an initial plateau during the first 15 epochs. After that, the validation loss starts increasing while the training loss still decreases. After roughly 50 epochs, the validation loss goes on a regime with unstable results, but still higher than the training loss. These observations are clues of *overfitting*. It means that the model exploits (non-informative) leakage not localized in the PoIs to memorize the training data and to improve the training loss. Such a strategy should not generalize well on the validation traces. As we are looking for models that implement a strategy that are generalizable on unseen traces, we propose to use a regularization technique called *early-stopping* [13]: the training is stopped after a number of epochs called *patience* (in our case 10) if no remarkable decrease (*i.e.* up to a *tolerance term*, 0.25 bits here) is observed in the validation loss. With this slight modification, the previous architectures are trained again from scratch, and a better GV is produced (see the left-hand side of Fig. 6). As the main peaks are separated enough, an evaluator may conclude that they represent different leakages.

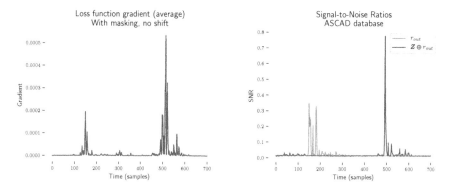

Fig. 6. Early-stopping is applied. Left: GV. Right: corresponding SNR.

6.4   Comparison in the Context of Template Attacks

A careful observation of Fig. 6 shows that the main peaks given by the GV are not exactly aligned with those given by the SNR characterization (performed under the hypothesis that the masks are known). For GV, the main peak appears at the points corresponding to the 20-th clock cycle, which is one cycle after the one previously targeted by both the GV and the SNR in the previous case where no countermeasure was considered (Sect. 6.1). We validated that this phenomenon occurred for every successful visualization produced by GV. Furthermore, concerning the peaks related to the mask leakage, the GV only emphasizes one clock cycle (the 6-th) whereas the SNR highlights two of them: the 6-th and the 7-th. It implies that the GV should not be taken as an exact equivalent to the SNR. We have not found any track of explanation to justify this slight shift but it raises the question whether the PoIs highlighted by GV represent relevant leakages and can be used in the context of Template Attacks.

To give an answer, we decided to use our characterization method as a pre-processing for a Template Attack, and compare it to two pre-processing methods: SNR (through PoIs selection) and PCA (through dimensionality reduction).

The input dimension of the traces are reduced to $2^n, n \in \{1, 2, 3, 4, 5\}$ points, based on the following methods:

- **SNR strategy**: the 2^{n-1} highest PoIs from the mask SNR and the 2^{n-1} highest PoIs from the masked data SNR are selected;
- **PCA strategy**: the 2^n first components in a decreasing order of contribution are selected;
- **GV strategy**: the 2^{n-1} highest PoIs from the GV are selected from the area around the 6-th clock cycle. Likewise, the other half comes from the peaks in the area around the 20-th clock cycle.

Remark 1. To make a fair comparison in the context of a first order masking, we assume that we know the mask during the characterization phase for SNR, so that we can localize PoIs for the mask and the masked data. Notice that we do not assume the mask knowledge neither during the profiling phase nor for the other strategies. Obviously, this scenario is not realistic as if one has access to the mask during characterization, then the latter one is very likely to be also available during the profiling phase.

Once reduced, the traces are processed with a first order Template Attack [7], and the GE is estimated. The results are given on Fig. 7. The plain curves denote the GE for GV whereas the dotted curves denote either GE obtained with SNR (left) or PCA (right).

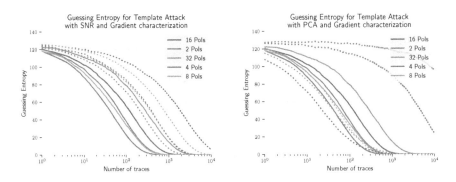

Fig. 7. Comparison of the guessing entropy for GV based attacks in plain lines and: (left) SNR based attacks, or (right) PCA based attacks in dotted lines.

From Fig. 7 we can observe several things:

- Only a few PoIs from the GV strategy are needed to get a successful attack. The optimal number of extracted PoIs is 4. Beyond that, the other PoIs bring more difficulty in the Template Attack than they bring new information (due to the increasing dimensionality).
- When the SNR strategy is followed, the optimal attack is done with 2 PoIs and the more PoIs are used, the less efficient are the attacks. This observation confirms that SNR selects relevant PoIs as expected. However, when comparing the SNR and GV strategies with a same number of PoIs, the latter one appears to be always better, except for 32 PoIs where both strategies seem equal.
- The PCA strategy does not work well for the two or four first extracted components. However, when considering eight components and above, it achieves an efficiency as good as the GV strategy, and even sometimes better.
- In any case, the Template Attacks need much more traces to get a GE converging towards zero than the optimal CNN attack presented in Table 2.

Based on the presented experiments, we may draw several conclusions on the GV efficiency. First of all, it seems to be an accurate characterization method, almost always much better than that based on an SNR. This first conclusion enables to answer the question previously asked: the targeted PoIs in GV are relevant leakages and can be used in the context of Template Attacks. A possible and informal explanation would be that choosing the couples of samples that maximize the information about the sensitive variable is not equivalent as selecting the single samples that independently maximize the information on each share.

Secondly, GV can be used as a reliable dimensionality reduction preprocessing in presence of counter-measures, even more reliable than PCA in our cases where one makes a reduction to a very few dimensions (2 or 4). However, this conclusion has a minor interest, as the GV seen as a pre-processing method is done *post-mortem*, and the training of a CNN model did not suffer from a high dimension input. And last, but not least, the GV method unfortunately faces a drawback: if the trained CNN overfits, then the GV might suffer from the presence of ghost peaks. That is why the overfitting must be carefully monitored. In this sense, visualizing the gradient can hopefully help to assess whether it is the case or not.

7   Conclusion

In this paper, we have theoretically shown that a method called Gradient Visualization can be used to localize Points of Interest. This result relies on two assumptions that can be considered as realistic in a Side Channel context.

Generally, the efficiency of the proposed method only depends on the ability of the profiling model to succeed in the attack. In the case where countermeasures like masking or misalignment are considered, CNNs are shown to still build good pdf estimations, and thereby the Gradient Visualization provides a good characterization tool. In addition, such a visualization can be made for each trace individually, and the method does not require more work than needed to perform a profiling with CNNs leading to a successful attack. Therefore, characterization can be done after the profiling phase whereas profiling attacks with Templates often requires to proceed a characterization phase before.

We verified the efficiency of our proposed method on simulated data. It has been shown that as long as a Neural Network is able to have slightly better performance than randomness, it can localize points that contain the informative leakage.

On experimental traces, we have empirically shown that Gradient Visualization is at least as good as state-of-the-art characterization methods, in different cases corresponding to the presence or not of different countermeasures. Not only it can still localize Points of Interest in presence of desynchronization or masking but it has also been shown that different PoIs can be emphasized compared to the first ones highlighted by SNR. These new PoIs have been shown to be at least as relevant as the ones proposed by SNR.

Further work would study such a technique in presence of both desynchronization and masking, or in presence of higher order masking scheme.

A   Profiling Attacks

As the model is aiming at approximating the conditional pdf, a Maximum Likelihood score can be used for the guessing:

$$\mathbf{d}_{S_a}[k] \triangleq \sum_{i=1}^{N_a} \log\left(\mathbf{y}_i[z_i]\right) \text{ where } z_i = \mathbf{C}(p_i, k). \tag{8}$$

Based on these scores, the key hypotheses are ranked in a decreasing order. Finally, the attacker chooses the key that is ranked first (resp. the set of first o ranked keys). More generally, the *rank* $g_{S_a}(k^\star)$ of the correct key hypothesis $k^\star$ is defined as:

$$g_{S_a}(k^\star) \triangleq \sum_{k \in \mathcal{K}} 1_{\mathbf{d}_{S_a}[k] > \mathbf{d}_{S_a}[k^\star]}. \tag{9}$$

Remark 2. In practice, to compute $\mathrm{GE}(N_a)$, sampling many attack sets may be very prohibitive in an evaluation context, especially if we need to reproduce the estimations for many values of N_a; one solution to circumvent this problem is, given a validation set S_v of N_v traces, to sample some attack sets by permuting the order of the traces into the validation set. $\mathbf{d}_{S_a}$ can then be computed with a cumulative sum to get a score for each $N_a \in [\![1, N_v]\!]$, and so is $g_{S_a}(k^\star)$. While this trick gives good estimations for $N_a \ll N_v$, one has to keep in mind that the estimates become biased when $N_a \to N_v$. This problem also happens in Machine Learning when one lacks data to validate a model. A technique called *Cross-Validation* [34] enables to circumvent this problem by splitting the dataset into q parts called *folds*. The profiling is done on $q - 1$ folds and the model is evaluated with the remaining fold. By repeating this step q times, the measured results can be averaged so that they are less biased.

B   Study of an Optimal Model

Informally, Assumption 1 tells that the leaking information is non-uniformly distributed over the trace $\mathbf{X}$, *i.e.* only a few coordinates contain clues about the attacked sensitive variable. Assumption 1 has been made in many studies such as [4]. Depending on the countermeasures implemented into the attacked device, the nature of $\mathcal{I}_Z$ may be precised. Without any countermeasure, and supposing that the target sensitive variable only leaks once, Assumption 1 states that $\mathcal{I}_Z$ is only a set of contiguous and constant coordinates, regardless the input traces.

Adding masking will split $\mathcal{I}_Z$ into several contiguous and fixed sets whose number is equal to the number of shares in the masking scheme (or at least equal to the number of shares if we relax the hypothesis of one leakage per share). For example if M (resp. $Z \oplus M$) denotes the mask (resp. masked data) variable leaking at coordinate t_1 (resp. t_2), then M and $X[t]$ with $t \neq t_1$ are independent (resp. Z and $X[t]$ with $t \neq t_2$ are independent). The conditional probability $\Pr[Z = z | \mathbf{X} = \mathbf{x}]$ satisfies:

$$\Pr[Z = z | \mathbf{X} = \mathbf{x}]$$
$$= \sum_m \Pr[Z \oplus M = z \oplus m | \mathbf{X}[t_1] = \mathbf{x}[t_1]] \Pr[M = m | \mathbf{X}[t_2] = \mathbf{x}[t_2]] \quad (10)$$

Adding de-synchronization should force $\mathcal{I}_Z$ to be non-constant between each trace.

Likewise, Assumption 2 is realistic because it is a direct corollary of a Gaussian leakage model for the traces [7,9]. Such an hypothesis is common for Side Channel Analysis [7]. It implies that $\mathbf{x} \mapsto \Pr[\mathbf{X} = \mathbf{x} | Z = z]$ is differentiable and:

$$\nabla_\mathbf{x} \Pr[\mathbf{X} = \mathbf{x} | Z = z] = \Sigma_z^{-1}(\mathbf{x} - \mu_z) \Pr[\mathbf{X} = \mathbf{x} | Z = z] \quad (11)$$

where μ_z and Σ_z^{-1} respectively denote the mean vector and the covariance matrix of the normal probability distribution related to the target sensitive value hypothesis z. Then, from Bayes' theorem, (11) and the basic rules for derivatives computation, it gives an analytic expression of $\nabla_\mathbf{x} F^*(\mathbf{x})$, thereby proving that F^* is differentiable with respect to the input trace.

C   Neural Networks

Neural Networks (NN) are nowadays the privileged tool to address the classification problem in Machine Learning [19]. They aim at constructing a function $F \colon \mathcal{X} \to \mathcal{P}(\mathcal{Z})$ that takes data $\mathbf{x}$ and outputs vectors $\mathbf{y}$ of scores. The classification of $\mathbf{x}$ is done afterwards by choosing the label $z^* = \mathrm{argmax}_{z \in \mathcal{Z}} \, \mathbf{y}[z]$, but the output can be also directly used for soft decision contexts, which corresponds more to Side Channel Analysis as the NN outputs on attack traces will be used to compute the score vector in (8). In general F is obtained by combining several simpler functions, called *layers*. An NN has an *input layer* (the identity over the input datum $\mathbf{x}$, an output layer (the last function, whose output is the scores vector $\mathbf{y}$ and all other layers are called *hidden* layers. The nature (the number and the dimension) of the layers is called the *architecture* of the NN. All the parameters that define an architecture, together with some other parameters that govern the training phase, have to be carefully set by the attacker, and are called *hyper-parameters*. The so-called *neurons*, that give the name to the NNs, are the computational units of the network and essentially process a scalar product between the coordinate of its input and a vector of *trainable weights* (or simply *weights*) that have to be *trained*. We denote θ the vector containing all the trainable weights. Therefore, for a fixed architecture, an NN is completely parameterized by θ. Convolutional Neural Networks (CNN) implement other operations, but can be rewritten as regular NN with specific constraints on the weights [18]. Each layer processes some neurons and the outputs of the neuron evaluations will form new input vectors for the subsequent layer.

The ability of a Neural Network to approximate well a target probabilistic function F^* by minimizing a loss function on sampled training data with Stochastic Gradient Descent is still an open question. This is what we call the *mystery of Deep Learning*. It theoretically requires a huge quantity of training data so that the solution obtained by loss minimization generalizes well, though it empirically works with much less data. Likewise, finding the minimum with Stochastic Gradient Descent is theoretically not proved, but has been empirically shown to be a good heuristic. For more information, see [14]. Indeed, though it raises several theoretical issues, it has been empirically shown to be efficient, especially in SCA with CNN based attacks [5,30].

D   Experimental Results

D.1   The Jacobian Matrix

In this appendix, we present the Jacobian matrix visualization, equivalent to the GV. It shows, in addition, that some target values seem more sensitive, especially those whose Hamming weight is shared by only few other values (so it gives clues about how the traces leak sensitive information). Figure 8 (top) shows such a matrix in application context (Exp. 1) as described in Sect. 6, while Fig. 8 (bottom) shows the Jacobian matrix corresponding to the application context (Exp. 2). Fig. 9 shows the SNR computed on de-synchronized traces.

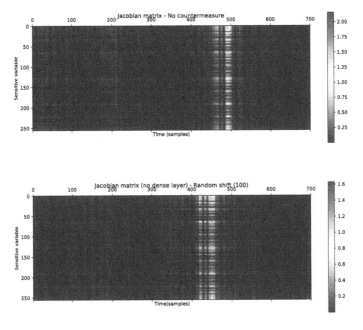

Fig. 8. Jacobian matrix for the best models in application contexts (Exp. 1) (top) and (Exp. 2) (bottom).

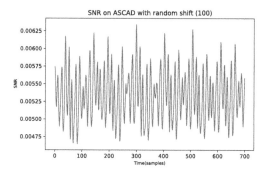

Fig. 9. The SNR in the case where de-synchronization is considered.

References

1. Sensitivity analysis - Wikipedia. https://en.wikipedia.org/wiki/Sensitivity_analysis
2. Abadi, M., et al.: TensorFlow: a system for large-scale machine learning. arXiv:1605.08695 [cs], 27 May 2016
3. Brier, E., Clavier, C., Olivier, F.: Correlation power analysis with a leakage model. In: Joye, M., Quisquater, J.-J. (eds.) CHES 2004. LNCS, vol. 3156, pp. 16–29. Springer, Heidelberg (2004). https://doi.org/10.1007/978-3-540-28632-5_2
4. Cagli, E., Dumas, C., Prouff, E.: Enhancing dimensionality reduction methods for side-channel attacks. In: Homma, N., Medwed, M. (eds.) CARDIS 2015. LNCS, vol. 9514, pp. 15–33. Springer, Cham (2016). https://doi.org/10.1007/978-3-319-31271-2_2
5. Cagli, E., Dumas, C., Prouff, E.: Convolutional neural networks with data augmentation against jitter-based countermeasures. In: Fischer, W., Homma, N. (eds.) CHES 2017. LNCS, vol. 10529, pp. 45–68. Springer, Cham (2017). https://doi.org/10.1007/978-3-319-66787-4_3
6. Cagli, E., Dumas, C., Prouff, E.: Kernel discriminant analysis for information extraction in the presence of masking. In: Lemke-Rust, K., Tunstall, M. (eds.) CARDIS 2016. LNCS, vol. 10146, pp. 1–22. Springer, Cham (2017). https://doi.org/10.1007/978-3-319-54669-8_1
7. Chari, S., Rao, J.R., Rohatgi, P.: Template attacks. In: Kaliski, B.S., Koç, K., Paar, C. (eds.) CHES 2002. LNCS, vol. 2523, pp. 13–28. Springer, Heidelberg (2003). https://doi.org/10.1007/3-540-36400-5_3
8. Choudary, M.O., Kuhn, M.G.: Efficient stochastic methods: profiled attacks beyond 8 bits. In: Joye, M., Moradi, A. (eds.) CARDIS 2014. LNCS, vol. 8968, pp. 85–103. Springer, Cham (2015). https://doi.org/10.1007/978-3-319-16763-3_6
9. Choudary, O., Kuhn, M.G.: Efficient template attacks. In: Francillon, A., Rohatgi, P. (eds.) CARDIS 2013. LNCS, vol. 8419, pp. 253–270. Springer, Cham (2014). https://doi.org/10.1007/978-3-319-08302-5_17
10. Durvaux, F., Renauld, M., Standaert, F.-X., van Oldeneel tot Oldenzeel, L., Veyrat-Charvillon, N.: Efficient removal of random delays from embedded software implementations using hidden Markov models. In: Mangard, S. (ed.) CARDIS 2012. LNCS, vol. 7771, pp. 123–140. Springer, Heidelberg (2013). https://doi.org/10.1007/978-3-642-37288-9_9

11. Eisenbarth, T., Paar, C., Weghenkel, B.: Building a side channel based disassembler. In: Gavrilova, M.L., Tan, C.J.K., Moreno, E.D. (eds.) Transactions on Computational Science X. LNCS, vol. 6340, pp. 78–99. Springer, Heidelberg (2010). https://doi.org/10.1007/978-3-642-17499-5_4

12. Gilmore, R., Hanley, N., O'Neill, M.: Neural network based attack on a masked implementation of AES. In: 2015 IEEE International Symposium on Hardware Oriented Security and Trust (HOST), pp. 106–111, May 2015. https://doi.org/10.1109/HST.2015.7140247

13. Goodfellow, I., Bengio, Y., Courville, A.: Deep Learning. Adaptive Computation and Machine Learning Series. MIT Press, Cambridge (2017)

14. Hardt, M.: Off the convex path. http://offconvex.github.io/

15. Kingma, D.P., Ba, J.: Adam: a method for stochastic optimization. arXiv:1412.6980 [cs], 22 December 2014

16. Kocher, P., Jaffe, J., Jun, B.: Differential power analysis. In: Wiener, M. (ed.) CRYPTO 1999. LNCS, vol. 1666, pp. 388–397. Springer, Heidelberg (1999). https://doi.org/10.1007/3-540-48405-1_25

17. Krizhevsky, A., Sutskever, I., Hinton, G.E.: ImageNet classification with deep convolutional neural networks. In: Advances in Neural Information Processing Systems, pp. 1097–1105 (2012)

18. LeCun, Y., Bengio, Y.: Convolutional networks for images, speech, and time series. In: The Handbook of Brain Theory and Neural Networks, pp. 255–258. MIT Press, Cambridge (1998). http://dl.acm.org/citation.cfm?id=303568.303704

19. LeCun, Y., Bengio, Y., Hinton, G.: Deep learning. Nature **521**(7553), 436–444 (2015). https://doi.org/10.1038/nature14539. http://www.nature.com/articles/nature14539

20. Lerman, L., Bontempi, G., Markowitch, O.: A machine learning approach against amasked AES: reaching the limit of side-channel attacks with a learningmodel. J. Cryptographic Eng. **5**(2), 123–139 (2015). https://doi.org/10.1007/s13389-014-0089-3

21. Maghrebi, H., Portigliatti, T., Prouff, E.: Breaking cryptographic implementations using deep learning techniques. In: Carlet, C., Hasan, M.A., Saraswat, V. (eds.) SPACE 2016. LNCS, vol. 10076, pp. 3–26. Springer, Cham (2016). https://doi.org/10.1007/978-3-319-49445-6_1

22. Mangard, S., Oswald, E., Popp, T.: Power Analysis Attacks: Revealing the Secrets of Smart Cards. Springer, Boston (2007). https://doi.org/10.1007/978-0-387-38162-6. OCLC: ocm71541637

23. Martinasek, Z., Dzurenda, P., Malina, L.: Profiling power analysis attack based on MLP in DPA contest v4.2. In: 2016 39th International Conference on Telecommunications and Signal Processing (TSP), pp. 223–226, June 2016. https://doi.org/10.1109/TSP.2016.7760865

24. Mather, L., Oswald, E., Bandenburg, J., Wójcik, M.: Does my device leak information? An *a priori* statistical power analysis of leakage detection tests. In: Sako, K., Sarkar, P. (eds.) ASIACRYPT 2013. LNCS, vol. 8269, pp. 486–505. Springer, Heidelberg (2013). https://doi.org/10.1007/978-3-642-42033-7_25

25. Montavon, G., Samek, W., Müller, K.R.: Methods for interpreting and understanding deep neural networks. Digit. Sig. Process. **73**, 1–15 (2018). https://doi.org/10.1016/j.dsp.2017.10.011. http://linkinghub.elsevier.com/retrieve/pii/S1051200417302385

26. Moradi, A., Richter, B., Schneider, T., Standaert, F.X.: Leakage detection with the x2-test. IACR Trans. Cryptographic Hardware Embed. Syst. **2018**(1), 209–237 (2018)

27. Nagashima, S., Homma, N., Imai, Y., Aoki, T., Satoh, A.: DPA using phase-based waveform matching against random-delay countermeasure. In: 2007 IEEE International Symposium on Circuits and Systems, pp. 1807–1810, May 2007. https://doi.org/10.1109/ISCAS.2007.378024

28. Paszke, A., et al.: Automatic differentiation in Pytorch. In: NIPS-W (2017)

29. Picek, S., Heuser, A., Jovic, A., Bhasin, S., Regazzoni, F.: The curse of class imbalance and conflicting metrics with machine learning for side-channel evaluations. IACR Trans. Cryptographic Hardware Embed. Syst. **2019**(1), 209–237 (2018). https://doi.org/10.13154/tches.v2019.i1.209-237. https://tches.iacr.org/index.php/TCHES/article/view/7339

30. Picek, S., Samiotis, I.P., Heuser, A., Kim, J., Bhasin, S., Legay, A.: On the performance of deep learning for side-channel analysis. IACR Cryptology ePrint Archive 2018, 4 (2018). http://eprint.iacr.org/2018/004

31. Prouff, E., Rivain, M., Bevan, R.: Statistical analysis of second order differential power analysis. IEEE Trans. Comput. **58**(6), 799–811 (2009). https://doi.org/10.1109/TC.2009.15. http://ieeexplore.ieee.org/document/4752810/

32. Prouff, E., Strullu, R., Benadjila, R., Cagli, E., Dumas, C.: Study of deep learning techniques for side-channel analysis and introduction to ASCAD database. IACR Cryptology ePrint Archive 2018, 53 (2018). http://eprint.iacr.org/2018/053

33. Rivain, M., Prouff, E., Doget, J.: Higher-order masking and shuffling for software implementations of block ciphers. In: Clavier, C., Gaj, K. (eds.) CHES 2009. LNCS, vol. 5747, pp. 171–188. Springer, Heidelberg (2009). https://doi.org/10.1007/978-3-642-04138-9_13

34. Shalev-Shwartz, S., Ben-David, S.: Understanding Machine Learning: From Theoryto Algorithms. Cambridge University Press (2014). https://doi.org/10.1017/CBO9781107298019. http://ebooks.cambridge.org/ref/id/CBO9781107298019

35. Simonyan, K., Vedaldi, A., Zisserman, A.: Deep inside convolutional networks: visualising image classification models and saliency maps. arXiv:1312.6034 [cs], 20 December 2013

36. Springenberg, J.T., Dosovitskiy, A., Brox, T., Riedmiller, M.: Striving for simplicity: the all convolutional net. arXiv:1412.6806 [cs], 21 December 2014

37. Standaert, F.-X., Archambeau, C.: Using subspace-based template attacks to compare and combine power and electromagnetic information leakages. In: Oswald, E., Rohatgi, P. (eds.) CHES 2008. LNCS, vol. 5154, pp. 411–425. Springer, Heidelberg (2008). https://doi.org/10.1007/978-3-540-85053-3_26

38. Standaert, F.-X., Malkin, T.G., Yung, M.: A unified framework for the analysis of side-channel key recovery attacks. In: Joux, A. (ed.) EUROCRYPT 2009. LNCS, vol. 5479, pp. 443–461. Springer, Heidelberg (2009). https://doi.org/10.1007/978-3-642-01001-9_26

39. van Woudenberg, J.G.J., Witteman, M.F., Bakker, B.: Improving differential power analysis by elastic alignment. In: Kiayias, A. (ed.) CT-RSA 2011. LNCS, vol. 6558, pp. 104–119. Springer, Heidelberg (2011). https://doi.org/10.1007/978-3-642-19074-2_8. http://dl.acm.org/citation.cfm?id=1964621.1964632

40. Zeiler, M.D., Fergus, R.: Visualizing and understanding convolutional networks. arXiv:1311.2901 [cs], 12 November 2013

41. Zhou, B., Khosla, A., Lapedriza, A., Oliva, A., Torralba, A.: Learning deep features for discriminative localization. In: 2016 IEEE Conference on Computer Vision and Pattern Recognition (CVPR), pp. 2921–2929, June 2016. https://doi.org/10.1109/CVPR.2016.319

Fast Analytical Rank Estimation

Liron David[(✉)] and Avishai Wool[(✉)]

School of Electrical Engineering, Tel Aviv University, 69978 Ramat Aviv, Israel
lirondavid@gmail.com, yash@eng.tau.ac.il

Abstract. Rank estimation is an important tool for a side-channel evaluations laboratories. It allows estimating the remaining security after an attack has been performed, quantified as the time complexity and the memory consumption required to brute force the key given the leakages as probability distributions over d subkeys (usually key bytes). These estimations are particularly useful when the key is not reachable with exhaustive search. We propose a new framework for rank estimation that is conceptually simple, and more time and memory efficient than previous proposals. Our main idea is to bound each subkey distribution by an analytical function, and estimate the rank by a closed formula. To demonstrate the power of the framework, we instantiate it with Pareto-like functions to create the PRank algorithm. Pareto-like functions have long-tails that model empirical SCA distributions, and they are easily calculable. We evaluated the performance of PRank through extensive simulations based on two real SCA data corpora, and compared it to the currently-best histogram-based algorithm. We show that PRank gives a good rank estimation with much improved time and memory efficiency, especially for large ranks: For ranks between $2^{80} - 2^{100}$ PRank estimation is at most 10 bits above the histogram rank and for ranks beyond 2^{100} the PRank estimation is only 4 bits above the histogram rank—yet it runs in milliseconds, and uses negligible memory. One could employ our framework with other classes of functions and possibly achieve even better results.

1 Introduction

1.1 Background

Side-channel attacks (SCA) represent a serious threat to the security of cryptographic hardware products. As such, they reveal the secret key of a cryptosystem based on leakage information gained from physical implementation of the cryptosystem on different devices. Information provided by sources such as timing [16], power consumption [15], electromagnetic radiation [2,12,28] and other sources, can be exploited by SCA to break cryptosystems.

A security evaluation of a cryptographic device should determine whether an implementation is secure against such an attack. To do so, the evaluator needs to determine how much time, what kind of computing power and how

© Springer Nature Switzerland AG 2019
I. Polian and M. Stöttinger (Eds.): COSADE 2019, LNCS 11421, pp. 168–190, 2019.
https://doi.org/10.1007/978-3-030-16350-1_10

much storage a malicious attacker would need to recover the key given the side-channel leakages. The leakage of cryptographic implementations is highly device-specific, therefore the usual strategy for an evaluation laboratory is to launch a set of popular attacks, and to determine whether the adversary can break the implementation (i.e., recover the key).

Most of the attacks that have been published in the literature are based on a "divide-and-conquer" strategy. In the first "divide" part, the cryptanalyst recovers multi-dimensional information about different parts of the key, usually called subkeys (e.g., each of the $d = 16$ AES key bytes can be a subkey). In the "conquer" part the cryptanalyst combines the information all together in an efficient way via key enumeration [7, 26, 29]. In the attacks we consider in this paper, the information that the SCA provides for each subkey is a probability distribution over the N candidate values for that subkey, and the SCA probability of a full key is the product of the SCA probabilities of its d subkeys.

A security evaluator knows the secret key and aims to estimate the number of decryption attempts the attacker needs to do before he reaches to the correct key, assuming the attacker uses the SCA's probability distribution. Clearly enumerating the keys in the optimal SCA-predicted order is the best strategy the evaluator can follow. However, this is limited to the computational power of the evaluator. This is a worrying situation because it is hard to decide whether an implementation is "practically secure". For example, one could enumerate the 2^{50} first keys for an AES implementation without finding the correct key, and then to decide that the implementation is practically secured because the attacker needs to enumerate beyond 2^{50} number of keys. But, this does not provide any hint whether the concrete security level is 2^{51} or 2^{120}. This makes a significant difference in practice, especially in view of the possibility of improved measurement setups, signal processing, information extraction, etc., that should be taken into account for any physical security evaluation, e.g., via larger security margins.

In this paper, we introduce a new method to estimate the rank of a given secret key in the optimal SCA-predicted order. Our algorithm enjoys simplicity and much improved time and memory efficiency.

The rank estimation problem: Given d independent subkey spaces each of size N with their corresponding probability distributions $P_1, ..., P_d$ such that P_i is sorted in non-increasing order of probabilities, and given a key k^* indexed by $(k_1, ..., k_d)$, let $p^* = P_1(k_1) \cdot P_2(k_2) \cdot ... \cdot P_d(k_d)$ be the probability of k^* to be the correct key. The evaluator would like to estimate the number of full keys with probability higher than p^*, when the probability of a full key is defined as the product of its subkey's probabilities.

In other words, the evaluator would like to estimate k^*'s rank: the position of the key k^* in the sorted list of N^d possible keys when the list is sorted in non-increasing probability order, from the most likely key to the least. If the dimensions, or k^*'s rank are small, one can easily compute the rank of the correct key by a straightforward key enumeration. However, for a key with a high rank r optimal-order key enumeration requires $\Omega(r)$ time which may be prohibitive, and the best currently-known optimal-order key enumeration algorithms require $\Omega(N^{d/2})$ space, which again may be prohibitive. Hence developing fast and low-memory algorithms to estimate the rank without enumeration is of great interest.

1.2   Related Work

The best key enumeration algorithm so far, in terms of optimal-order, was presented by Veyrat-Charvillon, Gérard, Renauld and Standaert in [29]. However, its worst case space complexity is $\Omega(N^{d/2})$ when d is the number of subkey dimensions and N is the number of candidates per subkey - and its space complexity is $\Omega(r)$ when enumerating up to a key at rank $r \leq N^{d/2}$. Thus its space complexity becomes a bottleneck on real computers with bounded RAM in realistic SCA attacks.

Since then several near-optimal key enumeration were proposed [5,7,17–19,22–24,27,32]. However, none of these key enumeration algorithms enumerate the whole key space within a realistic amount of time and with a realistic amount of computational power: enumerating an exponential key space will always come at an exponential cost. Hence the need for efficient and accurate rank estimation for keys that have a high rank.

The first rank estimation algorithm was proposed by Veyrat-Charvillon et al. [30]. They suggested to organize the keys by sorting their subkeys according to the a-posteriori probabilities provided, and to represent them as a high-dimensional dataspace. The full key space can then be partitioned in two volumes: one defined by the key candidates with probability higher than the correct key, one defined by the key candidates with probability lower than the correct key. Using this geometrical representation, the rank estimation problem can be stated as the one of finding bounds on these "higher" and "lower" volumes. It essentially works by carving volumes representing key candidates on each side of their boundary, progressively refining the lower and upper bounds on the key rank. Refining the bounds becomes exponentially difficult at some point.

A number of works have investigated solutions to improve upon [30]. In particular, Glowacz et al. [13] presented a rank estimation algorithm that is based on a convolution of histograms and allows obtaining tight bounds for the key rank of (even large) keys. This Histogram algorithm is currently the best rank estimation algorithm we are aware of. The space complexity of this algorithm is $O(dB)$ where d is the number of dimensions and B is a design parameter controlling the number of the histogram bins. A comparable result was developed independently by Bernstein et al. [3].

Martin et al. [24] used a score-based rank enumeration, rather than a probability based rank estimation. They mapped the rank estimation to a knapsack problem, which can be simplified and expressed as path counting. In [22] the algorithm was further simplified and made more efficient by slightly changing the recurrence relation that iterates through the graph. Subsequently, in [21] Martin et al. show that their (latter) algorithm is mathematically equivalent to the Histogram algorithm [13] for a suitable choice of their respective discretization parameter, thus they can both be equally accurate. Since the two algorithms are equivalent we compared our algorithm's performance only to that of the Histogram algorithm [13]. Besides, Martin et al. show in [20] a large class of functions that enables the comparison of research utilizing scores with those which utilize probabilities.

Ye et al. investigated an alternative solution based on a weak Maximum Likelihood (wML) approach [32], rather than a Maximum Likelihood (ML) one for the previous examples. They additionally combined this wML approach with the possibility to approximate the security of an implementation based on "easier to sample" metrics, e.g., starting from the subkey Success Rates (SR) rather than their likelihoods. Later Duc et al. [10] described a simple alternative to the algorithm of Ye et al. and provided an "even easier to sample" bound on the subkey SR, by exploiting their formal connection with a Mutual Information metric. Recently, Wang et al. [31] presented a rank estimation for dependent score lists.

Choudary et al. [6] presented a method for estimating Massey's guessing entropy (GM) which is the statistical expectation of the position of the correct key in the sorted distribution. Their method allows to estimate the GM within a few bits. However, the *actual* guessing entropy (GE), i.e., the *rank* of the correct key, is sometimes quite different from the expectation. In contrast, our algorithm focuses on the real GE.

David et al. show in [8] a different rank estimation algorithm. Their main idea is to use exponential sampling to drastically reduce the algorithm's complexity. They showed that their results are on-par with the histograms results [13].

Grosso presents in [14] a simple trick to reduce the cost of rank estimation for a large number of subkeys based on the rank estimation of [13].

1.3   Contribution

We propose a new framework for rank estimation that is conceptually simple, and more time and memory efficient than previous proposals. Our main idea is to bound each subkey distribution by an analytical function, and then estimate the rank by a closed formula.

To instantiate the framework, we selected Pareto-like functions to upper-bound the subkey distributions. Pareto-like functions have long-tails that model empirical SCA probability distributions, and they are easily calculable. We first prove that one can always upper-bound a sorted probability distribution P by a Pareto-like function f that is anchored at 2 indexes at which $f(x) = P[x]$. We then fully characterize such upper-bounding functions, prove that there can only be $O(N)$ of them, and develop an efficient algorithm to find them.

Since Pareto-like functions are amenable to analysis, the instantiated framework provides an upper bound on the rank of a given key, as an explicit *closed formula*. Combined with the algorithm to find the upper-bounding Pareto-like functions, we obtain an $O(dN^2)$ rank upper-bound estimation algorithm we call PRank.

We evaluated the performance of PRank through extensive simulations based on two SCA data corpora of [25] and of [11], and compared it to the currently-best histogram rank estimation algorithm of [13]. We show that PRank gives a good rank estimation with much improved time and memory efficiency, especially for large ranks: For ranks between $2^{80} - 2^{100}$ the median PRank estimation is at most 10 bits above the histogram rank and for ranks beyond 2^{100} the median PRank estimation is only 4 bits above the histogram rank—yet it runs faster, and uses negligible memory.

Our framework, instantiated as the PRank algorithm, provides a new way to solve the rank estimation problem based on a reduction to analytical functions and the calculation of one closed formula, using negligible time and space. It is therefore a useful addition to the SCA evaluator's toolbox. We believe one could employ our framework with other classes of functions to upper-bound the empirical SCA distributions, and possibly achieve even better results.

2   An Analytical Framework for Bounding the Rank

Throughout the paper we always assume that the probability distributions P_i are sorted in non-increasing order: e.g., $P_i[1]$ is the probability of the most likely value for subkey i. For notational convenience when we discuss a key $k = (k_1, .., k_d)$ we mean that k_i is the rank, in the sorted distribution P_i, of the relevant subkey value.

Definition 1 (*Rank(k^*)*). *Let d non-increasing subkey probability distributions P_i for $1 \leq i \leq d$ and the correct key $k^* = (k_1, ..., k_d)$ be given. Let $p^* = P_1[k_1] \cdot ... \cdot P_d[k_d]$ be the probability of the correct key. Then, define Rank(k^*) to be the number of keys $(x_1, ..., x_d)$ s.t. $P_1[x_1] \cdot ... \cdot P_d[x_d] \geq p^*$.*

2.1   The Box Bound

Given the correct key k^*, we start with an observation restricting the search space in which key candidates with probabilities above p^* may be found.

Theorem 1. *Let d non-increasing subkey probability distributions P_i for $1 \leq i \leq d$ be given and let the correct key be $k^* = (k_1, ..., k_d)$. Let $p^* = P_1[k_1] \cdot ... \cdot P_d[k_d]$ be the probability of the correct key. Then, it holds that all the keys $(x_1, ..., x_d)$ s.t. $P_1[x_1] \cdot ... \cdot P_d[x_d] \geq p^*$ have subkeys in the range $1 \leq x_i \leq n_i^*$ where $n_i^* = max_{1 \leq l \leq N}\{l : P_i(l) \cdot \prod_{j \neq i} P_j(1) \geq p^*\}$.*

Proof: In Appendix A.

This bound n_i^* can be easily computed in $O(\log N)$ time using a binary search. Theorem 1 gives us an upper bound on the rank of the correct key, that is tighter than the trivial bound of [30]:

Corollary 1. *(Box Upper Bound) Given d non-increasing subkey probability distributions P_i for $1 \leq i \leq d$ then, the rank of the correct key $k^* = (k_1, ..., k_d)$ whose probability p^* is bounded as follows*

$$Rank(k^*) \leq \prod_{i=1}^{d} n_i^* - \prod_{i=1}^{d} (n_i^* - k_i).$$

2.2 Upper Bound Functions

As we shall see in Sect. 4, our general idea is to upper bound each subkey's probability distribution P_i by an integrable function f_i, such that $P_i[j] \leq f_i(j)$ for all $1 \leq j \leq N$. Then, given the correct key $k^* = (k_1, ..., k_d)$ and using analytical methods, we can estimate the rank of k^* by a closed formula. To do this, let us first define $Rank_f(k^*)$:

Definition 2. *A function is an upper bound function f of a sorted probability distribution P of size N if for all $j = 1, ..., N$, $P[j] \leq f(j)$.*

Definition 3 ($Rank_f(k^*)$)**.** *Given d non-increasing subkey probability distributions P_i and their corresponding d upper bound functions f_i s.t. $P_i[j] \leq f_i(j)$ for all $1 \leq i \leq d$ and $1 \leq j \leq N$, and let the correct key be $k^* = (k_1, ..., k_d)$. Let $p^* = P_1[k_1] \cdot ... \cdot P_d[k_d]$ be the probability of the correct key. Then, define $Rank_f(k^*)$ to be the number of keys $(x_1, ..., x_d)$ s.t. $f_1(x_1) \cdot ... \cdot f_d(x_d) \geq p^*$.*

Proposition 1. *Given d subkey probability distributions P_i and their d upper-bound functions f_i and given the correct key $k^* = (k_1, ..., k_d)$ and its probability $p^* = P_1[k_1] \cdot ... \cdot P_d[k_d]$, it holds that $Rank(k^*) \leq Rank_f(k^*)$*

Proof: Omitted.   □

Our idea is to calculate $Rank_f(k^*)$ of the correct key k^* whose probability is p^*, by integrating the volume under the manifold derived by the d upper bound functions f_i, subject to the isotropic curve defined by $\prod_{i=1}^{d} f_i(x_i) \geq p^*$:

$$Rank(k^*) \leq Rank_f(k^*) \leq \int\limits_{\substack{0 \leq x_1, ..., x_d \leq N, \\ \prod_{i=1}^{d} f_i(x_i) \geq p^*}} \cdots \int 1 \, dx_1 \ldots dx_d. \tag{1}$$

3 Instantiating the Framework with Pareto-Like Functions

We decided to select the integrable upper-bound functions to be based on Pareto distributions, since, like empirical SCA probability distributions, they have long-tails, and they are easily calculable. However, for an upper bound function we do not need to use an actual probability distribution. Therefore we focus on Pareto-*like* functions, without the requirement that $\int f(x)dx = 1$ and without the requirement that $\alpha > 1$.

Definition 4. *A function $f(x)$ is Pareto-like if $f(x) = a/x^\alpha$ for some $a > 0$ and $\alpha \geq 0$.*

Given a probability distribution P we find it useful to consider *anchored* Pareto-like functions, that are defined by two indexes $l < r$, as follows.

Definition 5. *Let P be a distribution, and let indexes $1 \le l < r \le N$ be given. Then a function $f(x)$ is anchored at l, r if $f(l) = P[l]$ and $f(r) = P[r]$. We call the indexes l, r the anchors of f.*

Lemma 1. *Let P be a distribution, and let indexes $1 \le l < r \le N$ be given. Let $\alpha = \log_{r/l}(P[l]/P[r])$ and let $a = P[r]r^\alpha$, or equivalently, $a = P[l]l^\alpha$. Then $f(x) = a/x^\alpha$ is the unique Pareto-like function that is anchored at l, r.*

3.1   The Existence of Pareto-Like Upper Bound Functions

Proposition 2. *Given a sorted non-increasing probability distribution P, there exists an index $r > 1$ such that the Pareto-like function $f(x)$ that is anchored at $1, r$ is an upper bound function.*

Proof: In Appendix B.

3.2   Efficient Search for Pareto-Like Upper Bound Functions

In this section we prove a complete characterization of all the different Pareto-like upper bound functions that are anchored to indexes of the distribution P. This characterization is described by the following theorem:

Theorem 2. *Given a non-increasing sorted probability distribution P, there exist $m < N$ indexes $t_1, \ldots, t_m$ such that every unique Pareto-like upper bound function for P that is anchored at some $l < r$ obeys $l = t_j$ and $r = t_{j+1}$ for some $1 \le j < m$.*

Proof: In Appendix C.

From Theorem 2 we get an efficient search method (Algorithm 1) to find all the different Pareto-like upper-bound functions.

For a given l, the algorithm finds its leftmost matching $r > l$ so the Pareto-like function anchored at l, r is an upper bound function, and then for the next candidate pair it sets $l = r$. Theorem 2 guarantees that no valid candidate pairs are missed by this skip. To do this, the algorithm starts with $l = 1$ and $r = 2$. In order to check whether this pair defines a Pareto-like upper bound the algorithm iterates over all $k \ge r$. If $f_{l,r}(k) \ge P[k]$, then $d > 0$ (line 11) and the algorithm "jumps forward". It calculates the intersection point between the Pareto function and $P[k]$, i.e., the algorithm calculates k' such that $a/k'^\alpha = P[k]$ (line 12) and "jumps" to this k'. The reason this jump is valid is as follows: For each $h \in [k, k'], P[k] \ge P[h] \ge P[k']$ and for each $t \in [k, k'], a/k^\alpha \ge a/t^\alpha \ge a/k'^\alpha$. Since $a/k'^\alpha = P[k]$ it holds $a/t^\alpha \ge P[h]$, for each $t \in [k, k']$ and $h \in [k, k']$. Therefore $f_{l,k}$ is guaranteed to be an upper bound for each $h \in [k, k']$ and we only need to check whether it is an upper bound beyond k', therefore k is updated to be k' (line 12). If $d < 0$ (line 15), the algorithm finds the first violation, i.e., $P[k] > f_{l,r}(k)$ therefore, it stops on this k. Since k is the violation, all the pairs (l, t) such that $t < k$ do not anchor Pareto-like upper bounds: clearly any such (l, t) anchors a Pareto-like function with a violation at k. Therefore, the next candidate for the leftmost matching $r > l$ is k and we only need to check whether $f_{l,k}$ is also an upper bound for the indices

---

Algorithm 1. The function ParetoUpperEstimation().

Input: Subkey distributions P.
Output: A set C of candidate pairs.
1 $C = \emptyset$; $l = 1$;
2 **while** *(l < N)* **do**
3 | $r = l + 1$;
4 | $found = False$;
5 | **while** *(r ≤ N and found == False)* **do**
6 | | $\alpha = \log_{r/l}(P[l]/P[r])$;
7 | | $a = P[l] \cdot l^{\alpha}$;
8 | | $k = r$;
9 | | **while** $k < N$ **do**
10 | | | $d = a/k^{\alpha} - P[k]$;
11 | | | **if** $d \geq 0$ **then**
12 | | | | $k = \min(N, \lfloor (a/P[k])^{1/\alpha} \rfloor) + 1$;   // $f(k) \geq P[k]$: jump forward
13 | | | **if** $d < 0$ *or* $k == N$ **then**
14 | | | | break;
15 | | **if** $d < 0$ **then**
16 | | | $r = k$;   // violation of upper bound: switch to (l, k)
17 | | **else**
18 | | | $found = True$;
19 | | | $C = C \cup \{(l, r)\}$;
20 | | | $l = r$;
21 return C;

$t > k$. So the algorithm sets r to k (line 16) and repeats till it finds a Pareto-like upper bound. Then, the algorithm sets the l of the next pair to be r, according to Theorem 2, and continues in the same way.

Proposition 3. *Let P be a non-increasing sorted probability distribution and let m be the number of its anchors as in Theorem 2. The running time of Algorithm 1 is $O(m \cdot N)$.*

Proof: In Appendix D.

Note that since typically $m \ll N$ the algorithm is almost linear in N and very quick in practice. Furthermore, while the "forward jumps" in the algorithm do not affect the asymptotic running time, they have a dramatic impact in practice since they often allow skipping hundreds of candidates per jump.

3.3 Choosing the Best Pareto-Like Upper Bound Function

In general, Algorithm 1 identifies multiple candidates for Pareto-like upper bound functions for each distribution P_i. We need to select the 'best' function per distribution in the sense that it will lead to a tight bound in the volume computed in Eq. (1). To do so, we need to select the criteria for the 'best' Pareto-like upper bound function.

Algorithm 2. PickBest: Choosing the best Pareto-like upper bounds.

Input: A set C_i of candidate pairs for each Subkey distribution $\{P_i\}_{i=1}^d$, and
the correct key $k^* = \{k_i\}_{i=1}^d$

Output: $(\{a_i\}_{i=1}^d, \{\alpha_i\}_{i=1}^d)$

1 **for** $i = 1$ *to* d **do**

2      $(l_i, r_i) = \arg\min_{(l,r) \in C_i^{10}}\{|P_i[k_i] - f_{l,r}(k_i)|\}$;

3      $\alpha_i = \log_{r_i/l_i}(P_i[l_i]/P_i[r_i])$;

4      $a_i = P_i[l_i] \cdot l_i^\alpha$;

5 **return** $\{a_i\}_{i=1}^d, \{\alpha_i\}_{i=1}^d$;

We tested many criteria for selecting the upper-bound functions. Overall we found that there is no clear 'best' upper bound function for a given probability distribution: rather, the best bound usually depends on the rank k_i of the correct subkey value, with larger ranks k_i requiring upper-bound functions anchored at larger indices. After much experimentation we arrived at the following choice: Given the indices of the correct key $k^* = (k_1, k_2, ..., k_d)$, for each P_i we choose the pair (l_i, r_i) which anchors a Pareto-like upper bound function f_{l_i,r_i} such that $f_{l_i,r_i}(k_i)$ will be the closest to $P_i[k_i]$. Since larger k_i require larger indices (l_i, r_i) which provide larger a_i which directly influences on the upper bound (as we shall see in Sect. 4.1), we limit the chosen pair to be one of the first w pairs. Note that the choice of w impacts the running time (a smaller w means fewer options to minimize over in Algorithm 2 line 2) and potentially impacts the accuracy of the resulting bounds. In our experiments we tested values $w \in [5, 50]$ and found that in fact the bounds were quite insensitive to the choice of w. Therefore we selected $w = 10$ arbitrarily. We denote the set of the first 10 pairs of C_i by C_i^{10}. Algorithm 2 shows the pseudo code for the selection method.

Note that instead of first building the whole set C_i as in Algorithm 1, we can build C_i incrementally until we find the 'best' pair.

4 PRank: The Pareto Rank Estimation Algorithm

Now that we know how to efficiently obtain Pareto-like upper bound functions for all the subkey distributions, we describe the details of our rank estimation algorithm (See Algorithm 3). First, we upper bound each one of the d probability distributions by a Pareto-like upper bound function. Then, given the probability of the correct key, we compute the upper bound rank by a closed formula.

4.1 Estimating the Volume

We solve the multiple integral Eq. (1) for the Pareto-like upper bound functions f_i, for the general case $d \geq 2$. We assume a general configuration in which $\alpha_i \neq \alpha_j$ for all $i \neq j$. The analysis appears in Appendix E. The final solution is

Algorithm 3. Pareto Rank Estimation.

Input: Subkey distributions $\{P_i\}_{i=1}^d$, the correct key $k^* = \{k_i\}_{i=1}^d$
Output: Upper bound rank of the correct key.
1 Let $p^* = \prod_{i=1}^d P_i[k_i]$;
2 $\{a_i\}_{i=1}^d, \{\alpha_i\}_{i=1}^d = ParetoUpperEstimation(\{P_i\}_{i=1}^d, k^*)$;
3 return $UpperBound(\{a_i\}_{i=1}^d, \{\alpha_i\}_{i=1}^d, \{P_i\}_{i=1}^d, p^*)$;

the following closed formula:

$$\sum_{i=1}^d \left[\left(\frac{1}{p^*} \cdot \prod_{j=1}^d a_j \right)^{\frac{1}{\alpha_i}} \cdot \prod_{j=1, j\neq i}^d \left(\frac{\alpha_i}{\alpha_i - \alpha_j} \cdot N^{\frac{\alpha_i - \alpha_j}{\alpha_i}} \right) \right]. \tag{2}$$

The same analysis can also be done assuming each dimension has a different bound—and then we can use the n_i^* of the Box Bound (Theorem 1) to yield a closed formula for the upper bound:

$$Rank(k^*) \leq \sum_{i=1}^d \left[\left(\frac{1}{p^*} \cdot \prod_{j=1}^d a_j \right)^{\frac{1}{\alpha_i}} \cdot \prod_{j=1, j\neq i}^d \left(\frac{\alpha_i}{\alpha_i - \alpha_j} \cdot n_j^{*\frac{\alpha_i - \alpha_j}{\alpha_i}} \right) \right]. \tag{3}$$

Notes: (i) The formulas of Eqs. (3) and (2) are analogous to the results of [4] obtained via Laplace transforms. (ii) In our data we did not encounter cases in which $\alpha_i = \alpha_j$ so the "general configuration" assumption did not restrict us.

4.2 Theoretical Worst-Case Performance

Running Time: Equation (3) consists of d additions and in each sum we have d multiplications and d calls to the real-value power function. Therefore, assuming that calculating x^y takes constant time, the running time of computing the formula is $O(d^2)$. According to Proposition 3 the running time of finding a Pareto-like upper bound function f_i for each probability distribution P_i, takes $O(m_i \cdot N)$. Let $\hat{m} = \max_i\{m_i\}$, then the running time in total is $O(\hat{m} \cdot d \cdot N)$, assuming that computing formula (3) is negligible. Since typically $\hat{m} \ll N$ the algorithm is almost linear in $d \cdot N$ and very quick in practice.

Space Complexity: The algorithm needs to keep for each probability distribution its corresponding Pareto-like upper bound function. In other words, it only needs to keep the corresponding a_i, α_i and n_i^* for every $1 \leq i \leq d$. Therefore the space complexity is $O(d)$.

5 Performance Evaluation

We evaluated the performance of the PRank estimation algorithm through an extensive simulation study. We compared the new PRank algorithm to the currently best rank estimation algorithm: the histogram algorithm of [13]. We implemented both in Matlab, our PRank code is available in [9]. We ran both algorithms on a 2.80 GHz i7 PC with 8 GB RAM running Microsoft windows 7, 64bit.

5.1   Data Corpus I

To evaluate PRank, we used the data of [11]. Within this data, there are 611 probability distribution sets gathered from a specific SCA. The SCA of [11] was against AES [1] with 128-bits keys. The sets represent various setting of the SCA: number of traces used, whether the clock was jittered, and the values of tunable attack parameters. The attack grouped the key bits into 16 8-bit subkeys, and hence its output probability distributions are over these byte values. Each set in the corpus consists of the correct secret key and 16 distributions, one per subkey. The distributions are sorted in non-increasing order of probability, each of length 2^8.

Since we don't know the real rank of the correct keys, we used the histogram rank as the x axis in our resulting graphs (Figs. 1 and 2). We measured the time and the upper bound for each trace using PRank and the histograms rank estimation.

We checked PRank's accuracy and running time for different configurations. We started with $d = 16$ and $n = 2^8$. As we shall see, the computed upper bound is noticeably higher than the histogram rank, however the running time is a fraction of that of the histogram algorithm.

Next, in order to improve the accuracy, we applied a technique suggested in [13]: merge the $d = 16$ probability lists of size $n = 2^8$ into $d = 8$ lists of size $n = 2^{16}$. As we shall see we found that reducing the number of dimensions indeed significantly improved the accuracy with a marginal increase in the PRank running time.

Bound Tightness. Figure 1 illustrates the PRank upper bound with $d = 16$, the PRank upper bound with $d = 8$ and the histogram rank, all in number of bits ($\log_2$). All these values are shown as function of the number of bits of histogram rank, hence its curve is a straight line. The figure clearly shows that it is advantageous to reduce the dimension d. As we can see in the Figure, the accuracy of PRank's estimation is quite good: for ranks between 2^{80}–2^{100} the median PRank bound is less than 10 bits above the histogram rank, and for the very high ranks (above 2^{100}) median PRank bound is only 4 bits more. For small ranks, around 2^{20}, PRank gave a bound which is roughly 20 bits greater than that of the histogram—however we argue that such ranks are within reach of key enumeration so rank estimation is not particularly interesting there.

Runtime Analysis. Figure 2 shows the running times (in seconds) of the histogram rank estimation (with B = 5K and B = 50K) and the PRank estimation for $d = 16$ and $d = 8$. The running time of the PRank consists of the preprocessing time of finding the Pareto-like upper bound function of each probability distribution, plus the running time of calculating the closed formula bound of Eq. (3) given the secret key. The histogram running time consists of the preprocessing of converting each probability distribution into a histogram plus the running time of finding the sum of the corresponding bins given the secret key. The figure shows that PRank, for both $d = 8$ and $d = 16$, typically takes only a few milliseconds to

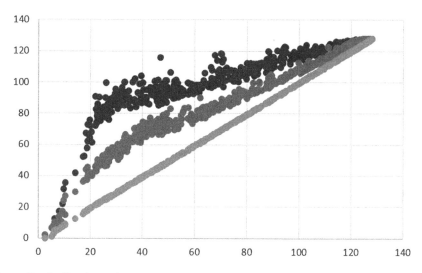

Fig. 1. Ranks ($\log_2$) as a function of histogram rank. The curves are, from top to bottom: PRank upper bound for $d = 16$ (blue), PRank upper bound for $d = 8$ (orange) and Histogram rank for B = 5K (gray). (Color figure online)

Table 1. Space complexity of PRank and Histograms in four configurations. The left side of each column in the table is the PRank space and the right is the Histograms space.

	B = 5K		B = 50K	
$d = 8$	24 bytes	80 KB	24 bytes	800 KB
$d = 16$	48 bytes	160 KB	48 bytes	1.6 MB

complete, and runs faster than the Histograms in its 4 configurations. Looking at the PRank itself we can see, as we expected, that $d = 16$ runs faster than $d = 8$ since the length N of each distribution is shorter. Looking at the Histograms runtimes, we can see that the number of buckets B is dominant: $B = 5K$ is 10 times faster than $B = 50K$ and for $B = 50K$ we can also see that $d = 16$ is faster than $d = 8$. However, notice that both PRank and Histograms run in less than 1 s.

Space Utilization. Table 1 illustrates the space used by the 2 algorithms' data structures. As we can see, the memory consumption of PRank algorithm is drastically lower than the histogram space consumption. PRank space consumption is trivial $3 \cdot d$ while the histogram space requirements are around $2 \cdot B \cdot d$.

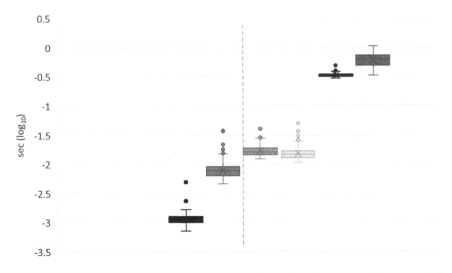

Fig. 2. The running times of the algorithms as a box plot: the top and bottom of the boxes represent the 3rd and 1st quartiles, respectively, and the line inside the box represents the median. The left side represents the PRank running time in two configurations: $d = 16$ (black) and $d = 8$ (orange). The right side represents the histograms running time in four configurations: $d = 16$, B = 5K (gray), $d = 8$, B = 5K (yellow), $d = 16$, B = 50K (blue) and $d = 8$, B = 50K (green), all in seconds (log scale). (Color figure online)

5.2   Data Corpus 2

The second set of experiments uses the data of [25]. Within this data, there are 936 probability distribution sets gathered from another SCA. The SCA of [25] was against AES [1] with 128-bits keys. The attack grouped the key bits into 4 32-bit subkeys, and hence its output probability distributions are over these 32-bit values. Each set in the corpus consists of the correct secret key and 4 distributions, one per sub-key. The distributions are sorted in non-increasing order of probability. The SCA of [25] discards subkey candidates it finds to be unacceptable hence the probability distributions all have much fewer than 2^{32} values: the distribution length N is at most 2^{16}. This means that the largest rank that the data could predict is $N^4 \approx 2^{64}$.

We again used the histogram rank as the x axis in our resulting graphs. We measured the time, the space consumption and the upper bound for each trace using PRank and the histograms rank estimation.

Bound Tightness. Figure 3 illustrates the number of bits ($\log_2$) of the PRank upper bound and the histogram rank. The ranks depicted in Fig. 3 for both algorithms are significantly lower than those in Fig. 1 (nearly all the ranks are below 2^{40}). This is a feature of the SCA of [25], which produces sharp distributions and assigns high probabilities to the correct subkey values. In Fig. 1 we saw that PRank

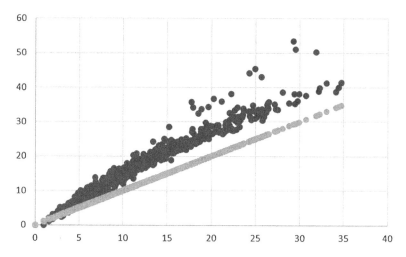

Fig. 3. Ranks ($\log_2$) as a function of histogram rank. The curves are show the PRank upper bound for $d = 4$ (blue) and Histogram rank (orange). (Color figure online)

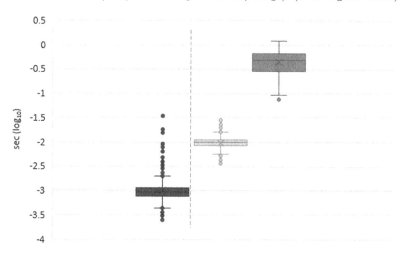

Fig. 4. The left side represents the PRank running time for $d = 4$ (blue). The right side represents the histograms running time in two configurations: $d = 4$, B = 5K (orange) and $d = 4$, B = 50K (gray), all in seconds (log scale). (Color figure online)

accuracy was up to 20 bits above the Histogram rank for keys with low ranks: Fig. 3 shows that when the distributions are sharper, PRank accuracy improves: The figure shows that the accuracy of PRank's estimation for most of the keys in this data is around 4 bits above the histograms bound.

Runtime Analysis. Figure 4 shows the ($\log_{10}$) time (in seconds) of histogram rank estimation [13] and PRank estimation.

The figure shows that on this data corpus too the PRank algorithm runs in a few milliseconds, and is faster than the histogram algorithm—by about 1 order of magnitude—but both algorithms are very efficient, taking under 1 s to complete.

6   Conclusions and Future Work

In this paper we proposed a new framework for rank estimation, that is conceptually simple, and more time and memory efficient than previous proposals. Our main idea is to bound each subkey distribution by an analytical function, and then estimate the rank by a closed formula.

To instantiate the framework we use Pareto-like functions to upper-bound the empirical distributions. Pareto-like functions are suitable, since like the SCA-based probability distributions, they have long-tails, and they are easily calculable. We fully characterized such upper-bounding functions and developed an efficient algorithm to find them. We then used Pareto-like functions to develop a new explicit upper bound on the rank of a given key. Combined with the algorithm to find the upper-bounding Pareto-like functions, we obtained an $O(dN^2)$ rank upper-bound estimation algorithm we call PRank.

We evaluated the performance of PRank through extensive simulations based on two real SCA data corpus, and compared it to the currently-best histogram-based algorithm. We showed that PRank gives a good rank estimation with much improved time and memory efficiency, especially for large ranks: For ranks between $2^{80} - 2^{100}$ the median PRank estimation is at most 10 bits above the histogram rank and for ranks beyond 2^{100} the median PRank estimation is only 4 bits above the histogram rank—yet it runs in milliseconds, and uses negligible memory. It is therefore a useful addition to the SCA evaluator's toolbox.

As we demonstrated, our choice of Pareto-like functions is clearly very effective. However, one could employ our framework with other classes of functions to upper-bound the non-increasing empirical distributions, and possibly achieve even better results. The criteria for selecting a good class of functions include: (i) the ability to derive a closed formula for the bounded volume; (ii) the tightness of the resulting rank estimates; and (iii) the computational complexity of finding the best bounding functions per distribution. We leave this direction for future research.

Acknowledgments. Liron David was partially supported by The Yitzhak and Chaya Weinstein Research Institute for Signal Processing.

A   Proof for Theorem 1

For any dimension i, if we choose the most likely value in all dimensions $j \neq i$, we can find the minimum probability in dimension i that still fulfills the condition $P_1[x_1] \cdot ... \cdot P_d[x_d] \geq p^*$. Therefore, any index l s.t. $P_i(l)$ is smaller than this minimum probability will never be part of a key whose probability is higher than or equal to p^*. Since P_j is non-increasing, the most likely value is at index 1, hence for all dimensions $j \neq i$, the most likely value has probability $P_j(1)$. We look for the farthest index l in dimension i such that the product $P_i(l) \cdot \prod_{j \neq i} P_j(1)$ is still higher than or equal to p^*. Therefore, the number of subkey indexes for dimension i that are needed in order to compute the rank of a key whose probability p^* is

$$n_i^* = max_{1 \leq l \leq N} \{l : P_i(l) \cdot \prod_{j \neq i} P_j(1) \geq p^*\}.$$

$\square$

B   Proof for Proposition 2

Let $f^{\alpha,a} = a/x^\alpha$ be a Pareto-like function with parameters α and a. Since P is a sorted non-increasing probability distribution, $P[1]$ is greater than or equal to any other $P[j]$ for $1 \leq j \leq N$. Therefore, a trivial Pareto-like upper bound function for P is $f^{0,P[1]}(x) = P[1]$. If $P[2] = P[1]$ then $f^{0,P[1]}(x)$ fulfills the requirements with anchors 1,2.

Else, we shall construct an upper-bound function $f^{\alpha,P[1]}$, that is anchored at $1, r$ for some $r > 1$. Given any index $r > 1$ and the value $P[r]$, let $\alpha_r = \log_r (P[1]/P[r])$. Then, the function $f^{\alpha_r,P[1]}(x) = P[1]/x^{\alpha_r}$ is the unique Pareto-like function that is anchored at $1, r$. Hence we need to find $1 < r \leq N$ s.t. $f^{\alpha_r,P[1]}(x)$ is an upper-bound function: $f^{\alpha_r,P[1]}(x) \geq P[x]$ for all $1 \leq x \leq N$. For a fixed index $r > 1$, the function $g(\alpha) = f^{\alpha,P[1]}(r) = P[1]/r^\alpha$ for $\alpha \geq 0$ is monotone decreasing, with $g(0) = P[1]$. Clearly $g(\alpha_r) = P[r]$, hence for all $0 \leq \alpha \leq \alpha_r$ we have $f^{\alpha,P[1]}(r) \geq P[r]$. Let $\alpha^* = \min_r \{\alpha_r\}$ and let $r^* = \arg\min_r \{\alpha_r\}$ be the minimal index at which α^* is achieved. Then, $f^{\alpha^*,P[1]}$ is an upper bound function for P which obeys $f^{\alpha^*,P[1]}(1) = P[1]$ and $f^{\alpha^*,P[1]}(r^*) = P[r^*]$ - at all other indices $r \neq 1$, $r \neq r^*$ we have $\alpha^* \leq \alpha_r$ by definition, so $f^{\alpha^*,P[1]}(r) = g(\alpha^*) \geq g(\alpha_r) = P[r]$.

$\square$

C   Proof for Theorem 2

We prove this theorem using induction. The base case is Proposition 2, which shows that $t_1 = 1$, and whose proof describes how to find $t_2 = r$.

For the induction step we assume that we have a Pareto-like upper bound function f that is anchored at indexes l, r. We prove that if there exists another Pareto-like upper bound function $\hat{f} \neq f$ that is anchored at $\hat{l}, \hat{r}$ s.t. $\hat{l} > l$ then there exists some $r < t \leq \hat{l}$ s.t. the Pareto-like function anchored at r, t is an upper-bound function for P.

We shall prove this in 3 steps: in Theorem 3 we prove that the anchors of f and $\hat{f}$ cannot be nested. In Theorem 4 we prove that if the anchors of f and $\hat{f}$ are interleaved then the intermediate anchors coincide, i.e., $t = r = \hat{l}$. Finally in Theorem 5 we prove that if the anchors of f and $\hat{f}$ obey $r < \hat{l}$ then the required t exists and obeys $t \leq \hat{l}$.

To prove these theorems, we first state two simple lemmas, and prove Propositions 4 and 5 showing that two different Pareto-like upper bound functions cannot "share" only their left anchors l, or only their right anchor r.

Lemma 2. *Let $f_1 = a/x^\alpha$ and $f_2 = b/x^\beta$ be Pareto-like functions s.t. $\alpha > \beta$. Then, $f_1(x) = f_2(x)$ only at the crossover point $x_c = (a/b)^{\frac{1}{\alpha-\beta}}$.*

Lemma 3. *Let $f_1 = a/x^\alpha$ and $f_2 = b/x^\beta$ be Pareto-like functions s.t. $\alpha > \beta$ and let x_c be their crossover point. Then for $x > x_c$ $f_1 < f_2$ and for $x < x_c$ $f_2 < f_1$.*

Proposition 4. *Given a non-increasing sorted probability distribution P and a Pareto-like upper bound function f of P anchored at l, r, then any Pareto-like function $\hat{f} \neq f$ that is anchored at $l, \hat{r}$ s.t. $\hat{r} > r$ will violate the upper bound condition at index r, i.e., $\hat{f}(r) < P[r]$.*

Proof: Let $f(x) = a/x^\alpha$ and $\hat{f}(x) = \hat{a}/x^{\hat{\alpha}}$ be defined as above, "sharing" the anchor l. Since f is a Pareto-like upper bound function $f(\hat{r}) \geq P[\hat{r}]$. By definition $P[\hat{r}] = \hat{f}(\hat{r})$, therefore $f(\hat{r}) \geq \hat{f}(\hat{r})$, which is equivalent to

$$a \cdot \hat{r}^{\hat{\alpha}} \geq \hat{a} \cdot \hat{r}^{\alpha}.$$

Substituting $a = P[l] \cdot l^\alpha$ and $\hat{a} = P[l] \cdot l^{\hat{\alpha}}$ for the same l we get

$$\hat{r}^{\hat{\alpha}-\alpha} \geq l^{\hat{\alpha}-\alpha}.$$

Since $\hat{r} \geq l$, we get $\hat{\alpha} > \alpha$. Since $P[r] = f(r)$ by definition, in order to prove $P[r] > \hat{f}(r)$, it suffices to prove $f(r) > \hat{f}(r)$, which is equivalent to

$$\hat{a} \cdot r^\alpha < a \cdot r^{\hat{\alpha}}.$$

By substituting $a = P[l] \cdot l^\alpha$ and $\hat{a} = P[l] \cdot l^{\hat{\alpha}}$ we get the equivalent inequality

$$l^{\hat{\alpha}-\alpha} < r^{\hat{\alpha}-\alpha},$$

which holds since $l < r$ and $\hat{\alpha} > \alpha$. □

Proposition 5. *Given a non-increasing sorted probability distribution P and a Pareto-like upper bound function f of P anchored at l, r, then any Pareto-like function $\hat{f} \neq f$ that is anchored at $\hat{l}, r$ for some $\hat{l} < l$ will violate the upper bound condition at index l, i.e., $\hat{f}(l) < P[l]$.*

Proof: Analogous to that of Proposition 4.

Theorem 3. *(No nested anchors). Let P be a non-increasing sorted probability distribution and let two index pairs $l < r$ and $\hat{l} < \hat{r}$ s.t. $l \leq \hat{l} < \hat{r} \leq r$. There cannot exist two Pareto-like upper bound functions $f \neq \hat{f}$ s.t. f is anchored at l, r and $\hat{f}$ is anchored at $\hat{l}, \hat{r}$.*

Proof: From Proposition 4, we see that there cannot exist two different Pareto-like upper bound functions $f, \hat{f}$ s.t. $f(l) = P[l] = \hat{f}(l)$ (i.e., the crossover point is at l) but $f(r) = P[r]$ and $\hat{f}(\hat{r}) = P[\hat{r}]$ for $r < \hat{r}$. In the same way, from Proposition 5 we see that there cannot exist two different Pareto-like upper bound functions $f, \hat{f}$ s.t. $f(r) = P[r] = \hat{f}(r)$ (i.e., the crossover point is at r) but $f(l) = P[l]$ and $\hat{f}(\hat{l}) = P[\hat{l}]$ for $l < \hat{l}$. Therefore the only option is that $l < \hat{l} < \hat{r} < r$. However, this option also cannot exist since then we get

$$\hat{f}(l) \geq P[l] = f(l), \quad f(\hat{l}) \geq P[\hat{l}] = \hat{f}(\hat{l}),$$
$$f(\hat{r}) \geq P[\hat{r}] = \hat{f}(\hat{r}), \quad \hat{f}(r) \geq P[r] = f(r).$$

However, since $f \neq \hat{f}$ at least 3 of these 4 inequalities must be sharp, which means we need to have at least two crossover points, contrary to Lemma 2.   □

Theorem 4. *(Interleaved anchors). Let P be a non-increasing sorted probability distribution and let two index pairs $l < r$ and $\hat{l} < \hat{r}$ be such that $l \leq \hat{l} \leq r \leq \hat{r}$ and s.t. there exist two different Pareto-like upper bound functions, f anchored at l, r and $\hat{f}$ anchored at $\hat{l}, \hat{r}$. Then, $l < \hat{l} = r < \hat{r}$.*

Proof: From properties of f and $\hat{f}$, it holds that:

$$\hat{f}(l) \geq P[l] = f(l), \quad f(\hat{l}) \geq P[\hat{l}] = \hat{f}(\hat{l}),$$
$$\hat{f}(r) \geq P[r] = f(r), \quad f(\hat{r}) \geq P[\hat{r}] = \hat{f}(\hat{r}). \tag{4}$$

In other words, we get $f(l) \leq \hat{f}(l)$, $f(\hat{l}) \geq \hat{f}(\hat{l})$, $f(r) \leq \hat{f}(r)$ and $f(\hat{r}) \geq \hat{f}(\hat{r})$. Notice that f and $\hat{f}$ are different, therefore they have a single crossover point. To obtain a contradiction, assume that $l < \hat{l} < r < \hat{r}$. If two or more of the inequalities in Eq. (4) are equalities then $f \equiv \hat{f}$, contrary to the premise. Therefore at least 3 of the inequalities in Eq. (4) are sharp. However since $f \neq \hat{f}$ there is a unique crossover point x_c between them, and regardless of where x_c is located with respect to $l, \hat{l}, r, \hat{r}$, there will be two indices $u, v \in \{l, \hat{l}, r, \hat{r}\}$ either to its left or to its right, such that $f(u) > \hat{f}(u)$ and $f(v) < \hat{f}(v)$, contradicting Lemma 2. Therefore at least two indices need to be equal to each other. As we've seen in Proposition 4 there cannot exist two upper bound Pareto-like functions f and $\hat{f}$ such that $f(l) = P[l] = \hat{f}(l)$ (i.e., the crossover point is at l) but $f(r) = P[r]$ and $\hat{f}(\hat{r}) = P[\hat{r}]$ for $r < \hat{r}$. Therefore l cannot be equal to $\hat{l}$. In the same way, Proposition 5 shows that there cannot exist two Pareto-like upper bound functions f and $\hat{f}$ such that $f(r) = P[r] = \hat{f}(r)$ (i.e., the crossover point is at r) but $f(l) = P[l]$ and $\hat{f}(\hat{l}) = P[\hat{l}]$ for $l < \hat{l}$. Therefore, r cannot be equal to $\hat{r}$. Therefore, the only option is $\hat{l} = r$. □

Theorem 5. *(Disjoint anchors). Let P be a non-increasing sorted probability distribution and let two index pairs $l < r$ and $\hat{l} < \hat{r}$ be such that $l < r \leq \hat{l} < \hat{r}$ and s.t. there exist two different Pareto-like upper bound functions, f anchored at l, r and $\hat{f}$ anchored at $\hat{l}, \hat{r}$. Then there exists $r < t \leq \hat{l}$ such that the Pareto-like function $\bar{f}$ anchored at r, t is an upper-bound function.*

Proof: Omitted.   □

The combination of Theorems 3, 4 and 5 completes the proof of Theorem 2. □

D   Proof for Proposition 3

To find the first pair $(t_1 = 1, t_2)$ that anchors a Pareto-like upper bound takes $N - 1$ steps. Then, starting at t_2, looking for its leftmost matching $t_3 > t_2$, the algorithm tests for violations at indices between t_2 and N, taking at most $N - t_2$ steps and similarly till finding last pair takes $N - t_m$ steps. In total we get at most $(N - t_1) + (N - t_2) + ... + (N - t_m) = m \cdot N - \sum_{i=1}^{m} t_i = O(m \cdot N)$. □

E   Derivation of the Rank Upper-Bound Formula

We start by solving the multiple integral Eq. (1) for the Pareto-like upper bound functions f_i, for the first non-trivial case which is $d = 3$. Then, we will generalize it for any d. Plugging the Pareto-like function $f_i = a_i/x_i^{\alpha_i}$ for each $1 \le i \le d$ into Eq. (1) we get:

$$\int_0^N \int_0^N \int_0^N 1 \, dx_3 dx_2 dx_1. \qquad (5)$$
$$\left(\frac{a_1}{x_1^{\alpha_1}} \cdot \frac{a_2}{x_2^{\alpha_2}} \cdot \frac{a_3}{x_3^{\alpha_3}}\right) \ge p^*$$

We assume the general case in which $\alpha_i \ne \alpha_j$ for all $i \ne j$. The range of the multiple integrals in Eq. (5) is equivalent to

$$\left(\frac{a_1}{x_1^{\alpha_1}} \cdot \frac{a_2}{x_2^{\alpha_2}} \cdot \frac{a_3}{p^*}\right)^{\frac{1}{\alpha_3}} \ge x_3.$$

Therefore, we can plug x_3 into Eq. (5) to get

$$\int_0^N \int_0^N \left(\frac{a_1}{x_1^{\alpha_1}} \cdot \frac{a_2}{x_2^{\alpha_2}} \cdot \frac{a_3}{p^*}\right)^{\frac{1}{\alpha_3}} dx_2 dx_1. \qquad (6)$$

The lower bound of each dimension x_i is 0, but Pareto-like functions are not defined at 0. However, in order to maintain $x_3 \le N$ we require:

$$x_3 \le \left(\frac{a_1}{x_1^{\alpha_1}} \cdot \frac{a_2}{x_2^{\alpha_2}} \cdot \frac{a_3}{p^*}\right)^{\frac{1}{\alpha_3}} \le N,$$

which provides a bound on x_2

$$x_2 \ge \left(\frac{a_1}{x_1^{\alpha_1}} \cdot \frac{a_2}{N^{\alpha_3}} \cdot \frac{a_3}{p^*}\right)^{\frac{1}{\alpha_2}}. \qquad (7)$$

We denote this lower bound on x_2 by x_2':

$$x_2' \triangleq \left(\frac{a_1}{x_1^{\alpha_1}} \cdot \frac{a_2}{N^{\alpha_3}} \cdot \frac{a_3}{p^*}\right)^{\frac{1}{\alpha_2}}.$$

For all $x_2 < x_2'$, we get $x_3 > N$ which is out of range, therefore for $x_2 < x_2'$ we take $x_3 = N$. By splitting the inner-most integral in Eq. (6) into two ranges we get:

$$\int_0^N \left[\int_0^{x_2'} N \, dx_2 + \int_{x_2'}^N \left(\frac{a_1}{x_1^{\alpha_1}} \cdot \frac{a_2}{x_2^{\alpha_2}} \cdot \frac{a_3}{p^*}\right)^{\frac{1}{\alpha_3}} dx_2\right] dx_1. \qquad (8)$$

We repeat the procedure and divide the next dimension x_1. In order to maintain $x_2 \leq N$, from Eq. (7)

$$(\frac{a_1}{x_1^{\alpha_1}} \cdot \frac{a_2}{N^{\alpha_3}} \cdot \frac{a_3}{p^*})^{\frac{1}{\alpha_2}} \leq x_2 \leq N,$$

so x_1 should maintain

$$x_1 \geq (\frac{a_1}{N^{\alpha_2}} \cdot \frac{a_2}{N^{\alpha_3}} \cdot \frac{a_3}{p^*})^{\frac{1}{\alpha_1}}.$$

Denote this lower bound of x_1 by x_1'

$$x_1' \triangleq (\frac{a_1}{N^{\alpha_2}} \cdot \frac{a_2}{N^{\alpha_3}} \cdot \frac{a_3}{p^*})^{\frac{1}{\alpha_1}}.$$

For all $x_1 < x_1'$, we get $x_2 > N$ which is out of range, therefore for $x_1 < x_1'$ we take $x_2 = N$. Plugging this into Eq. (8)

$$\int_0^{x_1'} \int_0^N N \, dx_1 + \int_{x_1'}^N \left[\int_0^{x_2'} N \, dx_2 + \int_{x_2'}^N \left(\frac{a_1}{x_1^{\alpha_1}} \cdot \frac{a_2}{x_2^{\alpha_2}} \cdot \frac{a_3}{p^*} \right)^{\frac{1}{\alpha_3}} dx_2 \right] dx_1. \quad (9)$$

To solve this integral we solve each term separately, starting with the inner-right term of Eq. (9):

$$\int_{x_2'}^N \left(\frac{a_1}{x_1^{\alpha_1}} \cdot \frac{a_2}{x_2^{\alpha_2}} \cdot \frac{a_3}{p^*} \right)^{\frac{1}{\alpha_3}} dx_2,$$

which is straightforward:

$$\left(\frac{a_1 \cdot a_2 \cdot a_3}{x_1^{\alpha_1} \cdot p^*} \right)^{\frac{1}{\alpha_3}} \int_{x_2'}^N x_2^{-\frac{\alpha_2}{\alpha_3}} dx_2 = \left(\frac{a_1 \cdot a_2 \cdot a_3}{x_1^{\alpha_1} \cdot p^*} \right)^{\frac{1}{\alpha_3}} \cdot \frac{\alpha_3}{\alpha_3 - \alpha_2} \cdot x_2^{1-\frac{\alpha_2}{\alpha_3}} \Big|_{x_2'}^N.$$

After substituting the limits, since $\alpha_2 \neq \alpha_3$, we get:

$$\left(\frac{a_1 \cdot a_2 \cdot a_3}{x_1^{\alpha_1} \cdot p^*} \right)^{\frac{1}{\alpha_3}} \cdot \frac{\alpha_3}{\alpha_3 - \alpha_2} \cdot \left[N^{\frac{\alpha_3-\alpha_2}{\alpha_3}} - \left(\frac{a_1 \cdot a_2 \cdot a_3}{x_1^{\alpha_1} \cdot p^*} \right)^{\frac{1}{\alpha_2}-\frac{1}{\alpha_3}} \cdot N^{\frac{\alpha_2-\alpha_3}{\alpha_2}} \right]$$

which equals to

$$\left(\frac{a_1 \cdot a_2 \cdot a_3}{x_1^{\alpha_1} \cdot p^*} \right)^{\frac{1}{\alpha_3}} \cdot \frac{\alpha_3}{\alpha_3 - \alpha_2} \cdot N^{\frac{\alpha_3-\alpha_2}{\alpha_3}} - \left(\frac{a_1 \cdot a_2 \cdot a_3}{x_1^{\alpha_1} \cdot p^*} \right)^{\frac{1}{\alpha_2}} \cdot \frac{\alpha_3}{\alpha_3 - \alpha_2} \cdot N^{\frac{\alpha_2-\alpha_3}{\alpha_2}}. \quad (10)$$

Now, we calculate the inner-left term of Eq. (9):

$$\int_0^{x_2'} N \, dx_2 = \left(\frac{a_1 \cdot a_2 \cdot a_3}{x_1^{\alpha_1} \cdot p^*} \right)^{\frac{1}{\alpha_2}} \cdot N^{\frac{\alpha_2-\alpha_3}{\alpha_2}}. \quad (11)$$

Plugging in Eqs. (10) and (11) into the right term of Eq. (9), we get:

$$\int_{x_1'}^N \left(\frac{a_1 \cdot a_2 \cdot a_3}{x_1^{\alpha_1} \cdot p^*} \right)^{\frac{1}{\alpha_3}} \cdot \frac{\alpha_3}{\alpha_3 - \alpha_2} \cdot N^{\frac{\alpha_3-\alpha_2}{\alpha_3}} + \left(\frac{a_1 \cdot a_2 \cdot a_3}{x_1^{\alpha_1} \cdot p^*} \right)^{\frac{1}{\alpha_2}} \cdot \frac{\alpha_2}{\alpha_2 - \alpha_3} \cdot N^{\frac{\alpha_2-\alpha_3}{\alpha_2}} \, dx_1.$$

Calculating the integral we get:

$$\left(\frac{a_1 \cdot a_2 \cdot a_3}{p^*}\right)^{\frac{1}{\alpha_3}} \cdot \frac{\alpha_3}{\alpha_3 - \alpha_2} \cdot N^{\frac{\alpha_3 - \alpha_2}{\alpha_3}} \cdot \frac{\alpha_3}{\alpha_3 - \alpha_1} \cdot x_1^{\frac{\alpha_3 - \alpha_1}{\alpha_3}}\Bigg|_{x_1'}^{N} +$$

$$\left(\frac{a_1 \cdot a_2 \cdot a_3}{p^*}\right)^{\frac{1}{\alpha_2}} \cdot \frac{\alpha_2}{\alpha_2 - \alpha_3} \cdot N^{\frac{\alpha_2 - \alpha_3}{\alpha_2}} \cdot \frac{\alpha_2}{\alpha_2 - \alpha_1} \cdot x_1^{\frac{\alpha_2 - \alpha_1}{\alpha_2}}\Bigg|_{x_1'}^{N}.$$

Solving this and adding the solution of the left term of Eq. (9) we get the final formula for $d = 3$:

$$\left(\frac{a_1 \cdot a_2 \cdot a_3}{p^*}\right)^{\frac{1}{\alpha_1}} \cdot \frac{\alpha_1}{\alpha_1 - \alpha_2} \cdot \frac{\alpha_1}{\alpha_1 - \alpha_3} \cdot N^{\frac{\alpha_1 - \alpha_2}{\alpha_1}} \cdot N^{\frac{\alpha_1 - \alpha_3}{\alpha_1}} +$$

$$\left(\frac{a_1 \cdot a_2 \cdot a_3}{p^*}\right)^{\frac{1}{\alpha_2}} \cdot \frac{\alpha_2}{\alpha_2 - \alpha_3} \cdot \frac{\alpha_2}{\alpha_2 - \alpha_1} \cdot N^{\frac{\alpha_2 - \alpha_1}{\alpha_1}} \cdot N^{\frac{\alpha_2 - \alpha_3}{\alpha_2}} + \qquad (12)$$

$$\left(\frac{a_1 \cdot a_2 \cdot a_3}{p^*}\right)^{\frac{1}{\alpha_3}} \cdot \frac{\alpha_3}{\alpha_3 - \alpha_1} \cdot \frac{\alpha_3}{\alpha_3 - \alpha_2} \cdot N^{\frac{\alpha_3 - \alpha_1}{\alpha_3}} \cdot N^{\frac{\alpha_3 - \alpha_2}{\alpha_3}}$$

For the general case $d \geq 2$ the analysis is analogous so we omit the details. The final solution for any $d \geq 2$ is the following closed formula:

$$\sum_{i=1}^{d}\left[\left(\frac{1}{p^*} \cdot \prod_{j=1}^{d} a_j\right)^{\frac{1}{\alpha_i}} \cdot \prod_{j=1, j\neq i}^{d}\left(\frac{\alpha_i}{\alpha_i - \alpha_j} \cdot N^{\frac{\alpha_i - \alpha_j}{\alpha_i}}\right)\right].$$

References

1. FIPS PUB 197, advanced encryption standard (AES), U.S. Department of Commerce/National Institute of Standards and Technology (NIST) (2001)
2. Agrawal, D., Archambeault, B., Rao, J.R., Rohatgi, P.: The EM Side—Channel(s). In: Kaliski, B.S., Koç, K., Paar, C. (eds.) CHES 2002. LNCS, vol. 2523, pp. 29–45. Springer, Heidelberg (2003). https://doi.org/10.1007/3-540-36400-5_4
3. Bernstein, D.J., Lange, T., van Vredendaal, C.: Tighter, faster, simpler side-channel security evaluations beyond computing power. IACR Cryptology ePrint Archive, 2015:221 (2015)
4. Bibinger, M.: Notes on the sum and maximum of independent exponentially distributed random variables with different scale parameters. arXiv preprint, arXiv:1307.3945 (2013)
5. Bogdanov, A., Kizhvatov, I., Manzoor, K., Tischhauser, E., Witteman, M.: Fast and memory-efficient key recovery in side-channel attacks. In: Dunkelman, O., Keliher, L. (eds.) SAC 2015. LNCS, vol. 9566, pp. 310–327. Springer, Cham (2016). https://doi.org/10.1007/978-3-319-31301-6_19
6. Choudary, M.O., Popescu, P.G.: Back to massey: impressively fast, scalable and tight security evaluation tools. In: Fischer, W., Homma, N. (eds.) CHES 2017. LNCS, vol. 10529, pp. 367–386. Springer, Cham (2017). https://doi.org/10.1007/978-3-319-66787-4_18

7. David, L., Wool, A.: A bounded-space near-optimal key enumeration algorithm for multi-subkey side-channel attacks. In: Handschuh, H. (ed.) CT-RSA 2017. LNCS, vol. 10159, pp. 311–327. Springer, Cham (2017). https://doi.org/10.1007/978-3-319-52153-4_18

8. David, L., Wool, A.: Poly-logarithmic side channel rank estimation via exponential sampling. In: RSA Conference Cryptographers' Track, CT-RSA (2019, to appear)

9. David, L., Wool, A.: Prank: Fast analytical rank estimation matlab code (2019)

10. Duc, A., Faust, S., Standaert, F.-X.: Making masking security proofs concrete. In: Oswald, E., Fischlin, M. (eds.) EUROCRYPT 2015. LNCS, vol. 9056, pp. 401–429. Springer, Heidelberg (2015). https://doi.org/10.1007/978-3-662-46800-5_16

11. Fledel, D., Wool, A.: Sliding-window correlation attacks against encryption devices with an unstable clock. In: Cid, C., Jacobson Jr., M. (eds.) SAC 2018. LNCS, vol. 11349, pp. 193–215. Springer, Cham (2018). https://doi.org/10.1007/978-3-030-10970-7_9

12. Gandolfi, K., Mourtel, C., Olivier, F.: Electromagnetic analysis: concrete results. In: Koç, Ç.K., Naccache, D., Paar, C. (eds.) CHES 2001. LNCS, vol. 2162, pp. 251–261. Springer, Heidelberg (2001). https://doi.org/10.1007/3-540-44709-1_21

13. Glowacz, C., Grosso, V., Poussier, R., Schüth, J., Standaert, F.-X.: Simpler and more efficient rank estimation for side-channel security assessment. In: Leander, G. (ed.) FSE 2015. LNCS, vol. 9054, pp. 117–129. Springer, Heidelberg (2015). https://doi.org/10.1007/978-3-662-48116-5_6

14. Grosso, V.: Scalable key rank estimation (and key enumeration) algorithm for large keys. https://eprint.iacr.org/2018/175.pdf

15. Kocher, P., Jaffe, J., Jun, B.: Differential power analysis. In: Wiener, M. (ed.) CRYPTO 1999. LNCS, vol. 1666, pp. 388–397. Springer, Heidelberg (1999). https://doi.org/10.1007/3-540-48405-1_25

16. Kocher, P.C.: Timing attacks on implementations of Diffie-Hellman, RSA, DSS, and other systems. In: Koblitz, N. (ed.) CRYPTO 1996. LNCS, vol. 1109, pp. 104–113. Springer, Heidelberg (1996). https://doi.org/10.1007/3-540-68697-5_9

17. Li, Y., Meng, X., Wang, S., Wang, J.: Weighted key enumeration for em-based side-channel attacks. In: 2018 IEEE International Symposium on Electromagnetic Compatibility and 2018 IEEE Asia-Pacific Symposium on Electromagnetic Compatibility (EMC/APEMC), pp. 749–752. IEEE (2018)

18. Li, Y., Wang, S., Wang, Z., Wang, J.: A strict key enumeration algorithm for dependent score lists of side-channel attacks. In: Eisenbarth, T., Teglia, Y. (eds.) CARDIS 2017. LNCS, vol. 10728, pp. 51–69. Springer, Cham (2018). https://doi.org/10.1007/978-3-319-75208-2_4

19. Longo, J., et al.: How low can you go? Using side-channel data to enhance brute-force key recovery. Cryptology ePrint Archive, Report 2016:609 (2016). https://eprint.iacr.org/2016/609

20. Martin, D.P., Martinoli, Marco: A note on key rank. IACR Cryptology ePrint Archive, 2018:614 (2018)

21. Martin, D.P., Mather, L., Oswald, E.: Two sides of the same coin: counting and enumerating keys post side-channel attacks revisited. In: Smart, N.P. (ed.) CT-RSA 2018. LNCS, vol. 10808, pp. 394–412. Springer, Cham (2018). https://doi.org/10.1007/978-3-319-76953-0_21

22. Martin, D.P., Mather, L., Oswald, E., Stam, M.: Characterisation and estimation of the key rank distribution in the context of side channel evaluations. In: Cheon, J.H., Takagi, T. (eds.) ASIACRYPT 2016. LNCS, vol. 10031, pp. 548–572. Springer, Heidelberg (2016). https://doi.org/10.1007/978-3-662-53887-6_20

23. Martin, D.P., Montanaro, A., Oswald, E., Shepherd, D.: Quantum key search with side channel advice. In: Adams, C., Camenisch, J. (eds.) SAC 2017. LNCS, vol. 10719, pp. 407–422. Springer, Cham (2018). https://doi.org/10.1007/978-3-319-72565-9_21

24. Martin, D.P., O'Connell, J.F., Oswald, E., Stam, M.: Counting keys in parallel after a side channel attack. In: Iwata, T., Cheon, J.H. (eds.) ASIACRYPT 2015. LNCS, vol. 9453, pp. 313–337. Springer, Heidelberg (2015). https://doi.org/10.1007/978-3-662-48800-3_13

25. Oren, Y., Weisse, O., Wool, A.: A new framework for constraint-based probabilistic template side channel attacks. In: Batina, L., Robshaw, M. (eds.) CHES 2014. LNCS, vol. 8731, pp. 17–34. Springer, Heidelberg (2014). https://doi.org/10.1007/978-3-662-44709-3_2

26. Pan, J.: Improving DPA by peak distribution analysis. In: Biryukov, A., Gong, G., Stinson, D.R. (eds.) SAC 2010. LNCS, vol. 6544, pp. 241–261. Springer, Heidelberg (2011). https://doi.org/10.1007/978-3-642-19574-7_17

27. Poussier, R., Standaert, F.-X., Grosso, V.: Simple key enumeration (and rank estimation) using histograms: an integrated approach. In: Gierlichs, B., Poschmann, A.Y. (eds.) CHES 2016. LNCS, vol. 9813, pp. 61–81. Springer, Heidelberg (2016). https://doi.org/10.1007/978-3-662-53140-2_4

28. Quisquater, J.-J., Samyde, D.: ElectroMagnetic Analysis (EMA): measures and counter-measures for smart cards. In: Attali, I., Jensen, T. (eds.) E-smart 2001. LNCS, vol. 2140, pp. 200–210. Springer, Heidelberg (2001). https://doi.org/10.1007/3-540-45418-7_17

29. Veyrat-Charvillon, N., Gérard, B., Renauld, M., Standaert, F.-X.: An optimal key enumeration algorithm and its application to side-channel attacks. In: Knudsen, L.R., Wu, H. (eds.) SAC 2012. LNCS, vol. 7707, pp. 390–406. Springer, Heidelberg (2013). https://doi.org/10.1007/978-3-642-35999-6_25

30. Veyrat-Charvillon, N., Gérard, B., Standaert, F.-X.: Security evaluations beyond computing power. In: Johansson, T., Nguyen, P.Q. (eds.) EUROCRYPT 2013. LNCS, vol. 7881, pp. 126–141. Springer, Heidelberg (2013). https://doi.org/10.1007/978-3-642-38348-9_8

31. Wang, S., Li, Y., Wang, J.: A new key rank estimation method to investigate dependent key lists of side channel attacks. In: 2017 Asian Hardware Oriented Security and Trust Symposium, AsianHOST, pp. 19–24. IEEE (2017)

32. Ye, X., Eisenbarth, T., Martin, W.: Bounded, yet sufficient? How to determine whether limited side channel information enables key recovery. In: Joye, M., Moradi, A. (eds.) CARDIS 2014. LNCS, vol. 8968, pp. 215–232. Springer, Cham (2015). https://doi.org/10.1007/978-3-319-16763-3_13

Security Aspects of Post-Quantum Schemes

Fault Attacks on UOV and Rainbow

Juliane Krämer[(✉)] and Mirjam Loiero

TU Darmstadt, Darmstadt, Germany
`jkraemer@cdc.informatik.tu-darmstadt.de`

Abstract. Multivariate cryptography is one of the main candidates for creating post-quantum public key cryptosystems. Especially in the area of digital signatures, there exist many practical and secure multivariate schemes. The signature schemes UOV and Rainbow are two of the most promising and best studied multivariate schemes which have proven secure for more than a decade. However, so far the security of multivariate signature schemes towards physical attacks has not been appropriately assessed. Towards a better understanding of the physical security of multivariate signature schemes, this paper presents fault attacks against SingleField schemes, especially UOV and Rainbow. Our analysis shows that although promising attack vectors exist, multivariate signature schemes inherently offer a good protection against fault attacks.

Keywords: Multivariate cryptography · Rainbow · UOV · Fault attacks

1 Introduction

Cryptographic techniques are an essential tool to guarantee the security of communication in modern society. Until recently, the security of nearly all cryptographic schemes used in practice was based on number theoretic problems such as factoring large integers and solving discrete logarithms, e.g., RSA and ECC. However, schemes like these will become insecure once large enough quantum computers are built. This is due to Shor's algorithm [21], which solves the integer factorization problem and discrete logarithms in polynomial time on a quantum computer. Therefore, we need alternative public key schemes which are based on hard mathematical problems that remain hard in the presence of quantum computers: post-quantum cryptosystems.

Besides cryptography based on lattices, hash functions, codes, and isogenies, multivariate cryptography is one of the main candidates for this. The security of multivariate schemes is based on the hardness of the MQ-problem - solving a randomly generated system of multivariate quadratic polynomial equations over finite fields - which is NP-hard [13]. Depending on the size of the finite field, a distinction is made between SingleField schemes and BigField schemes [20]. The public key of multivariate schemes is a set of multivariate polynomials and the private key is mainly the trapdoor that allows to invert the public key.

© Springer Nature Switzerland AG 2019
I. Polian and M. Stöttinger (Eds.): COSADE 2019, LNCS 11421, pp. 193–214, 2019.
https://doi.org/10.1007/978-3-030-16350-1_11

Unfortunately, most of the proposed multivariate encryption schemes have been broken. This is due to the fact that the construction in this case must be based on an injective trapdoor function. As a consequence, the multivariate system of the public key is not a hard instance of the MQ-problem. On the other hand, constructions of multivariate signature schemes allow to add some randomness to the secret trapdoor which leads to a harder public key. Multivariate signature schemes are in general very fast and require only modest computational resources, which makes them attractive for the use on low cost devices like smart cards and RFID chips [4,8]. Therefore, developing fast and lightweight implementations of multivariate signature schemes became an active field of research [9,23,25]. Among many practical alternatives, UOV [16] and Rainbow[1] [11] are two of the oldest, most efficient, and most promising multivariate signature schemes.

When it comes to implementing post-quantum cryptography and using it in practical applications, however, relying only on the mathematical security of the schemes is not sufficient, but the physical security of the schemes and their implementations has to be ensured as well. Since post-quantum cryptography is only rarely used in practice as of 2019, and especially not in widespread use on smart cards and in embedded systems so far, research about side channel attacks and fault attacks on these schemes is still in the early stages of development. For multivariate schemes in particular, only few publications exist, most of which target (passive) side channel attacks rather than (active) fault attacks: Already in 2001, it was theoretically shown how the signature schemes FLASH and SFLASH can be attacked with differential power analysis (DPA) [22]. Steinwaldt et al. reveal the secret 80-bit seed Δ for SHA-1 and subsequently the affine bijections S and T by analyzing the power consumption of involved $\oplus$ operations. Okeya et al. propose another side channel attack on SFLASH in 2004 [18]. They also learn Δ through a DPA and then break SFLASH by reducing its security to the C^* problem, which is broken. They verify their results experimentally. Many years later, Yi and Li present a DPA against the enTTS signature scheme [24]. The DPA attack is facilitated by a fault attack which fixes certain unknown values to known ones. The DPA part of the attack is verified experimentally against a naive ASIC implementation of enTTS. Only recently, Park et al. presented side channel attacks on the Rainbow and UOV signature schemes [19]. They use correlation power analysis together with algebraic key recovery attacks and demonstrate the practical feasibility of their attack on an 8-bit AVR microcontroller. Regarding fault attacks on multivariate cryptography, only a single work exists: Hashimoto et al. describe general methods how to attack multivariate cryptography with fault attacks [14][2]. These methods provide the basis for our work.

---

[1] Rainbow has been submitted to the call for post-quantum cryptography standardization by the US American National Institute of Standards and Technology (NIST) in November 2017 [10] and was selected Round 2 Candidate in January 2019 [1].

[2] The same authors published their work additionally in [15].

Our Contribution. The authors of [14] focus on BigField schemes and STS-type schemes, which form a specific subclass of SingleField schemes. We complement their work by comprehensively analyzing how the attacks can be applied to SingleField schemes in general. In particular, we apply the attacks to UOV and Rainbow. We find that several special cases exist where the attacks do not work. From these findings we deduce countermeasures to protect multivariate signature schemes against fault attacks. With this, we pave the way for future fault attack resistant (implementations of) multivariate signature schemes.

Our analysis shows that although promising attack vectors exist, the randomness induced by the vinegar variables - and in case of Rainbow also by the different layers - proves to be an inherent protection against fault attacks.

Organization. In Sect. 2, we introduce the mathematics of multivariate cryptosystems and summarize the work [14]. In the subsequent Sects. 3 and 4, we discuss the applicability of the attacks from [14] to SingleField schemes and in particular to UOV and Rainbow. We provide success probabilities for the attacks and detect cases where the attacks do not work. We present countermeasures to protect multivariate signature schemes against such attacks in Sect. 5.

2   Background

First, we provide an introduction to multivariate cryptosystems in Sect. 2.1. Then, in Sect. 2.2 we give an overview about the ideas of the attacks in [14].

2.1   Multivariate Cryptosystems

The basic objects of multivariate cryptography are systems of multivariate quadratic polynomials, see Eq. 1.

$$p^{(1)}(x_1, \ldots, x_n) = \sum_{i=1}^{n} \sum_{j=i}^{n} p_{ij}^{(1)} \cdot x_i x_j + \sum_{i=1}^{n} p_i^{(1)} \cdot x_i + p_0^{(1)}$$

$$\vdots$$

$$p^{(m)}(x_1, \ldots, x_n) = \sum_{i=1}^{n} \sum_{j=i}^{n} p_{ij}^{(m)} \cdot x_i x_j + \sum_{i=1}^{n} p_i^{(m)} \cdot x_i + p_0^{(m)} \tag{1}$$

The security of multivariate schemes is based on the MQ problem: Given m quadratic polynomials $p^{(1)}(\mathbf{x}), \ldots, p^{(m)}(\mathbf{x})$ in n variables $x_1, \ldots, x_n$ as shown in Eq. 1, find a vector $\bar{\mathbf{x}} = (\bar{x}_1, \ldots, \bar{x}_n)$ such that $p^{(1)}(\bar{\mathbf{x}}) = \ldots = p^{(m)}(\bar{\mathbf{x}}) = 0$. The MQ problem (for $m \approx n$) is proven to be NP-hard [13].

To build a public key cryptosystem on the basis of the MQ problem, one starts with an easily invertible quadratic map $\mathcal{F} : \mathbb{F}^n \to \mathbb{F}^m$, the central map, where $\mathbb{F}$ is a finite field. To hide the structure of $\mathcal{F}$ in the public key, one composes it with two invertible affine maps $\mathcal{T} : \mathbb{F}^m \to \mathbb{F}^m$ and $\mathcal{S} : \mathbb{F}^n \to \mathbb{F}^n$. These affine maps can be written as $\mathcal{T}(y) = Ty + t$ and $\mathcal{S}(x) = Sx + s$, where $T \in \mathbb{F}^{m \times m}$ and $S \in \mathbb{F}^{n \times n}$ are linear transformations and $t \in \mathbb{F}^m$ and $s \in \mathbb{F}^n$ are constant vectors. The *public key* of the scheme is given by $\mathcal{P} = \mathcal{T} \circ \mathcal{F} \circ \mathcal{S} : \mathbb{F}^n \to \mathbb{F}^m$. The *private key* consists of $\mathcal{T}$, $\mathcal{F}$, and $\mathcal{S}$ and thereby allows to invert the public key[3].

Signature Generation. To generate a signature for a message d, the signer uses a hash function $\mathcal{H} : \{0,1\}^\star \to \mathbb{F}^m$ to compute the hash value $\mathbf{w} = \mathcal{H}(d) \in \mathbb{F}^m$ and computes recursively $\mathbf{x} = \mathcal{T}^{-1}(\mathbf{w}) \in \mathbb{F}^m$, $\mathbf{y} = \mathcal{F}^{-1}(\mathbf{x}) \in \mathbb{F}^n$, and $\mathbf{z} = \mathcal{S}^{-1}(\mathbf{y})$. The signature of the message d is $\mathbf{z} \in \mathbb{F}^n$. Here, $\mathcal{F}^{-1}(\mathbf{x})$ means finding one (of possibly many) preimages of $\mathbf{x}$ under the central map $\mathcal{F}$.

Verification. To check if $\mathbf{z} \in \mathbb{F}^n$ is indeed a valid signature for a message d, one computes $\mathbf{w} = \mathcal{H}(d)$ and $\mathbf{w}' = \mathcal{P}(\mathbf{z}) \in \mathbb{F}^m$. If $\mathbf{w}' = \mathbf{w}$ holds, the signature is accepted, otherwise it is rejected.

In Appendix A, we describe the signature schemes Rainbow and UOV.

2.2   General Fault Attacks on Multivariate Public Key Cryptosystems

In [14] the authors propose two approaches for fault attacks on multivariate signature schemes. In both attacks, the goal of the attackers is to reveal the affine maps $\mathcal{T}$ and $\mathcal{S}$, respectively, via a linear algebra attack [16]. By a preceding fault attack, they decrease the complexity of the linear algebra attack considerably.

The goal of the first attack, which we analyze in Sect. 3, is to gain partial information about the affine map $\mathcal{T}$ via fault injection on the central map $\mathcal{F}$. It is assumed that the fault changes a single coefficient during signature generation. By changing an additional coefficient in each following signature generation and using message-signature pairs for random messages, the attacker deduces information about the affine map $\mathcal{T}$.

The second attack aims at the random values which are used during signature generation. If an attacker manages to fix (some of) those values for several signature generations, he can transform the affine map $\mathcal{S}$ by using several pairs of random messages and corresponding signatures to facilitate the subsequent linear algebra attack. We analyze this attack in Sect. 4.

3   Fault Attack on the Central Map

In this section we analyze the fault attack on the central map. We introduce the attacker model in Sect. 3.1 and give a detailed description how the attack is intended to work for SingleField schemes in Sect. 3.2. In Sect. 3.3, we show that UOV schemes - contrary to what is claimed in [14] - are immune to this attack. In Sect. 3.4 we explain how the attack can be applied to Rainbow schemes and in Sect. 3.5 we analyze special cases of the attack.

---

[3] Due to the above construction, the security of multivariate public key schemes is not only based on the MQ-Problem, but also on the EIP-Problem (Extended Isomorphism of Polynomials) of finding the composition of $\mathcal{P}$ [20].

3.1   Attacker Model

We assume in this attack that the attacker targets the signature generation process and randomly changes a coefficient in the central map $\mathcal{F}$. He either modifies $\mathcal{F}$ directly or he attacks the public key $\mathcal{P}$ to modify $\mathcal{F}$. (For a discussion about the distinguishability of the faulty place in the latter case, we refer to [14, Section 3.2.3].) The fault that the attacker induces is permanent. He then receives the signature of a random message, i.e., this signature is generated with a faulty central map, and applies the correct public key to it. Afterwards, he again induces a fault into the central map - hence, the central map used in the next step to generate a signature on another random message includes two faults, and so on. By comparing the random messages with the messages yielded by signing the random messages with the faulty central map and then applying the correct public key to them, the attacker gains information about the affine map $\mathcal{T}$.

In a successful attack, all faults would affect pairwise different equations of the central map $\mathcal{F}$. The attacker would need $m - 1$ faults, see Sect. 3.2. As of 2018, we have $m = 28$ in the Rainbow scheme for $\mathbb{F} = GF(256)$ [20, Table 6.13].

3.2   Detailed Description of the Attack for SingleField Schemes

In [14], the authors describe the attack for Stepwise Triangular System (STS) schemes. Schemes of this type form a subset of the SingleField family. However, our findings show that the applicability and the success of this attack highly depend on the concrete scheme it is targeting. Therefore, we first generalize the attack to SingleField schemes, and then approach the schemes UOV and Rainbow in a more concrete way.

For each message that is to be signed, i.e., for each iteration of the attack, in case of SingleField schemes four steps have to be performed[4]. They are displayed in Algorithm 1. Since we do not know which kind of coefficient $\alpha_{ij}^{(k)}, \beta_{ij}^{(k)}, \gamma_i^{(k)}$ or $\eta^{(k)}$ - the coefficients of the quadratic and linear variables and the constant part of the central map $\mathcal{F}$, see Appendices A.2 and A.3 - is changed, we write $\xi^{(k)}$ for any of those. We denote faulty values with an apostrophe, e.g., $\xi'^{(k)}$.

We denote with $l \in \mathbb{N}$ the iteration of the attack, i.e., in iteration l the lth fault is induced and the lth message is signed. Thus, $\delta^{(l)}$ is the difference between the lth message and the message obtained from signing this message with the faulty central map $\mathcal{F}'$ and then applying the correct public key $\mathcal{P}$ to it. Hence, $\delta^{(l)}$ contains information about the difference between the correct and the faulty central map.

---

[4] To clarify Step 2. of [14, p. 9]: It is essential to cause a new fault on the central map for each message (i.e., for each iteration over Steps 1 - 4) and not use the same faulty map for all messages. Using the same faulty map for more than one message will not reveal new information about T, as for two messages $h^{(l_1)}$ and $h^{(l_2)}$ - signed with the same faulty central map - $\delta^{(l_1)}$ and $\delta^{(l_2)}$ will be multiples component-wise, since the attack would both times target the same column of T.

Algorithm 1. One iteration of the attack on the central map

1: Change a coefficient $\xi^{(k)}$ into $\xi'^{(k)}$ to get a faulty central map $\mathcal{F}'$ out of $\mathcal{F}$. Then
   $\Delta\mathcal{F} = \mathcal{F}' - \mathcal{F}$.
2: Sign a randomly chosen message $h^{(l)} = (h_1^{(l)}, \ldots, h_m^{(l)})$ via the faulty central map
   $\mathcal{F}'$ by $z'^{(l)} := S^{-1}(\mathcal{F}'^{-1}(T^{-1}(h^{(l)})))$, where $z'^{(l)} = (z'^{(l)}_1, \ldots, z'^{(l)}_n)$.
3: Verify $z'^{(l)}$ by using the correct public key $\mathcal{P}$ as $h'^{(l)} := \mathcal{P}(z'^{(l)})$.
4: Set $\delta^{(l)} := h'^{(l)} - h^{(l)}$.

First, we show that during the whole attack it suffices to consider T, the linear part of $\mathcal{T}$, cf. Sect. 2.1. This is due to the fact that the constant part t cancels out, see Eq. 2. For $z'^{(l)}$, the faulty signature in iteration l, correct public key $\mathcal{P} = \mathcal{T} \circ \mathcal{F} \circ \mathcal{S}$, and faulty public key $\mathcal{P}' = \mathcal{T} \circ \mathcal{F}' \circ \mathcal{S}$, we have

$$
\begin{aligned}
\delta^{(l)} &= h^{(l)} - h'^{(l)} = \mathcal{P}'(z'^{(l)}) - \mathcal{P}(z'^{(l)}) = (\mathcal{T} \circ \mathcal{F}' \circ \mathcal{S})(z'^{(l)}) - (\mathcal{T} \circ \mathcal{F} \circ \mathcal{S})(z'^{(l)}) \\
&= (\mathcal{T} \circ \mathcal{F}' \circ \mathcal{S}(z'^{(l)})) - (\mathcal{T} \circ \mathcal{F} \circ \mathcal{S}(z'^{(l)})) \\
&= [T(\mathcal{F}'((\mathcal{S}(z'^{(l)}) + s))) + t] - [T(\mathcal{F}((\mathcal{S}(z'^{(l)}) + s))) + t] \\
&= T(\mathcal{F}' - \mathcal{F})((\mathcal{S}(z'^{(l)})) + s) \\
&= (T \circ (\mathcal{F}' - \mathcal{F}) \circ \mathcal{S})(z'^{(l)}).
\end{aligned}
\tag{2}
$$

Note that in the last three rows of Eq. 2, we do not use $\mathcal{T}$ and $\mathcal{S}$, but T and S. Now we show how T is transformed: We assume that in the first iteration $(l = 1)$, a coefficient $\xi^{(k_1)}$ in $\mathcal{F}$ is changed to $\xi^{(k_1)'}$. In the resulting difference between the correct and the faulty central map, there will be only one nonzero entry, exactly at position k_1: $(\mathcal{F}' - \mathcal{F})(x) = (0, \ldots, 0, (\xi^{(k_1)'} - \xi^{(k_1)})x_i x_j, 0, \ldots, 0)^T$[5]. For the faulty signature $z'^{(1)}$ of the first message $h^{(1)}$, with Eq. 2 we have:

$$
\delta^{(1)} = (\delta_1^{(1)}, \ldots, \delta_m^{(1)}) = T \circ (\mathcal{F}' - \mathcal{F}) \circ S(z'^{(1)}) = T(0, \ldots, 0, c_1, 0, \ldots, 0)^T, \tag{3}
$$

where c_1 at position k_1 is an unknown constant resulting from $S(z'^{(1)})$ plugged into $\mathcal{F}' - \mathcal{F}$. All other entries are zero, since the central map consists of m quadratic equations $f^{(1)}, \ldots, f^{(m)}$ and in the faulty central map only in the k_1^{th} equation one coefficient was changed by the fault. $\delta^{(1)}$ has length m and as we can see from Eq. 3, it coincides with a constant multiple of the k_1^{th} column vector of

the $m \times m$ matrix T. Hence, T can be written as $T = \begin{pmatrix} * \ldots * & \delta_1^{(1)}/c_1 & * \ldots * \\ \vdots & \vdots & \vdots \\ * \ldots * & \delta_m^{(1)}/c_1 & * \ldots * \end{pmatrix}$,

where $(\delta_1^{(1)}/c_1, \ldots, \delta_m^{(1)}/c_1)^T$ is its k_1^{th} column. The idea is now to stepwise transform T into a triangular matrix. To do so, in each iteration l a matrix $T^{(l)}$ is

---

[5] Note that this does not imply that one of the quadratic coefficients is changed. This representation only serves as an illustration.

multiplied to T, which by construction annihilates all entries in the k_i^{th} column except for the lth. For the construction of this matrix, we define the vector

$$\delta(l) := (-\delta_{l+1}^{(l)}/\delta_l^{(l)}, \ldots, -\delta_m^{(l)}/\delta_l^{(l)})^T, \tag{4}$$

which has length $m - l$ in each step. Each matrix $T^{(l)}$ consists of four blocks, the sizes and structure of which change in each step depending on the value l of the iteration. The upper left block is the $l \times l$ identity matrix, the upper right block consists of zeroes of dimension $l \times (m - l)$, the lower right block contains the $(m - l) \times (m - l)$ identity matrix and the lower left block, which has the size $(m - l) \times l$, includes the vector defined in Eq. 4 in column l and a number of $l - 1$ zero vectors of length $m - l$ in columns 1 to $l - 1$, i.e.,

$$T^{(l)} = \left(\begin{array}{c|c} [I]_{l \times l} & [0]_{l \times (m-l)} \\ \hline & \\ [0]_{(m-l) \times (l-1)} \quad \begin{matrix} \delta(l)_1 \\ \vdots \\ \delta(l)_{m-l} \end{matrix} & [I]_{(m-l) \times (m-l)} \end{array} \right).$$

Hence, for $l = 1$ the matrix is $T^{(1)} = \begin{pmatrix} 1 & 0 & \cdots & 0 \\ -\delta_2^{(1)}/\delta_1^{(1)} & & & \\ \vdots & & [I_{m-1}] & \\ -\delta_m^{(1)}/\delta_1^{(1)} & & & \end{pmatrix}$ and $T^{(1)}T =$

$$\begin{pmatrix} * \cdots * & \delta_1^{(1)}/c_1 & * \cdots * \\ * \cdots * & 0 & * \cdots * \\ \vdots & \vdots & \vdots \\ * \cdots * & 0 & * \cdots * \end{pmatrix}, \text{ where } (\delta_1^{(1)}/c_1, 0, \cdots, 0)^T \text{ is the } k_1^{th} \text{ column.}$$

This calculation is performed at least $m - 1$ times[6], until in the last step we have

$$T^{(m-1)} = \begin{pmatrix} & & 0 \\ & [I_{m-1}] & \vdots \\ & & 0 \\ 1\ 0 \cdots & -\frac{\delta_m^{(m-1)}}{\delta_{m-1}^{(m-1)}} & 1 \end{pmatrix} \text{ and } T^{(m-1)}T = \begin{pmatrix} * \cdots * & \delta_1^{(m-1)}/c_{m-1} & * \cdots * \\ \vdots & \vdots & \vdots \\ * \cdots * & \delta_{m-1}^{(m-1)}/c_{m-1} & * \cdots * \\ * \cdots * & 0 & * \cdots * \end{pmatrix},$$

where $(\delta_1^{(m-1)}/c_{m-1}, \ldots, \delta_{m-1}^{(m-1)}/c_{m-1}, 0)^T$ is the k_{m-1}^{th} column. If we put together T from the $m - 1$ transformed matrices $T^{(1)}T, \ldots, T^{(m-1)}T$, we obtain a permutation of a triangular matrix with at most $\frac{m(m+1)}{2}$ nonzero entries. All other entries are expressed as quotients of some entry of δ^l and constants c_l.

---

[6] In Table 1 of [14] the authors state that the number of faults for STS type schemes - they erroneously consider UOV and Rainbow to be STS schemes - is exactly $n - 1$. This is incorrect in two different ways: (1) According to the dimension of T, the number of faults does not depend on n, but on m. (2) The number of faults is not exactly $m - 1$, but at least $m - 1$. In Sect. 3.5, we describe a special case where more faults need to be injected.

By using the MinRank attack [16] we can now recover T by using the rank of the central equations $f^{(k)}$. The MinRank attack uses the fact that the rank of $\mathcal{F}^{(k)}$ is invariant under S (the transformation of variables), but changed by T (the transformation of equations). Since the entries of T have been reduced by this attack, the complexity of the MinRank attack is reduced as well [14].

3.3 UOV Schemes Are Immune to This Attack

The authors of [14] state that the attack can be applied to UOV. However, in UOV the second affine map T can be omitted since using it does not increase the overall security of the scheme while increasing the key sizes and complexity [6].

This leaves us with a UOV public key of $\mathcal{F} \circ S$. Thus, applying the proposed attack on a UOV scheme does not work, as the goal was to restore parts of the affine map T. Interestingly, because of the different roles of the dimensions n and m and since S is computed before the central map in the public key, the attack can not be transferred to S.

3.4 Applying the Attack to Rainbow Schemes

In this section we adapt the attack on the central map to a Rainbow scheme with parameters v_i for the vinegar variables and o_i for the oil variables with $i = 1, \ldots, u$, a central map $\mathcal{F} : \mathbb{F}^n \to \mathbb{F}^m$ with $m = n - v_1$, and two affine maps $T : \mathbb{F}^m \to \mathbb{F}^m$ and $S : \mathbb{F}^n \to \mathbb{F}^n$, see Appendix A.3.

First, we consider the case that the attacker does not know which map is affected by the fault and is only able to randomize values. Therefore, we compute the success probability for hitting a coefficient in the central map $\mathcal{F}$.

Success Probability. The attack on the central map is only successful if actually an element in $\mathcal{F}$ is changed by the fault. However, we assume that the attacker can only randomly alter elements of either S, $\mathcal{F}$, or T without knowing anything about the changed values. In order to estimate the success probability for hitting an element of the central map $\mathcal{F}$ we need to determine the number of all entries of the three matrices representing the maps S, $\mathcal{F}$, and T. We revise and detail the information hereof given in [14].

The affine map $T : \mathbb{F}^m \to \mathbb{F}^m$ consists of a quadratic $m \times m$ matrix and a linear vector of length m. This gives a total of $m \cdot m + m = m(m+1)$ elements. Analogously, the affine map $S : \mathbb{F}^n \to \mathbb{F}^n$ has a total of $n(n+1)$ elements. The central map $\mathcal{F} : \mathbb{F}^n \to \mathbb{F}^{n-v_1}$ contains m equations each theoretically in n variables. All variables that are not assigned in an equation, e.g., all terms of the form oil-oil, have the coefficient 0. The number of assigned variables depends on the layer. First, we provide the formula for the number of nonzero variables summed up over all layers: $\sum_{i=1}^{u} \frac{o_i(v_i+1)(v_i+2)}{2} - (n - v_i)$. This formula describes the actual combination of n variables quadratically, linearly, and constantly, considering that there are no oil-oil variables and the number of vinegar-vinegar variables depends on the layer.

In the general case, however, we assume that the attacker can change any of the coefficients stored in a coefficient matrix as depicted in [9, Figure 3], e.g., he could "create" an oil-oil variable that does not exist (i.e., is zero) by changing the corresponding coefficient from 0 to another value. In the general case, for a single equation we have $n(n + 1)/2$ quadratic terms, n linear terms, and one constant term. For m equations this sums up to a total of at most $m\frac{n(n+1)+2n+2}{2} = m\frac{(n+1)(n+2)}{2}$. Hence, we obtain the success probability[7]

$$p = \frac{m(n + 1)(n + 2)}{m(n + 1)(n + 2) + 2m(m + 1) + 2n(n + 1)}. \tag{5}$$

Since the parameter q does not appear in this formula, the success probability for this attack does not depend on the field $\mathbb{F}^8$. It rather depends on the ratio between the number of equations m and the number of variables n.

To learn the concrete success probability of the attack against the Rainbow scheme, we computed examples for different reasonable parameters. In [2], lower bounds for n, depending on the value of m, are given for finite fields with $q \in \{16, 31, 256\}$. For these fields, we selected four values for (m, n) from the literature [11, 20][9] and computed the success probability for the attack against schemes instantiated with theses parameters. The results are given in Table 1.

Table 1. Success probability of hitting the central map in Rainbow schemes.

Rainbow parameters	Success probability
$\mathbb{F}_{16}, m = 42, n = 61$	$p \sim 0.936$
$\mathbb{F}_{31}, m = 35, n = 52$	$p \sim 0.926$
$\mathbb{F}_{256}, m = 28, n = 48$	$p \sim 0.916$
$\mathbb{F}_{256}, m = 33, n = 27$	$p \sim 0.895$

We conclude with the result that for Rainbow schemes in common fields and with up-to-date parameter choices, the success probability for hitting a coefficient in the central map $\mathcal{F}$ is more than 90%.

Assuming a Stronger Attacker. On the one hand, a stronger attacker can target $\mathcal{F}$ (instead of only $\mathcal{P}$) or even specific coefficients in $\mathcal{F}$ directly. This allows him to perform the attack in a more structured way and to avoid unwanted scenarios. On the other hand, a stronger attacker can not only randomize values, but zero them or even set them to a chosen value. In case an attacker is more

---

[7] The same formula holds for UOV schemes.
[8] Actually the parameters q and n are indirectly connected, since in fields with small q the parameter n has to be chosen larger in order to ensure security.
[9] The first three tuples of parameters are taken from [20] for the year 2018, the last one is the original suggestion from [11].

powerful in both ways, he can directly find values of $\mathcal{F}$: He chooses a random message and successively assigns all values from the underlying field to a certain entry of $\mathcal{F}$ before signing the message with that modified $\mathcal{F}$. As soon as a $\delta^{(l)}$ consists of only zeroes, the right entry of $\mathcal{F}$ is found.

3.5   Special Cases

During anaylzing how the attack can be applied to a Rainbow scheme, we detected some special cases that can occur and which are not covered by the descriptions in [14].

Specific Vinegar Variable Assigned 0. In each signature generation process there are a number of values randomly assigned to the vinegar variables over the field $\mathbb{F}$. Let us assume v_i to be the number of vinegar variables. If the coefficient changed by the fault attack belongs to a variable that contains a vinegar-monomial (i.e., vinegar-vinegar or vinegar-oil) and furthermore exactly this vinegar variable takes the value 0 during the step in the inversion of the central map where random values are assigned to the vinegar variables, then this term with the faulty coefficient drops out during signature generation. As a consequence, there is no difference in a signature generated with the correct central map and one generated with the faulty central map, resulting in $\delta^{(k)} = 0$ in all entries. When the attacker computes $\delta^{(k)} = 0$, he realizes that this case occurred[10] but gains no information in the sense of the attack.

We computed the probability for this special case to occur for an example Rainbow scheme. In the original paper of Ding and Schmidt [11], a set of parameters for practical implementation is proposed. For these parameters, we derived a probability of approximately 1.1%, as explained in Appendix B.

l^{th} Entry of $\delta^{(l)}$ Equals 0. The second special case concerns that in each iteration l of the attack $\delta^{(l)} = h'^{(l)} - h^{(l)}$ is computed, with $\delta^{(l)} = (\delta_1^{(l)}, \ldots, \delta_m^{(l)})$. These entries are a constant multiple of the k_l^{th} column of the matrix T. This implies that if the k_l^{th} entry of a column in T equals 0, then for the lth entry of $\delta^{(l)}$ it holds $\delta_l^{(l)} = 0$. In this case it is not possible to construct the vector in Eq. 4 in order to perform the transformation since all other entries of $\delta^{(l)}$ would have to be divided by $\delta_l^{(l)} = 0$. An attacker would detect this occurrence by computing $\delta^{(l)}$, but could discard the values and start over.

The probability for this special case to occur depends on m, the number of multivariate quadratic polynomials, and on the size of the finite field. For each column separately, the probability is $\frac{1}{|\mathbb{F}|}$, since the values in T were assigned randomly from $\mathbb{F}$. Performing this step at least $m - 1$ times, the probability p_2

---

[10] The same situation would occur if an entire column of $\mathcal{T}$ was equal zero. However, this cannot happen since the maps are expected to have full rank.

for this special case to occur can be computed via the complementary event:
$p_2 \geq 1 - \left(\frac{|\mathbb{F}|-1}{|\mathbb{F}|}\right)^{m-1}$. For the example schemes from Table 1, this yields $p_2 \geq$
0.928 ($q = 16$, $m = 42$), $p_2 \geq 0.672$ ($q = 31, m = 35$), and $p_2 \geq 0.100$ ($q =$
$256, m = 28$). With increasing field size, the probability decreases drastically.

Coefficients in Same Equation Targeted More Than Once. The third special
case concerns redundant faults: It can happen that an attacker injects faults
that affect an equation that had already been altered with a previous fault, i.e.,
the same column of T is affected several times. The attacker would detect this
situation if a newly computed $\delta^{(k)}$ is linearly dependent to any of the already
computed ones. Since the goal is to transform T into a triangular matrix where
the k_l^{th} column vector contains information about the k_l^{th} column of T, it is
necessary to target each equation (at least) once. Hence, an attacker would
abort this step and try to target another equation which is yet untouched.

4   Fault Attack on the Random Values

In this section we show how the attack on the random values can be applied
to the SingleField schemes UOV and Rainbow. First, we introduce the attacker
model in Sect. 4.1. Then, we explain how the attack can be applied to Single-
Field signature schemes. The explanation of the attack method is similar to
the description in [14, Section 3.3.2] with a slightly different notation and more
details. In Sect. 4.3, we discuss a special case of the attack that has not been
covered in [14], and from this deduce the success probability of the attack.

4.1   Attacker Model

In each signature generation the vinegar variables are instantiated with random values. In this attack, which targets the signature generation process, we
assume that the attacker fixes some (or all) of these random values with a single
permanent fault. He does not know how many variables he fixed, and he does
not know the value of these variables. Afterwards, he receives several message-
signature pairs where each signature has been computed with the fixed variables
and, in case he did not fix all of the variables, additional random ones. The more
variables he fixes, the less message-signature pairs he needs. By analyzing these
pairs, the attacker gains partial information of S.

4.2   Detailed Description of the Attack for SingleField Schemes

We denote the random values with $r_1, \ldots, r_{u_1} \in \mathbb{F}, u_1 \in \mathbb{N}$ and assume that the
attacker fixes the first u_2 variables $r_1, \ldots, r_{u_2}$ for $u_2 \leq u_1$.
    Consider a UOV scheme over a finite field $\mathbb{F}$ with v vinegar and o oil variables
satisfying $v > o$ or a Rainbow scheme with v_i vinegar and o_i oil variables per layer
$i = 1, \ldots, u$. Since the attack works analogously for both schemes, we simply

---

Algorithm 2. Attack on the random values

1: Cause a fault that fixes $r_1,\ldots,r_{u_2}$ and suppose that $\bar{r}_1,\ldots,\bar{r}_{u_2} \in \mathbb{F}$ are exactly these unknown fixed values.
2: Generate signatures $z^{(1)},\ldots,z^{(n-u_2+1)}$ for randomly chosen messages $h^{(1)},\ldots,h^{(n-u_2+1)}$ with $r = (\bar{r}_1,\ldots,\bar{r}_{u_2},r_{u_2+1},\ldots,r_n)$.
3: Recover parts of S by using the pairs $(z^{(k)}, h^{(k)})$.

---

write v. Let $h^{(1)},\ldots,h^{(n-u_2+1)} \in \mathbb{F}^m$ be the messages and $z^{(1)},\ldots,z^{(n-u_2+1)} \in \mathbb{F}^n$ the corresponding signatures with $u_2 \leq v$ variables that have been fixed by the attacker. Let $x^{(k)} = (x_1^{(k)},\ldots,x_v^{(k)}) \in \mathbb{F}^v$ be the vinegar variables in step k. W.l.o.g. we assume that the first u_2 variables $(x_1,\ldots,x_{u_2})$ are fixed to the values $(\bar{x}_1\ldots,\bar{x}_{u_2})$, yielding the vector $x^{(k)} = (\bar{x}_1\ldots,\bar{x}_{u_2},x_{u_2+1}^{(k)},\ldots,x_v^{(k)})^T$ for each step k. We write $x^{(k)} = (\bar{x},r^{(k)})^T$, where $\bar{x}$ denotes the fixed part and $r^{(k)} \in \mathbb{F}^{v-u_2}$ denotes the random values that differ in each step.

Below we will show that a total of $n - u_2 + 1$ message-signature pairs are needed to perform the attack.

Reducing the Number of Nonzero Elements in a Specific Representation of S. Signatures in UOV and Rainbow are computed by $z = S^{-1}(\mathcal{F}^{-1}(y))$ and $z = S^{-1}(\mathcal{F}^{-1}(\mathcal{T}^{-1}(y)))$, respectively. In both cases we can write

$$z = S^{-1}\begin{pmatrix} x \\ w \end{pmatrix}$$

for some $x \in \mathbb{F}^v$ and $w \in \mathbb{F}^{n-v}$. With the above notation we can rewrite

$$Sz^{(k)} + s = \begin{pmatrix} \bar{x} \\ r^{(k)} \\ w^{(k)} \end{pmatrix}. \tag{6}$$

We want to see how the fixed values $\bar{x}$ can be used to express S, so we split up S, $z^{(k)}$, and s into

$$S = \begin{pmatrix} A & B \\ C & D \end{pmatrix} \text{ and } z^{(k)} = \begin{pmatrix} z^{(k,1)} \\ z^{(k,2)} \end{pmatrix} \text{ and } s = \begin{pmatrix} s_1 \\ s_2 \end{pmatrix},$$

where $z^{(k,1)}, s_1 \in \mathbb{F}^{u_2}$ and $z^{(k,2)}, s_2 \in \mathbb{F}^{n-u_2}$ and $A \in \mathbb{F}^{u_2 \times u_2}$, $B \in \mathbb{F}^{u_2 \times (n-u_2)}$, $C \in \mathbb{F}^{(n-u_2) \times u_2}$, and $D \in \mathbb{F}^{(n-u_2) \times (n-u_2)}$. We now use Eq. 6 to write $Sz^{(k)} + s =$

$$\begin{pmatrix} A & B \\ C & D \end{pmatrix} \cdot \begin{pmatrix} z^{(k,1)} \\ z^{(k,2)} \end{pmatrix} + \begin{pmatrix} s_1 \\ s_2 \end{pmatrix} = \begin{pmatrix} Az^{(k,1)} + Bz^{(k,2)} + s_1 \\ Cz^{(k,1)} + Dz^{(k,2)} + s_2 \end{pmatrix} = \begin{pmatrix} \bar{x} \\ r^{(k)} \\ w^{(k)} \end{pmatrix}.$$

From the dimensions of A, B, C, and D we deduce $Az^{(k,1)} + Bz^{(k,2)} + s_1 = \bar{x}$. As s_1 and $\bar{x}$ are fixed from the beginning, we write $Az^{(k,1)} + Bz^{(k,2)} = \bar{x} - s_1$ and with setting $\bar{z}^{(k,1)} := z^{(k,1)} - z^{(1,1)}$ and $\bar{z}^{(k,2)} := z^{(k,2)} - z^{(1,2)}$ for $2 \leq k \leq n - u + 1$, we obtain $A\bar{z}^{(k,1)} + B\bar{z}^{(k,2)} = A(z^{(k,1)} - z^{(1,1)}) + B(z^{(k,2)} - z^{(1,2)}) = Ax^{(k,1)} - Bz^{(k,2)} - (Az^{(1,1)} + Bz^{(1,2)}) = \bar{x} - s_1 - (\bar{x} - s_1) = 0$. Based on this we are able to express $A^{-1}B$ with the aid of the signatures $z^{(k)}$ by using $\bar{z}^{(k,1)}$, $k \in \{2,\ldots,n-u_2+1\}$, as column $k-1$ of the $u_2 \times (n-u_2)$-matrix Z_1 and accordingly $\bar{z}^{(k,2)}$ as column $k-1$ of the $(n-u_2) \times (n-u_2)$-matrix Z_2. It follows

$$AZ_1 + BZ_2 = 0 \Leftrightarrow AZ_1 = -BZ_2 \Leftrightarrow Z_1 = -A^{-1}BZ_2 \Leftrightarrow -Z_1 Z_2^{-1} = A^{-1}B \quad (7)$$

if A and Z_2 are invertible. The facilitated representation of S is then given by $\begin{pmatrix} A & B \\ C & D \end{pmatrix} \cdot \begin{pmatrix} I_{u_2} & -A^{-1}B \\ 0 & I_{n-u_2} \end{pmatrix} = \begin{pmatrix} A & 0 \\ C & -CA^{-1}B + D \end{pmatrix}$. Hence, the attack on the random values can be used to reduce the number of nonzero elements in the facilitated representation of S. Subsequently, the MinRank attack [16] can be used to compute S [12].

4.3   Special Case and Success Probability of the Attack

The attack does not work if A is a singular matrix, as can be seen in Eq. 7. To discuss the probability of this special case, we determine the probability that an $(n \times n)$-matrix with random entries from $\mathbb{F}$ is invertible, i.e., not singular. Following [7], we estimate this probability under the assumption that the entries are uniformly distributed in $\mathbb{F}$ as

$$\prod_{i=0}^{n-1} \frac{(q^n - q^i)}{q^{n^2}} = \prod_{i=1}^{n}(1 - \frac{1}{q^i}).$$

In the attack, matrix A has dimension $u_2 \times u_2$, where u_2 is the number of random variables that the attacker fixed. For common parameters for UOV and Rainbow schemes, we get high success probabilities that A is invertible, see Table 2. With u_2 increasing, the probability decreases only slightly.

Table 2. Success probability that the matrix $A \in \mathbb{F}^{u_2 \times u_2}$ is invertible, depending on different sizes of the finite field $\mathbb{F}$, as suggested for UOV and Rainbow [20], and different numbers u_2 of fixed vinegar variables.

Finite field	Number of fixed vinegar variables	Success probability
$\mathbb{F}_{16}$	$u_2 \in \{1,\ldots,16\}$	$p \geq 0.933$
$\mathbb{F}_{31}$	$u_2 \in \{1,\ldots,31\}$	$p \geq 0.966$
$\mathbb{F}_{256}$	$u_2 \in \{1,\ldots,256\}$	$p \geq 0.996$

On the other hand, the number of fixed values u_2 affects how many messages need to be signed, cf. Sect. 4.2. This is related to the complexity of the MinRank attack (which is used to learn S completely) which initially is $\mathcal{O}(q^{v-o-1}o^4) = \mathcal{O}(q^{n-2o-1}o^4)$ [5] with $n = v + o$. For each fixed vinegar variable the complexity is reduced by the factor q, i.e., in total by q^{u_2}. Hence, if an attacker fixes a number u_2 of vinegar variables, the complexity decreases to $\mathcal{O}(q^{(v-u_2)-o-1}o^4) = \mathcal{O}(q^{n-2o-u_2-1}o^4)$.

Consequently, an attacker should fix as many vinegar variables as possible.

5   Countermeasures

Derived from the fault attacks explained in the previous sections, we present algorithmic countermeasures to protect multivariate SingleField signature schemes against these attacks.

5.1   Securing the Central Map

Check for a Faulty Central Map. An approach that has already been proposed in [14] is to test the central map for modifications before starting signature generation. The idea is to store a checksum $c_{\mathcal{F}}$ of the coefficients in $\mathcal{F}$ and compare it at the beginning of each signature generation with a checksum $c_{\mathcal{F}'}$ of the coefficients of the central map used during that signature generation. In case the checksums differ, the message is not signed. This countermeasure can be applied to all SingleField schemes. However, the checking procedure has to be carefully implemented, i.e., protected, so that it cannot be skipped by an experienced attacker [3].

Increase the Chances for Vinegar Variables to be 0. As shown in Sect. 3.5, a situation can occur where the faulty coefficient in the central map coincides with the choice of a vinegar variable to be 0 during the signature generation process. In this case the whole expression with the faulty coefficient and the vinegar variable evaluates to 0. We learned that each time this happens, the attacker has to start over again since this step does not yield new information. The idea of this countermeasure is to increase the probability of the vinegar variables to be assigned 0 in order to increase the overall probability for it to coincide with the exact faulty coefficient. (This of course requires the faulty coefficient to be of vinegar-type.) The vinegar variables are assigned with random values from the underlying finite field $\mathbb{F}$. Hence, signature schemes that use smaller finite fields are better protected against the attack on the central map.

Increase the Number of 0-entries in T. As discussed in Sect. 3.5, it can happen that in the lth iteration the lth entry of $\delta^{(l)}$ equals 0. Then the attacker cannot proceed with the attack, since in order to reduce the elements of T it is necessary to divide all other entries of $\delta^{(l)}$ by $\delta_l^{(l)}$. To make the attack less likely to work, we can thus increase the number of 0-entries in T, so that it gets more probable to have such a 0-entry at the according position. However, there are several problems involved: Too many 0-entries result in sparseness of the matrix and while a sparse matrix might impede this attack, it simultaneously facilitates rank attacks. Also, when the attacker learns which entries are 0 he might use this knowledge to adjust the attack accordingly. We leave for future work to analyze if indeed it is reasonable to increase the number of 0-entries in T.

Change the Ratio of m and n. In Sect. 3.4 we showed that the success probability for changing an entry in $\mathcal{F}$ is around 90% for Rainbow schemes. This high probability comes from the fact that the size of $\mathcal{F}$ is relatively large in comparison to

$\mathcal{T}$ and $\mathcal{S}$. This depends on the ratio of n and m. So it seems to be a reasonable idea to make the attack less successful by changing the ratio of the variables m and n and thus increase the probability that an attacker targets parameters of $\mathcal{T}$ or $\mathcal{S}$ instead of $\mathcal{F}$. This can be achieved by minimizing Eq. 5. However, if an attacker is able to distinguish the faulty place (c.f. Scenario 2 in Sect. 3.4), he realizes if the fault injection was successful and can repeat the attack in case it was not. Again, we leave for future work to determine how this countermeasure impairs the security of the scheme. This countermeasure is also applicable for other schemes of SingleField type.

5.2 Securing the Random Values

Saving the Values. The first idea to prevent the attack on the random values has already been roughed out in [14]. This countermeasure consists in saving the randomly chosen values for each step and compare them with the variables of every current signature. If a certain threshold of coincidences between old and new values occurs, the signature generation has to be aborted. The countermeasure can be applied to all SingleField schemes which use random values.

This threshold has to be chosen carefully, since, as we show in Appendix C, also without fault injection coincidences are frequent. The choice of this threshold depends, among others, on the underlying field: the smaller the field, the more likely a coincidence in the random variables occurs. Considering the specifics of the attack, it might moreover be reasonable to count coincidences column-wise and abort further signature generations once the threshold is reached in one of the columns.

Matrix A not Invertible. In Eq. 7 we showed that the matrix A is required to be invertible, otherwise the transformation of S to reduce the number of nonzero elements does not work. A is the upper left part of the matrix S with dimension $u_2 \times u_2$, with $0 \leq u_2 \leq v$, where u_2 is the number of fixed variables. A powerful attacker would try to fix as many variables as possible. Since we do not know the value of u_2, but u_2 is bounded above by v, this countermeasure consists in filling the upper v entries of the first column of S with zeroes and thereby force A to be singular without necessarily making S singular (as $v < n$). Although this countermeasure completely prevents the attack against the random values, we leave for future work to analyze any security implications this might entail.

6 Conclusion

With this paper, we complement the research on the physical attack security of multivariate signature schemes. We presented to fault attacks on SingleField schemes with an emphasis on UOV and Rainbow. We showed that the success probability of both attacks is rather high. Nevertheless, since both attacks do not lead to complete key recovery, we conclude that multivariate signature schemes inherently offer a good protection against fault attacks.

Acknowledgments. This work has been co-funded by the DFG as part of project P1 within the CRC 1119 CROSSING. We thank Mohamed Saied Emam Mohamed for his contribution to a preliminary version of this work and Albrecht Petzold for his diligent proofreading of this paper.

A   The Signature Schemes UOV and Rainbow

A.1   Signature Generation and Verification of Multivariate Schemes

The standard signature generation and verification process of a multivariate signature scheme works as shown in Fig. 1.

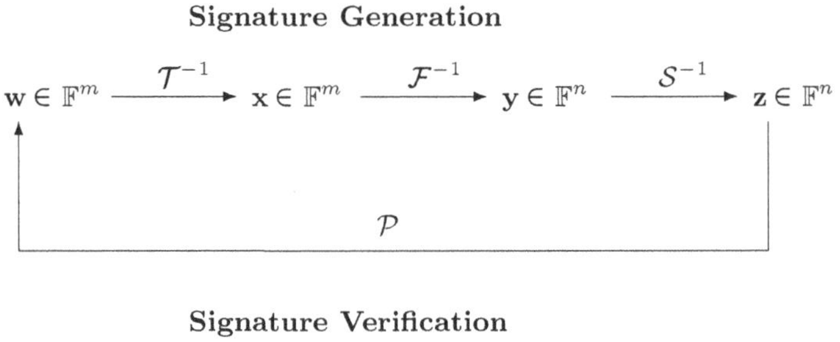

Signature Generation

$$\mathbf{w} \in \mathbb{F}^m \xrightarrow{\mathcal{T}^{-1}} \mathbf{x} \in \mathbb{F}^m \xrightarrow{\mathcal{F}^{-1}} \mathbf{y} \in \mathbb{F}^n \xrightarrow{\mathcal{S}^{-1}} \mathbf{z} \in \mathbb{F}^n$$

$$\mathcal{P}$$

Signature Verification

Fig. 1. General workflow of multivariate signature schemes.

A.2   Unbalanced Oil and Vinegar Signature Scheme

The Unbalanced Oil and Vinegar signature scheme (UOV) is a modified version of the Oil and Vinegar scheme. It was designed by Kipnis and Patarin and presented at EUROCRYPT'99 [16] after the original scheme was broken by Kipnis and Shamir in 1998 [17] via linear algebra attacks.

Unlike in the Oil and Vinegar scheme, where the number of vinegar and oil variables are equal, the advantage of UOV consists in choosing the number of vinegar variables to be greater than the number of oil variables in order to guarantee better security against known attacks. The formal notation, the choice of variables, and the structure of the scheme is described in the following.

Notation. All computations are performed in a finite field $\mathbb{F}$ with q elements. Let $o := m \in \mathbb{N}$ be the number of oil variables and $v \in \mathbb{N}$ the number of vinegar variables, hence $n = o + v$. The corresponding index sets for the variables be $V = \{1,...,v\}$ and $O = \{v+1,...,n\}$. $x_i (i \in V)$ are called vinegar variables and $x_j (j \in O)$ oil variables. The message (or its hash) to be signed is denoted by $h = (h_1,...,h_m) \in \mathbb{F}^m$ and the signature itself by $z = (z_1,...,z_n) \in \mathbb{F}^n$.

Central Map and Affine Maps. The central map $\mathcal{F} : \mathbb{F}^n \to \mathbb{F}^o$ of the UOV-scheme consists of m quadratic polynomials $f^{(1)},...,f^{(m)} \in \mathbb{F}[x_1,...,x_n]$ of the form

$$f^{(k)}(x) = \sum_{\substack{i,j \in V \\ i \leq j}} \alpha_{ij}^{(k)} x_i x_j + \sum_{\substack{i \in V \\ j \in O}} \beta_{ij}^{(k)} x_i x_j + \sum_{i \in V \cup O} \gamma_i^{(k)} x_i + \eta^{(k)}$$

where $k \in \{1,...,m\}$ and the $\alpha_{ij}^{(k)}$ are the coefficients of the quadratic vinegar-vinegar, the $\beta_{ij}^{(k)}$ of the quadratic oil-vinegar, the $\gamma_i^{(k)}$ of the linear oil and vinegar variables and $\eta^{(k)}$ is the constant part. All coefficients are chosen randomly from the underlying field $\mathbb{F}$ and stored in a matrix, see, e.g., [9, Figure 2].

In order to hide the structure of the central map $\mathcal{F}$, it is composed with an affine bijective map $\mathcal{S} : \mathbb{F}^n \to \mathbb{F}^n$, which can be written as $\mathcal{S}(x) = Sx + s$, where $S \in \mathbb{F}^{n \times n}$ is a linear transformation and $s \in \mathbb{F}^n$ is a vector.

Note that unlike in other multivariate signature schemes of SingleField type like Rainbow (cf. Sect. A.3), in UOV the second affine map $\mathcal{T} : \mathbb{F}^m \to \mathbb{F}^m$ can be omitted (or similarly treated like the identity map $\mathcal{T} = id$) since applying it to the polynomials would not change the structure of the central map $\mathcal{F}$ at all and thus would not increase the overall security.

Public Key and Private Key. The public key of the UOV scheme is given by $\mathcal{P} = \mathcal{F} \circ \mathcal{S}$ with $\mathcal{P} : \mathbb{F}^n \xrightarrow{\mathcal{S}} \mathbb{F}^n \xrightarrow{\mathcal{F}} \mathbb{F}^m$, consisting of m public quadratic polynomials in n variables. The private key is the tuple $(\mathcal{F}, \mathcal{S})$. As both $\mathcal{F}$ and $\mathcal{S}$ can be inverted efficiently, knowledge of the private key allows for inversion of the public key and therefore signature generation.

Inversion of the Central Map. In order to create a valid signature, inversion of the central map is required (compare Eq. 8 below), which is done by performing the following steps:

1. Assign random values to the vinegar variables $x_1,...,x_v$.
2. Substitute them into the polynomials $f^{(1)},...,f^{(m)}$, resulting in a system of m linear equations in the oil variables $x_{v+1},...,x_n$.
3. Solve the system of linear equations, e.g., by using Gaussian elimination.
4. If the system does not have a solution, go back to Step 1 and try again with different random values.

Signature Generation and Verification. To sign a document $h = (h_1,..., h_m) \in \mathbb{F}^m$, solve the equation

$$\mathcal{F} \circ \mathcal{S} z = h$$

for $z \in \mathbb{F}^n$. First, find a pre-image of h under the central map $\mathcal{F}$ with the method described above to get

$$\mathcal{S} z = \mathcal{F}^{-1} h =: y \tag{8}$$

with $y \in \mathbb{F}^n$. Then invert S to obtain the signature

$$z = S^{-1}y.$$

For signature verification it has to be checked whether $\mathcal{P}(z) = h$ holds. If this is the case, the signature is accepted, if not, rejected.

A.3   Rainbow

In 2005, Ding and Schmidt published a new signature scheme named Rainbow, which is a generalization of the Unbalanced Oil and Vinegar scheme [11]. The basic idea is to combine several layers of Oil and Vinegar in one scheme in order to improve the security and efficiency of the scheme. Compared to UOV, in Rainbow key and signature sizes can be reduced.

Notation. Let $\mathbb{F}$ be a finite field with q elements. Let S be the set $\{1,...,n\}$ and $v_1,...,v_{u+1}$ integers with the property

$$0 < v_1 < v_2 < ... < v_{u+1} = n,$$

where u stands for the number of layers. Define the sets of integers $S_i = \{1,...,v_i\}$ for each $i = 1,...,u$. The number of elements in set S_i is v_i and by construction we have

$$S_1 \subset S_2 \subset ... \subset S_{u+1} = S.$$

We set $o_i := v_{i+1} - v_i$ and $O_i := S_{i+1} - S_i = \{v_i + 1,...,v_{i+1}\}$ for $i = 1,...,u$. Then we have $|O_i| = o_i$.

Central Map and Affine Maps. The central map $\mathcal{F} : \mathbb{F}^n \to \mathbb{F}^{n-v_1}$, which is an easily invertible quadratic map, consists of $m := n - v_1$ polynomials $(f^{(v_1+1)},...,f^{(n)})$, each of the form

$$f^{(k)}(x_1,...,x_n) = \sum_{\substack{i,j \in S_l \\ i \leq j}} \alpha_{ij}^{(k)} x_i x_j + \sum_{\substack{i \in O_l \\ j \in S_l}} \beta_{ij}^{(k)} x_i x_j + \sum_{i \in O_l \cup S_l} \gamma_i^{(k)} x_i + \eta^{(k)}$$

with $k = v_1 + 1,...,n$ and where l denotes the layer. For $i \in O_l$ we call x_i an lth-layer oil variable and for $i \in S_l$ an lth-layer vinegar variable. The central map of a Rainbow scheme consists of u different layers, the ith layer of which consists of the polynomials $f^{(j)}$ for $j \in O_i$.

The name Rainbow refers to the fact that the number of variables increases with each layer and can be arranged like the layers of a rainbow:

$$[x_1,...,x_{v_1}]\{x_{v_1+1},...,x_{v_2}\}$$
$$[x_1,...,x_{v_1},x_{v_1+1},...,x_{v_2}]\{x_{v_2+1},...,x_{v_3}\}$$
$$\vdots \qquad\qquad\qquad \vdots$$
$$[x_1,...,...,...,...,...,...,...,...,...,x_{v_{u-1}}]\{x_{v_{u-1}+1},...,x_n\}.$$

Each row represents a layer of the Rainbow scheme with the vinegar variables in squared and the oil variables in curly brackets.

In order to hide the structure of the central map, two invertible affine maps are composed to $\mathcal{F}$ from both sides:

$$S : \mathbb{F}^n \to \mathbb{F}^n \quad \text{with } S(x) = Sx + s \text{ for } x \in \mathbb{F}^n$$

$$T : \mathbb{F}^m \to \mathbb{F}^m \quad \text{with } T(y) = Ty + t \text{ for } y \in \mathbb{F}^m, \tag{9}$$

where $T \in \mathbb{F}^{m \times m}$ and $S \in \mathbb{F}^{n \times n}$ are linear transformations and $t \in \mathbb{F}^m$ and $s \in \mathbb{F}^n$ are constant vectors.

Public Key and Private Key. The public key is given by $\mathcal{P} = T \circ \mathcal{F} \circ S$ with $\mathcal{P} : \mathbb{F}^n \xrightarrow{S} \mathbb{F}^n \xrightarrow{\mathcal{F}} \mathbb{F}^m \xrightarrow{T} \mathbb{F}^m$. The field $\mathbb{F}$ and its additive and multiplicative structure are also publicly known. The private key consists of $(T, \mathcal{F}, S)$.

Inversion of the Central Map. In order to generate a signature, one needs to be able to invert $\mathcal{F}$. This can be done by the following steps, similar to the method for UOV, cf. Sect. A.2.

1. Assign values to the vinegar variables $x_1, \ldots, x_{v_1}$ at random and substitute them into the equations given by $f^{(v_1+1)}, \ldots, f^{(n)}$.
2. Solve the system of o_1 linear equations in the o_1 unknowns $x_{v_1+1}, \ldots, x_{v_2}$, e.g., via Gaussian elimination. This gives all the values x_i with $i \in S_2$.
3. Insert these values into the second layer of polynomials (i.e., $f^{(k)}$ with $k > v_2$) to obtain a system of o_2 linear equations in the o_2 unknowns $x_i, i \in O_2$. Solving the systems yields the x_i with $i \in S_3$.
4. Repeat this process until a solution for all variables is found. If in any step no solution for the systems of equations can be found, again random values for the variables $x_1, \ldots, x_{v_1}$ are chosen.

Signature Generation and Verification. To sign a document $h = (h_1, \ldots, h_m) \in \mathbb{F}^m$, the equation

$$T \circ \mathcal{F} \circ S(z_1, \ldots, z_n) = h$$

needs to be solved for $z = (z_1, \ldots, z_n)$. To do this, first the inverse T^{-1} is applied

$$\mathcal{F} \circ Sz = T^{-1}h =: x.$$

Next invert the central map $\mathcal{F}$ via the method described above to get

$$Sz = \mathcal{F}^{-1}x =: y.$$

Finally apply the inverse S^{-1} to obtain a signature z

$$z = S^{-1}y.$$

To verify a signature one simply checks whether $\mathcal{P}(z) = h$ holds. In this case the signature is accepted, otherwise rejected.

B   Probability for the Special Case of Sect. 3.5

We are interested in the following case: A fault is caused on a coefficient of the multivariate system. Coincidentally, during the signature generation process, a vinegar variable belonging to this coefficient is assigned 0.

The probability of a certain vinegar variable x_i to be assigned 0 is $\frac{1}{q}$, where $q = |\mathbb{F}|$. So the probability that at least one variable is chosen 0 is $1 - (1 - \frac{1}{q})^{v_l}$, where l is a layer in the Rainbow scheme. In the system of equations we have quadratic and linear terms with vinegar variables. The number of terms in the central map including a certain vinegar variable is $n + 1$ for one equation or $m(n + 1)$ for the whole system of equations. The total number of terms in the system consisting of $\mathcal{S}, \mathcal{T}$ and $\mathcal{F}$ thereby is given by $n(n + 1)$, $m(m + 1)$ and $\frac{m(n+1)(n+2)}{2}$, respectively.

The probability p for all u layers is then computed by

$$p = \left(\sum_{l=1}^{u} (1 - (1 - \frac{1}{q})^{v_l}) \right) \cdot \frac{m(n + 1)}{m(m + 1) + n(n + 1) + \frac{m(n+1)(n+2)}{2}}$$

To get an idea of the concrete probability, we apply the considerations above to an example Rainbow scheme. Ding and Schmidt proposed in the original paper [11] a set of parameters for practical implementation. The finite field has $q = 2^8$ elements and $n = 33, S = \{1,2,...,33\}$. The number of layers is given by $u = 4$, the number of vinegar variables by $v_1 = 6, v_2 = 12, v_3 = 17, v_4 = 22, v_5 = 33$, and the number of oil variables by $o_1 = 6, o_2 = 5, o_3 = 5, o_4 = 11$, $m = n - v_1 = 27$. This yields:

$$p = \left(\sum_{l=1}^{4} (1 - (1 - \frac{1}{256})^{v_l}) \right) \cdot \frac{27 \cdot 34}{27 \cdot 28 + 33 \cdot 34 + \frac{27 \cdot 34 \cdot 35}{2}} \approx 0.011.$$

Hence, with the parameter choice given above, this special case approximately occurs in 1.1% of signature generations.

Table 3. Probability for coincidences in random variables for different fields for UOV and Rainbow.

Parameters	$p_1 \approx$	$i \geq 2 \to p_2 \geq$
UOV($\mathbb{F}_{16}, v = 128$)	0.99	0.99
UOV($\mathbb{F}_{31}, v = 104$)	0.97	0.99
UOV($\mathbb{F}_{256}, v = 90$)	0.30	0.50
Rainbow($\mathbb{F}_{16}, v_1 = 19$)	0.71	0.92
Rainbow($\mathbb{F}_{31}, v_1 = 17$)	0.43	0.68
Rainbow($\mathbb{F}_{256}, v_1 = 20$)	0.075	0.14

C   Probability for Equal Random Variables

For a field with q elements and a number of v_1 vinegar variables, the event that two randomly generated sets of v_1 vinegar variables have at least one coincidence is the complementary event of no coincidences at all. The probability for this is $p_1 = 1 - \left(\frac{q-1}{q}\right)^{v_1}$. If we compute this for a number of $i \leq k$ sets of random values, then we get the probability that at least in one comparison at least one coincidence occurs by $p_2 = 1 - (1 - p_1)^i$. If we use common parameters for UOV and Rainbow schemes, we see that such occurrences are quite frequent.

As we can see in Table 3, it is quite probable that one or more variables have a value in common with older sets of variables. So one should not deny any signature where a coincidence occurs, but define a threshold value.

References

1. Round 2 submissions - post-quantum cryptography—CSRC (2019). https://csrc. nist.gov/projects/post-quantum-cryptography/round-2-submissions. Accessed 14 Feb 2019
2. Albrecht, Bulygin, S., Buchmann, J.A.: Selecting parameters for the rainbow signature scheme - extended version. IACR Cryptology ePrint Archive 2010, p. 437 (2010)
3. Blömer, J., da Silva, R.G., Günther, P., Krämer, J., Seifert, J.P.: A practical second-order fault attack against a real-world pairing implementation. In: 2014 Workshop on Fault Diagnosis and Tolerance in Cryptography, pp. 123–136 (2014)
4. Bogdanov, A., Eisenbarth, T., Rupp, A., Wolf, C.: Time-area optimized public-key engines: $\mathcal{MQ}$-cryptosystems as replacement for elliptic curves? In: Oswald, E., Rohatgi, P. (eds.) CHES 2008. LNCS, vol. 5154, pp. 45–61. Springer, Heidelberg (2008). https://doi.org/10.1007/978-3-540-85053-3_4
5. Braeken, A., Wolf, C., Preneel, B.: A study of the security of unbalanced oil and vinegar signature schemes. In: Menezes, A. (ed.) CT-RSA 2005. LNCS, vol. 3376, pp. 29–43. Springer, Heidelberg (2005). https://doi.org/10.1007/978-3-540-30574-3_4
6. Bulygin, S., Petzoldt, A., Buchmann, J.: Towards provable security of the unbalanced oil and vinegar signature scheme under direct attacks. In: Gong, G., Gupta, K.C. (eds.) INDOCRYPT 2010. LNCS, vol. 6498, pp. 17–32. Springer, Heidelberg (2010). https://doi.org/10.1007/978-3-642-17401-8_3
7. Charlap, L.S., Rees, H.D., Robbins, D.P.: The asymptotic probability that a random biased matrix is invertible. Discrete Math. **82**(2), 153–163 (1990)
8. Chen, A.I.-T., et al.: SSE implementation of multivariate PKCs on modern x86 CPUs. In: Clavier, C., Gaj, K. (eds.) CHES 2009. LNCS, vol. 5747, pp. 33–48. Springer, Heidelberg (2009). https://doi.org/10.1007/978-3-642-04138-9_3
9. Czypek, P., Heyse, S., Thomae, E.: Efficient implementations of MQPKS on constrained devices. In: Prouff, E., Schaumont, P. (eds.) CHES 2012. LNCS, vol. 7428, pp. 374–389. Springer, Heidelberg (2012). https://doi.org/10.1007/978-3-642-33027-8_22
10. Ding, J., Chen, M., Petzoldt, A., Schmidt, D., Yang, B.: Rainbow - algorithm specification and documentation, November 2017. https://csrc.nist.gov/Projects/Post-Quantum-Cryptography/Round-1-Submissions

11. Ding, J., Schmidt, D.: Rainbow, a new multivariable polynomial signature scheme. In: Ioannidis, J., Keromytis, A., Yung, M. (eds.) ACNS 2005. LNCS, vol. 3531, pp. 164–175. Springer, Heidelberg (2005). https://doi.org/10.1007/11496137_12

12. Faugère, J.-C., Levy-dit-Vehel, F., Perret, L.: Cryptanalysis of MinRank. In: Wagner, D. (ed.) CRYPTO 2008. LNCS, vol. 5157, pp. 280–296. Springer, Heidelberg (2008). https://doi.org/10.1007/978-3-540-85174-5_16

13. Garey, M.R., Johnson, D.S.: Computers and Intractability: A Guide to the Theory of NP-Completeness. W. H. Freeman & Co., New York (1990)

14. Hashimoto, Y., Takagi, T., Sakurai, K.: General fault attacks on multivariate public key cryptosystems. In: Yang, B.-Y. (ed.) PQCrypto 2011. LNCS, vol. 7071, pp. 1–18. Springer, Heidelberg (2011). https://doi.org/10.1007/978-3-642-25405-5_1

15. Hashimoto, Y., Takagi, T., Sakurai, K.: General fault attacks on multivariate public key cryptosystems. IEICE Trans. **96-A**(1), 196–205 (2013)

16. Kipnis, A., Patarin, J., Goubin, L.: Unbalanced oil and vinegar signature schemes. In: Stern, J. (ed.) EUROCRYPT 1999. LNCS, vol. 1592, pp. 206–222. Springer, Heidelberg (1999). https://doi.org/10.1007/3-540-48910-X_15

17. Kipnis, A., Shamir, A.: Cryptanalysis of the oil and vinegar signature scheme. In: Krawczyk, H. (ed.) CRYPTO 1998. LNCS, vol. 1462, pp. 257–266. Springer, Heidelberg (1998). https://doi.org/10.1007/BFb0055733

18. Okeya, K., Takagi, T., Vuillaume, C.: On the importance of protecting Δ in SFLASH against side channel attacks. In: Proceedings of the International Conference on Information Technology: Coding and Computing, ITCC 2004, vol. 2, pp. 560–568 (2004)

19. Park, A., Shim, K.A., Koo, N., Han, D.G.: Side-channel attacks on post-quantum signature schemes based on multivariate quadratic equations. IACR Trans. Crypt. Hardware Embed. Syst. **2018**(3), 500–523 (2018)

20. Petzoldt, A.: Selecting and reducing key sizes for multivariate cryptography. Ph.D. thesis, Darmstadt University of Technology, Germany (2013)

21. Shor, P.W.: Polynomial-time algorithms for prime factorization and discrete logarithms on a quantum computer. SIAM J. Comput. **26**(5), 1484–1509 (1997)

22. Steinwandt, R., Geiselmann, W., Beth, T.: A theoretical DPA-based cryptanalysis of the NESSIE candidates FLASH and SFLASH. In: Davida, G.I., Frankel, Y. (eds.) ISC 2001. LNCS, vol. 2200, pp. 280–293. Springer, Heidelberg (2001). https://doi.org/10.1007/3-540-45439-X_19

23. Tang, S., Yi, H., Ding, J., Chen, H., Chen, G.: High-speed hardware implementation of rainbow signature on FPGAs. In: Yang, B.-Y. (ed.) PQCrypto 2011. LNCS, vol. 7071, pp. 228–243. Springer, Heidelberg (2011). https://doi.org/10.1007/978-3-642-25405-5_15

24. Yi, H., Li, W.: On the importance of checking multivariate public KeyCryptography for side-channel attacks: the case of enTTS scheme. Comput. J. **60**(8), 1197–1209 (2017)

25. Yi, H., Nie, Z.: High-speed hardware architecture for implementations of multivariate signature generations on FPGAs. EURASIP J. Wirel. Commun. Networking **2018**(1), 93 (2018)

Towards Optimized and Constant-Time CSIDH on Embedded Devices

Amir Jalali[1(✉)], Reza Azarderakhsh[1], Mehran Mozaffari Kermani[2], and David Jao[3]

[1] Department of Computer and Electrical Engineering and Computer Science, Florida Atlantic University, Boca Raton, FL, USA
{ajalali2016,razarderakhsh}@fau.edu
[2] Department of Computer Science and Engineering, University of South Florida, Tampa, FL, USA
mehran2@usf.edu
[3] Department of Combinatorics and Optimization, University of Waterloo, Waterloo, ON, Canada
djao@uwaterloo.ca

Abstract. We present an optimized, constant-time software library for commutative supersingular isogeny Diffie-Hellman key exchange (CSIDH) proposed by Castryck et al. which targets 64-bit ARM processors. The proposed library is implemented based on highly-optimized field arithmetic operations and computes the entire key exchange in constant-time. The proposed implementation is resistant to timing attacks. We adopt optimization techniques to evaluate the highest performance CSIDH on ARM-powered embedded devices such as cellphones, analyzing the possibility of using such a scheme in the quantum era. To the best of our knowledge, the proposed implementation is the first constant-time implementation of CSIDH and the first evaluation of this scheme on embedded devices. The benchmark result on a Google Pixel 2 smartphone equipped with 64-bit high-performance ARM Cortex-A72 core shows that it takes almost 12 s for each party to compute a commutative action operation in constant-time over the 511-bit finite field proposed by Castryck et al. However, using uniform but variable-time Montgomery ladder with security considerations improves these results significantly.

Keywords: Commutative supersingular isogeny · Constant-time · Embedded devices · Post-quantum cryptography

1 Introduction

The construction of public-key cryptography schemes based on the elliptic curves isogeny problem was proposed by Couveignes in 1997 [11] which described a non-interactive key exchange based on the isogeny classes of ordinary elliptic curves defined over a finite field $\mathbb{F}_p$. In 2004, Rostovtsev and Stolbunov [26]

© Springer Nature Switzerland AG 2019
I. Polian and M. Stöttinger (Eds.): COSADE 2019, LNCS 11421, pp. 215–231, 2019.
https://doi.org/10.1007/978-3-030-16350-1_12

Table 1. Comparison of SIDH and CSIDH over NIST's level 1 quantum security [12]

Scheme	Speed	Key size (Bytes)	Constant-time	Quantum attack	Active attacks	Non-interactive
SIDH	$\sim 10\,\mathrm{ms}$	378 B	Yes	$p^{1/6}$	Yes	No
CSIDH	$\sim 100\,\mathrm{ms}$	64 B	Not yet	Subexponential	Not known	Yes

independently came up with the same construction which later led to the design of other primitives such as isogeny-based digital signature [29]. Although the isogeny-based public-key cryptography construction by Couveignes-Rostovtsev-Stolbunov is attractive in many aspects such as key size, in 2010, Childs, Jao and Soukharev [7] showed that there exists a subexponential quantum algorithm that can solve the ordinary curve isogeny underlying problem. The proposed attack targeted the commutative ideal class group $\mathrm{cl}(\mathcal{O})$ for isogeny of ordinary curves; thus made this primitive unsuitable for the post-quantum era.

In 2006, Charles-Lauter-Goren [6] proposed a set of secure cryptographic hash functions from the supersingular curves isogeny graphs. Inspired by their work, in 2011, Jao and De Feo [22] proposed a Diffie-Hellman key exchange protocol from the isogeny of supersingular elliptic curves which was not vulnerable to Childs's quantum attack because of the non-commutative ring of endomorphisms in supersingular curves. Their interactive Supersingular Isogeny Diffie-Hellman (SIDH) key exchange is the fundamental basis of CCA secure Supersingular Isogeny Key Encapsulation (SIKE) mechanism [21] which was submitted to NIST PQC standardization project.

Due to the Child's quantum attack and impractical performance results of Couveignes-Rostovtsev-Stolbunov scheme, this primitive has been disregarded by community. Even the recent effort by De Feo-Kieffer-Smith [15] still takes several minutes to perform a single commutative action, in spite of using optimized state-of-the-art techniques.

Recently, Castryck et al. [5] proposed a new modification on the Couveignes-Rostovtsev-Stolbunov original scheme by adopting it to supersingular elliptic curves. However, instead of defining the supersingular curve over full ring of endomorphisms, the proposed scheme is restricted to the prime field $\mathbb{F}_p$ which preserves the commutative action of isogeny. They named the Diffie-Hellman key exchange scheme constructed over the commutative action as CSIDH (Commutative Supersingular Isogeny Diffie-Hellman). The main motivation behind using supersingular curves is to accelerate the commutative action rather than to address the security concerns on the Couveignes-Rostovtsev-Stolbunov raised by Child's quantum attack. In fact, CSIDH proposal can still be solved *theoretically* in subexponential time using the quantum algorithm as it is discussed by Biasse-Jao-Sankar [3] which targets the abelian hidden shift problem in the context of isogeny of supersingular curves [5]. However, as it is stated in [5], since the CSIDH public-key, in contrast to SIDH, contains only a single curve coefficient, it is not vulnerable to torsion point images attacks presented by Petit [25]. Furthermore, CSIDH simple key validation makes it inherently secure against CCA attacks proposed by Galbraith et al. [17]. Table 1 provides an abstract comparison between CSIDH and SIDH over NIST's level 1 security. The performance metrics provided in this table are based on optimized implementations on Intel Skylake processors. The performance of SIDH scheme on embedded devices is also investigated in detail in [18–20,23,27].

Recent detailed analysis in [4] shows that the CSIDH may have some security concerns with respect to quantum attacks. However, it offers efficient and fast key validation as well as extremely small key size. Moreover, other cryptography applications can be derived from the commutative group action similar to traditional Diffie-Hellman. For instance, De Feo and Galbraith [14] recently proposed SeaSign, a set of compact signatures from supersingular isogeny group action. Therefore, it is important to evaluate and analyze different aspects of this scheme such as performance and security on the practical settings.

The initial performance report of the commutative group action in [1,5] is based on a variable-time, mixed C and ASM implementation on Intel Skylake processors. Recent performance improvement of CSIDH by Meyer et al. [24] was also designed on top of the proof of concept implementation of CSIDH [5] and thus is variable-time. Note that as it is stated clearly in [5], the proof of concept implementation of CSIDH is unfit for production and it is totally vulnerable to timing and power analysis attacks.

In this work, we present a constant-time software library for CSIDH which targets 64-bit ARM-powered embedded devices. The main motivation behind this work is to evaluate the performance and the feasibility of using CSIDH in the real setting while the proposed software is secure against timing analysis attacks due to the constant-time implementation. We provide a set of modifications to the initial implementation of CSIDH in [5] over different layers from field arithmetic to group operations.

Since the proposed commutative action operation is implemented in constant-time, it can be simply adopted inside other applications of commutative supersingular isogeny to evaluate their performance in real settings.

The paper is organized as follows. Section 2 provides preliminaries on the isogeny of supersingular elliptic curves and explains the CSIDH scheme in a nutshell. Section 3 describes our approach to implement the entire commutative Diffie-Hellman key exchange efficiently and constant-time on embedded devices. The CSIDH benchmark results on two popular cellphones are presented in Sect. 4 and a comparison of constant- and variable-time implementations is provided. We conclude this work in Sect. 5.

2   Background

In this section, a brief description of supersingular curves isogeny and its application to construct a Diffie-Hellman key exchange protocol is presented. We refer the readers to [5,13,16,28] for more details.

2.1 Isogeny of Supersingular Curves

An ℓ-degree isogeny ϕ_ℓ is a rational function that maps an elliptic curve E defined over a field K to another curve E'. E' is a unique curve up to isomorphism and the map can be defined by a kernel which is a point P of order ℓ on E.

$$\phi_\ell : E \to E'/\langle P \rangle, P \in E[\ell].$$

The ring of endomorphisms of E is defined over the algebraic closure of K and denoted as $\mathrm{End}(E)$. Considering an elliptic curve E defined over a finite field $\mathbb{F}_p$, in case of ordinary elliptic curves, the $\mathrm{End}(E)$ is defined only over the base field $\mathbb{F}_p$, while for supersingular curves, it is defined over some extension field.

In contrast to Couveignes-Rostovtsev-Stolbunov scheme, CSIDH is constructed on supersingular curves. Therefore, only the subring of $\mathrm{End}(E)$ which is defined over $\mathbb{F}_p$, i.e., $\mathrm{End}_{\mathbb{F}_p}(E)$, is considered [5]. We have $\mathrm{End}_{\mathbb{F}_p}(E) \cong \mathcal{O}$ where $\mathcal{O}$ is an order in an imaginary quadratic field [14].

2.2 Class Group Action

For a supersingular elliptic curve E defined over $\mathbb{F}_p$ with $\mathrm{End}_{\mathbb{F}_p}(E) \cong \mathcal{O}$, the $\mathrm{cl}(\mathcal{O})$ is the ideal class group of $\mathcal{O}$. The action of an $\mathcal{O}$-ideal $\mathfrak{a}$ can be defined by an isogeny $\phi : E \to E'$ and denoted as $\mathfrak{a} * E$; its kernel $\ker(\phi)$ is presented by a torsion subgroup of points $E[\mathfrak{a}]$ on the curve E. The j-invariant, $j(E)$, of a curve E divides the $\mathrm{End}(E)$ into isomorphism classes where the isomorphic curves share the j-invariant value. Moreover, according to [11], the set of $j(E)$ constructs a hard homogeneous space which immediately implies the construction of a Diffie-Hellman like protocol.

2.3 Commutative Isogeny Diffie-Hellman Key Exchange

Considering the isogeny group action as described above on supersingular curves, CSIDH is defined over a finite field $\mathbb{F}_p$ with the prime p of the form $p = 4.\ell_1 \cdots \ell_n - 1$. Here ℓ_i are small odd primes and in the proposed parameter setting in [5] contain 74 primes which together construct a 511-bit prime value. Since the curve is supersingular, all ℓ_i are Elkies primes.

Using supersingular curves in CSIDH in contrast to Couveignes-Rostovtsev-Stolbunov original scheme makes it easy to find a curve with cardinality equal to $\#E(\mathbb{F}_p) = p+1$ and $\ell_i | p + 1$. Thus $\#E(\mathbb{F}_p)$ is congruent to 0 modulo all primes.

Similar to SIDH efficient implementation [10], in order to take advantage of fast and compact Montgomery arithmetic, the starting curve is defined as $E_0 : y^2 = x^3 + x$ which is an instance of Montgomery curve and therefore all the corresponding isomorphic curves are also in Montgomery form.

Private Key. The private key is defined as an n-tuple $(e_1, \cdots, e_n)$ of integers chosen from $[-m, m]$ where m is a small integer. Note that the value of m is defined by the provided security level as it is discussed in details in [5, Section 7]. According to their security analysis, $m = 5$ is sufficient to provide 125-bit and

61-bit of classical and quantum security, respectively. De Feo and Galbraith also provide the estimation of range for m regarding the NIST higher security levels [14, Table 1].

Public Key. Each n-tuple private key represents the ideal class $[\mathfrak{a}] = [\mathfrak{l}_1^{e_1} \cdots \mathfrak{l}_n^{e_n}]$ on the ideal class group $\mathrm{cl}(\mathcal{O})$ and generates a public key by applying the group action on the base curve E_0. The isomorphic curve generated by this group action is a Montgomery curve $[\mathfrak{a}]E : y^2 = x^3 + Ax^2 + x$ which whose coefficient $A \in \mathbb{F}_p$ is the corresponding public key.

Shared Secret. Since the group action is commutative, Alice and Bob compute the shared secret in a non-interactive procedure. They generate their key pairs as $([\mathfrak{a}], E_A)$ and $([\mathfrak{b}], E_B)$. Alice applies the action using her secret $[\mathfrak{a}]$ on the Bob's public key E_B and computes $[\mathfrak{a}]E_B$. Conversely, Bob computes $[\mathfrak{b}]E_A$ using his action and Alice's public key. The shared secret is the final curve coefficient $[\mathfrak{a}][\mathfrak{b}]E_0 = [\mathfrak{a}]E_B = [\mathfrak{b}]E_A$. Figure 1 demonstrates the key exchange procedure in a nutshell.

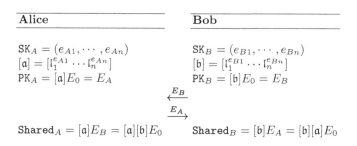

Fig. 1. CSIDH key exchange.

3   Constant-Time CSIDH Implementation

In this section, we outline our strategy for implementing an optimized and constant-time CSIDH on 64-bit ARMv8 processors. We engineered the underlying finite field arithmetic for the proposed field size and adopted different optimizations to evaluate a high performance and constant-time implementation of CSIDH on embedded devices.

All the field arithmetic operations described in this work are implemented using hand-written ARMv8 assembly to reduce the compiler overhead and provide the most-optimized results.

3.1   Field Arithmetic Modulo p_{511}

Starting from simple field arithmetic, modular addition and subtraction modulo p_{511} are implemented in constant-time. In contrast to the CSIDH proof of concept implementation [5] in which the modulo operation is only performed when the results are required to be corrected, our addition result is always subtracted from p_{511} and tested for borrow overflow. Based on the last borrow value, either p_{511} or 0 is added to the result for final correction. The same strategy is adopted for modular subtraction in order to have constant-time modular addition/subtraction.

Montgomery Modular Multiplication. Following the optimized SIDH implementation by Castello-Longa-Naehrig [10], Castryck et al. designed the entire curve operations in x-only arithmetic to take advantage of the optimized and compact Montgomery formulas. Accordingly, field multiplication and reduction are implemented using the Montgomery multiplication which is expected to offer the optimal performance since the p_{511} does not have any special form to enable further optimization techniques.

Since the prime is 511-bit, there is only one bit space left for any overflows and it is impossible to use optimization techniques such as lazy reduction to postpone the reduction operation. Therefore, using the Montgomery multiplication seems to be a better option rather than separate multiplication and Montgomery reduction due to the optimal memory usage and compactness.

The p_{511} is not a *Montgomery-friendly* prime which means that $p' = -p^{-1}$ mod r is not equal to 1 for the target radix, i.e., $r = 2^{64}$. This adds extra multiplication operations to the reduction part.

Because of the special shape of the CSIDH prime $p = 4.\ell_1 \cdots \ell_n - 1$, a straightforward strategy to find a Montgomery-friendly primes suggests the form

$$p = r.\ell_1 \cdots \ell_n - 1,$$

where r is the implementation target radix. This adds a considerable length (an extra word) to the field size without enhancing security level. Therefore, searching for a Montgomery-friendly prime in the context of CSIDH does not seem to add any performance improvement and the prime p_{511} is a proper choice for the target security level.

Since the filed elements over $\mathbb{F}_{p_{511}}$ are stored in an array of 8×64-bit words, 32 available 64-bit general registers inside the ARMv8 cores are adequate for implementing the modular multiplication efficiently using operand-scanning method. Therefore, we implement a compact and constant-time operand-scanning Montgomery multiplication using ARMv8 assembly, taking advantage of 64-bit wide general registers. Similar to our constant-time addition, the final result of the multiplication is always subtracted from p_{511} and according to the borrow overflow it adds to either p_{511} or 0 for the final correction.

Field Inversion. The constant-time field inversion is implemented using FLT algorithm in which for a field element a, the inverse of the element is computed as $a^{-1} = a^{p-2} \mod p$. Surprisingly, the variable-time CSIDH proof of concept implementation uses the same approach for computing the inverse of an operand, while faster non-constant algorithm such as Extended Euclidean

Algorithm (EEA) could have been utilized. Moreover, they used binary square-and-multiply method to compute such exponentiation which is not an efficient approach in terms of performance, but it offers slightly less memory usage.

We implemented the exponentiation using fixed-window method with precomputed table. We set the window length to 6-bit which led to a table with 28 $\mathbb{F}_p$ elements. This consumes roughly 1.8 KB of memory which is negligible to the obtained performance improvement. The proposed addition chain is highly-optimized for the 6-bit window and it costs $29\mathbf{M} + 2\mathbf{S}$ operations[1] for generating the table, and $73\mathbf{M} + 510\mathbf{S}$ for computing addition chain. Therefore, a field inversion costs $102\mathbf{M} + 512\mathbf{S}$ in our window method, while it costs $255\mathbf{M} + 510\mathbf{S}$ for binary method which is used in the CSIDH proof of concept.

Square Root. The square root test over $\mathbb{F}_{p511}$ for a field element a is implemented in constant-time by computing $a^{\frac{p-1}{2}} \bmod p$. Instead of using binary method in the CSIDH proof of concept implementation, we adopted the window method. The proposed addition chain computes the square root test using $71\mathbf{M} + 510\mathbf{S}$ in addition to $27\mathbf{M} + 2\mathbf{S}$ for the precomputed table generation. This leads to the total $98\mathbf{M} + 512\mathbf{S}$ computations, in contrast to $255\mathbf{M} + 510\mathbf{S}$ cost of binary method.

Note that in contrast to projective implementation of SIDH which only requires one inversion at the very end of each round, projective CSIDH requires several field inversion and square root computations inside each group action. Therefore, the above optimizations provide considerable enhancement in overall performance and efficiency of the protocol.

3.2   Scalar Multiplication

The Montgomery curve and x-only arithmetic offer a set of fast and compact formulas for computing curve arithmetic and isogeny computations. The CSIDH proof of concept implementation [5] is implemented based on the Montgomery group arithmetic. However, since the proposed implementation is non-constant time, it is entirely vulnerable to DPA and SPA attacks. In particular, the Montgomery ladder implementation for computing scalar multiplication is totally vulnerable to the power attacks and the exact value of scalar can be retrieved easily by power trace analysis [8].

To mitigate this vulnerability, we adopted the constant-time Montgomery ladder using the constant-time conditional `cswap` function. Since the point scalars in the CSIDH scheme have variable length, the constant-time ladder adds a significant extra operations to the scheme compared to non-constant version, but since the scalar in the commutative action operation is directly related to the private key, this modification is necessary.

The constant-time left-to-right Montgomery ladder is illustrated in Algorithm 1. It computes the scalar multiplication using $n - 1$ number of operations for different bit-length scalars where n is the finite field bit-length.

---

[1] **M** and **S** stand for field multiplication and field squaring, respectively.

Algorithm 1. Constant-time variable length scalar multiplication

---

Input : $k = \sum_{i=0}^{n-1} k_i 2^i$ and $\mathbf{x}(P)$ for $P \in E(\mathbb{F}_p)$.
Output: $(X_k, Z_k) \in \mathbb{F}_p^2$ s.t. $(X_k : Z_k) = \mathbf{x}([k]P)$.

1: $X_R \leftarrow X_P, Z_R \leftarrow Z_P$
2: $X_Q \leftarrow 1, Z_Q \leftarrow 0$
3: **for** $i = n - 2$ **downto** 0 **do**
4:     $(Q, R) \leftarrow \mathtt{cswap}(Q, R, (k_i \ \mathtt{xor} \ k_{i+1}))$
5:     $(Q, R) \leftarrow \mathtt{xDBLADD}(Q, R, P)$
6: **end for**
7: $(Q, R) \leftarrow \mathtt{cswap}(Q, R, k_0)$
8: **return** Q

As it is already implemented in [10] and pointed out in [24], the xDBLADD function inside Algorithm 1 computes the simultaneous point addition and doubling using precomputed $(A + 2C : 4C)$ values to reduce the number of operations. We state that the effect of this optimization on the overall performance of our constant-time CSIDH is negligible.

Remark 1. The constant-time Montgomery ladder in Algorithm 1 is computationally expensive. However, using this algorithm guarantees the DPA and SPA resistance. Alternatively, to achieve significant better performance results, we can adopt a uniform ladder with various number of iterations for different scalars such that $k_{n-1} = 1$ as it is outlined in Algorithm 2. Since the algorithm is uniform, it does not reveal any information about the scalar bit values. However, the scalar bit-length can still be exposed by DPA. We included both implementations in our software to illustrate the difference in performance results of the CSIDH scheme. Further details are provided in Sect. 4.

Remark 2. In order to be resistant against DPA, Coron [8] proposed different countermeasures for scalar multiplication in the context of elliptic curve cryptography. According to his analysis, the countermeasures do not significantly impact efficiency. However, they also do not thwart all kinds of power attacks. Moreover, adopting such techniques results in variable-time software which is dependent to the inputs. Therefore, we choose to use fully constant-time Montgomery ladder inside our software to be resistant against all kinds of timing and power attacks.

The rest of Montgomery arithmetic such as xDBL, xADD, are constant-time and therefore no modifications are needed. However, we note that depending on the inputs, the number of group operations and subsequently field arithmetic counts can vary in the CSIDH variable-time implementation. Accordingly, in order to make the scheme entirely constant-time, we need to modify the key exchange operations and make them independent of inputs. In the next section, we describe these modifications.

Algorithm 2. Uniform and variable-time scalar multiplication

Input : $k = \sum_{i=0}^{n-1} k_i 2^i$ with $k_{n-1} = 1$ and $\mathbf{x}(P)$ for $P \in E(\mathbb{F}_p)$.
Output: $(X_k, Z_k) \in \mathbb{F}_p^2$ s.t. $(X_k : Z_k) = \mathbf{x}([k]P)$.

1: $X_R \leftarrow X_P, Z_R \leftarrow Z_P$
2: $Q \leftarrow \mathtt{xDBL}(P)$
3: **for** $i = n - 2$ **downto** 0 **do**
4:    $(Q, R) \leftarrow \mathtt{cswap}(Q, R, (k_i \mathtt{\ xor\ } k_{i+1}))$
5:    $(Q, R) \leftarrow \mathtt{xDBLADD}(Q, R, P)$
6: **end for**
7: $(Q, R) \leftarrow \mathtt{cswap}(Q, R, k_0)$
8: **return** Q

3.3 Key Exchange Operations

As it is discussed in details in [5, Section 8], the most prominent operation inside CSIDH is the commutative group action. This operation computes the resulting curve coefficient given a starting curve and an n-tuple private key. The provided proof of concept implementation of group action in [5] is fast and optimized. However, as it is discussed before, its timing and performance directly depend on the input which makes it impossible to utilize in the practical settings. In this section, we provide a set of modifications to make key exchange operations constant-time. These modifications result in notable performance degradation to the scheme. However, they are necessary to be resistant against timing and power attacks.

Constant-Time Commutative Action. In order to compute an ℓ-degree isogeny using Vélu's formulas [30], we need to find a kernel point of order ℓ from torsion subgroup $E[\ell]$ on the curve. On Montgomery curves, a set of projective x-only formulas for arbitrary degree isogenies were proposed by Costello and Hisil [9] which the CSIDH proof of concept implementation is constructed upon.

In the context of SIDH, since the exact degree of isogeny is defined prior to the key exchange (2^{e_A} and 3^{e_B} for Alice and Bob, respectively), two pairs of base points are chosen from each torsion subgroups $P_A, Q_A \in E[2^{e_A}]$ and $P_B, Q_B \in E[3^{e_B}]$ as public parameters. Using these bases, Alice and Bob simply compute their secret isogeny kernel points $R_A = Q_A + [n_A]P_A$ and $R_B = Q_B + [n_B]P_B$ which accelerate the computation. However, this is not the case in the CSIDH scheme since the degree of isogeny action $[\ell_1^{e_1} \cdots \ell_n^{e_n}]$ is directly related to the each party's secret key $(e_1, \cdots, e_n)$. Therefore, as it is noted in [5] the kernel of each small degree isogeny $\ell_i^{e_i}$ in each step of isogeny computation is retrieved by sampling a random x-coordinate followed by a square root test (to check whether it is defined over $\mathbb{F}_p$ or imaginary $\mathbb{F}_{p^2}$) and a multiplication by $(p+1)/\ell_i$ which because of the special shape of p outputs a point of order ℓ_i or the point at infinity $\mathcal{O}$ with the probability of $1 - 1/\ell_i$ and $1/\ell_i$, respectively. After finding a kernel for each small degree isogeny ϕ_{ℓ_i}, the isogeny map is computed on the

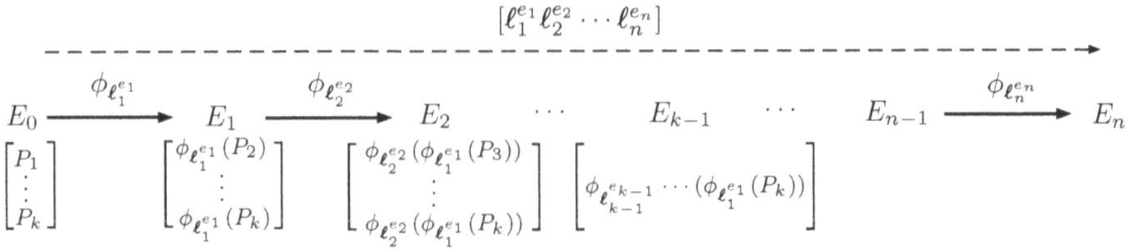

$$[\ell_1^{e_1}\ell_2^{e_2}\cdots\ell_n^{e_n}]$$

Fig. 2. Computing action using auxiliary base points on E_0.

current curve. This procedure is consecutively performed for all the small degree isogeny maps which together construct the action.

The random sampling procedure is expensive and it significantly affects the performance of the action operation, especially when it fails to provide an ℓ_i order point. It is possible to define a set of base points with predefined orders $\{P_1 \in E[\ell_1], \cdots, P_k \in E[\ell_k]\}$ such that $\{\ell_1, \cdots, \ell_k\}$ are a subgroup of primes from $\{\ell_1, \cdots, \ell_n\}$ on the base curve E_0 similar to SIDH. Furthermore, in each step of isogeny computations, the image of these base points can be computed on the next curve. Therefore, for the small degree isogenies $(\ell_1, \cdots, \ell_k)$ with higher probability of failure in random sampling $(1/\ell_1, \cdots, 1/\ell_k)$, the kernel points are ready at each step to use for the isogeny computations.

For the larger degrees, since the failure probability is relatively small, we can stick to the random sampling to reduce the memory usage. Figure 2 illustrates this procedure for some predefined value of k^2. In each step of isogeny computation, one of the image points is dropped and its image is not needed for the further isogeny computations.

Therefore, at the beginning of the procedure, the x-coordinate of k points is stored while at the k-th step, only one point is required. As a result, the isogeny evaluations of the auxiliary points are reduced as the algorithm steps forward.

However, this adds some security concerns to the scheme since the isogeny kernels are the image of some public base points through small degree isogenies. Moreover, a set of extra isogeny evaluations in each step is added to the scheme. Therefore, more investigation on the security and performance of the proposed method is needed. We leave the possibility of using such a technique for the future work.

To be able to practically evaluate the variation of the main loop in variable-time group action implementation, we performed a statistical analysis on the number of required iterations for uniformly random inputs. We conducted 10^6 experiments of variable-time group action from random inputs and recorded the number of iterations. Figure 3 presents the result of this experiment. We observed that the number of iterations for different private keys can be as large as 60 (only once in 10^6 experiments), while some inputs only require 9 iterations. This is

---

[2] The optimal value for k is directly related to the prime and the trade-off between memory usage and performance.

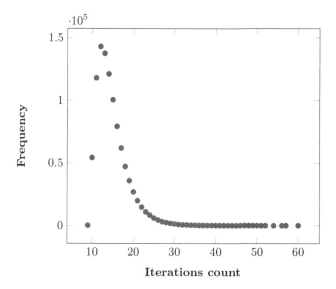

Fig. 3. The frequency of different iterations count over 10^6 experiments of group action.

the result of the variation in the n-tuple secret key and the failure probability of computing the point of order ℓ_i for some ℓ_is.

To mitigate this variation, the variant number of iterations should be replaced with an upper bound value. The straightforward value for the upper bound is n (the number of e_is). However, this is very conservative which significantly degrades the performance of the software. In fact, the recent detailed analysis of CSIDH in [2] shows that it is sufficient to iterate $r = 59$ iterations of the main loop to obtain a negligible failure probability ($<2^{-32}$) of the group action, considering the range of $e \in \{-5, \cdots, 5\}$.

To evaluate the performance of constant-time CSIDH on the target embedded devices, we modified the CSIDH variable-time action operation algorithm by removing all the conditional and while loop statements in an efficient way to provide a constant-time implementation of this algorithm inside our software. We outline the procedure in Algorithm 3. We refer the readers to our implementation for further details.

Using cswap in Algorithm 3 implies useless point multiplication and isogeny computations. However, the frequency of these operations may directly reveal the sign and the value of private key in a detailed power analysis trace. In fact, the detailed analysis of variable-time implementation of CSIDH in the Fig. 3 indeed demonstrates that the main loop iteration can have notable variation depending on the value of private key.

Algorithm 3. Constant-time commutative class group action

Input : $A \in \mathbb{F}_p$ and a list of integers $(e_1, \cdots, e_n)$.
Output: $B \in \mathbb{F}_p$ s.t. $[\mathfrak{l}_1^{e_1} \cdots \mathfrak{l}_n^{e_n}]E_A = E_B$.

1: // Decoding private key
2: **for** $i = 0$ **to** $n - 1$ **do**
3:     Set $s \leftarrow 1$ if e_i is negative, otherwise $s \leftarrow 0$.
4:     Set $v \leftarrow 0$ if e_i is 0, otherwise $v \leftarrow 1$.
5:     $e_i(s) \leftarrow e_i - (2 \cdot s \cdot e_i)$.
6:     $e_i(\bar{s}) \leftarrow 0$.
7:     $k(\bar{s}) \leftarrow \ell_i \cdot k(\bar{s})$.
8:     $k(\bar{v}) \leftarrow (\ell_i - v \cdot (\ell_i - 1)) \cdot k(\bar{v})$.
9: **end for**
10: // Action
11: **for** $i = 0$ **to** $n - 1$ **do**
12:     $A' \leftarrow A$.
13:     Sample a random $x = \mathbf{x}(P) \in \mathbb{F}_p$.
14:     Set $u \leftarrow 0$ if $x^3 + Ax^2 + x$ is a square in $\mathbb{F}_p$, otherwise $u \leftarrow 1$.
15:     $R \leftarrow [k(u)]P$.
16:     $d(u) \leftarrow 1$.
17:     **for** $j = 0$ **to** $n - 1$ **do**
18:         $f \leftarrow 1, r \leftarrow e_j(u)$.
19:         **for** $z = j + 1$ **to** $n - 1$ **do**
20:             $f \leftarrow f \times (\ell_z - (\bar{e}_z(u).(\ell_z - 1)))$.
21:         **end for**
22:         $Q \leftarrow [f]R$.
23:         Set $t \leftarrow 1$ if $Z_Q = 0$, otherwise $t \leftarrow 0$.
24:         Compute $\phi_{\ell_j} : A \to B$ s.t. $\ker(\phi_{\ell_j}) = Q$.
25:         cswap$(B, A, (\bar{t} \vee e_j(u)))$.
26:         $e_j(u) \leftarrow e_j(u) - 1$.
27:         $m \leftarrow (e_j(u) \vee t \vee \bar{r})$.
28:         $e_j(u) \leftarrow e_j(u) + t$.
29:         $k(u) \leftarrow k(u) \times (\ell_j - (m \cdot (\ell_j - 1)))$.
30:         $d(u) \leftarrow (d(u) \wedge e_j(u))$.
31:     **end for**
32:     $q \leftarrow q \oplus q$.
33:     cswap(A', A, q).
34:     $q \leftarrow (d(0) \wedge d(1))$.
35: **end for**
36: **return** A

We observe that the scalar multiplications in lines 15 and 22 of Algorithm 3 directly generate the secret isogeny kernel. Therefore, from the security viewpoint, the scalar multiplication indeed requires to be resistant against side-channel attacks. However, as we see in this algorithm, the point P is randomly generated in each iteration.

This makes it very hard for an attacker to retrieve the value of the kernel point using power analysis. Therefore, using a uniform but variable-time Montgomery ladder can be an option since it improves the performance results notably. We leave the further investigations for future work.

Constant-Time Key Generation. The CSIDH key generation algorithm is straightforward. First, private keys are randomly generated as an n-tuple integers from $[-m, m]$ interval, where in case of our implementation $m = 5$. Next, the public key is computed by performing the group action using the generated private key on the base curve E_0.

The CSIDH proof of concept implementation generates both private and public keys in variable-time. Since our proposed group action in Sect. 3.3 is constant-time, the public key generation is indeed constant-time. We made some trivial changes using constant-time conditional instructions on the private key random generation procedure to make the entire key generation resistant to timing attacks. We refer the reader to our implementation for further details.

Public Key Validation. The CSIDH scheme offers a fast and straightforward public key validation by examining whether the given curve is supersingular or not. Based on [5, Proposition 8], the supersingularity check justifies that the represented curve (public key) has the right endomorphism ring and therefore is a valid public key.

Since the public key validation procedure only uses public values, it does not require to be resistant against power and timing attacks and therefore it can be designed and implemented in variable-time as it is already implemented efficiently in [5]. Accordingly, we adopted the same implementation of the public key validation inside our software and used the fast variable-time Montgomery ladder algorithm for point multiplication inside the cofactor multipliers algorithm. We refer the readers to [5] for further details on the implementation of public key validation.

4 Performance Results and Discussion

In this section, we present our implementation[3] results on the two popular cell-phones, Google Pixel 2 and Huawei Nexus 6P equipped with 64-bit ARM Cortex-A72 and Cortex-A57, respectively. Our software is designed in a way that can be simply compiled to either constant-time or variable-time executable using `gcc` preprocessors.

We used `aarch64-linux-gnu-gcc` compiler for cross-compiling the executable with `-static -O3` flags and ran it using `adb shell` on the cellphones. Table 2 presents the performance of our constant-time and variable-time software on target platforms. Note that the variable-time implementation is also based on our optimized hand-written assembly field arithmetic and provides an optimized performance estimation of CSIDH proof of concept implementation on embedded devices. Moreover, the total CSIDH results are obtained by running the entire protocol, containing key generations and key validation on the target processors. The difference between timing and the number of clock cycles for target

---

[3] Our library is publicly available at: https://github.com/amirjalali65/ARMv8-CSIDH.

Table 2. Performance results of constant-time (with constant-time Montgomery ladder) and variable-time CSIDH. (Benchmarks were obtained on 1.95 GHz Cortex-A57 and 2.4 GHz Cortex-A72 cores running Android 7.1.1 and 8.1.0, respectively)

		Constant-time		Variable-time [5]	
		Cortex-A57	Cortex-A72	Cortex-A57	Cortex-A72
Key validation	Cycles $\times 10^6$	-	-	38	23
	Seconds	-	-	0.02	0.01
Group action	Cycles $\times 10^6$	30,459	28,872	624	552
	Seconds	**15.6**	**12.03**	**0.32**	**0.23**
Total CSIDH	Cycles $\times 10^6$	61,054	57,912	1,326	1,224
	Seconds	31.3	24.1	0.68	0.51

Table 3. Performance results of constant-time (with uniform but variable-time Montgomery ladder) CSIDH.

Operation	Cortex-A57	Cortex-A72
Group action	$11,286 \cdot 10^6$ cc	$10,824 \cdot 10^6$ cc
	5.94 s	**4.51 s**
Total CSIDH	$22,819 \cdot 10^6$ cc	$21,744 \cdot 10^6$ cc
	12.01 s	9.06 s

platforms refers to the processor's working frequency and its micro-architecture technology. Cortex-A72 core is the new high-performance 64-bit ARM core with optimized pipeline and micro-architecture which is used inside many embedded devices recently.

We also benchmarked our constant-time software with uniform but variable-time Montgomery ladder as it is discussed in Sect. 3.2. Table 3 presents the performance results of this experiment on our target platforms. We observed more than 2.5 times performance improvement just by using uniform variable-time ladder. This implies that the main challenge for designing a constant-time isogeny group action is to find an optimized and secure way of computing scalar multiplication. Considering the countermeasure techniques for uniform variable-time ladder, the performance results become more practical.

4.1 Discussion

Although the performance results of the constant-time CSIDH is not extremely promising, but since it is constructed on a commutative action, it offers a set of cryptographic applications such as digital signature which can be very useful in the quantum era. Based on the estimations in [14], such signatures are not very high-performance even by using fast and variable-time commutative action.

Therefore, in order to be able to practically adopt the isogeny commutative group action, its performance should be enhanced. The main bottleneck lies in the constant-time Montgomery ladder for computing point multiplication. Furthermore, useless computations inside the constant-time group action is undesirable.

One significant improvement to the algorithm can be achieved by using a faster but insecure ladder as it is discussed in the previous section. We can also reduce the number of useless operations and point sampling inside the group action by defining a set of base points as CSIDH public parameters and compute the image of these points in each step. While this may improve the performance notably, it adds some concerns regarding the security of the scheme. We believe that using the above suggestions and imposing security countermeasures can make the CSIDH and isogeny group action a suitable candidate for different applications, specifically because of its small key sizes and fast key validation.

5 Conclusion

In this work, we presented an efficient and constant-time implementation of CSIDH scheme on embedded devices. We engineered a set of constant-time and highly-optimized field and group arithmetic implementation using ARM assembly and provided a CSIDH software which is secure against SPA and DPA attacks. We benchmarked our software on two popular cellphones equipped with 64-bit high-performance ARM Cortex-A57 and Cortex-A72 cores. To the best of our knowledge, this work is the first constant-time implementation of CSIDH and the first evaluation of this scheme on embedded devices.

The implementation results imply that the fully constant-time implementation of the scheme may not be practical for many applications and it needs more investigations on the performance improvement and security analysis. However, because of many advantages of the isogeny commutative group action, the proposed software can still be used inside the applications with static keys and restricted band-width, taking advantage of fast key validation and small key size of CSIDH. Since side-channel attacks resistance is one of the fundamental requirements for any cryptographic scheme, we hope this work attracts engineers and researchers to investigate the performance improvement and security of the constant-time isogeny group action as it seems to be one of the promising candidates for designing different cryptographic applications in the future.

Acknowledgment. This work is supported in parts by NSF CNS-1801341, NIST-60NANB17D184, NIST-60NANB16D246, and ARO W911NF-17-1-0311, as well as NSERC, CryptoWorks21, Public Works and Government Services Canada, Canada First Research Excellence Fund, and the Royal Bank of Canada.

References

1. An Efficient Post-quantum Commutative Group Action. https://csidh.isogeny.org/software.html
2. Bernstein, D.J., Lange, T., Martindale, C., Panny, L.: Quantum Circuits for the CSIDH: Optimizing Quantum Evaluation of Isogenies. https://quantum.isogeny.org/qisog-20181031.pdf
3. Biasse, J.-F., Jao, D., Sankar, A.: A quantum algorithm for computing isogenies between supersingular elliptic curves. In: Meier, W., Mukhopadhyay, D. (eds.) INDOCRYPT 2014. LNCS, vol. 8885, pp. 428–442. Springer, Cham (2014). https://doi.org/10.1007/978-3-319-13039-2_25
4. Bonnetain, X., Schrottenloher, A.: Quantum security analysis of CSIDH and ordinary isogeny-based schemes. IACR Cryptology ePrint Archive (2018). https://eprint.iacr.org/2018/537
5. Castryck, W., Lange, T., Martindale, C., Panny, L., Renes, J.: CSIDH: an efficient post-quantum commutative group action. IACR Cryptology ePrint Archive (2018). https://eprint.iacr.org/2018/383
6. Charles, D.X., Lauter, K.E., Goren, E.Z.: Cryptographic hash functions from expander graphs. J. Cryptol. $22(1)$, 93–113 (2009)
7. Childs, A.M., Jao, D., Soukharev, V.: Constructing elliptic curve isogenies in quantum subexponential time. J. Math. Cryptol. $8(1)$, 1–29 (2014)
8. Coron, J.-S.: Resistance against differential power analysis for elliptic curve cryptosystems. In: Koç, Ç.K., Paar, C. (eds.) CHES 1999. LNCS, vol. 1717, pp. 292–302. Springer, Heidelberg (1999). https://doi.org/10.1007/3-540-48059-5_25
9. Costello, C., Hisil, H.: A simple and compact algorithm for SIDH with arbitrary degree isogenies. In: Takagi, T., Peyrin, T. (eds.) ASIACRYPT 2017. LNCS, vol. 10625, pp. 303–329. Springer, Cham (2017). https://doi.org/10.1007/978-3-319-70697-9_11
10. Costello, C., Longa, P., Naehrig, M.: Efficient algorithms for supersingular isogeny Diffie-Hellman. In: Robshaw, M., Katz, J. (eds.) CRYPTO 2016. LNCS, vol. 9814, pp. 572–601. Springer, Heidelberg (2016). https://doi.org/10.1007/978-3-662-53018-4_21
11. Couveignes, J.M.: Hard Homogeneous Spaces. IACR Cryptology ePrint Archive (2006). http://eprint.iacr.org/2006/291
12. Feo, L.D.: Isogeny Graphs in Cryptology. http://defeo.lu/docet/assets/slides/2018-05-31-gdr-securite.pdf
13. Feo, L.D.: Mathematics of isogeny based cryptography. CoRR abs/1711.04062 (2017). http://arxiv.org/abs/1711.04062
14. De Feo, L., Galbraith, S.D.: SeaSign: compact isogeny signatures from class group actions. IACR Cryptology ePrint Archive (2018). https://eprint.iacr.org/2018/824
15. Feo, L.D., Kieffer, J., Smith, B.: Towards practical key exchange from ordinary isogeny graphs. CoRR (2018). http://arxiv.org/abs/1809.07543
16. Galbraith, S.D.: Mathematics of Public Key Cryptography. Cambridge University Press, Cambridge (2012)
17. Galbraith, S.D., Petit, C., Shani, B., Ti, Y.B.: On the security of supersingular isogeny cryptosystems. In: Cheon, J.H., Takagi, T. (eds.) ASIACRYPT 2016. LNCS, vol. 10031, pp. 63–91. Springer, Heidelberg (2016). https://doi.org/10.1007/978-3-662-53887-6_3

18. Jalali, A., Azarderakhsh, R., Mozaffari-Kermani, M.: Efficient post-quantum unde-
    niable signature on 64-Bit ARM. In: Adams, C., Camenisch, J. (eds.) SAC 2017.
    LNCS, vol. 10719, pp. 281–298. Springer, Cham (2018). https://doi.org/10.1007/
    978-3-319-72565-9_14
19. Jalali, A., Azarderakhsh, R., Kermani, M.M.: NEON SIKE: supersingular isogeny
    key encapsulation on ARMv7. In: Security, Privacy, and Applied Cryptography
    Engineering - 8th International Conference, SPACE, pp. 37–51 (2018)
20. Jalali, A., Azarderakhsh, R., Kermani, M.M., Jao, D.: Supersingular isogeny Diffie-
    Hellman key exchange on 64-bit ARM. IEEE Trans. Depend. Secure Comput.
    (2017)
21. Jao, D., et al.: Supersingular isogeny key encapsulation. Submission to the NIST
    Post-Quantum Standardization project (2017). https://csrc.nist.gov/Projects/
    Post-Quantum-Cryptography/Round-1-Submissions
22. Jao, D., De Feo, L.: Towards quantum-resistant cryptosystems from supersingular
    elliptic curve isogenies. In: Yang, B.-Y. (ed.) PQCrypto 2011. LNCS, vol. 7071, pp.
    19–34. Springer, Heidelberg (2011). https://doi.org/10.1007/978-3-642-25405-5_2
23. Koziel, B., Jalali, A., Azarderakhsh, R., Jao, D., Kermani, M.M.: NEON-SIDH:
    efficient implementation of supersingular isogeny Diffie-Hellman key exchange pro-
    tocol on ARM. In: Cryptology and Network Security - 15th International Confer-
    ence, CANS, pp. 88–103 (2016)
24. Meyer, M., Reith, S.: A faster way to the CSIDH. IACR Cryptology ePrint Archive,
    p. 782 (2018). https://eprint.iacr.org/2018/782
25. Petit, C.: Faster algorithms for isogeny problems using torsion point images. In:
    Takagi, T., Peyrin, T. (eds.) ASIACRYPT 2017. LNCS, vol. 10625, pp. 330–353.
    Springer, Cham (2017). https://doi.org/10.1007/978-3-319-70697-9_12
26. Rostovtsev, A., Stolbunov, A.: Public-key cryptosystem based on isogenies. IACR
    Cryptology ePrint Archive (2006). http://eprint.iacr.org/2006/145
27. Seo, H., Liu, Z., Longa, P., Hu, Z.: SIDH on ARM: faster modular multiplica-
    tions for faster post-quantum supersingular isogeny key exchange. IACR Trans.
    Cryptogr. Hardw. Embed. Syst. 3, 1–20 (2018)
28. Silverman, J.H.: The Arithmetic of Elliptic Curves. GTM, vol. 106. Springer, New
    York (2009). https://doi.org/10.1007/978-0-387-09494-6
29. Stolbunov, A.: Constructing public-key cryptographic schemes based on class group
    action on a set of isogenous elliptic curves. Adv. Math. Commun. 4(2), 215–235
    (2010). https://doi.org/10.3934/amc.2010.4.215
30. Vélu, J.: Isogénies entre courbes elliptiques. CR Acad. Sci. Paris, Séries A 273,
    305–347 (1971)

Number "Not Used" Once - Practical Fault Attack on *pqm4* Implementations of NIST Candidates

Prasanna Ravi[1,2(✉)], Debapriya Basu Roy[3], Shivam Bhasin[1],
Anupam Chattopadhyay[2], and Debdeep Mukhopadhyay[3]

[1] Temasek Laboratories, Nanyang Technological University, Singapore, Singapore
PRASANNA.RAVI@ntu.edu.sg, sbhasin@ntu.edu.sg
[2] School of Computer Science and Engineering, Nanyang Technological University,
Singapore, Singapore
anupam@ntu.edu.sg
[3] Indian Institute of Technology, Kharagpur, India
dbroy24@gmail.com, debdeep.mukhopadhyay@gmail.com

Abstract. In this paper, we demonstrate practical fault attacks over a number of lattice-based schemes, in particular NewHope, Kyber, Frodo, Dilithium which are based on the hardness of the Learning with Errors (LWE) problem. One of the common traits of all the considered LWE schemes is the use of nonces as domain separators to sample the secret components of the LWE instance. We show that simple faults targeting the usage of nonce can result in a nonce-reuse scenario which allows key recovery and message recovery attacks. To the best of our knowledge, we propose the first practical fault attack on lattice-based Key encapsulation schemes secure in the CCA model. We perform experimental validation of our attack using Electromagnetic fault injection on reference implementations of the aforementioned schemes taken from the *pqm4* library, a benchmarking and testing framework for post quantum cryptographic implementations for the ARM Cortex-M4. We use the instruction skip fault model, which is very practical and popular in microcontroller based implementations. Our attack requires to inject a very few number of faults (numbering less than 10 for recommended parameter sets) and can be repeated with a 100% accuracy with our Electromagnetic fault injection setup.

1 Introduction

Ever since the discovery of the Shor's algorithm [26], there has always been an imminent danger of the possibility of large scale quantum computers threatening our existing public key infrastructure. The cryptographic community has long felt the need to replace the existing public key cryptosystems with quantum resistant alternatives, which is also justifiable given that research in the quantum computing field has grown by leaps and bounds [24].

© Springer Nature Switzerland AG 2019
I. Polian and M. Stöttinger (Eds.): COSADE 2019, LNCS 11421, pp. 232–250, 2019.
https://doi.org/10.1007/978-3-030-16350-1_13

NIST recently initiated the process for standardization of post quantum cryptographic alternatives for public key encryption (PKE), Key Exchange (KEX) and digital signatures (DS) [21]. Among the 64 submissions which still remain in the competition, lattice-based cryptography fields the largest contingent in terms of the number of submissions. This is due to the fact that they provide a very good balance of a number of attributes like key sizes, ciphertext sizes, computational performance which are on par with existing public key cryptographic primitives based on RSA and ECC along with providing post-quantum security.

The assessment of each candidate is being done based on multiple aspects such as classical security, post-quantum security, performance on a wide-range of devices (from Desktop PCs to resource constrained 8-bit microcontrollers) among other parameters. Another crucial aspect that is being looked at is the implementation security of post quantum cryptographic alternatives against active and passive physical attacks. In this regard, there have been a number of works that have reported physical attacks over lattice-based schemes through exploitation of a number of side channels like power/EM side [15,23], cache timing [10] and induced faults [11].

In this work, we try to analyze the fault vulnerabilities of multiple lattice-based schemes which base their security on the Learning with Errors (LWE) problem. One of the crucial components with respect to the implementation of all the LWE based schemes is the error sampling procedure. We analyzed the implementations of multiple lattice-based schemes such as NewHope [3], Kyber [6], Frodo [9] Key Encapsulation (KEM) schemes & Dilithium digital signature (DS) scheme [19] and observed common traits with respect to the usage of fixed nonces as simple domain separators in the error sampling procedure. The simplistic use of nonce to generate the secret components in the scheme raises questions concerning security against potential fault attacks. Though nonce-reuse based attacks such as the ones reported on ECDSA are well known in literature [12], surprisingly, none of the specification documents of any of the schemes discuss possible issues due to misuse of the nonces. Thus, we extend the applicability of nonce-reuse based fault attacks to cryptographic schemes based on the LWE problem. *In this work, we mainly focus on targeting the simplistic use of nonces through fault injection to create weak faulty LWE instances, resulting in key recovery and message recovery attacks in multiple lattice-based schemes.*

The contribution of this work are as follows:

- We extend the applicability of nonce-misuse based attacks to lattice-based LWE schemes mainly targeting nonces used as domain separators during generation of LWE instances.
- We analyze four lattice-based LWE schemes such as NewHope, Kyber, Frodo and Dilithium and demonstrate how nonce-misuse in these schemes could result in key recovery (long term key) and message recovery (session key) attacks. To the best of our knowledge, we perform the first fault analysis of lattice-based KEM schemes while all prior works focussed on fault attacks on lattice-based digital signatures [11,14].

- We propose a novel fault assisted Man-In-The-Middle (MITM) attack to perform message recovery in the considered KEM schemes secure in the Chosen Ciphertext Attacker (CCA) model. We fault the encapsulation procedure to perform successful message recovery, which is counter-intuitive given the fact that a re-encapsulation is done at the decapsulator's side in a Chosen Cipehertext secure KEM scheme which might detect tampering due to fault injection.
- We validated the vulnerabilities using electromagnetic fault injection on the ARM Cortex-M4 microcontroller. We performed practical fault attacks over reference implementations of the aforementioned NIST candidates taken from the *pqm4*[1] public library, a testing and benchmarking framework for post quantum cryptographic schemes on the ARM Cortex-M4 microcontroller.

The rest of the paper is organized as follows. Section 2 provides a brief description of various lattice-based LWE cryptosystems. The identified fault vulnerabilities and the associated key recovery and message recovery attacks are described in Sect. 3 with practical experimental results using our EMFI setup covered in Sect. 4. Possible countermeasures against the proposed fault attacks are discussed in Sect. 5 with final conclusions drawn in Sect. 6.

2   Background on Lattice Based Cryptography

2.1   Lattice Preliminaries

This section provides a brief background on the Learning With Errors problem and the LPR encryption scheme, which is the first Ring-LWE based PKE scheme [20] that has been the foundation of a number of efficient lattice-based PKE and KEM schemes including the schemes considered in this work. This section also further touches upon known insecure instantiations of the LWE problem and prior work done with respect to fault analysis on lattice-based cryptographic schemes.

We denote the polynomial ring $\mathbb{Z}_q[X]/(X^n + 1)$ as R_q for $q \in \mathbb{Z}^+$. Polynomials in R_q are denoted using bold lower case letters while matrices $(\mathbb{Z}_q^{k \times l})$ and vectors$(\mathbb{Z}_q^l)$ are denoted using bold upper case letters. Multiplication of two polynomials $\mathbf{a}$ and $\mathbf{b}$ is denoted as $\mathbf{c} = \mathbf{a} \times \mathbf{b}$ while point wise multiplication of two entities is denoted as $\mathbf{c} = \mathbf{a} * \mathbf{b}$. We use the notation $\mathcal{B}^p$ to denote an array of p bytes and $\mathcal{D}_\sigma$ to denote the zero-centered Gaussian distribution with standard deviation σ.

2.2   The Learning with Errors Problem

The Learning With Errors (LWE) problem, introduced by Regev in 2006 [25] is a versatile average case problem related to worst case hard lattice problems like the Shortest Vector Problem (SVP) and the Bounded Distance Decoding

---

[1] Available on https://github.com/mupq/pqm4.

Problem (BDD) on related lattices. The general LWE problem can be briefly defined as follows: Given a small secret $\mathbf{S} \in \mathbb{Z}_q^n$, an LWE distribution consists of ordered pairs $(\mathbf{A}, t) \in \mathbb{Z}_q^n \times \mathbb{Z}_q$ where $\mathbf{A} \in \mathbf{Z}_q^n$ is public and $t = (\mathbf{A} \times \mathbf{S} + e) \in \mathbb{Z}_q$ where $e \leftarrow \mathcal{D}_\sigma$. Given polynomially many pairs $(\mathbf{A}, t)$, the search LWE problem requires one to find a solution for $\mathbf{S}$ and the decision LWE problem requires one to distinguish structured ordered pairs $(\mathbf{A}, t)$ from random ones in $\mathbb{Z}_q^n \times \mathbb{Z}_q$. Its more structured variants like the Ring-LWE problem [20] and the Module-LWE problem [18] that compute over polynomial rings R_q possess greatly reduced key-sizes and computational time. All the four schemes considered in this paper except for FRODO, base their hardness on these structured variants of the LWE problem. There is another variant of the LWE problem, called the Learning With Rounding (LWR) problem wherein deterministic noise is generated by rounding every coefficient of the product $(\mathbf{A} \times \mathbf{S})$ to a lower modulus and their subsequent expansion back to the higher modulus. It is also interesting to note that this rounding/modulus switching technique has been used in all the considered LWE schemes in the paper, as an effort to reduce the key or ciphertext sizes.

We classify the LWE instances in general into two types, based on the purpose for which they are utilized in the considered schemes.

1. An LWE instance can serve as the public key of a KEM/DS scheme. Such an LWE instance is denoted as LWE_{PK}.
2. An LWE instance which is indistinguishable from random, can help hide a suitably encoded message in a KEM scheme. Ciphertexts are formed by adding an encoded message with an LWE instance, thus obscuring the message. Such an LWE instance is denoted as LWE_{OBS}.

We will henceforth utilize this terminology for LWE instances throughout this paper.

2.3   LPR Encryption Scheme [20]

The three LWE based KEM schemes (i.e) NewHope, Frodo and Kyber contain in their core, the LPR public key encryption scheme which is based on the hardness of the Ring-LWE problem. The key generation procedure of all the three KEM schemes (including Dilithium) and the encryption procedure of all the three KEM schemes follow the same framework as that of the LPR encryption scheme. It would be sufficient to describe the LPR encryption scheme, as it captures the essence of our attack analysis in all the considered schemes. The LPR encryption scheme can be briefly described as follows:

– KeyGen($\mathbf{a}$): Generate random polynomials $\mathbf{a} \leftarrow R_q$ and $\mathbf{e}, \mathbf{s} \leftarrow \mathcal{D}_\sigma^n$. The public-key polynomial is calculated as follows: $\mathbf{p} = \mathbf{e} + \mathbf{a} \times \mathbf{s} \in R_q$ with $\mathbf{s}$ being the private key.

- Encrypt($\mathbf{a}, \mathbf{p}, \mathbf{m}$): Three polynomials $\acute{s}$, $\acute{e}$, $\acute{e} \in R_q$ are sampled from $\mathcal{D}_\sigma^n$. The message m $(m_0, m_1, m_2, \ldots, m_{n-1})$ to be encrypted is encoded coefficient-wise into a polynomial as follows: The bit m_i is encoded to coefficient $q/2$ if it is 1, else it is encoded to 0. Ciphertext $\mathbf{c}_1$ is calculated as $\mathbf{a} \times \acute{s} + \acute{e}$ while ciphertext $\mathbf{c}_2$ is formed by embedding the message into an LWE instance as $\mathbf{c}_2 = \mathbf{p} \times \acute{s} + \acute{e} + \mathbf{m}$.
- Decrypt($\mathbf{c}_1, \mathbf{c}_2, \mathbf{r}_2$): $\hat{\mathbf{m}} \in R_q$ is computed as $\mathbf{c}_2 - \mathbf{c}_1 \times \mathbf{s}$. The decoder further retrieves the message m one bit at a time as $m = \mathcal{D}(\hat{\mathbf{m}})$ such that $m_i = 1$ if the corresponding coefficient is on $[q/4, 3q/4]$ else $m_i = 0$. This encoding procedure can withstand a coefficient wise error in $\hat{\mathbf{m}}$ upto $q/4$.

Our attack works by targeting appropriate variants of the aforementioned KeyGen and Encrypt procedures instantiated within the considered KEM (NewHope, Frodo and Kyber) and signature schemes (Dilithium).

2.4   Insecure Instantiations of the LWE Problem

The error component plays a major role in ensuring the hardness of the LWE instance. An LWE instance without the error component is nothing but a system of well defined modular linear equations, which can be solved by Gaussian elimination. There are indeed certain other trivially solvable instantiations of the LWE problem. If the error component only has values in a fixed interval $[z + \frac{1}{2}, z - \frac{1}{2}]$, then one can just "round away" the non-integral part and subtract z to remove the error from every sample [22]. From a given set of n LWE instances, if k of the n error components add up to zero, then one can simply add the corresponding samples to cancel the error and obtain an error-free sample. It is also possible to solve an LWE instance in roughly n^d time and space using n^d samples if the error in the samples lies in a known set of size d [5]. For a very small d, this yields a very practical attack. Our attack works by realizing such an insecure instance of LWE through faults to mount key recovery and message recovery attacks in the considered schemes.

2.5   Error Sampling Procedure

Almost all of the earlier lattice-based schemes like BLISS [13], LPR Encryption scheme [20] resorted to using complex discrete Gaussian samplers for their error sampling procedures [17]. But, Gaussian samplers turned out to be inefficient and very difficult to be implemented in constant time. Adding to that, implementations of discrete Gaussian samplers came under heavy scrutiny owing to a number of side channel attacks [10,15]. Moreover, Alkim *et al.* [4] reported that high precision Gaussian sampling is overkill for encryption schemes and that it was only required for schemes that require zero-knowledge proofs. Subsequently, all the newer lattice-based proposals (including the schemes considered in this paper) resorted to sampling from simpler and more secure noise distributions like the centered Binomial distribution (CBD) [3,6]. All the schemes considered in this paper expand a given small seed using XOF's such as SHAKE256, CSHAKE (Extendable Output Functions) from the SHA3 family of cryptographic primitives to random outputs of the desired length, which is further processed to generate samples from simpler distributions like the CBD or uniform distribution. Alternatively, coefficient-wise modulus switching is also used to generate a deterministic error in schemes based on the hardness of the LWR problem.

2.6   Prior Work on Fault Analysis of Lattice-Based Cryptographic Schemes

Bindel *et al.* [8] proposed the first fault analysis of a number of lattice-based signature schemes like the GLP [16], BLISS [13] and Ring-Tesla [2] schemes that follow the Fiat-Shamir framework. They identified a number of fault vulnerabilities in multiple operations across the various key generation, signing and verification procedures of lattice-based digital signature schemes. Later, Espitau *et al.* [14] reported a generic and a stronger fault attack based on loop abort faults on both the Fiat-Shamir type and Hash-and-Sign type signature schemes. It worked by converting the signature component into a solvable closest vector problem (CVP) instance when the error polynomial is limited to low degrees using loop-abort faults. The first differential style fault attacks on Dilithium and qTESLA signatures that are potential NIST standards, have been reported by Bruinderink and Pessl [11] that mainly targets the deterministic nature of the signing procedure by inducing random faults that can be injected during a large section of the execution time. They utilize clock glitches to realize their faults on an ARM Cortex-M4 based microcontroller. To the best of our knowledge, while all related prior works have only reported fault attacks on lattice-based signature schemes, our work is the first practical fault attack on lattice-based KEM schemes.

3   Fault Attacks on LWE Schemes

3.1   General Attack Idea

The core idea of our attack is to create a nonce-reuse scenario using faults to generate a trivially solvable LWE instance. One of the common traits of all the considered schemes in this paper is the error sampling procedure. We explain the intuition of our attack using the NewHope KEM scheme as an example. The same vulnerability also applies to all the other considered schemes in this paper. Refer to the key generation procedure of the NewHope KEM scheme in Algorithm 2. We observe that both the secret (s) and error (e) components of the LWE instance $\hat{b}$ (in the NTT domain) are generated using the seeds which differ only based on a single nonce value (Line 8,10). These seeds are further input to the Sample function which generates the required polynomials through use of XOF functions from the SHA3 family. The most important observation being the use of almost similar seeds that differ only based on the nonce value, to generate the secret and error components of the LWE instance.

For example, assume a Ring-LWE instance as created in the LPR encryption scheme as follows:

$$\mathbf{t} = \mathbf{a} \times \mathbf{s} + \mathbf{e} \in \mathbf{R}_q$$

The above equation can be alternatively seen as a modular linear system of equations with n equations and $2n$ unknowns. Assume that the attacker injects faults to create a nonce-reuse scenario where both $\mathbf{s}$ and $\mathbf{e}$ are generated using the same seed. The corresponding faulty LWE instance generated is

$$\mathbf{t} = \mathbf{a} \times \mathbf{s} + \mathbf{s} \in \mathbf{R}_q$$

The faulty LWE instance is a modular well defined linear system of equations with n equations and n unknowns ($\because$ n coefficients for each polynomial) which can be trivially solved using Gaussian elimination. This principle also applies to all the versions of the LWE problem such as the general-LWE, Ring-LWE and the Module-LWE problem. Thus, the modus operandi of our attack is to ensure that the nonces used for generation of both the secret and error are the same through injection of appropriate faults.

3.2   Key Recovery Attacks

In the following discussion, we will show how the identified vulnerabilities with respect to nonce reuse can result in key recovery attacks in the considered schemes. By key recovery attacks, we refer to the recovery of the long term secret key.

3.2.1   Attacking NewHope and Frodo

Refer to Algorithm 2 for the key generation procedure of the NewHope KEM scheme. The LWE instance $\hat{\mathbf{b}}$ formed as the public key in the key generation procedure is of type LWE_{PK}. Its corresponding secret and error components are created using the same seed, but with different nonces 0 and 1 respectively (Line 8 and 10 of KeyGen procedure of Algorithm 2). If faults can be injected to realize a nonce-reuse scenario, the secret key $\mathbf{s}$ can be trivially recovered from the public key, as per the analysis shown in Sect. 3.1. It is important to note that attack on the key generation procedure is applicable to both the CPA (Chosen Plaintext Attacker) and CCA (Chosen Ciphertext Attacker) secure model. The same attack can be very similarly adapted to the key generation procedure of the FRODO KEM scheme secure in both the CPA and CCA secure models. For brevity, we have not included the key generation algorithm of the FRODO scheme and hence please refer to [9] for the exact key generation procedure of the FRODO KEM scheme.

3.2.2   Attacking Dilithium

We also examine the applicability of our key recovery attack on schemes operating over modules (matrices/vectors of polynomials in ring) such as Dilithium and

Kyber. This section explains our key recovery attack on the Dilithium signature scheme which targets the key generation procedure (Refer Algorithm 1).

We can identify the LWE instance t as type LWE_{PK} (Line 14 in the KeyGen procedure of Algorithm 1). The multiple polynomials in its corresponding secret and error components are created using very similar seeds which only differ by a deterministically incrementing nonce value (Line 5–12 in the KeyGen procedure of Algorithm 1). If multiple faults can be injected to realize nonce-reuse during generation of both the secret and error components, t reduces to a set of well defined linear equations ($k \times n$ unknowns since $k > l$).

There is a subtle but considerable difference with respect to publicly revealed LWE instances in the Dilithium scheme. The public key reveals only t_1, the d higher order bits of t, while t_0 (the lower order component) is part of the secret key. Even on ensuring nonce-reuse, we would not be able to trivially solve for the secret s from the faulty public key. But, note that the security analysis of DILITHIUM is done with the assumption that the whole of t is declared as the public key. In addition to this, some information about t_0 is leaked with every published signature and thus the whole of t can be reconstructed by just observing several signatures generated using the same secret key [1]. Thus it is reasonable to assume that successful faults injected in the key generation procedure results in a key recovery attack over the Dilithium signature scheme.

3.2.3   Attacking Kyber

Refer to Algorithm 3 for the key generation procedure of Kyber KEM scheme. We identify the LWE instance t to be of type LWE_{PK} (Line 19 of KeyGen procedure of Algorithm 3). Its corresponding secret and error components are generated in a similar fashion as that of the key generation procedure of the Dilithium signature scheme (Line 10–17 of KeyGen procedure of Algorithm 3). But, similar to the compression technique used in Dilithium, we can also see that the LWE instance t is not directly published as the public key. A coefficient-wise modulus switching procedure is performed over the LWE instance t, which is subsequently revealed as the public key pk (Line 20 of KeyGen procedure of Algorithm 3).

This procedure adds a certain deterministic noise to the LWE instance similar to the Module-Learning-with-Rounding (Module-LWR) problem. But, the authors do not consider this as an added layer of security but simply as a technique to reduce the output size, due to the absence of a Ring/Module variant of a hardness reduction for LWR. The authors also state that they "believe" the compression technique adds some security, but this has not been quantified. Due to this compression technique, successful faults injected does not trivially result in key recovery, Our attack directly targets LWE hardness bringing down the security to LWR hardness. The attack on the residual LWR instance is out of scope of this work.

3.2.4   Applicability of Key Recovery Attacks

Among many aspects that are considered for evaluation in the standardization process, NIST also expects KEM schemes in particular, to provide *perfect forward secrecy.* This requires the KEM schemes to often perform key generation over frequent intervals to generate fresh public-private key pairs. It is often claimed that key generation is performed in certain secure locations thus removing the threat from possible physical attacks, especially side-channel/fault attacks. But, considering the use case of an IoT network housing a mesh of low power constrained devices, frequent communication of an end device with a server for a fresh public-private key pair would have a heavy toll on power-consumption of remote devices. Power is a very critical resource and thus communication of keys using power hungry RF transceiver modules would be much more expensive than performing key generation directly on the device. Thus, it is reasonable to assume that the key generation procedure will be performed over end-devices, thus leaving it prone to possible fault attacks.

3.3   Message Recovery Attacks

In this section, we will show how the identified vulnerabilities with respect to nonce reuse can result in message recovery attacks in the considered schemes. We specifically target the encryption procedures within the larger encapsulation procedures and our attack applies to the KEM schemes secure in both the CPA and CCA model. By message recovery, we refer to the recovery of the short term session key that is exchanged at the end of the encapsulation-decapsulation procedure.

Our message recovery attack directly applies to the considered CPA secure KEM schemes, similar to the analysis described for our key recovery attacks albeit involving some additional analysis to recover the message. But, intuition tells us that faulting the encapsulation procedure cannot be done in CCA secure version of KEM schemes. This is due to the employed Fujisaki-Okamoto (FO) transformation which performs a re-encapsulation during the decapsulation procedure to check for the validity of ciphertexts. This technique effectively thwarts use of chosen/faulted ciphertext attacks. But, we show that an MITM (Man-In-The-Middle) attacker can still perform valid message recovery attacks over CCA secure KEM schemes when faulting the encapsulation procedure.

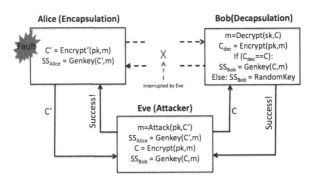

Fig. 1. Fault assisted MITM attack on CCA Secure KEM scheme

Refer to Fig. 1 for a pictorial description of our proposed fault assisted MITM attack on a CCA secure KEM scheme employing the FO transformation. Alice performs the encapsulation operation, Bob performs decapsulation with Eve being the MITM attacker. We have abstracted away the internal details of both the encapsulation and decapsulation procedures and have represented each of these procedures as composition of the functions Encrypt, Decrypt and GenKey. The Encrypt and Decrypt functions represent the encryption and decryption procedures underlying the considered KEM schemes. The GenKey function which is used to calculate the shared session key is a publicly known fixed transformation, varies according to the KEM scheme. The faulted encryption procedure is denoted as Encrypt'.

Lets assume that the attacker Eve performs a targeted fault into the Encrypt function of the encapsulation procedure to evoke a faulty ciphertext C' for an internally generated message m. The shared key ss_{Alice} is computed as GenKey(C',m). Lets assume that Eve receives the faulty ciphertext C' from Alice and recovers the message m using our analysis (Attack(C',pk)), whose details will be furnished later in this section. Further, Eve calculates Alice's shared secret key ss_{Alice} similar to Alice, now that Eve has the knowledge of both the faulted ciphertext C' and the message m. Having recovered the message, Eve now performs the correct encapsulation procedure with the recovered message m to generate the correct ciphertext C and the corresponding shared secret key which we denote as ss_{Bob}. The correct ciphertext is shared with Bob. Bob successfully decapsulates the ciphertext to generate the shared key ss_{Bob}.

Though the keys shared by both Bob and Alice and different, Eve has the knowledge of both the shared secret keys (session keys) ss_{Alice} and ss_{Bob} through which she can decrypt all communication transcripts between Alice and Bob during that session. To the best of our knowledge, we propose the first fault attack methodology to perform message recovery in CCA secure lattice-based KEM schemes. In the following discussion, we will show how nonce-reuse can be performed over encryption procedures to recover messages in the individual KEM schemes.

3.3.1   Attacking NewHope and Frodo

Refer to Algorithm 2 for the encryption procedure of the NewHope KEM scheme. We identify $\hat{u}$ as a compound LWE instance of type LWE_{OBS} which is used to hide the encoded message v (Line 11 of Encrypt procedure of Algorithm 2). Its corresponding secret $\acute{s}$ ($\hat{t}$ in the NTT form) is also used to create an LWE instance $\hat{u}$ (Line 9). We can also see that the secret and error components of this LWE instance $\hat{u}$ share the same input sampling seed while only differing by one byte on the nonce value (Line 5 and 6). It is important to note that $\hat{u}$ is encoded as part of the ciphertext, but is not tampered with (Not compressed). Thus, the attacker can directly access the LWE instance $\hat{u}$, as part of the ciphertext.

On ensuring the same nonce for both ś and é through faults, the resulting faulty LWE instance $\hat{\mathbf{u}}$ can be easily compromised, revealing $\hat{\mathbf{t}}$. Subsequently, we can calculate and retrieve message μ as follows:

$$\mathbf{m} = \mathsf{Decompress}(\mathbf{h}) - \mathsf{NTT}^{-1}(\hat{\mathbf{b}} * \hat{\mathbf{t}}) \ (\because \hat{\mathbf{t}} = \mathsf{NTT}(\acute{\mathbf{s}}))$$
$$\mu = \mathcal{D}(\mathbf{m})$$

where $\mathcal{D}$ denotes the corresponding message decoder used in the scheme.

Upon recovery of the message, an attacker can use our aforementioned attack methodology in an MITM setting to mount a successful message recovery attack on both the CCA and CPA secure versions of the NewHope KEM scheme. The same attack can be very similarly adapted to perform successful message recovery in both the CPA and CCA secure versions of the FRODO KEM scheme as well.

3.3.2   Attacking Kyber

Refer to Algorithm 3 for the encryption procedure of the Kyber KEM scheme. We identify a compound LWE instance $\mathbf{u}$ of type LWE$_{\mathrm{OBS}}$ is used to hide the encoded version of the message m (Line 15 of Encrypt procedure of Algorithm 3). Its corresponding secret $\mathbf{r}$ is also used to create another LWE instance $\mathbf{u}$ which is exposed as part of the ciphertext (Line 14 of Encrypt procedure of Algorithm 3). So, $\mathbf{u}$ can be appropriately faulted to enforce nonce-reuse. But, $\mathbf{u}$ is compressed using the modulus-switching technique (LWR) before it is revealed as part of the ciphertext. We thus reduce $\mathbf{u}$ to an LWR instance, whose security has not been analysed for the given parameters.

4   Experimental Validation

In this section, we perform an experimental validation of all our proposed attacks on a real device. We start by introducing our experimental setup, providing details of our device under target, implementation details and our attack setup. Since our attack requires to inject targeted faults, we further demonstrate our analysis of the various implementations to identify our target operation and ensure successful faults with very high repeatability.

4.1   Experimental Setup

For our experiments[2,3], we target the reference implementations of the considered schemes taken from the *pqm4* (see Footnote 1) library, a benchmarking and testing framework for PQC schemes on the ARM Cortex-M4 family of microcontrollers. We ported the reference implementations to the

---

[2] Our attack removes the hardness guarantees of the generated hard instance from the Module-LWE problem, while the Module-LWR problem remains to be solved.

[3] Attack works under the assumption that the attacker is able to reconstruct the whole of the generated instance $\mathbf{t}$ (Refer Algorithm 1).

STM32F4DISCOVERY board (DUT) housing the STM32F407, ARM Cortex-M4 microcontroller. All our implementations (compiled with `-O3 -mthumb -mcpu=cortex-m4 -mfloat-abi=hard -mfpu=fpv4-sp-d16`) were running at a clock frequency of 24 MHz. We use the ST-LINK/v2.1 add-on board for USART communication with our DUT. We used the OpenOCD framework for flash configuration and on-chip hardware debugging with the aid of the GNU debugger for ARM (arm-none-eabi-gdb). We use Electromagnetic Fault injection (EMFI) to inject faults into our device.

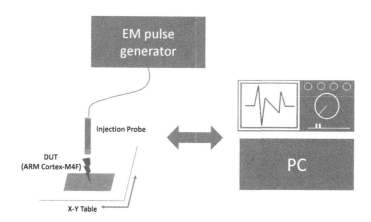

Fig. 2. Experimental setup for the fault injection

Refer Fig. 2 for our EMFI setup. The EMFI setup injects electromagnetic pulses with high voltage with low rise time (<4ns) in order to disturb the target operation. A controller software running on the laptop control both the EM pulse generator and the DUT and synchronizes their operation through serial communication. The EM pulse generator is directly triggered by an external trigger signal from the DUT. The EM pulse injector, which is a customized hand-made EM probe designed as a simple loop antenna. Refer to Fig. 3 for the EM probe used for our experiments.

4.2   Implementation of EMFI Attack

We first analyzed the operations within our target implementations that utilized the nonce value. The nonce value in implementations of all the considered schemes are used as inputs to Extendable Output Function (SHAKE256 for Kyber, NewHope, Dilithium and CSHAKE for FRODO) wherein they are simply stored to a given location in an array (say A). The array A determines the value of the sampled components. Different polynomials within the schemes are generated simply by changing the nonce value at the same index (memory location) while all the other elements of the array are fixed. The nonce updates in the array A were realized as store instructions (STR instruction for ARM) to

Fig. 3. (a) Hand-made probe used for our EMFI setup (b) Probe placed over the DUT

the memory. We attempt to skip all these store instructions and by doing so, we ensure that a single random value is used as a nonce to generate both the secret and error components, thus creating a nonce-reuse scenario.

Hence, we rely on the instruction skip fault model that has been widely studied and practically demonstrated on a range of devices (AVR and ARM microcontrollers) with high repeatability to satisfy our attack requirement [7,27]. It has been realized over different architectures through multiple fault injection methodologies like laser shots [7,27], clock [11] glitches and EM injection in addition to serving as a basis for multiple cryptanalytic efforts. We scanned

```
ldr     r3,[r5,#28]
stmia   r4!,{r0,r1,r2,r3}
strb.w  r7,[r6,#-132]!
movs    r1,#1
mov     r0,r6
```

```
movs    r1,#1
add     r0,sp,#52
strb.w  r9,[r6,#32]
movs    r2,#33
movs    r3,#0
```

(a) Target operation in NewHope   (b) Target operation in Kyber

```
lsrs    r2,r7,#8
ldr     r3,[pc,#264]
strb.w  r2,[sp,#7]
movw    r2,#4097
mov     r1,sp
```

```
movs    r1,#128
ldr     r0,[pc,#208]
strb.w  r7,[sp,#44]
add     r1,sp,#12
add     r0,sp,#48
```

(c) Target operation in Frodo   (d) Target operation in Dilithium

Fig. 4. Code snippet from reference implementations of the considered schemes. Our target store operation is highlighted in red. (Color figure online)

Table 1. Fault complexity (number of instruction skip faults) of our attack on the various recommended parameter sets of the considered schemes

Attack Objective	Fault Complexity			
	NEWHOPE		FRODO	
	NEWHOPE512	NEWHOPE1024	Frodo-640	Frodo-976
Key Recovery	1	1	1	1
Message Recovery	1	1	1	1

	KYBER			DILITHIUM			
	KYBER512	KYBER768	KYBER1024	Weak	Med.	Rec.	High
Key Recovery	4	6	8	5	7	9	11
Message Recovery	4	6	8	-	-	-	-

the entire top layer of the chip and could identify a precise location (close to the center of the chip near the ARM logo), where we could achieve *a 100% repeatability in skipping the same store instruction*, thus preventing update of the nonce. Since we are only skipping the update of the nonce, it is important to note that our attack works irrespective of the value of the nonce.

Refer to Fig. 4 for the assembly code snippets of the compiled reference implementations of the considered schemes. The faulted store operation in each implementation is highlighted in red. Refer Table 1 for the fault complexity of our nonce misuse attack when applied to the recommended parameter sets of all the schemes. Only a single fault is required in the case of NewHope and Frodo since it is enough to skip the update of the nonce for only the error component and not the secret component. But, in the case of Module-LWE schemes like Kyber and Dilithium, it is required to skip the update of all the nonces used for generation of polynomials. Thus, the number of faults amount to $(k + l)$ when the dimension of the public constant A in these schemes is assumed to $R_q^{k \times l}$.

5 Countermeasures

We have shown that the use of nonces in the reference implementations of all the aforementioned schemes can be easily targeted through fault attacks. The main reason however is due to use of seeds for generation of secret and error components which only vary by one or two bytes due to the nonce. The value of the nonce used primarily decide the difference between the secret and error components. Thus, it becomes important to perform a sanity check on the value of the nonce, which can possibly mitigate the attack. There are a lot of known vulnerable instances of the LWE problem (Refer Sect. 2.1 for some of them) and we have realized one of these instances using faults ($\mathbf{s} = \mathbf{e}$). Thus, performing simple checks on the secret and error components of the LWE instances for known trivial weaknesses could also be a potential countermeasure against our attack.

6   Conclusion

In this work, we present practical fault attacks on a number of potential NIST candidates for post quantum cryptography, mainly targeting schemes based on the LWE problem such as NewHope, Kyber, Dilithium, Frodo. We exploit the use of nonces in the sampling procedure in each of these schemes to demonstrate key recovery and message recovery attacks. While long term keys are directly recovered by faulting the key generation procedure, message recovery (session keys) is demonstrated through a novel fault assisted MITM attack on the encryption procedure on the CCA secure KEM schemes. We perform a practical validation of all our attacks on an ARM Cortex-M4F microcontroller running reference implementations taken from the *pqm4* library.

A   Appendix

Algorithm 1. Dilithium Signature scheme

---

1   **Procedure** Dilithium.KeyGen ()
2   $\quad \rho, \rho' \leftarrow \{0,1\}^{256}$
3   $\quad K \leftarrow \{0,1\}^{256}$
4   $\quad N = 0$
5   $\quad$ **for** i *from* 0 *to* $\ell - 1$ **do**
6   $\quad\quad$ $\mathbf{s}_1[i] = \mathsf{Sample}(\mathsf{PRF}(\rho', N))$
7   $\quad\quad$ $N := N + 1$
8   $\quad$ **end**
9   $\quad$ **for** i *from* 0 *to* $k - 1$ **do**
10 $\quad\quad$ $\mathbf{s}_2[i] = \mathsf{Sample}(\mathsf{PRF}(\rho', N))$
11 $\quad\quad$ $N := N + 1$
12 $\quad$ **end**
13 $\quad$ $\mathbf{a} \sim R_q^{k \times \ell} = \mathsf{ExpandA}(\rho)$
14 $\quad$ $\mathbf{t} = \mathbf{a} \times \mathbf{s}_1 + \mathbf{s}_2$
15 $\quad$ $\mathbf{t}_1 = \mathsf{Power2Round}_q(\mathbf{t}, d)$
16 $\quad$ $tr \in \{0,1\}^{384} = \mathsf{CRH}(\rho \| \mathbf{t}_1)$
17 $\quad$ **return** $pk = (\rho, \mathbf{t}_1), sk = (\rho, K, tr, \mathbf{s}_1, \mathbf{s}_2, \mathbf{t}_0)$

Algorithm 2. NewHope KEM scheme

---

 1   **Procedure** NewHope.KeyGen ()

 2      $seed \leftarrow \{0, \ldots, 255\}^{32}$

 3      $z \leftarrow \mathsf{SHAKE256}(64, seed)$

 4      $publicseed \leftarrow z[0:31]$

 5      $noiseseed \leftarrow z[32:63]$

 6      $\hat{\mathbf{a}} \leftarrow \mathsf{GenA}(publicseed)$

 7      $\mathbf{s} \leftarrow \mathsf{PolyBitRev}(\mathsf{Sample}(noiseseed, 0))$

 8      $\hat{\mathbf{s}} = \mathsf{NTT}(\mathbf{s})$

 9      $\mathbf{e} \leftarrow \mathsf{PolyBitRev}(\mathsf{Sample}(noiseseed, 1))$

10      $\hat{\mathbf{e}} = \mathsf{NTT}(\mathbf{e})$

11      $\hat{\mathbf{b}} = \hat{\mathbf{a}} * \hat{\mathbf{s}} + \hat{\mathbf{e}}$

12   **return** $(pk = \mathsf{EncodePK}(\hat{\mathbf{b}}, publicseed), sk = \mathsf{EncodePolynomial}(\mathbf{s}))$

 1   **Procedure** NewHope.Encrypt ($pk \in \mathcal{B}^{7 \cdot n/4 + 32}, \mu \in \mathcal{B}^{32}, coin \in \mathcal{B}^{32}$)

 2      $\hat{\mathbf{b}}, publicseed \leftarrow \mathsf{DecodePk}(pk)$

 3      $\hat{\mathbf{a}} \leftarrow \mathsf{GenA}(publicseed)$

 4      $\acute{\mathbf{s}} \leftarrow \mathsf{PolyBitRev}(Sample(coin, 0))$

 5      $\acute{\mathbf{e}} \leftarrow \mathsf{PolyBitRev}(Sample(coin, 1))$

 6      $\acute{\mathbf{e}} \leftarrow \mathsf{Sample}(coin, 2)$

 7      $\hat{\mathbf{t}} = \mathsf{NTT}(\acute{\mathbf{s}})$

 8      $\hat{\mathbf{u}} = \hat{\mathbf{a}} * \hat{\mathbf{t}} + \mathsf{NTT}(\acute{\mathbf{e}})$

 9      $\mathbf{v} = \mathsf{Encode}(\mu)$

10      $\acute{\mathbf{v}} = \mathsf{NTT}^{-1}(\hat{\mathbf{b}} * \hat{\mathbf{t}}) + \acute{\mathbf{e}} + \mathbf{v}$

11      $\mathbf{h} = \mathsf{Compress}(\acute{\mathbf{v}})$

12   **return** $c = \mathsf{EncodeC}(\hat{\mathbf{u}}, \mathbf{h})$

Algorithm 3. Kyber KEM scheme

---

1 **Procedure** Kyber.KeyGen()
2    $d \leftarrow \{0,1\}^{256}$
3    $(\rho, \sigma) := G(d)$
4    $N := 0$
5   **for** i *from* 0 *to* $k-1$ **do**
6   **for** j *from* 0 *to* $k-1$ **do**
7        $\mathbf{a}[i][j] \leftarrow \mathsf{Parse}(\mathsf{XOF}(\rho||j||i))$
8   **end**
9   **end**
10   **for** i *from* 0 *to* $k-1$ **do**
11      $\mathbf{s}[i] \leftarrow \mathsf{CBD}_\eta(\mathsf{PRF}(\sigma, N))$
12      $N := N + 1$
13   **end**
14   **for** i *from* 0 *to* $k-1$ **do**
15      $\mathbf{e}[i] \leftarrow \mathsf{CBD}_\eta(\mathsf{PRF}(\sigma, N))$
16      $N := N + 1$
17   **end**
18    $\hat{\mathbf{s}} \leftarrow \mathsf{NTT}(\mathbf{s})$
19    $\mathbf{t} = \mathsf{NTT}^{-1}(\hat{\mathbf{a}} * \hat{\mathbf{s}}) + \mathbf{e}$
20    $pk := (\mathsf{Encode}_{d_t}(\mathsf{Compress}_q(\mathbf{t}, d_t))||\rho)$
21    $sk := \mathsf{Encode}_{13}(\hat{\mathbf{s}} \bmod^+ q)$
22   **return** (pk, sk)

1 **Procedure** NewHope.Encrypt($pk \in \mathcal{B}^{d_t \cdot k \cdot n/8 + 32}$, $m \in \mathcal{B}^{32}$, $r \in \mathcal{B}^{32}$)
     $\vdots$
2
3    $N = 0$
4   **for** i *from* 0 *to* $k-1$ **do**
5      $\mathbf{r}[i] \leftarrow \mathsf{CBD}_\eta(\mathsf{PRF}(r, N))$
6      $N := N + 1$
7   **end**
8   **for** i *from* 0 *to* $k-1$ **do**
9      $\mathbf{e}_1[i] \leftarrow \mathsf{CBD}_\eta(\mathsf{PRF}(r, N))$
10      $N := N + 1$
11   **end**
12    $\mathbf{e}_2 \leftarrow \mathsf{CBD}_\eta(\mathsf{PRF}(r, N))$
13    $\hat{\mathbf{r}} = \mathsf{NTT}(\mathbf{r})$
14    $\mathbf{u} = \mathsf{NTT}^{-1}(\hat{a}^T * \hat{\mathbf{r}}) + \mathbf{e}_1$
15    $\mathbf{v} = \mathsf{NTT}^{-1}(\hat{t}^T * \hat{\mathbf{r}}) + \mathbf{e}_2 + \mathsf{Decode}_1(\mathsf{Decompose}_q(m, 1))$
16    $\mathbf{c}_1 = \mathsf{Encode}_{d_u}(\mathsf{Compress}_q(\mathbf{u}, d_u))$
17    $\mathbf{c}_2 = \mathsf{Encode}_{d_v}(\mathsf{Compress}_q(\mathbf{v}, d_v))$
18   **return** $\mathbf{c} = (\mathbf{c}_1, \mathbf{c}_2)$

References

1. Suppressed for blind review
2. Akleylek, S., Bindel, N., Buchmann, J., Krämer, J., Marson, G.A.: An efficient lattice-based signature scheme with provably secure instantiation. In: Pointcheval, D., Nitaj, A., Rachidi, T. (eds.) AFRICACRYPT 2016. LNCS, vol. 9646, pp. 44–60. Springer, Cham (2016). https://doi.org/10.1007/978-3-319-31517-1_3
3. Alkim, E., et al.: Algorithm specifcations and supporting documentation (2017)
4. Alkim, E., Ducas, L., Pöppelmann, T., Schwabe, P.: Post-quantum key exchange-a new hope. In: USENIX Security Symposium, pp. 327–343 (2016)
5. Arora, S., Ge, R.: New algorithms for learning in presence of errors. In: Aceto, L., Henzinger, M., Sgall, J. (eds.) ICALP 2011. LNCS, vol. 6755, pp. 403–415. Springer, Heidelberg (2011). https://doi.org/10.1007/978-3-642-22006-7_34
6. Avanzi, R., et al.: Crystals-kyber algorithm specifications and supporting documentation (2017)
7. Balasch, J., Gierlichs, B., Verbauwhede, I.: An in-depth and black-box characterization of the effects of clock glitches on 8-bit MCUs. In: 2011 Workshop on Fault Diagnosis and Tolerance in Cryptography (FDTC), pp. 105–114. IEEE (2011)
8. Bindel, N., Buchmann, J., Krämer, J.: Lattice-based signature schemes and their sensitivity to fault attacks. In: 2016 Workshop on Fault Diagnosis and Tolerance in Cryptography (FDTC), pp. 63–77. IEEE (2016)
9. Bos, J., et al.: Frodo: take off the ring! practical, quantum-secure key exchange from LWE. Technical report, National Institute of Standards and Technology (2017). https://csrc.nist.gov/projects/post-quantum-cryptography/round-1-submissions
10. Bruinderink, L.G., Hülsing, A., Lange, T., Yarom, Y.: Flush, gauss, and reload – a cache attack on the BLISS lattice-based signature scheme. In: Gierlichs, B., Poschmann, A.Y. (eds.) CHES 2016. LNCS, vol. 9813, pp. 323–345. Springer, Heidelberg (2016). https://doi.org/10.1007/978-3-662-53140-2_16
11. Bruinderink, L.G., Pessl, P.: Differential fault attacks on deterministic lattice signatures. IACR Trans. Cryptogr. Hardw. Embed. Syst. **2018**(3) (2018). https://eprint.iacr.org/2018/355.pdf
12. Bushing, S., Sven, M.: Console hacking 2010: PS3 epic fail. In: Talk at 27th Chaos Communication Congress (2010)
13. Ducas, L., Durmus, A., Lepoint, T., Lyubashevsky, V.: Lattice signatures and bimodal gaussians. In: Canetti, R., Garay, J.A. (eds.) CRYPTO 2013. LNCS, vol. 8042, pp. 40–56. Springer, Heidelberg (2013). https://doi.org/10.1007/978-3-642-40041-4_3
14. Espitau, T., Fouque, P.-A., Gérard, B., Tibouchi, M.: Loop-abort faults on lattice-based fiat-shamir and hash-and-sign signatures. In: Avanzi, R., Heys, H. (eds.) SAC 2016. LNCS, vol. 10532, pp. 140–158. Springer, Cham (2017). https://doi.org/10.1007/978-3-319-69453-5_8
15. Espitau, T., Fouque, P.A., Gérard, B., Tibouchi, M.: Side-channel attacks on bliss lattice-based signatures: exploiting branch tracing against strongswan and electromagnetic emanations in microcontrollers. In: Proceedings of the 2017 ACM SIGSAC Conference on Computer and Communications Security, pp. 1857–1874. ACM (2017)
16. Güneysu, T., Lyubashevsky, V., Pöppelmann, T.: Practical lattice-based cryptography: a signature scheme for embedded systems. In: Prouff, E., Schaumont, P. (eds.) CHES 2012. LNCS, vol. 7428, pp. 530–547. Springer, Heidelberg (2012). https://doi.org/10.1007/978-3-642-33027-8_31

17. Howe, J., Khalid, A., Rafferty, C., Regazzoni, F., O'Neill, M.: On practical discrete Gaussian samplers for lattice-based cryptography. IEEE Trans. Comput. **67**, 322–334 (2016)

18. Langlois, A., Stehlé, D.: Worst-case to average-case reductions for module lattices. Des. Codes Cryptogr. **75**(3), 565–599 (2015)

19. Lyubashevsky, V.,et al.: CRYSTALS-Dilithium. Technical report, National Institute of Standards and Technology (2017). https://csrc.nist.gov/projects/post-quantum-cryptography/round-1-submissions

20. Lyubashevsky, V., Peikert, C., Regev, O.: On ideal lattices and learning with errors over rings. J. ACM **60**(6), 43 (2013)

21. NIST: Submission requirements and evaluation criteria for the post-quantum cryptography standardization process (2016). https://csrc.nist.gov/csrc/media/projects/post-quantum-cryptography/documents/call-for-proposals-final-dec-2016.pdf

22. Peikert, C.: How (not) to instantiate ring-LWE. In: Zikas, V., De Prisco, R. (eds.) SCN 2016. LNCS, vol. 9841, pp. 411–430. Springer, Cham (2016). https://doi.org/10.1007/978-3-319-44618-9_22

23. Pessl, P.: Analyzing the shuffling side-channel countermeasure for lattice-based signatures. In: Dunkelman, O., Sanadhya, S.K. (eds.) INDOCRYPT 2016. LNCS, vol. 10095, pp. 153–170. Springer, Cham (2016). https://doi.org/10.1007/978-3-319-49890-4_9

24. Preskill, J.: Reliable quantum computers. Proc. R. Soc. Lond. A Math. Phys. Eng. Sci. **454**, 385–410 (1998). The Royal Society

25. Regev, O.: On lattices, learning with errors, random linear codes, and cryptography. J. ACM (JACM) **56**(6), 34 (2009)

26. Shor, P.W.: Polynomial time algorithms for discrete logarithms and factoring on a quantum computer. In: Adleman, L.M., Huang, M.-D. (eds.) ANTS 1994. LNCS, vol. 877, pp. 289–289. Springer, Heidelberg (1994). https://doi.org/10.1007/3-540-58691-1_68

27. Trichina, E., Korkikyan, R.: Multi fault laser attacks on protected CRT-RSA. In: 2010 Workshop on Fault Diagnosis and Tolerance in Cryptography (FDTC), pp. 75–86. IEEE (2010)

Countermeasures Against Implementation Attacks

Practical Evaluation of Masking
for NTRUEncrypt on ARM Cortex-M4

Thomas Schamberger[1]([✉]), Oliver Mischke[2], and Johanna Sepulveda[1]

[1] Technical University of Munich, Munich, Germany
{t.schamberger,johanna.sepulveda}@tum.de
[2] Infineon Technologies AG, Munich, Germany
oliver.mischke@infineon.com

Abstract. To protect against the future threat of large scale quantum computing, cryptographic schemes that are considered appropriately secure against known quantum algorithms have gained in popularity and are currently in the process of standardization by NIST. One of the more promising so-called post-quantum schemes is NTRUEncrypt, which withstood scrutiny from the scientific community for over 20 years.

Similar to classical algorithms like AES, implementations of NTRU-Encrypt must be protected against physical attacks. While different masking and hiding countermeasures have been proposed in the past, practical power analysis evaluations of masking for NTRUEncrypt are lacking. We therefore provide a practical evaluation of masking applied to index-based multiplication and a modern parameter set using trinary polynomials. With the use of SIMD instructions available in the Cortex-M4 microcontroller, we are able to implement additive masking without any significant performance overhead compared to an unmasked implementation. Our implementation showed no observable first-order leakage using a HW model and two million measurement traces. Successful second-order attacks are demonstrated for our implementation using SIMD instructions, which processes the mask and masked data simultaneously, as well as for a sequential implementation built for comparison. Finally, we show that applying both our low cost masking countermeasure together with a known and equally efficient shuffling scheme can provide a good trade-off achieving a high level of security without a large performance penalty.

Keywords: Post-quantum cryptography · Side-channel analysis ·
NTRUEncrypt · Countermeasures · Masking

1 Introduction

With the publication of the so called Shor's algorithm [11] established public key encryption algorithms are considered broken in the presence of a large-scale quantum computer. To mitigate this threat a transfer to cryptographic algorithms based on other quantum-safe mathematical problems has to be performed.

© Springer Nature Switzerland AG 2019
I. Polian and M. Stöttinger (Eds.): COSADE 2019, LNCS 11421, pp. 253–269, 2019.
https://doi.org/10.1007/978-3-030-16350-1_14

The research field of possible schemes for this transition is called post-quantum cryptography. Although the development of a large scale quantum computer is still an ongoing research field, NIST recognized this threat as serious enough to start a standardization process for post-quantum schemes.

A promising candidate for standardization is the public key encryption scheme NTRUEncrypt [14]. This lattice-based algorithm withstood mathematical cryptanalysis, with some parameter changes, for now twenty years since its original publication in [4]. Nevertheless, since the first publication of side-channel attacks by Kocher et al. [9], implementations can no longer be analyzed in a black box scenario. In order to provide secured implementations also the resistance against physical side-channel attacks has the be evaluated in an additional step.

The main side-channel attack against NTRUEncrypt is the correlation power analysis attack (CPA) published in [10]. This attack targets an implementation of the polynomial multiplication within the algorithm that utilizes the sparse structure of one multiplication operand in order to retrieve the corresponding secret key. In their paper the authors also propose different countermeasures of which the random initialization and shuffling countermeasures are shown to be broken in [10,15]. To the best of our knowledge there has been no practical evaluation of the proposed masking countermeasure. In this work we perform this evaluation for modern parameter sets. We show two different masked implementations of the polynomial multiplication together with successful second-order attack results on an ARM Cortex-M4 microcontroller.

Our Contributions. We adapt the CPA of [10] for modern parameter sets that make use of so called trinary polynomials and show successful attack results. For this we change the multiplication algorithm in order to utilize the sparse structure of trinary polynomials. In contrast to [10] we use the hamming weight power model for our attack after experiments verified that it is well suited for our attack target.

We show two different assembly implementations of the masking countermeasure of [10] for an implementation with trinary polynomials. No first-order leakage, that is exploitable through CPA, could be found on our setup for an attack up to two million traces in the hamming weight power model.

The first implementation performs the multiplication of the masked ciphertext and the update of masks in a sequential manner. This has the downside of an increased execution time of approximately a factor of two, since the same algorithm has to be executed twice. We show a successful bivariate second-order attack through combination of the leakage of the masked value with the leakage of the mask itself. Our second implementation computes the changes of the mask without performance penalty since it makes use of SIMD instructions of our ARM Cortex-M4 target platform. In this implementation the multiplication of the masked value as well as the update of the mask is performed in parallel. We show successful attack results with a zero-offset second-order CPA.

In a final step we show that a combination of the Random key rotation shuffling countermeasure [13] with our masked implementation provides a secured implementation against second-order attacks using two million traces on our setup.

Outline. In Sect. 2 we recall NTRUEncrypt together with its vulnerable multiplication operation. Then, in Sect. 3 we discuss previous work on power analysis attacks on NTRUEncrypt as well as proposed countermeasures. We adapt the published CPA for recent parameter sets, that make use of trinary polynomials, in Sect. 4. In Sect. 5 we describe our two masked implementations of the polynomial multiplication. First- and second-order attack results for both implementations are shown in Sect. 6. Finally, we conclude in Sect. 7.

2   NTRUEncrypt

The NTRU cryptosystem was first introduced by Hoffstein et al. in 1998 [4]. As the original algorithm has evolved substantially over the years this chapter gives an overview of the different aspects of the algorithm leading to its standardized version in the IEEE 1363.1-2008 [8] as well as the submission for the first round of the NIST Post-Quantum Cryptography competition [14].

2.1   Notation and Representation of Polynomials

The main elements of NTRUEncrypt are polynomials within one of the following convolution polynomial rings formally described as

$$R = \frac{\mathbb{Z}[x]}{(x^N - 1)}, \quad R_p = \frac{(\mathbb{Z}/p\mathbb{Z})[x]}{(x^N - 1)}, \quad R_q = \frac{(\mathbb{Z}/q\mathbb{Z})[x]}{(x^N - 1)}. \tag{1}$$

In essence this means every polynomial is at most of degree $N - 1$ and has integer coefficients. For the rings R_p and R_q the coefficients of the polynomials are reduced modulo p and respectively q. This results in polynomials of the following form:

$$a(x) = a_0 + a_1 x + a_2 x^2 + a_3 x^3 + \cdots + a_{N-1} x^{N-1} \in R, R_q, R_p \tag{2}$$

As the NTRUEncrypt algorithm has evolved over time, two different kinds of parameter sets were proposed. Their main difference is the choice of the modulo parameter p. This parameter defines the structure of the private key polynomial and therefore it is crucial to formalize a name for the different types of polynomials. In [1] the different types of a polynomial $a(x)$ are defined as:

– *Binary polynomial* ($p = 2$):

$$\mathcal{B}(d) : \begin{cases} a(x) \text{ has } d \text{ coefficients equal to 1} \\ a(x) \text{ has all other coefficients equal to 0} \end{cases}$$

- *Trinary polynomial* ($p = 3$):

$$\mathcal{T}(d+1, d) : \begin{cases} a(x) \text{ has } d+1 \text{ coefficients equal to } 1 \\ a(x) \text{ has } d \text{ coefficients equal to } -1 \\ a(x) \text{ with other coefficients equal to } 0 \end{cases}$$

It has to be noted that earlier parameter sets [7] propose the use of binary polynomials while more recent publications [3,14] as well as the standardized version [8] make use of trinary polynomials. Typical parameter sets given in the standard use a value of N that lies in the range of $401 < N < 1499$, while q is fixed to 2048.

2.2   Algorithm Description

This chapter describes the public key encryption variant of NTRUEncrypt according to the supporting document of the NIST submission in [14], where it is referred to as "ntru-pke". In order to provide CCA-2 security the authors instantiate NTRU with the NAEP encryption scheme as described in [7]. Additional padding operations by this scheme are abbreviated as they do not influence the side-channel discussion.

An instance of the algorithm is described by the parameter set $\{N, p, q\}$, which defines the used polynomial rings, as well as the parameter d, which describes the amount of non-zero coefficients in the used binary or trinary polynomials. Based on a specific parameter set the private key polynomial $\mathbf{f}$ and the corresponding public key $\mathbf{h}$ can be constructed. The encryption function uses the public key polynomial $\mathbf{h}$ to encrypt the message $\mathbf{m}$.

We limit the description of the algorithm to the decryption function, as this function is the only point during the algorithm where a known input, namely the ciphertext $\mathbf{e}$, is combined with the secret key polynomial $\mathbf{f}$, which is a necessary condition to mount side-channel attacks.

Decryption. The decryption of NTRUEncrypt is described in Algorithm 1. With the use of the private key $\mathbf{f}$ and the public key $\mathbf{h}$ a ciphertext $\mathbf{e}$ can be decrypted. It is important for later discussions that the private key $\mathbf{f}$ is a sparse polynomial in either $\mathcal{T}$ or $\mathcal{B}$, while the ciphertext $\mathbf{e}$ is element of R_q. The secret key is used in the form $p \cdot f + 1$ as this eliminates one multiplication step during decryption [6].

2.3   Operations on Polynomials

As discussed in the previous chapters all variables of the algorithm are element of a convolution polynomial ring. The main property of the used rings is that elements can be at most of degree $N - 1$. Therefore arithmetic operations on ring elements have to fulfill this property. An additional modulo operation has

---

Algorithm 1. NTRUEncrypt - Decryption

Input: Private key $\mathbf{f}$, public key $\mathbf{h}$ and ciphertext $\mathbf{e}$

1: $m' \leftarrow (p \cdot f + 1) * e \bmod p$
2: $t \leftarrow e - m'$
3: $m_{mask} \leftarrow \text{SAMPLER}(t)$ $\triangleright\ m_{mask} \in \mathcal{T}(d+1, d)$ or $\mathcal{B}(d)$
4: $m = m' + m_{mask} \bmod p$
5: $r \leftarrow \text{SAMPLER}(m|h)$ $\triangleright\ r \in \mathcal{T}(d+1, d)$ or $\mathcal{B}(d)$
6: **if** $p \cdot r * h = t$ **then**
7:      result $\leftarrow \mathbf{m}$
8: **else**
9:      result $\leftarrow \perp$

Output: result

---

to be performed on each coefficient of the resulting polynomial, depending on the respective ring.

Multiplication of two polynomials is performed with the circular convolution product in the corresponding ring. In [5] this product of two polynomials $a(x) * b(x)$ is defined as:

$$a(x) * b(x) = \sum_{k=0}^{N-1} \left(\sum_{i+j \equiv k \ (\bmod\ N)} a_i b_j \right) x^k \tag{3}$$

In other words, Eq. (3) can be seen as the multiplication of two polynomials with an additional reduction of the result by $(x^N - 1)$ through polynomial long division. The convolution product is denoted with the symbol $(*)$, while a simple multiplication with a factor is marked as $(\cdot)$.

As the convolution product is the bottleneck operation of NTRUEncrypt, there are several publications on optimized implementations of this multiplication. It has to be noted that neither the standardized version in IEEE-1363.1 [8] nor the NIST submission of NTRUEncrypt [14] defines a specific way of implementing the multiplication.

A popular type of implementation for resource constrained devices utilizes the sparse structure of binary or trinary polynomials. It is the case that all convolution products of the algorithm have one sparse polynomial as operand. This is also true for the first line of Algorithm 1 as $(p \cdot f + 1) * e$ can be rewritten to $(p \cdot f * e + e)$. In [1] the authors propose Algorithm 2 for the multiplication of a polynomial in $\mathcal{R}_q$ and a binary polynomial $\mathcal{B}(d)$. With this algorithm the authors substitute the multiplication of coefficients with additions based on the index of ones in the binary polynomial. As a binary polynomial is build to be sparse, the coefficients with the value zero can be skipped resulting in a lower number of additions to execute and therefore a faster multiplication. It has to be noted that the algorithm can be considered as constant time assuming a system without cache, as conditional branches are only dependent on known parameters of the algorithm.

Algorithm 2. Index-based binary multiplication

Input: $a(x) \in \mathcal{B}(d)$ (stored as an array a[d] with indexes a_i); $b(x) \in R_q$
1: Initialize a temporary array t of size $2N$
2: **for** $0 \leq j < 2N$ **do**   ▷ Initialize $t(x)$ with zero
3:    $t_j \leftarrow 0$
4: **for** $0 \leq j < d$ **do**
5:    **for** $0 \leq k < N$ **do**
6:        $t_{k+a[j]} \leftarrow t_{k+a[j]} + b_k$ ▷ Add polynomial $b(x)$ at position a[j]
7: **for** $0 \leq j < N$ **do**
8:    $c_j \leftarrow (t_j + t_{j+N}) \bmod q$ ▷ Reduction by $(x^N - 1)$ modulo q
Output: $c(x) \in R_q = a(x) * b(x)$

Algorithm 3. Index-based trinary multiplication

Input: $a(x) \in \mathcal{T}(d+1, d)$ (stored as arrays $a_{ones}[d+1]$ and $a_{mones}[d]$); $b(x) \in R_q$
1: Initialize a temporary array $t(x)$ of size $2N$
2: **for** $0 \leq j < 2N$ **do**   ▷ Initialize $t(x)$ to zero
3:    $t_j \leftarrow 0$
4: **for** $0 \leq j < d+1$ **do**
5:    **for** $0 \leq k < N$ **do**
6:        $t_{k+a_{ones}[j]} \leftarrow t_{k+a_{ones}[j]} + b_k$ ▷ Add $b(x)$ at position $a_{ones}[j]$
7: **for** $0 \leq j < d$ **do**
8:    **for** $0 \leq k < N$ **do**
9:        $t_{k+a_{mones}[j]} \leftarrow t_{k+a_{mones}[j]} - b_k$ ▷ Subtract $b(x)$ at position $a_{mones}[j]$
10: **for** $0 \leq j < N$ **do**
11:   $c_j \leftarrow (t_j + t_{j+N}) \bmod q$ ▷ Reduction by $(x^N - 1)$ modulo q
Output: $c(x) \in R_q = a(x) * b(x)$

As described in Sect. 2.1 recent parameter sets make use of trinary polynomials. As these polynomials also have a sparse nature, and therefore contain only ones and minus ones, the multiplication can again be abstracted by either addition or subtraction based on the index of nonzero coefficients. Our adaption of Algorithm 2 for trinary polynomials is given in Algorithm 3.

3   Related Work

In this work we focus on software implementations of NTRUEncrypt with the index based multiplication as described in Sect. 2.3. This chapter gives an overview of the previous work on power analysis attacks on such implementations with binary polynomials.

The main power analysis attack on NTRUEncrypt consists of a CPA published in [10]. With this attack the authors target the multiplication of the private key f with the ciphertext e, as this is the only operation on the private key with an attacker controllable input. If this multiplication is performed with the index-based method, as described in Algorithm 2, an attacker can exploit

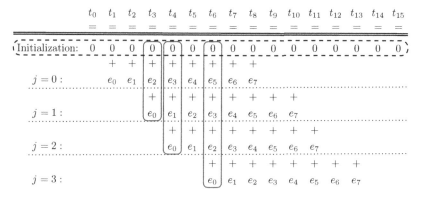

Fig. 1. Convolution product with binary polynomials according to Algorithm 2 for the parameters N = 8 and $f \in \mathcal{B}(4) = [1, 3, 4, 6]$. All targeted additions with the coefficient e_0 are marked.

the fact that the addition of the first ciphertext coefficient e_0 is determined by the indexes of ones in the private key f. An example of this multiplication is visualized in Fig. 1.

For all d rounds of additions the ciphertext coefficients e_i are added with the content of the corresponding temporary result array element t_i in a sequential manner, starting from e_0 to e_{N-1}. Based on the additions with e_0 (marked in Fig. 1) the difference between the key indexes of each round can be found. The attack of [10] performs a separate CPA for all rounds $j \geq 1$ with an attack on the hamming distance of the addition of t_i with e_0 ($HD(t_i, t_i + e_0)$). The corresponding values of t_i can be calculated based on a hypothesis for the difference in the associated key indexes. After the individual CPAs successfully retrieved all index differences w_i, the location of the first key index can be found by exhaustive search. We will denote the difference between the indexes $f[i]$ and $f[i + 1]$ with w_i for the rest of the paper. As an example, the difference between the first index $f[0]$ and second index $f[1]$ will be called w_0.

In addition to their attack the authors of [10] propose three different countermeasures:

1. **Random initialization of t:** The temporary result array t is initialized with different random values r_i, which can help during the first register overwrite in a HD scenario.
2. **Masking of ciphertext e:** With this countermeasure each individual coefficient e_i is masked with a random value through modular addition. We give a detailed evaluation of this countermeasure in this work.
3. **Shuffling:** The sequence of all d addition rounds can be shuffled randomly, as the order has no impact on the final result. In theory shuffling countermeasures can be defeated with an increased amount of traces, therefore the authors propose this countermeasure only in combination with masking.

Successful attacks have been shown against the random initialization countermeasure with a second-order CPA [10] and a first-order collision attack [15]. The second-order CPA still targets the $HD(t_i, t_i + e_0)$ which is changed by the countermeasure to $HD(t_i + r_i, t_i + r_i + e_0)$. The authors show that the subtraction of the power consumption of $HD(r_i, t_i + r_i)$ from $HD(t_i + r_i, t_i + r_i + e_0)$ can be used as a preprocessing function to mount an attack on the unmasked values with the hypothetical power consumption of $HW(t_i) - HW(e_0)$.

In order to perform the first-order collision attack an attacker has to observe the power consumption T_i during the initialization phase of t with the different masks r_i. The highest correlation of T_i with the power consumption during the addition of the last ciphertext coefficient e_{N-1} allows the calculation of the corresponding index of the private key. This can be done for all d rounds of addition.

More recently a countermeasure named *Random key rotation* is proposed in [13]. This countermeasure exploits the ring structure of the polynomials, which allows a rotation of the private key f and the ciphertext e in a way that does not change the multiplication result. As this rotation can be performed randomly without changing Algorithm 2, it can be seen as an efficient shuffling countermeasure. This countermeasure can in theory be defeated by an increased amount of traces and therefore we suggest to use it in addition with our masked implementations.

4   CPA on Trinary Polynomials

In this chapter we present the adaptation of the CPA attack from [10] for a convolution product with trinary polynomials. Even though the authors mention that their attack should also work against trinary polynomials they do not present the adaption or attack results. We implement the index-based multiplication for the trinary case with Algorithm 3.

An example of the trinary multiplication is shown in Fig. 2. It can be seen that the first part of the multiplication (light grey background) is performed exactly as in the binary case. Therefore, the differences between the ones in $f \in \mathcal{T}$, called w_i^1, can be found by using the CPA described in Sect. 3.

Our adaption works by first attacking the difference between the last index of ones $f_{ones}[d + 1]$ and the first index of minus ones $f_{mones}[0]$ during the first round of subtractions ($j = 0$). This difference will be called w^0. The correct w^0 is attacked by finding the index of e_i that is subtracted from the t_i corresponding to the last addition with e_0 (marked with a dotted line in Fig. 2). Based on the different hypothesis for w_0 the hamming weight of the corresponding intermediate values can be calculated and attacked through CPA. It has to be noted that there is the unlikely possibility of no subtraction from t_i corresponding to the last addition of e_0 for some constructions of the private key. This can also be defeated by successively evaluating different points of subtraction, for example the value of t_i corresponding to the last addition of e_1.

```
           t_0  t_1  t_2  t_3  t_4  t_5  t_6  t_7  t_8  t_9  t_10 t_11 t_12 t_13 t_14 t_15
           =    =    =    =    =    =    =    =    =    =    =    =    =    =    =    =

Initialization:  0    0    0    0   [0]   0  [0]   0    0    0    0    0    0    0    0    0
                      +    +    +    +    +    +    +    +    +
j = 0:               e_0  e_1  e_2  e_3  e_4  e_5  e_6  e_7
                                +    +    +    +    +    +    +    +
j = 1:                        e_0  e_1  e_2  e_3  e_4  e_5  e_6  e_7
                                        +    +    +    +    +    +    +
j = 2:                                  e_0  e_1  e_2  e_3  e_4  e_5  e_6  e_7

j = 0:              e_0  e_1  e_2  e_3  e_4  e_5  e_6  e_7

j = 1:                                       e_0  e_1  e_2  e_3  e_4  e_5  e_6  e_7
```

Fig. 2. Example of a convolution product with trinary polynomials for $N = 8$ and $f \in \mathcal{T}(3,2) = [1,3,4],[0,6]$.

With the correct w^0 the remaining differences between the indexes of minus ones w_i^{-1} can be found. Similar to the binary case different hypothetical intermediate results for the subtraction of e_0 during the rounds $j \geq 1$ can be constructed (see the attacked subtraction result marked with a solid line in Fig. 2). The correct hypothesis can be found through CPA, which reveals the corresponding w_i^{-1}.

The final private key f can be found through exhaustive search for $f_{ones}[0]$, as all relative index differences are known at this stage. The complexity of this search can be seen as negligible as an attacker has to try at most $N - (2d + 1)$ different combinations. This leads to at most 248 different combinations for the parameter set $NTRU\text{-}743$, which corresponds to the highest security level for a parameter set with trinary polynomials.

5 Masking the Ciphertext Polynomial

Since possible attacks for the random initialization countermeasure of [10] have already been shown and other approaches can be seen as shuffling and therefore hiding countermeasures, we focus on evaluating the masking of the ciphertext. Only a masking countermeasure is able to reliably provide a first-order secured implementation, as it makes the processed variables independent from the known input, in this case the ciphertext.

In accordance to [10] we use arithmetic masking with different masks on all coefficients of the ciphertext polynomial e. Arithmetic masking in our case can be defined as a modular addition of e with a polynomial $masks$, containing the different masks for each coefficient, as

$$e_m = e + masks \bmod 2^n. \tag{4}$$

For our implementations the modulus is set to 2^{16} as the elements of the temporary result array t are stored with 16-bit values. Arithmetic masking is

Sequential:

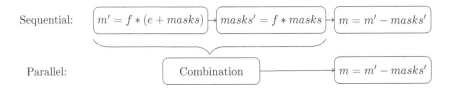

Parallel:

Fig. 3. Comparison of our sequential and parallel masked implementations. It can be seen that the parallel implementation combines the first two steps into one.

more suitable for the index-based multiplication as it only performs arithmetic operations and therefore changes to the mask are linear. In this case changes of a mask can be computed by performing the operations on the mask itself.

The masking countermeasure is implemented for the trinary index-based multiplication described in Algorithm 3. We provide two different masked implementations with the use of ARM assembly code. The first implementation performs the multiplication on the masked values and the mask itself sequentially. This approach has the downside of an increased execution time as the multiplication algorithm is executed twice in order to compute the mask changes. We eliminate this disadvantage in our second implementation, as it computes the multiplication on the masked value and the mask in parallel. To achieve this we utilize special SIMD instructions of the ARM Cortex-M4 architecture. The idea of the different implementations is visualized in Fig. 3.

5.1 Sequential Implementation

The sequential implementation first performs a multiplication of the masked ciphertext e_m with the private key f to get the masked result m':

$$m' = f * e_m = f * (e + masks) \qquad (5)$$

In a second step the changes to the masks are computed through a multiplication of f with the values of the masks as:

$$masks' = f * masks \qquad (6)$$

In order to retrieve the unmasked multiplication result m all coefficients of $masks'$ are subtracted from m' with the result reduced modulo q.

5.2 Parallel Implementation

The parallel implementation of the masking countermeasure makes use of SIMD instructions of the DSP extension of an ARM Cortex-M4 architecture. With these instructions a 32-bit word is split into smaller parts (two 16-bit or four 8-bit values) on which the corresponding arithmetic operation can be performed in parallel. For example the *SADD16* and *SSUB16* operation performs an addition respectively subtraction on the higher and lower 16-bit parts of the operand, taking care of suppressing a potential carry overflow between the two parts. An example of an addition with SADD16 is given in Fig. 4.

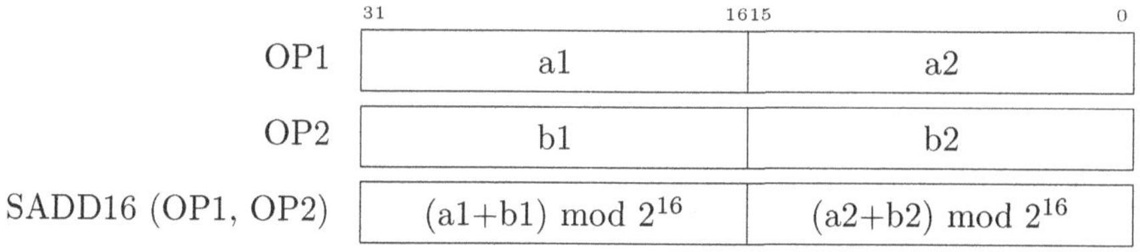

	31	1615	0
OP1	a1	a2	
OP2	b1	b2	
SADD16 (OP1, OP2)	(a1+b1) mod 2^{16}	(a2+b2) mod 2^{16}	

Fig. 4. Visualization of the SADD16 instruction of an ARM Cortex-M4 microcontroller. Two 16-bit additions of $(a1 + b1)$ and $(a2 + b2)$ are performed in parallel. The subtraction with SSUB16 works accordingly.

In order to benefit from these operations we construct the individual ciphertext coefficients e_i and corresponding mask $mask_i$ as a 32-bit word as shown in Fig. 5. By using this construction as an input for the ciphertext coefficients e_i in Algorithm 3, all additions and subtractions can be implemented with the corresponding SIMD instruction. In this case the update of the mask is computed in parallel, which is twice as fast as the sequential implementation. The implicit reduction modulo 2^{16} does not change the result of the multiplication as all coefficients of the result are reduced modulo 2^{11}, with $q = 2048$ for modern parameter sets.

31	16 15	0
$mask_i$	$e_i + mask_i$	

Fig. 5. Description of the input to Algorithm 3 as a combination of the masked ciphertext and the mask itself. The individual coefficients of the ciphertext e are constructed in this way.

6   Evaluation of Results

In this section we show the results of a CPA attack on a non-masked implementation using trinary polynomials as well as first and second-order attacks against the two masked implementations described in the previous chapter. In addition we show attack results for the masked implementations in combination with a shuffling countermeasure.

All attacks are performed with power measurements of a STM32F303RCT7 ARM Cortex-M4 microcontroller mounted on the NewAE CW308 UFO board. The target device is built with a $12\,\Omega$ shunt resistor placed in the VDD line and the corresponding power consumption can be measured through a SMA connector on the CW308 board. The measurements are performed with a Picoscope 6402D and a sampling frequency of 156.25 MHz. As the power is measured between VDD and GND, a Minicircuits BLK-89+ DC Block is used in order to utilize the whole input range of the oscilloscope. The clock for our DUT is fixed to 10 MHz provided by a Keysight 33500B waveform generator. In order to provide aligned traces the device clock and the sampling clock of the oscilloscope are synchronized through the waveform generator.

6.1 CPA on Trinary Polynomials

This section describes attack results on our assembly implementation of Algorithm 3 without any precaution against side-channel attacks. In contrast to the attack in [10] we show a working attack on a trinary multiplication with the hamming weight power model.

Some results for an attack on a multiplication with the private key $f \in T = [3, 7, 10], [1, 4]$ and a maximum degree of $N = 20$ are shown in Fig. 6. We exemplarily provide the correlation graphs that reveal w_0^1, w^0, and w_0^{-1}. However, all different CPA attacks on the corresponding key indexes are successful. The correlation over time is shown for the whole execution of lines 4 to 9 in Algorithm 3. It can be seen that the attack is successful even without the restriction of the measurements to the corresponding attacked operations. Nevertheless, a restriction would remove additional correlation peaks.

6.2 Second-Order Attacks on Masking Countermeasure

This section discusses results of second-order attacks against the two masked implementations. Attack results are only given for the second round ($j = 1$) in Algorithm 3 corresponding to the addition of ones in the ciphertext. In other words, results are shown for the difference between $f_{ones}[0]$ and $f_{ones}[1]$. The presented attacks are also applicable for the remaining key index differences. Measurements for the respective implementation are performed with the parameters $N = 20$ and $q = 2048$ together with a corresponding private key $f \in T(2, 1) = [3, 7], [5]$.

Sequential Implementation. In this implementation the masked value and the mask itself are processed during different moments in time. Therefore, a multivariate second-order attack is able to defeat the masking countermeasure through the combination of the corresponding leakages. In [12] the normalized product preprocessing function, which was initially proposed in [2], is stated to be the optimal way of combination for a hamming weight leakage model. As we are targeting hamming weight leakage, we make use of this combination function by multiplication of the corresponding mean-free sample points.

The location of the leakage points is found by a separate CPA on the masked intermediate value and the mask itself. Figure 7 shows the correlation of both attacks indicating the points in time where the individual values are processed. This is possible since we want to evaluate the attack under the best possible conditions and therefore we store the masks during the trace measurement. If an attacker does not know the corresponding mask he has to perform an educated guess on the possible leakage areas and try all possible combinations of samples, usually as a multiple of clock cycles.

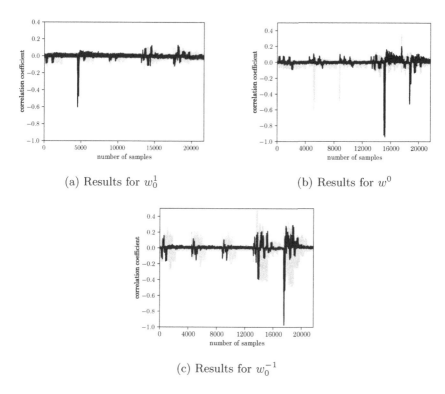

(a) Results for w_0^1

(b) Results for w^0

(c) Results for w_0^{-1}

Fig. 6. CPA results for $N = 20$ and $f \in \mathcal{T} = [3, 7, 10], [1, 4]$ with a total amount of 10000 traces.

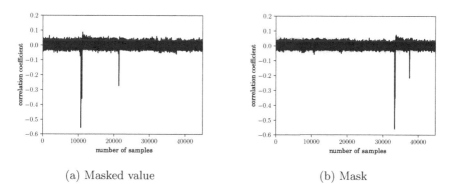

(a) Masked value

(b) Mask

Fig. 7. Leakage points of the masked value and the corresponding mask in time for the sequential masked implementation. The points with the highest correlation are used for the multivariate second-order attack.

Results for the first- and second-order attack are shown in Fig. 8. There is no significant correlation visible for the first-order attack using up to two million trace measurements. In contrast the second-order attack is successful with two hundred thousand traces.

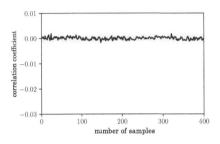
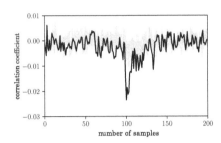

(a) First-order attack (2M traces)   (b) Second-order attack (200k traces)

Fig. 8. Result of attacks on the sequential masking implementation. Here a subsection of 200 samples centered around the leakage of the mask are shown. For the preprocessing step the traces were shifted 1445 clock cycles.

Parallel Implementation. As the parallel implementation processes the mask and the masked value at the same time, a zero-offset second-order attack can be used to attack this implementation. In order to perform this attack the individual samples of the traces are mean-free squared.

In Fig. 9 attack results for our masked implementation with the parallel construction are shown. No first-order leakage could be found using an amount of two million trace measurements. On the other hand it can be seen that the proposed second-order attack is successful in retrieving the correct key index difference w_0^1 for an amount of two hundred thousand traces.

Comparison. In order to compare both implementations we provide correlation plots of the corresponding main leakage points for an increasing number of trace measurements in Fig. 10. The correlation is shown for up to two hundred thousand measurements.

It can be seen that a second-order attack is less effective on the parallel implementation and therefore we recommend this implementation as it also shows an reduced execution time in comparison with the sequential one.

6.3   Second-Order Attack on the Combination of Masking and Shuffling

In this section we show attack results of our two masked implementations in combination with the *Random key rotation* shuffling countermeasure presented in [13]. In order to integrate the shuffling countermeasure we did not have to

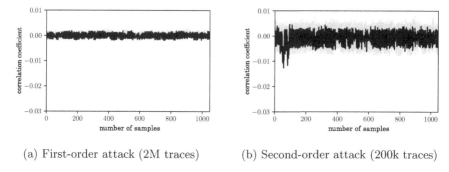

(a) First-order attack (2M traces)   (b) Second-order attack (200k traces)

Fig. 9. Attack results for the parallel masking implementation. The shown samples belong to the execution of the first two coefficient additions corresponding to $f_{ones}[1]$.

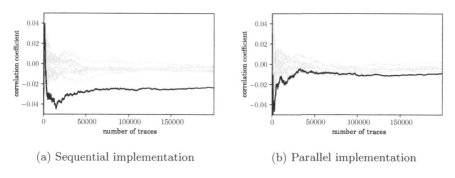

(a) Sequential implementation   (b) Parallel implementation

Fig. 10. Development of the correlation for both implementations with an increasing number of traces. The correlation of all hypotheses is shown for up to two hundred thousand measurements.

alter our implementation of the multiplication as the shuffling is done through changes to the input polynomials.

The shuffling method works by generating a random integer i in the range $0 \leq i < N - 1$ and circular shifting the coefficients of f to the right by i positions. In a second step the ciphertext e is shifted in the same way by $N - i$ positions. This randomizes the intermediate addition results but does not change the outcome of the multiplication.

For the shown attacks in Sect. 6.2 we used the parameter $N = 20$, which implies a shuffling with twenty possible ways of multiplication. Corresponding attack results for the parallel and sequential implementation are given in Fig. 11. It can be seen that a combination of both countermeasures shows no significant second-order leakage for up to two million trace measurements.

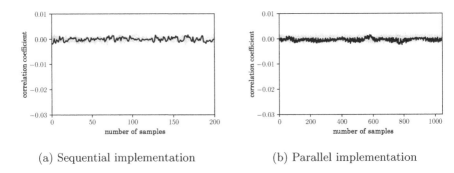

(a) Sequential implementation   (b) Parallel implementation

Fig. 11. Second-order attack results for both masked implementations in combination with the random key rotation countermeasure using two million trace measurements.

7 Conclusion

Typically, implementations of NTRUEncrypt that utilize the index-based multiplication are vulnerable to CPA attacks. We showed that this remains true for modern parameter sets that make use of trinary polynomials. We provided a practical evaluation of masking using both a sequential and a parallel implementation of processing mask and masked data, the later having negligible performance overhead compared to an unmasked implementation as it utilizes SIMD instructions of the used ARM Cortex-M4 microcontroller. Our evaluation showed that both implementations are secured against first-order attacks using our setup with up to two million traces. The parallel implementation showed less second-order leakage compared to the sequential one when no shuffling is applied. It is therefore an ideal fit to the shuffling countermeasure of [13] and we recommend applying both schemes in parallel.

Acknowledgment. This work was partly funded by the German Federal Ministry of Education and Research in the project HQS through grant number 16KIS0616.

References

1. Bailey, D.V., Coffin, D., Elbirt, A., Silverman, J.H., Woodbury, A.D.: NTRU in constrained devices. In: Koç, Ç.K., Naccache, D., Paar, C. (eds.) CHES 2001. LNCS, vol. 2162, pp. 262–272. Springer, Heidelberg (2001). https://doi.org/10.1007/3-540-44709-1_22
2. Chari, S., Jutla, C.S., Rao, J.R., Rohatgi, P.: Towards sound approaches to counteract power-analysis attacks. In: Wiener, M. (ed.) CRYPTO 1999. LNCS, vol. 1666, pp. 398–412. Springer, Heidelberg (1999). https://doi.org/10.1007/3-540-48405-1_26
3. Hoffstein, J., Pipher, J., Schanck, J.M., Silverman, J.H., Whyte, W., Zhang, Z.: Choosing parameters for NTRUEncrypt. In: Handschuh, H. (ed.) CT-RSA 2017. LNCS, vol. 10159, pp. 3–18. Springer, Cham (2017). https://doi.org/10.1007/978-3-319-52153-4_1

4. Hoffstein, J., Pipher, J., Silverman, J.H.: NTRU: a ring-based public key cryptosystem. In: Buhler, J.P. (ed.) ANTS 1998. LNCS, vol. 1423, pp. 267–288. Springer, Heidelberg (1998). https://doi.org/10.1007/BFb0054868

5. Hoffstein, J., Pipher, J., Silverman, J.H.: An Introduction to Mathematical Cryptography. UTM. Springer, New York (2014). https://doi.org/10.1007/978-1-4939-1711-2

6. Hoffstein, J., Silverman, J.: Optimizations for NTRU. In: Public-Key Cryptography and Computational Number Theory, Warsaw, pp. 77–88 (2001)

7. Howgrave-Graham, N., Silverman, J.H., Whyte, W.: Choosing parameter sets for NTRUEncrypt with NAEP and SVES-3. In: Menezes, A. (ed.) CT-RSA 2005. LNCS, vol. 3376, pp. 118–135. Springer, Heidelberg (2005). https://doi.org/10.1007/978-3-540-30574-3_10

8. IEEE: IEEE standard specification for public key cryptographic techniques based on hard problems over lattices. IEEE Std 1363.1-2008, pp. C1–69, March 2009. https://doi.org/10.1109/IEEESTD.2009.4800404

9. Kocher, P., Jaffe, J., Jun, B.: Differential power analysis. In: Wiener, M. (ed.) CRYPTO 1999. LNCS, vol. 1666, pp. 388–397. Springer, Heidelberg (1999). https://doi.org/10.1007/3-540-48405-1_25

10. Lee, M.K., Song, J.E., Choi, D., Han, D.G.: Countermeasures against power analysis attacks for the NTRU public key cryptosystem. IEICE Trans. Fundam. Electron. Commun. Comput. Sci. E93–A(1), 153–163 (2010). https://doi.org/10.1587/transfun.e93.a.153

11. Shor, P.W.: Polynomial-time algorithms for prime factorization and discrete logarithms on a quantum computer. SIAM J. Comput. 26(5), 1484–1509 (1997). https://doi.org/10.1137/s0097539795293172

12. Standaert, F.-X., et al.: The world is not enough: another look on second-order DPA. In: Abe, M. (ed.) ASIACRYPT 2010. LNCS, vol. 6477, pp. 112–129. Springer, Heidelberg (2010). https://doi.org/10.1007/978-3-642-17373-8_7

13. Wang, A., Wang, C., Zheng, X., Tian, W., Xu, R., Zhang, G.: Random key rotation: side-channel countermeasure of NTRU cryptosystem for resource-limited devices. Comput. Electr. Eng. 63, 220–231 (2017). https://doi.org/10.1016/j.compeleceng.2017.05.007

14. Zhang, Z., Chen, C., Hoffstein, J., Whyte, W.: NTRUEncrypt NIST Sumission. https://csrc.nist.gov/Projects/Post-Quantum-Cryptography/Round-1-Submissions

15. Zheng, X., Wang, A., Wei, W.: First-order collision attack on protected NTRU cryptosystem. Microprocess. Microsyst. 37(6–7), 601–609 (2013). https://doi.org/10.1016/j.micpro.2013.04.008

Shuffle and Mix: On the Diffusion of Randomness in Threshold Implementations of KECCAK

Felix Wegener[✉], Christian Baiker, and Amir Moradi

Horst Görtz Institute for IT Security, Ruhr University Bochum, Bochum, Germany
{felix.wegener,christian.baiker,amir.moradi}@rub.de

Abstract. Threshold Implementations are well known as a provably first-order secure Boolean masking scheme even in the presence of glitches. A precondition for their security proof is a uniform input distribution at each round function, which may require an injection of fresh randomness or an increase in the number of shares. However, it is unclear whether violating the uniformity assumption causes detectable leakage in practice. Recently, Daemen undertook a theoretical study of lossy mappings to extend the understanding of uniformity violations. We complement his work by entropy simulations and practical measurements of KECCAK's round function. Our findings shed light on the necessity of mixing operations in addition to bit-permutations in a cipher's linear layer to propagate randomness between S-boxes and prevent exploitable leakage. Finally, we argue that this result cannot be obtained by current simulation methods, further stressing the continued need for practical leakage measurements.

1 Introduction

Ensuring the integrity of a message is one of the central objectives in many cryptographic applications. It can be achieved by using a hash algorithm in conjunction with a secret key to compute a message authentication code (MAC). As the integrity of a MAC depends on the secrecy of the key, the need to protect against side-channel analysis (SCA), e.g. Differential Power Analysis (DPA) [14], arises. To thwart DPA in hardware implementations of cryptographic algorithms Nikova et al. [17] introduced Threshold Implementations (TI), a provable first-order secure Boolean masking scheme[1].

Later, Bertoni et al. [4] developed the KECCAK-family[2] of sponge-based hash-functions and suggested a three-share Threshold Implementation for their quadratic non-linear layer χ. Subsequently, Bilgin et al. [6] noted that the suggested TI violates the uniformity property and introduced two methods to alleviate this flaw. First, the injection of four bits of fresh randomness per invocation

---

[1] Later extended to higher-order security.
[2] Standardized for selected parameters as SHA-3 in 2015.

© Springer Nature Switzerland AG 2019
I. Polian and M. Stöttinger (Eds.): COSADE 2019, LNCS 11421, pp. 270–284, 2019.
https://doi.org/10.1007/978-3-030-16350-1_15

of the non-linear building block χ. Second, the expansion to four shares, which allows the authors to find a uniform TI. Orthogonally, Daemen [10] investigated the implications of uniformity violation on the overall entropy in KECCAK and the local entropy of individual bits and suggested a cheap method to re-mask the state bits with other state bits to prevent any exploitable leakage. Later, Daemen [11] suggested a re-masking scheme called *Changing of the Guards* to achieve uniformity of an arbitrary bijective S-box layer and noted the applicability to KECCAK.

Recently, De Meyer *et al.* [15] pointed out that uniformity is not a necessary condition for first-order security. In fact, information leakage takes place when any distribution observable by the attacker differs based on the unmasked secret value. In the setting of infeasible exhaustive computations, they suggest to evaluate this effect based on the χ^2-Test. Previously, Moradi *et al.* [16] demonstrated the applicability of the χ^2-test in leakage detection both for simulated traces of noisy Hamming-weight leakages and in practical measurements.

Our Contribution. We investigate the practical relevance of the diffusion layer to counteract the uniformity loss in masked KECCAK-f. In fact, we find that diffusion between S-boxes solely based on bit-permutations (ρ, π) does not prevent first-order leakage originating from the non-uniformity, while the mixing part (θ) of KECCAK-f alone is sufficient to counteract observable leakage through an FPGA evaluation. Further, we show that this effect cannot be revealed with state-of-the-art simulations, thereby indicating the need for practical SCA evaluations. To our knowledge, this is the first practical analysis of uniformity loss thereby complementing the theoretical foundation laid out by Daemen [10].

Organization of the Paper. In Sect. 2, we describe our notation, recall the specification of KECCAK, describe Threshold Implementations and total imbalance. In Sect. 3 we give an overview of the recent TI designs of KECCAK. In Sect. 4, we analyze the probability distributions of S-box inputs with the methods of [10] and [15]. We describe the architecture of our hardware implementation in Sect. 5, and our practical evaluations in Sect. 6.

2   Preliminaries

In this section we introduce relevant definitions and our notation for the rest of the paper.

Introduction to KECCAK. KECCAK [4] is a sponge-based hash function that operates on a state of $b = 25 \cdot 2^l$ bits for l between 0 and 6. We use the same terminology as the authors to refer to individual parts of the state (cf. Figure 1 of [18]). Its core is the permutation KECCAK-f[b] which iterates the round function R a fixed number of times. The round function

$$R = \iota \circ \chi \circ \pi \circ \rho \circ \theta$$

consists of five sub-functions which are defined in the following:

– *Theta*: XORs the parity of two columns to each bit of a different column to improve diffusion between columns.

$$\theta : a[x][y][z] = a[x][y][z] \oplus \bigoplus_{y'=0}^{4} a[x-1][y'][z] \oplus \bigoplus_{y'=0}^{4} a[x+1][y'][z-1]$$

– *Rho*: performs a circular shift of all lanes, by a fixed constant per lane.

$$\rho : a[x][y][z] = a[x][y][z - \mathrm{const}(x,y)]$$

– *Pi*: creates diffusion between rows in one slice.

$$\pi : a[x][y] = a[x'][y'], \quad \text{with } x = y', y = 2 \cdot x' + 3 \cdot y'$$

– *Chi*: is the only non-linear function. It operates as a 5-bit quadratic bijection on each row individually.

$$\chi : a[x] = a[x] \oplus (1 \oplus a[x+1]) \cdot a[x+2]$$

– *Iota*: XORs a round constant to the first lane.

$$\iota : a[0][0] = a[0][0] \oplus RC[r]$$

A visual illustration of all steps can be seen in Fig. 1. For the remainder of this paper we focus on KECCAK-f[200], which consists of 18 iterations of R.

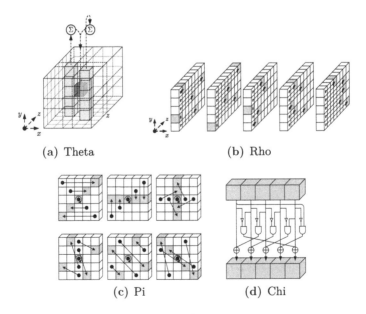

(a) Theta   (b) Rho

(c) Pi   (d) Chi

Fig. 1. The KECCAK subfunctions (a) θ, (b) ρ, (c) π, (d) χ, taken from [4]

Threshold Implementations. For brevity, we limit ourselves to three shares and first-order security in the following introduction to Threshold Implementations [17].

Let $x \in \mathbb{F}_2^n$, we call $X = (a, b, c) \in \mathbb{F}_2^{3n}$ a sharing or masking of x if

$$x = a \oplus b \oplus c.$$

Each part a, b and c is called a share. We denote $\int(x)$ for the set of all such sharings. A sharing is called uniform, if all elements from $\int(x)$ occur with equal likelihood.

Consider a Boolean function $f : \mathbb{F}_2^n \to \mathbb{F}_2^n$, we call $F = (F^A, F^B, F^C) : \mathbb{F}_2^{3n} \to \mathbb{F}_2^{3n}$ a *Threshold Implementation* if the following properties are present.

- *Correctness*: XORing all output shares reveals the output of the original function.

$$\forall x : \forall X \in \int(x) : F^A(X) \oplus F^B(X) \oplus F^C(X) = f(x)$$

- *Non-completeness*: Each output share is independent of at least one input share:

$$F^A(X) = F^A(b, c)$$
$$F^B(X) = F^B(c, a)$$
$$F^C(X) = F^C(a, b)$$

Provable security is achieved through the central theorem of TI [17] which states: Let f be a Boolean function and F a TI of f. Let $X_1, \ldots, X_T$ be a sequence of sharings of the value x, each uniformly drawn from $\int(x)$. Then, the evaluations of $F(X_i)$ do not reveal first-order information about x.

To ensure a uniform input share distribution during each round of an iterated cipher, it is beneficial to demand a third property of TI:

- *Uniformity*: F maps a uniform input distribution to a uniform output distribution.

$$\exists k : \forall x \in \mathbb{F}_2^n : \forall X \in \int(x) : \forall Y \in \int(f(x)) : Pr(F(X) = Y) = k$$

For KECCAK's non-linear function χ a uniform TI with four shares is known, while a uniform TI with three shares is either not possible or has not been found yet. Indeed, no statements about the existence of a uniform three share TI can be made due to the high computational complexity of an exhaustive search over all correction terms [5].

Entropy Study. We recall several definitions from Daemen's [9] work: Let P be a probability distribution over $\mathbb{F}_2^n$ and $v \in \mathbb{F}_2^n$ be a mask. The imbalance of P is defined as the Walsh-transformation of P and the total imbalance as its summation:

$$\widetilde{P}(v) := \sum_x P(x)(-1)^{v^\top x}, \qquad \phi_P := \sum_{\forall v \neq 0} \widetilde{P}(v)^2.$$

The evaluation of $\widetilde{P}$ in zero is omitted, as $\widetilde{P}(0) = 1$ regardless of the distribution of P. It can be shown that ϕ_P is zero if and only if P is a uniform distribution.

The chance that two elements drawn according to the probability distribution P over $\mathbb{F}_2^n$ are identical, is called the collision property $Pr_{\mathrm{coll}}(P)$, which is connected to ϕ_P via the relation

$$\phi_P = 2^n Pr_{\mathrm{coll}}(P) - 1.$$

It follows that $\phi_P \in [0, 2^n - 1]$ can be used as a metric to estimate the non-uniformity of a probability distribution P.

Pearson's χ^2-Test. Pearson's χ^2 test allows a comparison between categorical observations of multiple random variables. Consider a table T in which each column (j) corresponds to a category and each row (i) to a variable. The integer value in cell $T_{i,j}$ expresses the number of times the realization of variable i has been observed to adopt category j. To decide whether all variables follow the same distribution (which forms the null-hypothesis $\mathcal{H}_0$) we define the test statistic

$$X = \sum_{i=0}^{r-1} \sum_{j=0}^{c-1} \frac{(T_{i,j} - E_{i,j})^2}{E_{i,j}}$$

with the expected number of occurrences

$$E_{i,j} := \frac{(\sum_{k=0}^{c-1} T_{i,k})(\sum_{k=0}^{r-1} T_{k,j})}{\sum_{k=0}^{c-1}\sum_{l=0}^{r-1} T_{k,l}} \quad .$$

The test statistic X follows a χ^2-distribution

$$X \sim \sum_{i=1}^{\mathrm{df}} N_i^2, \qquad \mathrm{df} = (c-1)(r-1)$$

where N_i are independent, standard normal random variables and df denotes the degrees of freedom. To determine a confidence level, we compute the cumulative distribution for X from the density function:

$$f(x, df) = \begin{cases} \dfrac{x^{\frac{df}{2}-1} e^{-\frac{x}{2}}}{2^{\frac{df}{2}} \Gamma(\frac{df}{2})} & \text{if } x > 0 \\ 0 & \text{otherwise} \end{cases} \qquad p = \int_x^{\infty} f(x, \mathrm{df})$$

Under the assumption that $\mathcal{H}_0$ holds, p describes the likelihood that the observations in table T could have occurred. We reject the null-hypothesis to the level $p < 10^{-5}$, which constitutes the common threshold in leakage assessments.

3   TI of KECCAK

In this section, we summarize different shared constructions of χ. They all share the properties of correctness and non-completeness, hence they constitute valid TIs. The constructions differ in whether and how they achieve uniformity. In the following we indicate the i-th bit of x by x_i.

Original TI. As the non-linear χ was designed to enable efficient masking with TI by limiting the algebraic degree to two, Bertoni *et al.* [4] also introduced a three-share masking scheme, defined as $\chi' : \mathbb{F}_2^{15} \to \mathbb{F}_2^{15}, (A, B, C) = \chi'(a, b, c)$ with

$$A_i = b_i \oplus (b_{i+1} \oplus 1) \cdot b_{i+2} \oplus b_{i+1} \cdot c_{i+2} \oplus c_{i+1} \cdot b_{i+2}$$
$$B_i = c_i \oplus (c_{i+1} \oplus 1) \cdot c_{i+2} \oplus c_{i+1} \cdot a_{i+2} \oplus a_{i+1} \cdot c_{i+2}$$
$$C_i = a_i \oplus (a_{i+1} \oplus 1) \cdot a_{i+2} \oplus a_{i+1} \cdot b_{i+2} \oplus b_{i+1} \cdot a_{i+2}$$

Contra to the original belief of the authors, the given TI is not uniform. Hence, an iterated application reduces entropy. In the following we recall several methods repairing χ' to achieve uniformity.

Re-masking. A naive approach is to re-mask the entire output of χ' according to the equations

$$A_i = \chi'^A_i(b, c) \oplus r^b_i \oplus r^c_i$$
$$B_i = \chi'^B_i(c, a) \oplus r^c_i$$
$$C_i = \chi'^C_i(a, b) \oplus r^b_i.$$

This scheme requires 10 bits of fresh randomness (r^b and r^c) for every invocation of χ', which can easily surpass the available randomness in an embedded system, in case several instances of χ' are implemented to operate in parallel (e.g., a round-based implementation).

Better Re-masking. Bilgin *et al.* [6] observed that only some bits require re-masking. More precisely any choice of two successive bits to be re-masked yields a uniform sharing.

$$A_i = \chi'^A_i(b, c) \oplus r^b_i \oplus r^c_i \qquad\qquad i = 0, 1$$
$$B_i = \chi'^B_i(c, a) \oplus r^c_i \qquad\qquad i = 0, 1$$
$$C_i = \chi'^C_i(a, b) \oplus r^b_i \qquad\qquad i = 0, 1$$
$$A_i = \chi'^A_i(b, c) \qquad\qquad i = 2, 3, 4$$
$$B_i = \chi'^B_i(c, a) \qquad\qquad i = 2, 3, 4$$
$$C_i = \chi'^C_i(a, b) \qquad\qquad i = 2, 3, 4$$

Subsequently, the constructions by Daemen re-mask the same bits, but partially [10] or fully [11] recycle randomness to achieve uniformity with reduced fresh randomness. Further, Bilgin *et al.* [6] introduced a uniform four-share TI of χ.

In the following, our focus is to study the original non-uniform three-share TI χ' interleaved with parts of the linear layer of KECCAK-f to determine the practical impact of uniformity violation.

4   Simulations

In this section we characterize χ' as a lossy mapping by determining the number of sharings and total imbalance after a given number of successive iterations. Then, we sample the input distribution of χ' from simulations of KECCAK-200 with different linear layers.

Iterating χ' Alone. We iterated the three-share TI $\chi' : \mathbb{F}_2^{15} \rightarrow \mathbb{F}_2^{15}$ by feeding its output back into the function as an input, until the number of observed different sharings reached its minimum (5363) and the total imbalance its maximum (56.66). The extremes are attained after 54 iterations (cf. Fig. 2). In comparison, a uniform mapping would maintain a total imbalance of zero and a constant number of 2^{15} possible sharings.

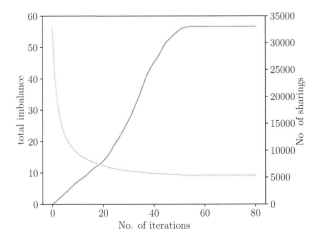

Fig. 2. Illustration of the rise of total imbalance over the number of iterations of χ' (red) in comparison with the decrease in the number of sharings (blue). (Color figure online)

The figure clearly shows that the violation of uniformity from one round to the next has a compounding effect over many rounds. In Sect. 6 we show that this reduction of entropy is sufficient to practically exhibit leakage. Fortunately, KECCAK-f consists of more functions than χ, namely a linear layer with three subfunctions:

- ρ - a bit-permutation for inter-slice diffusion
- π - a bit-permutation for intra-slice diffusion
- θ - a parity function to accelerate diffusion across columns

While ι is also a part of the linear layer, we disregard it for our analysis since it consists only of an addition with a round constant to counteract slide attacks and has limited relevance to SCA[3].

KECCAK-200. In our simulations we model the view of an attacker based on the glitch- extended 1-probing model [12, 20]. More specifically, the attacker may observe one output wire of the shared function χ' after a given number of rounds, which corresponds to observing the noise free values on two input wires to χ' resembling 1024 different potential observations. We determine whether the distribution seen on these wires is different between a fixed group consisting of sharings of the 200-bit all-zero plaintext and a random group in which the shared plaintext is chosen uniformly at random. Unfortunately, it is computationally infeasible to conduct an exhaustive computation of the distribution over all 3-sharing of 200 bits[4]. Hence, we follow the suggestion of [15] to conduct a χ^2-test on the histograms of the input values to determine whether a difference in the distributions of both groups is statistically significant. The results for 18 and 1800 iterations of variations of KECCAK-f and 200 million samples are displayed in Table 1. We simulated KECCAK-f with its original linear layer, only the bit-permuting part (ρ, π), only the mixing-part (θ) and without any linear layer. Note that in the first three cases a diffusion between all 40 instances of non-linear χ is achieved, while only in the last case no diffusion is present. Our simulations succeeded in finding the uniformity violation in the last (very obvious) case without diffusion. In the other three cases the null hypothesis that the input distribution is identical for both groups cannot be rejected given the common threshold of $p = 10^{-5}$ in a statistical test. Moreover, the null hypothesis cannot even be rejected given a very weak threshold of $p = 10^{-2}$. While the results clearly indicate that a linear layer is necessary to counteract the effects of uniformity violations, it remains unclear which parts of the linear layer are crucial and which are dispensable from an SCA perspective.

Table 1. χ^2-Test with degree of freedom $\mathsf{df} = 1023$ for 200 million samples. Only the uniformity violation of applying χ' alone is detected.

Enabled	p_{18}	p_{1800}
χ', π, ρ, θ	0.021	0.022
χ', π, ρ	0.018	0.016
χ', θ	0.022	0.020
χ'	0.000	0.000

---

[3] The addition of round constants would further increase the total imbalance in the χ'-only scenario, but it is of no interest for the investigation of full KECCAK.

[4] As it is already computationally infeasible for KECCAK-25, we kept the consistency between measurements and simulations by evaluating KECCAK-200.

5   Implementation

Although a round-based implementation would be a natural choice to implement KECCAK and would lead to short SCA traces (hence accelerating the evaluation), it would potentially increase the noise since the combinatorial circuit involving all KECCAK subfunctions would be active at all clock cycles. To achieve a compromise between a high signal-to-noise ratio (SNR) and a fast leakage evaluation, we chose to implement all variants of KECCAK in a slice-serial manner by having five instances of χ' in parallel.

Slice-Serial Implementation. In 2011 Jungk and Apfelbeck [13] introduced an area/latency trade-off for KECCAK by computing only eight slices in parallel instead of all 64 slices in a full round. Later Bilgin *et al.* [6] introduced a fully slice-serial architecture, which processes 25 state bits per clock cycle corresponding to the simultaneous execution of five χ functions (cf. Fig. 3). It contains a shift register for the state that operates on 25-bit chunks and an additional 5-bit register to keep track of the parity of the previously processed slice to realize θ. A specialty is the application of θ to the first slice, which happens as the last step of each round in parallel to processing the last slice, as it requires the parity of the last slice. We implemented KECCAK with a state size of 200 bits, which requires 144 clock cycles to process a given input for 18 rounds.

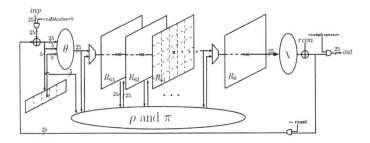

Fig. 3. Serial KECCAK-200 architecture [6], one of eight slices is processed per clock cycle. The computation completes after 18 rounds corresponding to 144 clock cycles.

Sharing the Implementation. We implemented several variants of three-share designs according to the χ constructions described in Sect. 3. Following the uncompressed design of [6], we maintained three shares throughout the entire computations. As ρ, π and θ are linear functions, they can be applied to each share of the state individually without modifications.

6   Practical Analysis

Measurement Setup. We synthesized our VHDL design in ISE Design Suite with the KEEP_HIERACHY attribute to ensure that non-completeness is maintained throughout the Place&Route process. For the practical evaluation, we used the SAKURA-G Side-Channel Evaluation Board [1] which includes two SPARTAN-6 FPGAs to separate controller and target functionality. We recorded power traces at a sampling rate of 625 MS/s by a Picoscope 6402 and an external amplifier (ZFL-1000LN+ from Mini-Circuits) in addition to the amplifier embedded on the SAKURA-G board. Following the methodology of [21] we performed a non-specific t-test "fixed vs. random"[5] over 100 million traces of the last round of KECCAK while operating the FPGA at a clock frequency of 1.5 MHz.

Results. A measurement of 100 million traces of full KECCAK-200 with non-uniform χ' and 18 rounds did not reveal first-order leakage as can be seen in Fig. 4. Even a drastic increase of the number of rounds to 1800 did not lead to first-order leakage (cf. Fig. 5). However, the removal of θ leads to detectable first-order leakage after 80 million traces (cf. Fig. 6)[6], while a removal of the ρ and π does not indicate first-order leakage as illustrated in Fig. 7. All measurements show leakage at orders two and three. Removing the entire linear layer causes each χ output to be taken as an input in the following round. Hence, an additional register is required to avoid transitional leakage, i.e., the leakage depending on the input of χ' being replaced by its output. This doubles the number of clock cycles to 288. Figure 8 shows the evaluation of 18 rounds of the non-uniform χ' function with 100 million traces. We observed, that the first-order t-value exceeds the threshold of 4.5 by far. We can also see an increase of the t-value along the time axis.

Summary. Table 2 summarizes our practical leakage investigation. Based on the results of our simulations in Sect. 4, we expected χ' alone without re-masking to show excessive first-order leakage which increases over time - this turned out to be true in practice. We also expected 18-round KECCAK-200 and 1800-round KECCAK-200 to show similar leakage behavior, which is also the case. Despite similar simulation results (see Table 1), the omission of permutations ρ and π led to no detectable first-order leakage, while leakage can be observed if θ is omitted. This indicates that although such theoretical analysis can be considered as the very first step, the results in practice might be slightly different.

Our results indicate that a diffusion between χ functions (S-boxes) should not solely employ bit-permutations to cope with uniformity loss. Instead, a good diffusion layer should apply additional linear mixing functions, that lead to partial re-masking by means of uncorrelated state bits.

---

[5] The groups fixed vs. random are formed over the entire 200-bit state.
[6] The peak coincides with the positive edge during the evaluation of χ'.

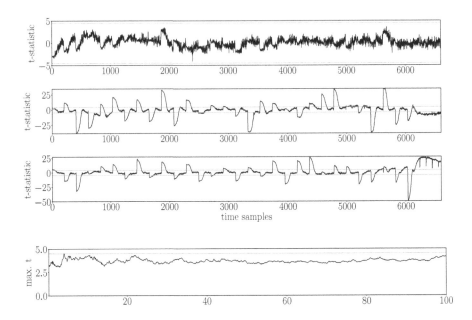

Fig. 4. 18 round KECCAK-f. top to bottom: t-test results first to third order over time axis. Maximal t-values first order over trace axis. Entire last round.

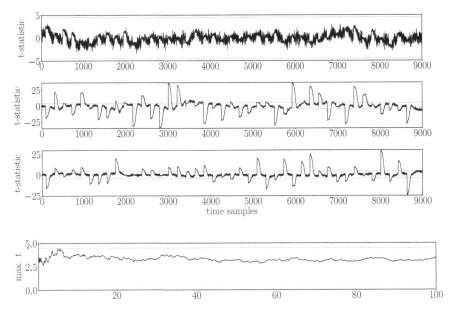

Fig. 5. 1800 round KECCAK-f. top to bottom: t-test results first to third order over time axis. Maximal t-values first order over trace axis. Entire last round.

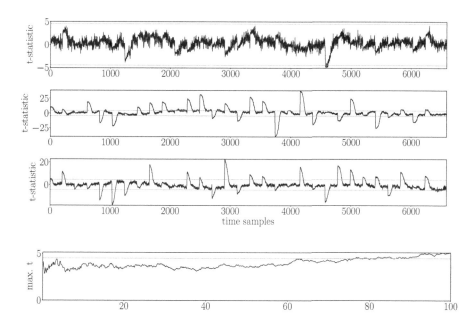

Fig. 6. 18 rounds of ρ, π and χ' (i.e., *KECCAK-f* without θ). top to bottom: t-test results first to third order over time axis. Maximal t-values first order over trace axis. Entire last round.

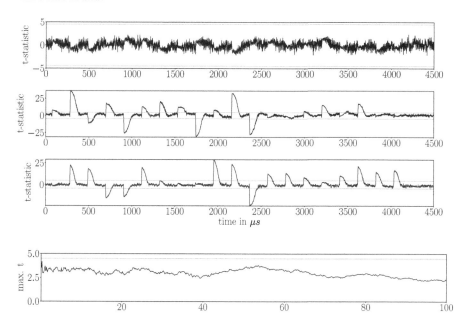

Fig. 7. 18 rounds of θ and χ' (i.e., *KECCAK-f* without ρ and π). top to bottom: t-test results first to third order over time axis. Maximal t-values first order over trace axis. Entire last round.

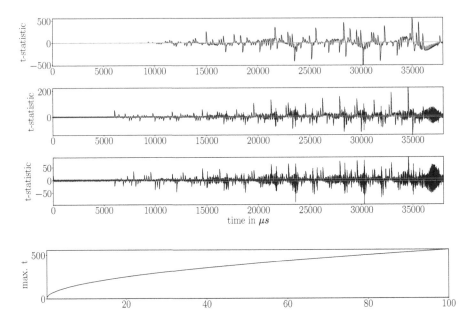

Fig. 8. 18 rounds of χ' alone. top to bottom: t-test results first to third order over time axis. Maximal t-values first to third order over trace axis. Entire last round.

Table 2. Summary of practical first-order evaluations.

Active layers	Leakage?
χ', ρ, π, θ	No
χ', θ	No
χ', ρ, π	**Yes**
χ'	**Yes**

Discussion. The linear layer of KECCAK has proven to mend a small violation of uniformity in Threshold Implementations of χ. However, extending this result to other security primitives with a non-linear of higher than quadratic degree is challenging. Consider the case of PRESENT [8], the cubic S-box can be decomposed into two quadratic bijections f, g each possessing a non-uniform TI F, G [19]. The non-uniformity caused by F cannot be alleviated by diffusion, before causing leakage in the evaluation of G. Hence, a strictly uniform TI remains important for decomposed non-linear layers.

While simulations of leakage behavior have already proven their utility in finding non-completeness violations in state-of-the-art implementations [2] and in known insecure constructions [3,7,15], finding a flaw based on uniformity violations can be computationally more intensive. On one hand, finding a uniformity flaw between S-box stages is easily possible by exhaustive computation [22]. On the other hand, any simulation of an entire round has to constrain itself to merely sampling the target distribution. It remains an open question how to obtain useful results with few samples. Hence, practical measurements stay a crucial part of leakage investigations.

7 Conclusion

We extended Daemen's theoretical study of lossy mappings [10] with entropy simulations and practical leakage evaluations of different variants of masked KECCAK-f. We conclude that our implementation of KECCAK-f achieves practical first-order security even with the non-uniform three-share TI χ' [4] since the diffusion property of its linear layer is sufficient to counteract the loss of entropy. We especially highlight the role of the mixing part (θ) in alleviating the non-uniformity in practical evaluations, whereas shuffling alone (ρ, π) cannot counteract the uniformity loss. Finally, a sampling-based simulation of input distributions is a fast method to falsify security claims, but cannot (and does not aim to) be a substitute for practical evaluation to intensify an indication of leakage absence.

Acknowledgments. The work described in this paper has been supported in part by the German Federal Ministry of Education and Research BMBF (grant nr. 16KIS0666 SysKit_HW).

References

1. Side-channel AttacK User Reference Architecture. http://satoh.cs.uec.ac.jp/SAKURA/index.html
2. Arribas, V., Nikova, S., Rijmen, V.: VerMI: verification tool for masked implementations. IACR Cryptology ePrint Archive, 2017:1227 (2017)
3. Barthe, G., Belaïd, S., Fouque, P.-A., Grégoire, B.: maskVerif: a formal tool for analyzing software and hardware masked implementations. IACR Cryptology ePrint Archive, 2018:562 (2018)
4. Bertoni, G., Daemen, J., Peeters, M., Van Assche, G.: Keccak. In: Johansson, T., Nguyen, P.Q. (eds.) EUROCRYPT 2013. LNCS, vol. 7881, pp. 313–314. Springer, Heidelberg (2013). https://doi.org/10.1007/978-3-642-38348-9_19
5. Beyne, T., Bilgin, B.: Uniform first-order threshold implementations. In: Avanzi, R., Heys, H. (eds.) SAC 2016. LNCS, vol. 10532, pp. 79–98. Springer, Cham (2017). https://doi.org/10.1007/978-3-319-69453-5_5
6. Bilgin, B., Daemen, J., Nikov, V., Nikova, S., Rijmen, V., Van Assche, G.: Efficient and first-order DPA resistant implementations of KECCAK. In: Francillon, A., Rohatgi, P. (eds.) CARDIS 2013. LNCS, vol. 8419, pp. 187–199. Springer, Cham (2014). https://doi.org/10.1007/978-3-319-08302-5_13
7. Bloem, R., Gross, H., Iusupov, R., Könighofer, B., Mangard, S., Winter, J.: Formal verification of masked hardware implementations in the presence of glitches. In: Nielsen, J.B., Rijmen, V. (eds.) EUROCRYPT 2018. LNCS, vol. 10821, pp. 321–353. Springer, Cham (2018). https://doi.org/10.1007/978-3-319-78375-8_11
8. Bogdanov, A., et al.: PRESENT: an ultra-lightweight block cipher. In: Paillier, P., Verbauwhede, I. (eds.) CHES 2007. LNCS, vol. 4727, pp. 450–466. Springer, Heidelberg (2007). https://doi.org/10.1007/978-3-540-74735-2_31

9. Daemen, J.: On non-uniformity in threshold sharings. In: Bilgin, B., Nikova, S., Rijmen, V. (eds.) Proceedings of the ACM Workshop on Theory of Implementation Security, TIS@CCS 2016, p. 41. ACM, New York (2016)

10. Daemen, J.: Spectral characterization of iterating lossy mappings. In: Carlet, C., Hasan, M.A., Saraswat, V. (eds.) SPACE 2016. LNCS, vol. 10076, pp. 159–178. Springer, Cham (2016). https://doi.org/10.1007/978-3-319-49445-6_9

11. Daemen, J.: Changing of the guards: a simple and efficient method for achieving uniformity in threshold sharing. In: Fischer, W., Homma, N. (eds.) CHES 2017. LNCS, vol. 10529, pp. 137–153. Springer, Cham (2017). https://doi.org/10.1007/978-3-319-66787-4_7

12. Ishai, Y., Sahai, A., Wagner, D.: Private circuits: securing hardware against probing attacks. In: Boneh, D. (ed.) CRYPTO 2003. LNCS, vol. 2729, pp. 463–481. Springer, Heidelberg (2003). https://doi.org/10.1007/978-3-540-45146-4_27

13. Jungk, B., Apfelbeck, J.: Area-efficient FPGA implementations of the SHA-3 finalists. In: Athanas, P.M., Becker, J., Cumplido, R. (eds.) 2011 International Conference on Reconfigurable Computing and FPGAs, ReConFig 2011, pp. 235–241. IEEE Computer Society, Washington, D.C. (2011)

14. Kocher, P., Jaffe, J., Jun, B.: Differential power analysis. In: Wiener, M. (ed.) CRYPTO 1999. LNCS, vol. 1666, pp. 388–397. Springer, Heidelberg (1999). https://doi.org/10.1007/3-540-48405-1_25

15. De Meyer, L., Bilgin, B., Reparaz, O.: Consolidating security notions in hardware masking. IACR Cryptology ePrint Archive, 2018:597 (2018)

16. Moradi, A., Richter, B., Schneider, T., Standaert, F.-X.: Leakage detection with the x2-test. IACR Trans. Cryptogr. Hardw. Embed. Syst. **2018**(1), 209–237 (2018)

17. Nikova, S., Rechberger, C., Rijmen, V.: Threshold implementations against side-channel attacks and glitches. In: Ning, P., Qing, S., Li, N. (eds.) ICICS 2006. LNCS, vol. 4307, pp. 529–545. Springer, Heidelberg (2006). https://doi.org/10.1007/11935308_38

18. National Institute of Standards and Technology: Sha-3 standard: permutation-based hash and extendable-output functions. FIPS Publikcation 2015:1–37 (2015)

19. Poschmann, A., Moradi, A., Khoo, K., Lim, C.-W., Wang, H., Ling, S.: Side-channel resistant crypto for less than 2, 300 GE. J. Cryptology **24**(2), 322–345 (2011)

20. Reparaz, O., Bilgin, B., Nikova, S., Gierlichs, B., Verbauwhede, I.: Consolidating masking schemes. In: Gennaro, R., Robshaw, M. (eds.) CRYPTO 2015. LNCS, vol. 9215, pp. 764–783. Springer, Heidelberg (2015). https://doi.org/10.1007/978-3-662-47989-6_37

21. Schneider, T., Moradi, A.: Leakage assessment methodology. In: Güneysu, T., Handschuh, H. (eds.) CHES 2015. LNCS, vol. 9293, pp. 495–513. Springer, Heidelberg (2015). https://doi.org/10.1007/978-3-662-48324-4_25

22. Wegener, F., Moradi, A.: A first-order SCA resistant AES without fresh randomness. In: Fan, J., Gierlichs, B. (eds.) COSADE 2018. LNCS, vol. 10815, pp. 245–262. Springer, Cham (2018). https://doi.org/10.1007/978-3-319-89641-0_14

Trade-offs in Protecting Keccak Against Combined Side-Channel and Fault Attacks

Antoon Purnal[✉], Victor Arribas, and Lauren De Meyer

KU Leuven, imec - COSIC, Leuven, Belgium
{antoon.purnal,victor.arribas,lauren.demeyer}@esat.kuleuven.be

Abstract. When deployed in a potentially hostile environment, security-critical devices are susceptible to physical attacks. Consequently, cryptographic implementations need to be protected against side-channel analysis, fault attacks and attacks that combine both approaches. CAPA (CRYPTO 2018) is an algorithm-level combined countermeasure, based on MPC, with provable security in a strong attacker model. A key challenge for combined countermeasures, and CAPA in particular, is the implementation cost. In this work, we use CAPA to obtain the first hardware implementations of Keccak (SHA-3) with resistance against combined side-channel and fault attacks. We systematically explore the speed-area trade-off and show that CAPA, in spite of its algorithmic overhead, can be very fast or reasonably small. In fact, for the standardized Keccak-$f[1600]$ instance, our low-latency version is nearly twice as fast as the previous implementations that only consider side-channel security, at the cost of area and randomness consumption. For all four presented designs, the protection level for side-channel and fault attacks can be scaled separately and to arbitrary order. To evaluate the physical security, we assess the side-channel leakage of a representative second-order secure implementation on FPGA. In addition, we experimentally validate the claimed fault detection probability.

Keywords: Side-channel analysis · Fault attacks · Masking · Combined countermeasure · Keccak · SHA-3 · CAPA

1 Introduction

Computing devices implement cryptographic algorithms. Traditionally, these devices are assumed to operate out of the attacker's reach. In practice, however, this condition is not upheld. Next to cryptanalytic attacks, the adversary can target the implementation of the algorithm directly. On the one hand, an adversary can employ *side-channel analysis* (SCA), which exploits the unintended leakage of sensitive information through one or more side-channels. Measurable physical channels include timing [28], power consumption [29] and electromagnetic emanation [16]. On the other hand, an adversary can mount devastating attacks by actively *injecting faults* in the cryptographic computations [12].

© Springer Nature Switzerland AG 2019
I. Polian and M. Stöttinger (Eds.): COSADE 2019, LNCS 11421, pp. 285–302, 2019.
https://doi.org/10.1007/978-3-030-16350-1_16

To thwart SCA attacks, masking [11,13,18,20,24,32,35,37] is a provably secure and scalable countermeasure. By randomizing the intermediate values processed by the cryptographic algorithm, masking decouples the side-channel information from the actual sensitive values.

The lion's share of countermeasures against fault attacks perform some redundant computations that allow the *detection* of faults. Proposed solutions include duplication of the computations in space or time [3], the use of error-detecting codes [5,26,30] and recomputing with permuted operands [22,34]. While such approaches are intuitively sound, they suffer from two fundamental problems. To begin with, if the redundancy is predictable, the attacker can evade detection by introducing well-crafted faults. Moreover, the detection mechanism itself constitutes an interesting point of attack [27,39]. Conceptually different from detection, *infection* [17,40] avoids the vulnerable check-before-output procedure. Instead, injected faults perturb the computation in such a way that the cryptographic output reveals no information about the implementation's secrets.

An attacker capable of separate side-channel and fault attacks, can also jointly exploit both attack vectors. Hence, cryptographic implementations also need to be protected against *combined attacks*. The combined countermeasures PRIVATE CIRCUITS II [14,23] and PARTI [38] are constructed by combining a masking scheme with fault-detecting redundancy. As a result, the fundamental problems of fault detection apply equally well to these schemes. The CAPA [36] and M&M [15] countermeasure methodologies avoid the latter problem by employing information-theoretic (i.e. perfectly unpredictable) MAC tags. CAPA draws inspiration from advances in the field of secure multi-party computation (MPC), resulting in provable security against combined physical attacks in a strong adversarial model. M&M is much cheaper to implement than CAPA, at the expense of a weaker attacker model. It additionally addresses the fundamental problem of fault checking by using the aforementioned infection strategy.

A key challenge for combined countermeasures is the implementation cost. We contribute to the evaluation of combined countermeasures by investigating the hardware trade-offs that govern the widely used KECCAK permutations [6] when protecting against combined physical attacks. We instantiate CAPA because it is the most resource-intensive methodology, but the implementation strategies and conclusions carry over to other (combined) countermeasures for which multiplications dominate the implementation cost. By extension, this work also covers the authenticated encryption ciphers KETJE [8] and KEYAK [9].

Our Contribution. In this work, we present the first implementations of KECCAK (SHA-3) with resistance to combined physical attacks, where previous works [1,7, 10,21] have considered only side-channel analysis. We systematically explore the speed-area trade-off in hardware, yielding a suite of protected implementations. We show that, in spite of the extremely strong adversarial model, CAPA can be very fast *or* reasonably compact. In particular, our low-latency implementation is almost twice as fast as all existing protected KECCAK-f[1600] implementations.

As a bonus, we discover a generic implementation optimization of the CAPA preprocessing stage. We illustrate and experimentally validate the overhead cost of the countermeasure as a function of the KECCAK permutation width and the side-channel and fault security parameters.

2 Preliminaries

2.1 KECCAK

Best known for their standardization as SHA-3, KECCAK [6] is a family of sponge functions, based on the KECCAK-$f[b]$ permutations. These permutations manipulate a state of b elements in $GF(2)$ (bits) for $b \in \{25, 50, 100, 200, 400, 800, 1600\}$ and consist of the iterative application of a round function R. Specifically, each of the seven instances of KECCAK-$f[b]$ has a fixed number of rounds $n_r = 12+2l$, where $l = \log_2(\frac{b}{25})$. The round function R, in turn, is defined by the consecutive application of five step mappings: $R = \iota \circ \chi \circ \pi \circ \rho \circ \theta$.

The effect of the step mappings is best explained by considering the state as a three-dimensional array $S(x, y, z)$ of dimensions $5 \times 5 \times w$, where $w = \frac{b}{25}$. This paper employs the established naming convention as introduced in [6]. In particular, we adopt the nomenclature of *planes, rows, lanes, slices and columns* to denote specific parts of the state.

The nonlinear part of the KECCAK-$f[b]$ permutation is confined to the χ step mapping, which is an S-box operating on 5-bit rows. Its algebraic degree is two, which is an attractive property in the context of masked implementations. The other step mappings are linear. For each column of the state, the θ mapping adds the parity of two neighbouring columns. The ι step mapping adds a round constant to one of the lanes. Finally, π reorganizes the lanes in the state and ρ shifts the bits within one lane.

2.2 CAPA: A Combined Countermeasure Against Physical Attacks

CAPA [36] is an algorithm-level countermeasure that achieves resistance against attacks that simultaneously exploit side-channel leakage and fault injection. As such, it claims security in the *tile-probe-and-fault* adversarial model [36]. We consider a computing architecture that has been partitioned in d tiles, resulting in side-channel security up to order $d - 1$. Let $\mathcal{T}_i$ denote one such tile and $\mathcal{T}$ the set of all tiles such that $\mathcal{T} = \bigcup_{i=0}^{d-1} \mathcal{T}_i$. The secure evaluation of an arbitrary arithmetic circuit occurs in two distinct stages. The *evaluation* stage comprises the actual cryptographic computations. The security of this stage depends on the presence of auxiliary random values, generated in the *preprocessing* stage.

The intermediate values of the cryptographic computation are referred to as sensitive variables x, y, z. The preprocessing stage generates auxiliary values a, b, c. Every sensitive or auxiliary value $x \in \mathbb{F}_q$ is shared as $\boldsymbol{x} = (x_0, x_1, \ldots, x_{d-1})$ where each tile $\mathcal{T}_i$ holds one share x_i and $\sum x_i = x$. The same sharing applies to every auxiliary value $a \in \mathbb{F}_q$. To detect faults injected in the evaluation stage, a MAC key $\alpha \in \mathbb{F}_q$, drawn uniformly at random, authenticates every sensitive or auxiliary value x with a multiplicative tag $\tau^x = \alpha \cdot x$, shared between the tiles as $\boldsymbol{\tau^x} = (\tau_0^x, \tau_1^x, \ldots, \tau_{d-1}^x)$. Note that α authenticates the secret value itself, not the shares. To protect α from being observed by the attacker, it is also shared between the tiles as $(\alpha_0, \alpha_1, \ldots, \alpha_{d-1})$. As α is secret, an attacker that alters a sensitive value is generally unable to forge a valid tag. The MAC key α changes for every new execution of the cryptographic algorithm.

To obtain a scalable security level against fault attacks, CAPA considers m independent MAC keys $\alpha[j]$, such that each sensitive value x is accompanied by m tags $\tau^x[j]$, for $j = 0, 1, \ldots, m-1$. Because KECCAK operates in $\mathbb{F}_q = GF(2)$, the CAPA fault detection probability in this work is $1 - 2^{-m}$.

Evaluation Stage. Next to establishing a shared representation $\langle x \rangle = (x, \boldsymbol{\tau^x})$ of every input value x of the arithmetic circuit, CAPA defines a computing procedure that yields a shared representation of the output. Linear operations, such as the parity additions in θ or the addition of the round constant in the ι step mapping, are easily evaluated by isolated computations in every tile. Nonlinear operations, like field multiplications, are more difficult to implement securely. In the CAPA methodology, multiplications require communication between the tiles and the consumption of an auxiliary triple $\langle a \rangle, \langle b \rangle, \langle c \rangle$ that satisfies $c = a \cdot b$.

To be secure in the presence of glitches, all communication between the tiles has to be synchronized by registers. Referring to [36] for the details, this implies that a multiplication operation has a two-cycle latency. However, multiplications can be organised in a pipeline, reducing the impact on the throughput of the implementation. To detect faults injected in the evaluation stage, every multiplication also features a check of the MAC tag. In an optimized implementation, this MAC check completes one cycle later than its corresponding multiplication.

Preprocessing Stage. Every multiplication instance in the evaluation stage incurs a corresponding preprocessing entity that produces the necessary auxiliary triple. In what follows, such an entity is denoted by a triple *factory*. The generation of an auxiliary triple goes as follows. First, the factory draws $\boldsymbol{a} = (a_0, a_1, \ldots, a_{d-1})$ and $\boldsymbol{b} = (b_0, b_1, \ldots, b_{d-1})$ uniformly at random from $\mathbb{F}_q^d$. To this end, every tile $\mathcal{T}_i$ randomly generates their share a_i, b_i. Next, the tiles securely compute a shared representation $\boldsymbol{c} = (c_0, c_1, \ldots, c_{d-1})$ of $c = a \cdot b$ by multiplying $\boldsymbol{a}$ and $\boldsymbol{b}$ with a *passively secure shared multiplier* [11,19,33,35]. The choice of multiplier is free, as long as the partition in tiles can be superimposed. In this work, we instantiate the DOM multiplier [19] because of its low randomness consumption. Shared multiplications of resp. $\boldsymbol{a}, \boldsymbol{b}, \boldsymbol{c}$ with the MAC key $\boldsymbol{\alpha}$ in turn yield the tags $\boldsymbol{\tau_a}, \boldsymbol{\tau_b}$ and $\boldsymbol{\tau_c}$. Note that each new triple thus requires $(1 + 3m)$ shared multiplications. To detect faults in the preprocessing and hence verify that the Beaver triples are genuine, the factory sacrifices another triple satisfying the same relation. This procedure is explained in more detail in [36].

3   Protected Implementations of KECCAK

Due to the substantial area and randomness cost of nonlinear operations in the CAPA methodology, the selection of the number of S-boxes is a crucial design decision. In this work, we explore the *speed-area trade-off* by presenting four secure designs of KECCAK-$f[b]$: BLAZE, FAST, FUR and KIT.

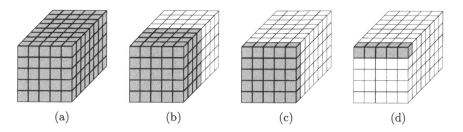

(a)   (b)   (c)   (d)

Fig. 1. Simultaneous processing of χ for the different designs.
(a) BLAZE. (b) FAST. (c) FUR. (d) KIT

The starting point for each design is the number of χ operations computed in parallel. Figure 1 marks the bits of the state that are treated simultaneously in the χ mapping. The design choices for the other step mappings follow from the speed-area characteristics implied by the number of S-boxes.

3.1   Evaluation Stage

BLAZE. The BLAZE design targets high throughput. Figure 2 (left) depicts a high-level overview of this round-based architecture. The delay elements in χ, unavoidable to be secure in the presence of glitches, are used as pipelining registers. Combinational logic implements the other step mappings. In the integrated $\pi \circ \rho \circ \theta$ stage, π and ρ are simple wirings.

The first cycle initiates the χ pipeline and hence only computes $\pi \circ \rho \circ \theta$. The subsequent cycles compute $\pi \circ \rho \circ \theta \circ \iota \circ \chi$ and the permutation finishes in the final cycle with $\iota \circ \chi$. Before the result can be shown at the output, the MAC tag check pertaining to the final computation cycle needs to be performed.

FAST. The baseline of the FAST design is a χ mapping that treats half of the state at a time. Figure 2 (right) presents the high-level architecture for FAST. The $\iota \circ \chi$ stage partitions the state in two equal parts by treating the first $w/2$ slices in the first cycle and the remaining $w/2$ slices in the second cycle. The ι mapping follows the pace dictated by χ and adds the round constant in two parts. Since the inter-slice shifts in ρ do not match with the slice-based partition for χ, the $\pi \circ \rho \circ \theta$ stage must consider the entire state at once.

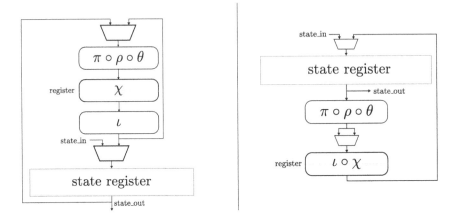

Fig. 2. High-level architectures for BLAZE (left) and FAST (right)

The computation of one round takes three cycles. In the first cycle, the first part of the state is loaded in the $\iota \circ \chi$ pipeline. During the second cycle, the now completed first part is written in the state register while the remaining part of the state enters the $\iota \circ \chi$ pipeline. In the third cycle, the now completed second part of the state also ends up in the state register. As with the BLAZE design, one extra cycle is needed to verify the tags of the last $\iota \circ \chi$.

FUR. As shown in Fig. 1, the baseline for the FUR design is a *slice-based* treatment of χ. Slice-based designs naturally lead to smaller implementations owing to the reuse of functional units. Moreover, a great deal of multiplexers are saved because only one slice during χ is written at once, as opposed to the entire state. The latter insight is key, given that storing the state dominates the implementation size as we move towards smaller designs. Although the architecture is not exactly the same, we acknowledge that a slice-based paradigm for KECCAK has been reported previously [25].

Schematically represented in Fig. 3, the slice-based $\iota \circ \chi$ stage takes one slice at a time, corresponding to one bit in every lane. At the same time, the slices are shifted and the result is written in the newly vacant position resulting from the shift. Because of the shift, the next slice is now in place to be processed. After repeating this process for all the slices, the results end up in the correct location. The $\pi \circ \rho \circ \theta$ mapping considers the whole state at once and its result is written to the state register to allow χ to be performed in a slice-based way. Due to its slice-based nature, χ takes $w + 1$ cycles, where the additional cycle stems from starting up the pipeline. One cycle suffices for $\pi \circ \rho \circ \theta$ and the ι mapping is computed concurrently with χ. In total, FUR takes $w + 2$ cycles per round, where one cycle for the MAC check must be added after the final round.

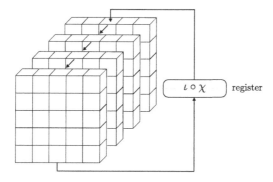

Fig. 3. Slice-based processing for the $\iota \circ \chi$ stage in FUR

KIT. The KIT design performs every step mapping in an iterated fashion and considers the minimal number of χ modules, i.e. *one*. In particular, KIT employs the slice-based paradigm for $\pi \circ \theta$ and ρ and even a *row-based* paradigm for χ. Row-based processing can be seen as an even more area-efficient extension of slice-based processing, resulting in the smallest design of this paper.

The KIT architecture comprises three distinct stages: $\pi \circ \theta$, ρ and $\iota \circ \chi$. Note that this interchanges the order of ρ and π. The $\pi \circ \theta$ stage is slice-based and implemented as in [10]. When processing one slice, its column parities are pre-computed for the next slice. The first slice features a special treatment as it requires the parities of the columns of the last slice. As a result, it is processed

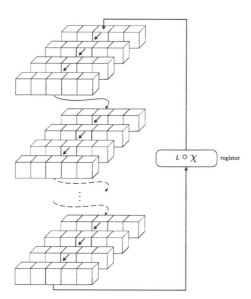

Fig. 4. Row-based processing for the $\iota \circ \chi$ stage in KIT

together with the last slice. The inter-slice diffusion in the ρ stage is also implemented iteratively. In particular, the lanes are shifted circularly until they reach the configuration dictated by ρ. It should be mentioned that a slice-based ρ mapping has been reported previously [21].

Figure 4 clarifies the row-based paradigm. The $\iota \circ \chi$ stage takes one row and shifts the remaining rows in the plane to fill the newly vacant position. In turn, this leaves a vacancy at the last row, which is filled by the first row of the next plane. Continuation of this reasoning results in a vacancy in the last row of the final plane, where the $\iota \circ \chi$ output is written. This process is repeated for every row. Care should be taken that the round constant is only added to the relevant lane. The row-based χ stage takes $5 \cdot w + 1$ cycles to treat the entire state. The other stages are slice-based and hence require w cycles each. In total, each round takes $(7w + 1)$ cycles.

Table 1. Summary of the designs, generic in the permutation width b. Recall that $w = b/25$ and that n_r denotes the number of rounds.

Design	# S-boxes (χ)	# Factories	Cycle count
BLAZE	$b/5$	b	$n_r + 2$
FAST	$b/10$	$b/2$	$3 \cdot n_r + 2$
FUR	5	25	$(w + 1) \cdot n_r + 1$
KIT	1	5	$(7w + 1) \cdot n_r + 1$

Pushing the Area Limits. Instead of providing a factory for every shared multiplication, five in the case of KIT, we can instantiate the design with only one factory. This implies that the evaluation stage waits for the preprocessing stage. Essentially, this is a *bit-based paradigm*, where only one bit of the state is processed at a time. As a result, the preprocessing stage is five times smaller and the design is five times slower. Given that the preprocessing stage is not dominant in size for many instances of KIT, this design has not been implemented.

Summary of the Designs. Table 1 summarizes the amount of S-boxes and factories of every implementation, and the number of cycles they take to execute.

3.2   Preprocessing Stage

In the computing procedure for the Beaver multiplication [36], the auxiliary value $\langle c \rangle$ is only needed *one cycle later* than its corresponding $\langle a \rangle$ and $\langle b \rangle$. However, a naive implementation of the preprocessing stage provides $\langle a \rangle$, $\langle b \rangle$ and $\langle c \rangle$ at the same time. By tolerating a one-cycle lag of the auxiliary values $\langle c \rangle$ with respect to $\langle a \rangle$ and $\langle b \rangle$ values, as depicted in Fig. 5, we save several storage elements at the boundary between evaluation and preprocessing stage. When the number of factories is large, this algorithm-independent optimization incurs a considerable resource saving.

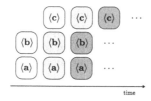

Fig. 5. The one-cycle lag of $\langle c \rangle$ w.r.t $\langle a \rangle$ and $\langle b \rangle$

4   Implementation Results and Cost Scalability

Our synthesis results are obtained with Synopsys Design Compiler N-2017.09 in conjunction with the freely available NANGATE 45 nm Open Cell technology library [31]. The compilation is done with the exact_map option enabled and clock gating disabled to prevent cross-tile optimizations.

Table 2. Synthesis results for KECCAK-f[200]

Design	Order	AREA [kGE]							Rand.	f_{max}	FoM
		Evaluation				Preprocessing		Total	[bpc]	[MHz]	[kbps/GE]
		χ	θ	State	Σ	Gen.	Ver.	Σ			
BLAZE	1	73.6	4.8	12.5	94.3	114.8	103.0	217.8	312.1	4400	806	25.8
	2	117.4	7.2	18.7	148.5	261.7	166.2	427.9	576.4	10800	806	14.0
	3	166.0	9.6	25.0	207.4	469.5	237.6	707.1	914.5	20000	751	8.2
FAST	1	36.8	4.8	11.1	56.1	57.4	51.5	108.9	165.0	2200	1333	28.9
	2	58.8	7.2	16.6	87.7	130.8	83.1	213.9	301.6	5400	1190	14.1
	3	83.1	9.6	22.2	121.6	234.7	118.8	353.5	475.2	10000	1190	8.9
FUR	1	9.2	4.8	13.2	27.9	14.3	12.9	27.2	55.1	550	1219	27.1
	2	14.7	7.2	19.9	42.7	32.7	20.8	53.5	96.2	1350	1098	14.0
	3	20.8	9.6	26.5	58.1	58.7	29.7	88.4	146.5	2500	1098	9.2
KIT	1	1.9	1.9	11.0	15.6	2.9	2.6	5.4	21.1	110	1315	12.1
	2	3.0	2.9	16.5	23.6	6.5	4.2	10.7	34.3	270	1162	6.6
	3	4.2	3.9	22.0	31.7	11.7	5.9	17.7	49.4	500	1176	4.6

KECCAK-f[200] in NANGATE 45 nm ($m = 2$)

Although the designs generally cover all seven KECCAK$-f[b]$ instances, for brevity, Table 2 reports the results for KECCAK-f[200], for variable side-channel protection orders. Recall that an implementation with d tiles achieves a side-channel protection order of $(d - 1)$. To conduct a consistent comparison of the different designs, we fix $m = 2$ and warn the reader that this security parameter does not correspond to a satisfactory practical protection against fault attacks.

The relevant metrics are the area of the implementation, the randomness consumption, the maximum clock frequency f_{max}, the number of cycles n_c (see Table 1) and a figure of merit (FoM) [25]. The area is reported in a hierarchical fashion so as to reveal how the total area is apportioned among the major parts of the design. The FoM jointly captures the performance in terms of speed and area and is given by $(b \cdot f_{max})/(A \cdot n_c)$, where A is the total area. As a measure of throughput per area (higher is better), the expression for the FoM directly follows from the reasoning that the throughput of KECCAK-f is proportional to the maximum clock frequency and the permutation width, but inversely proportional to the number of cycles.

Table 3. Comparison with side-channel only countermeasures. Note: the implementations of [21] are synthesized with UMC 90 nm and clock gating

Order	Design	AREA [kGE]						Rand.	f_{max}	Cycles
		Evaluation				Prep.	Total	[bpc]	[MHz]	[/]
		χ	θ	State	Σ					
	BLAZE	145.1	12.8	33.7	199.7	231.0	430.7	16000	892	25
	Parallel [21]	38.4	15.0	32.2	85.7	-	85.7	480	891	48
1	Parallel-3sh [10]	40.6	19.2	56.8	116.6	-	116.6	4	592	25
	KIT	0.5	0.6	26.1	29.1	0.7	29.8	50	1538	10776
	Serial-Area [21]	0.4	0.4	14.5	15.7	-	15.7	-	850	3160
	Serial-3sh [10]	0.6	0.3	38.1	39.0	-	39.0	< 1	645	1625
	BLAZE	235.2	19.2	50.5	317.1	449.3	766.4	28800	884	25
2	Parallel [21]	114.0	22.5	51.1	188.1	-	188.1	4800	898	48
	KIT	0.7	1.0	39.1	43.7	1.4	45.1	90	1351	10776
	Serial-Area [21]	2.2	0.6	21.4	24.2	-	24.2	75	898	3160
		KECCAK-f[200] in NANGATE 45 nm ($m = 0$)								
	BLAZE	18.1	1.6	4.2	25.2	28.9	54.0	2000	892	19
1	5-10-5 [1]	73.4	14.0	11.9	99.3	-	99.3	-	395.25	9
	6-6-6 [1]	44.6	11.3	14.2	70.1	-	70.1	-	436.7	9

KECCAK-f[1600] in NANGATE 45 nm ($m = 0$) (top section heading)

4.1   Comparison with the Literature

The literature already features protected implementations of KECCAK, although their protection scope is limited to side-channel analysis (SCA) in a weaker attacker model [1,10,21]. Table 3 compares these implementations with the ones introduced in this work, which are instantiated for $m = 0$, implying that the final MAC checking phase can be avoided and all implementations are one cycle faster. It should be stressed that this is not the intended setting for CAPA, but merely serves for comparison. When the fault protection capability is not used, one should indeed opt for another countermeasure. Although there are many trade-offs in the designs, the comparison features only the fastest and the smallest design of every source to cover the limits of high speed and low area. For this paper, the representative designs are BLAZE and KIT, which adopt the permutation width of the prior work they are compared to.

For the full permutation width $b = 1600$, BLAZE is nearly twice as fast as its competitors [10,21]. The price to pay is a larger area and a huge randomness consumption. For the $b = 200$ instance, BLAZE has a competitive speed and significantly smaller area than the unrolled implementations of [1] at the expense of a substantially larger randomness cost.

The first-order protected KIT design is clearly smaller than the Serial-3sh implementation [10] because the latter employs three shares. It would appear that the row-based efforts in the KIT design yield a (much) larger implementation than the Serial-Area implementation [21]. However, the difference can largely be attributed to *(1) different technology libraries* and *(2)* that the synthesis results for Serial-Area are obtained with *clock gating enabled*. We verify this hypothesis as follows for the first-order secure design. Without counting multiplexers, accommodating the state using scan flip-flops (SFF) in NANGATE 45 nm [31] already has an area cost of $8.0 \frac{\text{GE}}{\text{SFF}} \cdot 1600 \cdot 2\,\text{SFF} = 25.6\,\text{kGE}$. This is already in the same order of magnitude as the first-order KIT design as reported in Table 3.

4.2   Cost Scalability

Scaling with m. The implementation *area* is expected to scale linearly as a function of the fault security parameter m. Incrementally increasing m incurs an additional parallel computation in every arithmetic unit and an extra storage unit for every shared value $\langle x \rangle$. The control overhead is not expected to scale with m. To corroborate this intuition, we gather experimental evidence for KIT, the design where the control logic has the largest relative size. Figure 6a shows the results for KECCAK-f[200] with different values of d. Because of the near-perfect linear relationship, we take it as a given and fix m in the discussions that follow.

The *throughput* is affected, albeit slighty, by the value of m. The number of cycles is constant with respect to the fault security parameter m. Because the tags corresponding to different keys never interact, no significant increase in the critical path is to be expected either. However, Fig. 6b shows the contrary and reveals a monotonous increase of the critical path with respect to m. It can be attributed to the placement and routing of the cells.

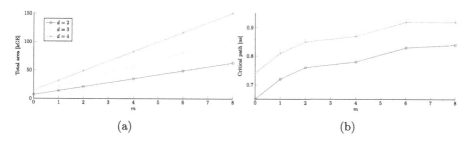

(a)   (b)

Fig. 6. (a) KECCAK-f[200] implementation size as function of m, for the KIT design. (b) The critical path increases monotonously with m

Scaling with d. The *area* of the evaluation stage scales linearly with the SCA protection parameter d. The preprocessing stage, on the other hand, scales asymptotically with d^2 due to the presence of the passively secure multipliers. Figure 7 presents experimental evidence for these claims. The FUR and KIT designs are particularly interesting for large SCA protection orders as the offline part, i.e. the part of the implementation that scales with d^2, is relatively small. The impact on the *throughput* can be determined as follows. Similar to m, the SCA security parameter d does not affect the number of cycles of the algorithm. To assess its influence on the critical path, consider Fig. 6b but now keeping m constant and varying d. There seems to be some dependency on d but there is no monotonous increase. The variations are likely due to placement and routing.

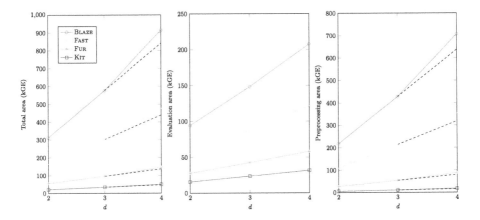

Fig. 7. Area of the designs (KECCAK-f[200]) w.r.t the SCA parameter d, for $m = 2$. From left to right: total area, evaluation stage, preprocessing stage

Scaling with b. As the KECCAK-f permutation width increases, a larger state has to be processed every round. As a result, the designs either become substantially larger (BLAZE, FAST) or suffer a considerable throughput penalty (FUR, KIT). Table 4 allows to interpret the influence of the permutation width on the *area* of the implementation. The last column features the interpolated numbers. In particular, the linear coefficient in b is of importance for this experiment. As expected, the slice- and row-based designs scale much less dramatically than the designs that consider the entire state or half of the state every round. The critical path is unaffected by b. This makes sense as the fundamental operations occur at the bit-level and remain unchanged. The *throughput* scaling can then simply be deduced from the number of cycles in Table 1.

Table 4. Area scaling of the designs for KECCAK-$f[b]$ w.r.t. b

	Area [kGE] of KECCAK-$f[b]$ for $d = 2, m = 2$				
Design	$b = 200$	$b = 400$	$b = 800$	$b = 1600$	Interpolation
BLAZE	312.1	623.9	1247.5	2494.6	$312.1 + \mathbf{1.56}(b - 200)$
FAST	165.0	329.7	659.1	1317.8	$165.0 + \mathbf{0.82}(b - 200)$
FUR	55.1	72.6	107.5	177.2	$55.1 + \mathbf{0.087}(b - 200)$
KIT	21.1	30.9	50.5	89.8	$21.1 + \mathbf{0.049}(b - 200)$

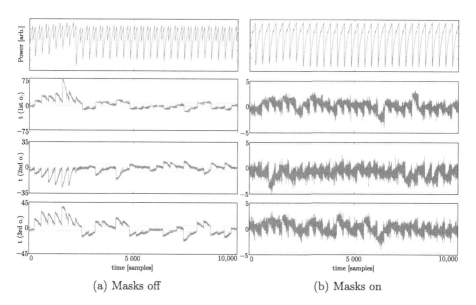

(a) Masks off   (b) Masks on

Fig. 8. Results of the non-specific leakage detection (t-test) for the KIT design of KECCAK-$f[200]$, where $d = 3$ and $m = 2$. Top row: average power trace (arbitrary units). Second until last row: resp. 1st, 2nd and 3rd order t-test

5   Security Evaluation

5.1   Side-Channel Resistance

To evaluate the side-channel resistance of the presented designs, we employ the *Test Vector Leakage Assessment* (TVLA) method [4]. Specifically, we consider a *non-specific* leakage detection test and adopt a t-test threshold of $|t| = 4.5$. The evaluation platform is a Sakura-G board, equipped with two 45 nm Xilinx Spartan-6 FPGAs that respectively host the cryptographic implementation and the control unit. By design, the board isolates the power supplies of the FPGAs, mitigating the noisy influence of the control unit on the power consumption measurements. The programming files for the cryptographic unit are obtained with the keep_hierarchy constraint to avoid that sources of out-of-model leakage are added by the synthesis of the design. The implementation is clocked at 3 MHz and the masks are produced by a KECCAK-f[1600]-based PRNG.

The evaluation is performed on the KECCAK-f[200] instance of the KIT design. This design should exhibit the fastest evidence of leakage as it only features a relatively small preprocessing phase, which contributes as a noise source in the context of this experiment. Because the implementations are general in b, the security claims carry over to the other KECCAK-f[b] instances. The implementation is parametrized with $d = 3$ tiles (offering a second-order secure design) and a fault security parameter $m = 2$. The specific value of m is unimportant, but is non-zero to ensure that the synthesis and implementation tools do not trim the preprocessing stage and MAC checks from the implementation.

To construct the power traces, an oscilloscope captures the voltage drop over a 1 Ω shunt resistor at 1 GS/s for 10000 samples. The traces correspond to the latter half of the ρ mapping and the first two slices of χ, obtaining a representative part of the round function, with linear and nonlinear operations. To ensure that the test setup is able to detect leakage, all masks are turned off in the first iteration of the experiment. In the subsequent iteration, the masks are turned on. The leakage reduction from the first experiment to the second on can then be fully attributed to the CAPA countermeasure.

The experiment where the masks are disabled, shown in Fig. 8a, shows serious leakage. Already after the first batch of 15000 traces, $|t|$ amply exceeds the threshold of $|t| = 4.5$. This observation validates that the measurement setup is reliable. When activating the masks, the t-test reveals no first-, second- or third-order leakage when presented 80 million traces (Fig. 8b). Although we do not claim that the implementation with three shares is secure against third-order attacks, no leakage is apparent from the statistical evidence contained within the supplied traces. This can be attributed to the measurement noise.

In Fig. 8b, the second-order t-test can be seen to approach the threshold value of $t = \pm 4.5$. To provide reassurance that this artefact stems from statistical variations as opposed to genuine leakage, Fig. 9 shows the maximum $|t|$-values over time. It can be seen to fluctuate around the threshold but no steady increase in its value is recognizable. In conclusion, the experiment does not provide evidence of second-order leakage.

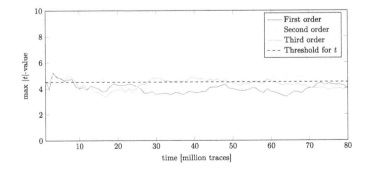

Fig. 9. Maximum t-test value over time

5.2   Fault Resistance

Resistance against fault attacks is difficult to evaluate as currently no established formal verification procedures exist. For a theoretical discussion on the fault resistance of CAPA, we refer to [36]. While not conclusive, we gain confidence in the implementation by experimentally verifying the fault detection probability.

Modelling the Attacker. Recall that CAPA considers the *tile-probe-and-fault* model, allowing the adversary to fault arbitrary bits in the implementation, given that at least one tile is not faulted nor probed. The adversarial goal is to introduce a fault f in the computations. To this end, she guesses a valid shared representation $\langle f \rangle$, denoted a *fault vector*, consisting of $d(1 + m)$ bits. This results in $2^{d(1+m)}$ possible fault vectors. In $GF(2)$, half of these correspond to $f = 0$ and are hence excluded. The attacker can simultaneously fault at several interesting locations in the implementation (preprocessing, the linear θ mapping, the MAC check and the S-box) but will stick to one guess of the MAC key; otherwise she will be detected with probability one. To cover the DFA attacks on KECCAK [2], we inject the faults in the penultimate round. We modify the HDL implementation in the targeted modules to introduce the fault vectors as additive differences as done in [15]. We simulate the design with GHDL 0.36-dev.

Experimental Results. We experimentally validate the claimed fault detection probability for the first-order $(d = 2)$ KECCAK-f[200] KIT implementation with $m \in \{2, 4, 6, 8\}$. The results can then be extrapolated to larger m as both CAPA and the KIT implementation itself are generically scalable in m. For these relatively small values of m, we need not follow a probabilistic approach. The fault coverage can be trivially parallelized and we can *exhaustively* cover all valid fault vectors in a few hours. This deterministic experiment is successful if the fraction of detected faults is *exactly* equal to $1 - 2^{-m}$. Table 5 covers the experimental results and demonstrates that the implementation is sound.

Table 5. Experimental fault resistance results

	$m = 2$	$m = 4$	$m = 6$	$m = 8$
# valid $\langle f \rangle$	32	512	8192	131072
# detected $\langle f \rangle$	24	480	8064	130560

6   Conclusion

Following the CAPA countermeasure methodology, this paper reports the first KECCAK implementations with resistance against combined side-channel and fault attacks. The fastest design competes with or even outperforms the state of the art in side-channel protected designs. As a drawback, the area and randomness requirements are prohibitively large. The smaller designs of this work have more attainable requirements, but incur a considerable throughput penalty. All four approaches are general in the KECCAK permutation width b, and scalable in the number of tiles d and the fault security parameter m. We have presented and validated the scaling laws as a function of these parameters. An advanced leakage detection test on the most intricate implementation of this paper has validated our confidence in its SCA resistance. The soundness of the implementation with respect to fault attacks has been supported by simulation.

Acknowledgements. The authors would like to thank the COSADE reviewers for their helpful comments. This work was supported in part by the Research Council KU Leuven: C16/15/058 and by the NIST Research Grant 60NANB15D346. Lauren De Meyer is funded by a PhD fellowship of the Fund for Scientific Research - Flanders (FWO). Antoon Purnal would like to thank Vincent Rijmen and Ingrid Verbauwhede for supervising the master's thesis that led to this paper.

References

1. Arribas, V., Bilgin, B., Petrides, G., Nikova, S., Rijmen, V.: Rhythmic Keccak: SCA security and low latency in HW. IACR Trans. Cryptogr. Hardw. Embed. Syst. **2018**(1), 269–290 (2018)
2. Bagheri, N., Ghaedi, N., Sanadhya, S.K.: Differential fault analysis of SHA-3. In: Biryukov, A., Goyal, V. (eds.) INDOCRYPT 2015. LNCS, vol. 9462, pp. 253–269. Springer, Cham (2015). https://doi.org/10.1007/978-3-319-26617-6_14
3. Bar-El, H., Choukri, H., Naccache, D., Tunstall, M., Whelan, C.: The sorcerer's apprentice guide to fault attacks. Proc. IEEE **94**(2), 370–382 (2006)
4. Becker, G., et al.: Test vector leakage assessment (TVLA) methodology in practice. In: International Cryptographic Module Conference, vol. 1001, p. 13 (2013)
5. Bertoni, G., Breveglieri, L., Koren, I., Maistri, P., Piuri, V.: Error analysis and detection procedures for a hardware implementation of the advanced encryption standard. IEEE Trans. Comput. **52**(4), 492–505 (2003)
6. Bertoni, G., Daemen, J., Peeters, M., Van Assche, G.: Keccak sponge function family main document. Submiss. NIST (Round 2) **3**(30) (2009)
7. Bertoni, G., Daemen, J., Peeters, M., Van Assche, G.: Building power analysis resistant implementations of Keccak. In: Second SHA-3 Candidate Conference, vol. 3, p. 2. Citeseer (2010)
8. Bertoni, G., Daemen, J., Peeters, M., Van Assche, G., Van Keer, R.: CAESAR submission: Ketje v2 (2015)
9. Bertoni, G., Daemen, J., Peeters, M., Van Assche, G., Van Keer, R.: CAESAR submission: Keyak v2 (2015)
10. Bilgin, B., Daemen, J., Nikov, V., Nikova, S., Rijmen, V., Van Assche, G.: Efficient and first-order DPA resistant implementations of KECCAK. In: Francillon, A., Rohatgi, P. (eds.) CARDIS 2013. LNCS, vol. 8419, pp. 187–199. Springer, Cham (2014). https://doi.org/10.1007/978-3-319-08302-5_13
11. Bilgin, B., Gierlichs, B., Nikova, S., Nikov, V., Rijmen, V.: Higher-order threshold implementations. In: Sarkar, P., Iwata, T. (eds.) ASIACRYPT 2014. LNCS, vol. 8874, pp. 326–343. Springer, Heidelberg (2014). https://doi.org/10.1007/978-3-662-45608-8_18

12. Boneh, D., DeMillo, R.A., Lipton, R.J.: On the importance of checking cryptographic protocols for faults. In: Fumy, W. (ed.) EUROCRYPT 1997. LNCS, vol. 1233, pp. 37–51. Springer, Heidelberg (1997). https://doi.org/10.1007/3-540-69053-0_4

13. Chari, S., Jutla, C.S., Rao, J.R., Rohatgi, P.: Towards sound approaches to counteract power-analysis attacks. In: Wiener, M. (ed.) CRYPTO 1999. LNCS, vol. 1666, pp. 398–412. Springer, Heidelberg (1999). https://doi.org/10.1007/3-540-48405-1_26

14. De Cnudde, T., Nikova, S.: More efficient private circuits II through threshold implementations. In: 2016 Workshop on Fault Diagnosis and Tolerance in Cryptography (FDTC), pp. 114–124. IEEE (2016)

15. De Meyer, L., Arribas, V., Nikova, S., Nikov, V., Rijmen, V.: M&M: Masks and Macs against physical attacks. IACR Trans. Cryptogr. Hardw. Embed. Syst. **2019**(1), 25–50 (2019)

16. Gandolfi, K., Mourtel, C., Olivier, F.: Electromagnetic analysis: concrete results. In: Koç, Ç.K., Naccache, D., Paar, C. (eds.) CHES 2001. LNCS, vol. 2162, pp. 251–261. Springer, Heidelberg (2001). https://doi.org/10.1007/3-540-44709-1_21

17. Gierlichs, B., Schmidt, J.-M., Tunstall, M.: Infective computation and dummy rounds: fault protection for block ciphers without check-before-output. In: Hevia, A., Neven, G. (eds.) LATINCRYPT 2012. LNCS, vol. 7533, pp. 305–321. Springer, Heidelberg (2012). https://doi.org/10.1007/978-3-642-33481-8_17

18. Goubin, L., Patarin, J.: DES and differential power analysis the "Duplication" method. In: Koç, Ç.K., Paar, C. (eds.) CHES 1999. LNCS, vol. 1717, pp. 158–172. Springer, Heidelberg (1999). https://doi.org/10.1007/3-540-48059-5_15

19. Groß, H., Mangard, S., Korak, T.: Domain-oriented masking: compact masked hardware implementations with arbitrary protection order. In: Proceedings of the ACM Workshop on Theory of Implementation Security, TIS@CCS 2016 Vienna, Austria, October 2016, p. 3 (2016)

20. Groß, H., Mangard, S., Korak, T.: An efficient side-channel protected AES implementation with arbitrary protection order. In: Handschuh, H. (ed.) CT-RSA 2017. LNCS, vol. 10159, pp. 95–112. Springer, Cham (2017). https://doi.org/10.1007/978-3-319-52153-4_6

21. Groß, H., Schaffenrath, D., Mangard, S.: Higher-order side-channel protected implementations of Keccak. In: Euromicro Conference on Digital System Design, DSD 2017, Vienna, Austria, 30 August – 1 September 2017, pp. 205–212 (2017)

22. Guo, X., Karri, R.: Recomputing with permuted operands: a concurrent error detection approach. IEEE Trans. CAD Integr. Circuits Syst. **32**(10), 1595–1608 (2013)

23. Ishai, Y., Prabhakaran, M., Sahai, A., Wagner, D.: Private circuits II: keeping secrets in tamperable circuits. In: Vaudenay, S. (ed.) EUROCRYPT 2006. LNCS, vol. 4004, pp. 308–327. Springer, Heidelberg (2006). https://doi.org/10.1007/11761679_19

24. Ishai, Y., Sahai, A., Wagner, D.: Private circuits: securing hardware against probing attacks. In: Boneh, D. (ed.) CRYPTO 2003. LNCS, vol. 2729, pp. 463–481. Springer, Heidelberg (2003). https://doi.org/10.1007/978-3-540-45146-4_27

25. Jungk, B., Apfelbeck, J.: Area-efficient FPGA implementations of the SHA-3 finalists. In: 2011 International Conference on Reconfigurable Computing and FPGAs, ReConFig 2011, Cancun, Mexico, 30 November – 2 December 2011, pp. 235–241 (2011)

26. Karpovsky, M.G., Kulikowski, K.J., Taubin, A.: Robust protection against fault-injection attacks on smart cards implementing the advanced encryption standard. In: 2004 International Conference on Dependable Systems and Networks (DSN 2004), 28 June – 1 July 2004, Florence, Italy, Proceedings, pp. 93–101 (2004)

27. Kim, C.H., Quisquater, J.-J.: Fault attacks for CRT based RSA: new attacks, new results, and new countermeasures. In: Sauveron, D., Markantonakis, K., Bilas, A., Quisquater, J.-J. (eds.) WISTP 2007. LNCS, vol. 4462, pp. 215–228. Springer, Heidelberg (2007). https://doi.org/10.1007/978-3-540-72354-7_18

28. Kocher, P.C.: Timing attacks on implementations of diffie-hellman, RSA, DSS, and other systems. In: Koblitz, N. (ed.) CRYPTO 1996. LNCS, vol. 1109, pp. 104–113. Springer, Heidelberg (1996). https://doi.org/10.1007/3-540-68697-5_9

29. Kocher, P., Jaffe, J., Jun, B.: Differential power analysis. In: Wiener, M. (ed.) CRYPTO 1999. LNCS, vol. 1666, pp. 388–397. Springer, Heidelberg (1999). https://doi.org/10.1007/3-540-48405-1_25

30. Kulikowski, K.J., Karpovsky, M.G., Taubin, A.: Robust codes and robust, fault-tolerant architectures of the advanced encryption standard. J. Syst. Architect. **53**(2–3), 139–149 (2007)

31. NANGATE: California. 45 nm open cell library (2008). http://www.nangate.com

32. Nikova, S., Rechberger, C., Rijmen, V.: Threshold implementations against side-channel attacks and glitches. In: Ning, P., Qing, S., Li, N. (eds.) ICICS 2006. LNCS, vol. 4307, pp. 529–545. Springer, Heidelberg (2006). https://doi.org/10.1007/11935308_38

33. Nikova, S., Rijmen, V., Schläffer, M.: Secure hardware implementation of non-linear functions in the presence of glitches. In: Lee, P.J., Cheon, J.H. (eds.) ICISC 2008. LNCS, vol. 5461, pp. 218–234. Springer, Heidelberg (2009). https://doi.org/10.1007/978-3-642-00730-9_14

34. Patel, J.H., Fung, L.Y.: Concurrent error detection in ALU's by recomputing with shifted operands. IEEE Trans. Comput. **31**(7), 589–595 (1982)

35. Reparaz, O., Bilgin, B., Nikova, S., Gierlichs, B., Verbauwhede, I.: Consolidating masking schemes. In: Gennaro, R., Robshaw, M. (eds.) CRYPTO 2015. LNCS, vol. 9215, pp. 764–783. Springer, Heidelberg (2015). https://doi.org/10.1007/978-3-662-47989-6_37

36. Reparaz, O., De Meyer, L., Bilgin, B., Arribas, V., Nikova, S., Nikov, V., Smart, N.: CAPA: the spirit of beaver against physical attacks. In: Shacham, H., Boldyreva, A. (eds.) CRYPTO 2018. LNCS, vol. 10991, pp. 121–151. Springer, Cham (2018). https://doi.org/10.1007/978-3-319-96884-1_5

37. Rivain, M., Prouff, E.: Provably secure higher-order masking of AES. In: Mangard, S., Standaert, F.-X. (eds.) CHES 2010. LNCS, vol. 6225, pp. 413–427. Springer, Heidelberg (2010). https://doi.org/10.1007/978-3-642-15031-9_28

38. Schneider, T., Moradi, A., Güneysu, T.: ParTI – towards combined hardware countermeasures against side-channel and fault-injection attacks. In: Robshaw, M., Katz, J. (eds.) CRYPTO 2016. LNCS, vol. 9815, pp. 302–332. Springer, Heidelberg (2016). https://doi.org/10.1007/978-3-662-53008-5_11

39. van Woudenberg, J.G.J., Witteman, M.F., Menarini, F.: Practical optical fault injection on secure microcontrollers. In: 2011 Workshop on Fault Diagnosis and Tolerance in Cryptography, FDTC 2011, Tokyo, Japan, 29 September 2011, pp. 91–99 (2011)

40. Yen, S., Joye, M.: Checking before output may not be enough against fault-based cryptanalysis. IEEE Trans. Comput. **49**(9), 967–970 (2000)

Author Index

Printed in the United States
By Bookmasters